CHICKENHAWK:
BACK IN
THE WORLD

CHICKEN

ROBERT MASON

H A W K

B A C K

I N

T H E

W O R L D

LIFE AFTER VIETNAM

V I K I N G

VIKING
Published by the Penguin Group
Penguin Books USA Inc., 375 Hudson Street,
New York, New York 10014, U.S.A.
Penguin Books Ltd, 27 Wrights Lane,
London W8 5TZ, England
Penguin Books Australia Ltd, Ringwood,
Victoria, Australia
Penguin Books Canada Ltd, 10 Alcorn Avenue,
Toronto, Ontario, Canada M4V 3B2
Penguin Books (N.Z.) Ltd, 182–190 Wairau Road,
Auckland 10, New Zealand

Penguin Books Ltd, Registered Offices:
Harmondsworth, Middlesex, England

First published in 1993 by Viking Penguin,
a division of Penguin Books USA Inc.

1 2 3 4 5 6 7 8 9 10

LIBRARY OF CONGRESS CATALOGING IN PUBLICATION DATA
Mason, Robert
Chickenhawk: Back in the World/ Robert
Mason.
p. cm.
ISBN 0 670 84835 2
1. Mason, Robert, 1942– . 2. Vietnamese Conflict, 1961–1975—
Veterans—United States. 3. Veterans—United States—Biography.
I. Title.
DS559.73.U6M37 1993
959.704'3—dc20   92–50518

Printed in the United States of America
Set in Meridien
Designed by Ann Gold

FOR PATIENCE AND JACK

AUTHOR'S NOTE

This is a personal narrative about my life after Vietnam, a period of twenty-six years from October 1966 to August 1992. I don't use a tape recorder, so the conversations in this book have been recreated from memory.

The names of my coconspirators on the *Namaste* and the inmates at staff at Eglin Federal Prison Camp, except for the superintendent, have been changed to protect their privacy. Everybody else, friends and foes alike, are (to their surprise in some cases) listed as I know them.

I'd like to thank Knox Burger for his ability to be a critical, hard-boiled literary agent and a sympathetic friend at the same time.

Al Silverman, my editor and now publisher at Viking Penguin, helped me shape this book, and for that I am grateful.

Patience, as always, was my first reader. Her editorial advice was offered with remarkable professional poise, considering some of the scenes about our life together. I am in her debt.

Finally, I'd like to thank my friends not mentioned here for being supportive of me while I was in trouble. That includes nearly everybody in High Springs, Florida, and the hundreds of people, most of whom I never met, who wrote to the judge. I thank you all from the bottom of my heart.

CHICKENHAWK:
BACK IN
THE WORLD

PROLOGUE

There's an ancient idea that when a man travels, he doesn't *go* anywhere. Instead, he performs a series of actions that, if done in the proper sequence, will bring his destination to him.

I'm walking a path in the woods where I live. I concentrate on the act of walking while keeping in mind that I am stationary, that it is the world that is moving. After several tries, it works. I move my body in precise ways and watch the ground pass beneath me and trees and bushes move by me until the steps of my cabin come to me and touch my feet. Doing this can make you dizzy, but once this perspective is accepted, you are in the center of it, focused on *what* you are doing, now. Walking is no longer the same. Neither is life. You walk, wriggle, love, and cry, and the path moves by bringing your destination to you—if you make the right moves.

I must have made the right moves: I'm alive. I moved the controls of my helicopter in Vietnam in just the right ways. Missed thousands of bullets because I did *something* right, instinctively, at just the right moments. Made impossible unlighted landings into deep midnight jungles to rescue soldiers, succeeding, perhaps, because we—me, my crew, even my helicopter—were the results of another soldier's right moves to make the jungle go away, to survive.

1

I have memories of others who made wrong moves, who were battered, burned, eviscerated in the war machine.

The war still rages on the far side of the planet.

I'm back in the world.

If I can just keep making the right moves—

PART ONE

FALSE
STARTS

CHAPTER 1

Octber 1966—The same old H-23 Hiller that had been here when
I was a student, two years before, squatted on a brickwork ped-
estal on the left side of the gate at the U.S. Army Primary Helicopter
School at Fort Wolters, Texas, so passersby would know this was not
just an ordinary Army base. It sagged a little and its paint looked dull,
but I'd trained in a Hiller and I liked it. Across the entrance, they'd
dragged off the other Hiller and set up in its place the school's new
trainer, a little bitty Hughes TH-55A, which looked to me like it should
be flown on the end of a string. "Above the Best" was the motto at
Wolters, and these helicopters were the ones which aspiring Army
aviators tried to fly.

A stringy swarm of skittering, buzzing, gnatlike machines—the
first batch of Hugheses, the smallest two-passenger helicopters in
existence—had arrived during my last week as a student. I'd never
flown one. The Hiller, a not-very-big three-passenger machine, looked
enormous by contrast. The Hughes was cheaper than the Hiller and
simpler to maintain. Of course it was cheaper. It used *rubber belts* in
its transmission system. The Hiller was overbuilt, complicated, hard to
fly, and practically indestructible—perfect for instruction. I was relieved to learn I was assigned to a training flight that used Hillers.

Wolters seemed entirely different to me as I drove from the main
gate to the flight line. For one thing, I was no longer a subhuman

warrant officer candidate—known as a WOC. I was a warrant officer pilot now. People, at least enlisted people, weren't fucking with me. Real officers believed warrants were kind of half-assed officers and allowed us our privileges because it was mandated. Any highest-ranking chief warrant officer, CW-4 (equivalent to a major), was outranked by any green second lieutenant. It's a mysterious system. If I wasn't a pilot, I wouldn't be here.

A lot more people were bustling around than when I went through flight training in 1964. Because my Volvo had a blue officer's parking sticker on the bumper, enlisted men and WOCs walking along the road saluted. The enlisted men's salutes were grudging and slovenly, as was expected. The WOC salutes were snappy and sharp and made you wonder if they ever whacked their heads. They saluted like their lives depended on doing it right. They were correct. Doing *everything* right was a big concern for WOCs. Half of them wouldn't make it through, and the prize for the runners-up was to be thrown out of flight school. They'd be sent to Vietnam as grunts, where they'd slog it out and get dirty, never mind killed. Dirty is bad; the Vietnam combat pilot's motto was "Die clean."

All this saluting was uncomfortable. In Vietnam anybody seen saluting in our aviation units was probably drunk or forced into it by a newbie field-grade officer trying to restore military discipline. I returned the salutes as I drove, feeling awkward.

I passed the post theater, the post library, the post craft shop, and the post commissary. As a WOC, I was only allowed in the commissary to buy necessities, like wax to shine my floor, my shoes, and my sink. I barely knew the other places existed. Now that I was a human being, I was interested in learning how to print photographs at the craft shop and build something at the woodshop. I'd done my war. As a stateside soldier, I wanted to coast, pursue mundane hobbies, and forget Vietnam. I still had some problems: I couldn't sleep, had boils from some vicious jungle infection, and got profoundly depressed each night seeing the war reported on television in banal snippets of violence before the weatherman, while the center of national attention was the new pop series, *Batman*. I thought these problems would go away. Just needed a little time to readjust, was all.

Down the hill from the commissary I passed four new student dormitories. A platoon of candidates were doing push-ups out front while a TAC (short for tactical) sergeant harangued them. Thank God I wasn't going to be a TAC officer. For a pilot, it was like a lobotomy. I was on the lookout for my old TAC sergeant, Wayne Malone, but hadn't seen him. The day I graduated from flight school I wanted to come to Wolters, find Malone, and make him do eight hundred push-ups for harassing me unmercifully while I was a WOC. Now I just wanted to say hello.

I passed the WOC Club at the bend in the road, an old white wood-frame building in which the candidates were allowed to visit for a few hours on the weekends with their wives or girlfriends. They served beer inside, but the candidates were usually outside driving their ladies to deserted places on the immense post to get laid. Patience and I had a Volkswagen when I was a candidate. One of our fondest memories is the time we didn't even make it to the car, stopping instead behind the big oak tree beside the club. It was the kind of scene in which you might imagine a large dog rushing up from nowhere to throw a bucket of water on us. I smiled when I drove past the tree.

As I drove along the road beside the main heliport, helicopters lurched into the air from the six takeoff pads and flew over me, flitting off in all directions over the central Texas hills. Twice a day, in the morning and afternoon training sessions, the school would put fifteen hundred aircraft in the air at the same time to crank out enough pilots to replace the ones getting killed in Vietnam. Wolters was dizzyingly crowded, and dangerous.

I had an eight o'clock aircraft orientation flight scheduled with War-rant Officer Gary Lineberry, a former classmate who had not yet gone to Vietnam. Actually, Lineberry hadn't gone anywhere. They'd as-signed him right back to flight school upon graduation from Fort Rucker, Alabama, the last stage of the Army's helicopter course, be-cause he was a superb pilot. While most of the rest of class 65-3 went to Vietnam, Lineberry became an instructor pilot (IP) and was now part of the Methods of Instruction (MOI) branch at Wolters that taught veteran pilots how to be IPs.

I pulled into a parking spot near the main hangar and got out, carrying my flight helmet—known also as a brain bucket—by its strap. It was the same one I'd used in Nam; still had the stupid picture of Snoopy I'd painted on the back. It was battered and chipped and looked awful. I had been told to exchange it for a new one, but I considered my helmet, my Zippo, my Nikonos camera, nearly all the objects I possessed in Vietnam, talismans that had helped keep me alive. A technician at the helmet shop, who seemed to understand my superstition—or was afraid to argue with a man with hollow eyes who spoke gravely of lucky helmets—had installed new earphones, new padding, a new microphone, and a new visor for me. I saw Lineberry putting his helmet inside the plastic bubble cockpit of a Hiller and walked over.

"Hey, Gary," I said, reaching out my hand. "Been a while."

Lineberry said hi, smiling as we shook hands. "Welcome back to the world."

"Yeah. Good to be here. Really missed the place; even Wolters." I smiled, looking around at the parched, paved-over central Texas waste-land called the main heliport. "Vietnam can do that to a person."

"I've heard." Lineberry shrugged. "But you got plenty of flying, right? Who were you with?"

"First Cav Division for eight months. Finished my tour with the Forty-eighth Aviation Company."

Lineberry nodded—the First Air Cavalry was pretty famous, but the Forty-eighth wasn't. "You got Huey time, too," he said, looking en-vious. "How was it?"

I shrugged. Lineberry the IP would want to know about the flying and the helicopters, not about the war, not until he got there. He figured he was stuck flying these little pissant trainers while we lucky fuckers flew the big turbine-powered hot-shit Hueys. "Great. You know, great ship. Saved my ass a bunch of times."

"Yeah?"

"Yeah. Got shot down once—took some rounds through a fuel line. But I took hits in the rotors, fuel tank—you name it—for a year. No problem," I said coolly, while my scrotum cinched itself tight at the memories.

"The armored seats work?"

"Well," I said with a shrug, "if you get hit from the back, the sides, or from underneath, they work great. But there's nothing up front, and that's were we take a lot of hits. The Viet Cong learned the best way to shoot down Hueys is to kill the pilots."

"Great to hear." Lineberry scowled and shook his head. "I'm going over there next month."

I nodded. What was there to say to that? Be careful? I pointed to the Hiller behind him. "That our ship?"

"Yeah." Lineberry smiled suddenly. "Let's go see if you remember how to fly one of these bone bruisers."

The Huey I'd flown in Vietnam was turbine powered and had hydraulically assisted controls. The Huey was huge compared to the Hiller—it carried a crew of four and could fly with eight or ten fully equipped grunts—but controlling it was effortless. The Hiller, I was instantly reminded, was powered by a noisy six-cylinder engine and controlled with direct mechanical linkages between the flight controls and the rotors. The controls vibrated, shook, and resisted every move. When I pulled up the collective—the control that raises and lowers the helicopter—and brought the ship to a hover, the stick pushed itself up in my left hand. Right, I remember: you have to pop the collective to release the sticky control ballast system that is supposed to neutralize the collective stick forces. I popped the collective down. Now it pulled down. It would take me a while to get used to it again, so I just let it tug for the moment. I was having enough problems with the cyclic, trying to balance the Hiller in the hover. The Hiller's cyclic—the stick between the pilot's knees—is connected, via a system of push-pull tubes and a rotating swash plate assembly, to two rotor paddles that stick out of the hub at right angles to the main rotors. The paddles are short, symmetrical wing sections on the ends of two short shafts. The idea behind Stanley Hiller's scheme was that a pilot would be strong enough to rotate these little paddles with the cyclic stick, and the paddles, in turn, would tilt the main rotors in the direction you wanted to fly using aerodynamic forces, eliminating the need for hydraulic assistance. It's really quite a clever idea. It worked, but it also doubled the normal delay in the cyclic control response that was common to all helicopters, and made the Hiller notoriously difficult to handle until you got used to it.

While I wrestled the ship into a hover, I glanced at Lineberry. He was laughing: ace Huey pilot can't fly his original trainer. The cyclic shook violently, jerking my hand around in a very rude, un-Hueylike manner. Two little tuning-fork things attached to the cyclic control system were supposed to dampen these feedback forces. I suppose they were working as well as they could. The only controls that felt reasonably normal were the foot pedals that controlled the pitch of the tail rotor, which let you point the helicopter where you wanted it to point.

The romantic memories of my first helicopter as a plucky, smooth-flying machine vanished. The Hiller was actually an ungainly, crude museum piece of a helicopter. I held it in a sort of hover, wallowing and pitching in a slight breeze, checking the tachometer and adjusting the throttle on the collective to keep the needles in the green because I'd forgotten how the engine sounded at the right RPM.

"Not bad," Lineberry said. "Let's go fly."

By the Christmas break I had been an IP for a month and Patience and I were pretty well settled. We'd rented a house in Mineral Wells, an all-American place with a garage and backyard. This was the first house we'd lived in together. We were married in 1963, just before I joined the Army. Patience and our son, Jack, had endured crummy apartments and trailers while I went through basic training, advanced infantry training, and flight school. They seldom saw me while I was a trainee soldier, and then I went to Vietnam. Jack, two years old now, was getting used to me again. I'd been away half his life and had missed the previous Christmas. I wanted to make him a present to show him I was just a regular dad. I was home. I was going to build things, pursue hobbies, do well at work. Forget.

I wasn't thinking about Vietnam, but it was there. Awake, in quiet moments, I felt a familiar dread in the pit of my stomach, even as I angrily informed myself that I was home. Asleep, my dreams were infected by what I'd seen. The explosive jump-ups I'd been having since the last month of my tour were getting more frequent. When Patience and Jack saw me leaping off the bed, Patience would make a joke of it: "Daddy's levitating again." But it scared her. I had asked the flight surgeon about it and he said I should be okay in a couple months.

During the two-week Christmas break I spent most of my time teaching myself how to print photographs at the craft shop or building Jack's present—a rocking horse I designed, which Patience said had to be big enough for her, too—at the woodshop. I thought I could obliterate memories of Vietnam by staying so busy I couldn't think about it.

A collection of my photographs began to assemble on our dining-room wall. A few were prints of pictures I'd taken in Vietnam, but most were of abandoned farm buildings, rusted farm equipment, and stark Texas still lifes taken when Patience and Jack and I went for drives. One of the Vietnam pictures was of a second lieutenant and three of his men, tired, dirty, but alive, sitting on a paddy dike. I called it "Ghosts." Patience asked why. "Because they are all dead. Everyone we dropped off in that LZ is dead."

The photographs were technically good.

The rocking horse turned out big and sturdy. Jack named it Haysup. Why Haysup? "It's his name!" Jack said.

I was staying busy, but fear, my familiar Vietnam companion, visited me at odd moments, even times when I should've been happy. Normal people didn't have these bouts with fear. I knew that because I had been normal once, long ago. I looked forward to flight school starting again so I could lose myself in my work, shake these feelings.

I drove Patience and Jack out into the country to fetch a Christmas tree. While I chopped it down and Patience and Jack happily collected small branches to trim our house, I searched the dark places in the woods where snipers could hide.

Our students had completed the primary stage of flight training when they got to us. Their civilian instructors had taught them the basics of flying the helicopter; our job was to teach them how to use it in the field. From Wolters they would go to Fort Rucker in Alabama and learn to fly Hueys. They'd take their final exam in Vietnam. I took my work seriously because the candidates who made it through this school needed to be very good pilots to survive. The government could send these eager guys to a stupid war, but I could help them live through it.

I was standing on a rock watching one of my four students pacing off a confined area to determine the best spot for the takeoff. The Hiller chugged nearby, its collective tied down, idling. I pulled out a cigarette from my flight suit and patted my pockets for my Zippo. Left it home. Student didn't smoke. Walked over to the Hiller, put the cigarette in my mouth, and strained my head in among the chugging machinery to press the cigarette against the engine exhaust manifold. Sucked until the end glowed. Stood back, drew a deep breath of smoke, looked at the Hiller. Why'd I do that? If any of that spinning shit had grabbed my clothes, I would've been chewed up. I *see* chewed up: guts and brains and green tin cans; muddy snapped bones and burned-off skin; bloody crotches and empty eye sockets—

"Sir, I've got it measured," student said to me, and gruesome images faded to his bright face. He turned around and told me his plan, pointing as he spoke. "I'll hover backward, following the trail of stones I laid out until I reach the marker stone—"

Right. Good, bright-faced kid had it figured out. "How far is the marker stone from the trees?"

"The length of the helicopter plus five paces, sir."

"Good. Let's try it." It was all by the numbers, but it worked. I'd gone through the same program thinking it was bullshit, this pacing business. But it actually built an indelible image of a process: getting a helicopter into a woodsy-tangled, confined area and back out again without snagging something. Confined areas would soon be known to the student as LZs—landing zones. By that time, the student wouldn't need to pace off the clearances, putting down markers where it was safe to hover and take off. He wouldn't have time, but would be able to judge them with extreme accuracy developed by going through this drill.

We got in the Hiller and belted up. The wind was gusty. The student hovered backward along his stone trail, overcontrolling the helicopter, making it lurch and wallow, afraid he'd bump into the trees behind him. No one trusts his own stone markers the first few times. He stopped over a rock, keeping it right in front of his feet. The wind was pushing him backward toward the brush and he was wallowing, getting sloppy, losing it. He could feel the wiry mesquite branches reaching for his tail rotor. "You sure that's the right rock?" I said. Added pressure.

His knuckles were white. The Hiller seemed to fight harder in the wind. He was wondering if it was the same goddamn rock he put at the end of his hover path. Why was the IP asking if it was the right rock? Maybe I went too far, he thought. Shit! But wait. There's that cow turd next to my marker. He loved seeing that cow flop. He clicked the intercom switch on the cyclic. "Yessir. It's the one."

"Okay."

My student let the Hiller down, banged around, hitting all four points of the landing skid; tail rocked back when it squatted down on the sloping ground. Not neat, this real world compared to the paved stage fields where he learned to fly. He searched the sky, making sure we were clear of other helicopters, rolled the throttle grip to bring the Hiller up to takeoff power, pulled up the collective, jerked to a hover, and lowered the nose into takeoff position. We hit translational lift almost immediately because the wind was so strong—the rotor system suddenly became more efficient as it translated (Army term) from the churning air under the rotors to the clean air ahead of it. The Hiller jerked up, eager to fly.

The student did well. We crossed the tree line with altitude to spare. He flew over rolling Texas brush country, home to tumbleweeds and jackrabbits, toward the Brazos River Valley a half mile away. When he crossed the edge of the two-hundred-foot drop-off into the river valley, I cut the power.

He slammed the collective down. Good. Late on the collective means the rotors, angled up for powered flight, will stop and you will die. Now. Had to find a place to land. Had twenty seconds before we hit the ground. The Hiller lost 1,750 feet a minute in a glide—called an autorotation in a helicopter. Nothing but a sheer wall of rocks and Texas brambles under him. Couldn't turn back—wouldn't make the ledge. He aimed the machine toward a sandbar in the middle of the river. I smiled. Fifty feet over the river, when I was sure he'd make it, I said "I've got it" and took control. I pulled in the power and skimmed across the sandbar.

I swooped up to the top of the far ridge of the river valley and landed on a little ledge, right in front of a wall of tall trees. The tail section of the Hiller jutted out into space. Just *knowing* that made you feel like you'd fall off.

"How can I get out of here?" I said into the intercom. "Have to take off into the wind, but the trees are too tall." I glanced at the student and then looked over my shoulder. "Can't back up, we're at the edge already." I looked left and right at the trees nearly touching the rotors. "No room to turn around, even. What would you do?"

Student turned to me and said he wouldn't have landed here in the first place. I liked this student.

I nodded. "Someday you will *have* to land here." I rolled on the throttle and pulled up the collective to lighten the Hiller on its skids. "We will *fall* out of here," I said.

"Sir?" the student said, looking worried.

We rose, rearing back—falling off the cliff. When the nose cleared the ledge, I fell into the valley. The trees and the ledge sailed above us as we sank. The tail naturally wanted to swap ends as we fell backward, like an arrow tossed feathers first. I pressed the right tail-rotor pedal and we snapped around. I dove to gain airspeed. At sixty knots, I swooped up and we soared up and out of the valley. Student said, "Wow!"

I am building a model airplane, a World War I Spad. A plastic Spad from a kit. It is three-thirty in the morning. Patience and Jack went to bed six hours ago. My tongue peeks out my mouth as I concentrate. I'm sticking pieces of cellophane onto the wings to create the effect of wrinkled fabric. My model is extremely detailed, but I left the little pilot head-and-shoulder figure in the box. The cockpit is empty. I rub silver paint on the tiny instrument panel.

While the Spad dries, I look at my photographs on the wall. They look dismal to me. Sad attempts to see the world as I once saw it. Patience picks flowers, wind blowing her hair. The gate to the old farmhouse swings as a blur, nobody there. The ghost second lieutenant is talking on his radio, full of plans. They are good, these photographs, but disturbing. I get up from the table and walk down the hall. Jack, bathed in moonlight, is tiny, his little chest breathing. Patience is beautiful; long dark hair hiding the pillow, she sprawls, taking up most of the bed. They are peaceful.

By four, the Spad's war-worn paint job is dry. I hold it and strafe the salt and pepper shakers. I'm aware that I am a grown man playing with a model airplane and that I don't make model airplanes. But it is a nice model. I take it to the corner cupboard and set it on a shelf. I stand back and admire my work, knowing I'll never do it again.

I open the cupboard to put the box of tools and glue and paint away. The top shelf is packed with bottles of bourbon my students have been giving me when they complete their cycles. Four students per cycle, one cycle every two months; lots of booze. Don't drink now. Drank some in Vietnam. Remembered how it tasted: warm canteen water and Old Granddad in a canteen cup, laughing friends. Good. Pull Old Granddad from the shelf and put him on the table. Get glass. Pour in three fingers of Old Granddad. Splash in water at the sink. Drink. Asleep beside Patience by four-thirty.

Flying in from the boonies with my last student of the day, I saw that a long grassy meadow we used for autorotation practice was clear. We were at cruising altitude, five hundred feet, and my student was concentrating on getting himself into the traffic jam of returning helicopters without hitting anyone—the last thing he needed was to have the engine quit. I rolled off the throttle, cutting the power.

The strip was to our right, the wind was coming from the right, so the student bottomed the pitch and turned to the right. I still didn't know for sure if he saw the strip, but he was doing everything okay so far. He did a few shallow turns on approach to lose altitude to get on the right glide angle, and I saw he knew where he was going. I decided to let him take it all the way to the ground—a rare treat because the brass said we were breaking too many helicopters teaching pilots how to autorotate to the ground. Something flickered in my peripheral vision. I looked. A Hiller was coming down on us.

I take the controls, telling the student I've got it. In a very strange way, I don't exactly mind this. Everything is happening in slow motion. It reminds me of the feelings I used to have during the assault landings. It is instantly obvious to me that there is no way to escape collision, but I want to be flying when I die. We're both autorotating to the same spot. The other Hiller is so close that if I try to get away my rotors will tilt up into his skids when I turn. He'd lose a skid; we'd lose our rotors. Can't go down any faster; we are both descending as fast as possible —we are both autorotating. His ship descends just a little faster than ours. We will hit soon. It is almost funny: Make it through Vietnam; killed in a peaceful meadow just outside Mineral Wells, Texas. One wrong move.

We're a little off course for the strip. The student in the ship above us turns slightly to correct and sees our rotors just below him. At about a hundred and fifty feet, his ship lurches away and we are safe. Total time for event: about ten seconds.

I come to a hover on the strip. My student is pale and pissed. Why didn't they clear themselves before they started their autorotation? I ask if he'd seen them. No. Good lesson, then, on keeping better lookout. He stares at me, nodding slightly.

It made a good story to tell my fellow instructor pilots back at the flight room. I jazzed it up with gestures and smiles, to make sure everybody knew I was scared shitless. They laughed. Been there, Bob.

It was Friday, so I decided to take both my flight suits home to wash. Grabbing my alternate flight suit that had been hanging in my locker for two weeks, I felt a bulge in one of the leg pockets. Zipped it open and found a thumb-sized barrel cactus wrapped in a slip of paper from my grade book. Ah, that was from that confined area on top of that hill toward Palo Pinto, I thought. I marveled at the plant, healthy and happy even in a stinking pocket. I took it home for Patience.

Patience liked the cactus. She put it in a pot and set it in the window. I was happy she liked little things.

Saturday morning we drove fifty miles to Fort Worth. We did this almost every Saturday: got a box of Kentucky Fried Chicken and ate it in a park. Went to the Fort Worth zoo and watched caged animals stare back, nutty and distracted. (We once saw a woman strenuously making faces at a gorilla, trying to get its attention. After watching her awhile, the gorilla gave her four bored claps and turned away.) Jack really liked the zoo. We rode in a miniature train that made him laugh. Patience rode the merry-go-round. Dinner was usually at Jimmy Dips, a Chinese place. We were on the road to Mineral Wells by nine or ten. Every Saturday, almost.

Sundays were quiet. I read, or worked on short stories. I wrote stories and thought of having them published someday. This Sunday I sat in a chair in the bedroom, reading. Suddenly my heart leapt and jerked. I sprang up, threw the book on the floor, and breathed out hard. I felt like I was dying.

"Patience," I hollered, "I must be having a heart attack." She rushed me to Beach Army Hospital, Jack in the back of the car. I took deep breaths with my face next to the air conditioner vents.

I explained what had happened. The flight surgeon felt my pulse and smiled. Funny stuff? "No," he said, "you've been hyperventilating."

"What's that?"

"You're accumulating more oxygen than you need because you're breathing wrong."

"Breathing wrong?" Been breathing for twenty-five years.

"Tension, maybe," the doctor said. "Next time you feel like this, try breathing in and out of a paper bag. That'll increase your carbon dioxide level and the feeling will go away."

Simple stuff. Drink myself to sleep at night and breathe out of paper bag to make it through the day. Could be worse: just met a classmate, Wavey Sharp, best-looking guy in our class, but not anymore; his face was burned away in Vietnam.

Hughes trainers were falling out of the sky and no one knew why. Only helicopters with instructors were crashing; solo students weren't going down. No clues. The ships were found, what was left of them, pointing straight down. Veteran instructor pilots and their students suddenly dove to the ground and ended up as wet stuff in the wreckage. A guy in the flight unit who found one of these mangled messes cried about it.

An IP radioed while crashing. In the few seconds he had left on the planet he said that if you push the cyclic stick forward in autorotation, the Hughes's nose tucked down and the controls didn't work—

A few weeks later, a test pilot at the Hughes factory in Culver City, California, took a Hughes up very high and tried duplicating the condition. The dead guy was right. The Hughes tucked and stayed there, straining like a dowsing rod to reach the ground. The Hughes test pilot (wearing a parachute) tried using the opposite control—pushed the cyclic forward. Worked. The Hughes came out of the dive, taking fifteen hundred feet to recover. They sent the word back to us: don't let your students push the cyclic forward in autorotation, and demonstrate the recovery to all Hughes instructors. Hoots in our Hiller flight room. Autorotations were done at five hundred feet, Pete. See it now: Peter Pilot pulls out of dive a thousand feet underground. Comical stuff.

My flight commander told me I had been *selected* to cross-train into the Hughes. I *will* fly a regular student load and learn Hughes in my off time. An honor, he said; he respected my flying skill.

Methods of Instruction again. Lineberry was gone. To Vietnam. A warrant officer pro-instructor took me out and tried to impress on me how nifty this little piece-of-shit helicopter was. Showed me the seven rubber belts that connected the engine to the transmission; claimed the system could operate even when only two belts were left. I nodded. We flew. Hughes buzzed a lot, but it was very maneuverable. I had trouble with the pedals. The tail rotor was too small and it was hard to move the tail around in strong wind. There was very little inertia in the lightweight main rotors, which made autorotations snappier, less forgiving of small errors than the Hiller. Pro-instructor climbed to three thousand feet and said, "You're supposed to see this." He cut the power and nudged the cyclic forward. *Whap!* Little shit dumped over on its nose. My goofy, friendly Hiller would never do that. (You can stop a Hiller on its tail during autorotation, slide backward, and then dump the nose down, accelerate, and get to where you're going—something you might have to do if you're already on top of the best spot to land, which you cannot do in a Hughes.) "Recovery is simple," pro-instructor said as we hurtled out of sky. "Just give the cyclic forward pressure, wait until the nose starts to come back up, and then resume normal control." He did that and the Hughes came out of kamikaze landing approach. Fun, but academic.

"Autorotations are always done from five hundred feet," I said.

Pro-instructor shrugged. "You won't be able to recover from five hundred feet, but this demonstration will make it hard to forget to keep your student from pushing the cyclic forward." Good point. *Still* haven't forgotten.

Two weeks later, when I finished the cross-training, my flight commander called me in again. They needed a substitute instructor in a Hughes flight—just one day. Just one day with *that* flight. But there was always a flight that needed a substitute. I now had a double load of work. I thought of the flight commander as an asshole.

I was having trouble at home. I drank more every night to get to sleep. I slept, but woke up exhausted. Argued with Patience—always cooked the same meals; sometimes forgot to cook at all; she wasn't sticking to our budget. Jack wanted to play.

Jack was learning to count. Sometimes I paid attention to his interests, but mostly not. He and I had a counting game. I held up my index finger and said, "One." Then I held up two fingers, "Two." And so on, until I popped up my thumb and said, "Five." He said he understood. We practiced: one, two, three, four, five. He said the right number when I added a finger. He understood. Quick-witted little guy. I held up my fist and raised my thumb. "Five," Jack said. Ah. Each finger was a number to Jack. We would have to work on this.

But I didn't. At least not very often. I didn't play with Jack enough, I didn't talk to Patience enough. I was drifting around in a fog of internalizations, talking to myself, fighting demons that kept coming back. Things just popped into my mind that I didn't want to see. I'm sitting alone in the living room at two A.M. I see twenty-one men trussed in a row, ropes at their ankles, hands bound under their backs—North Vietnamese prisoners. A sergeant, his face twisted with anger, stands at the first prisoner's feet. The North Vietnamese prisoner stares back, unblinking. The sergeant points a .45 at the man. He kicks the prisoner's feet suddenly. The shock of the impact jostles the prisoner inches across the ground. The sergeant fires the .45 into the prisoner's face. The prisoner's head bounces off the ground like a ball slapped from above, then flops back into the gore that was his brains. The sergeant turns to the next prisoner in the line.

"He tried to get away," says a voice at my side.

"He can't get away; he's tied!"

"He moved. He was trying to get away."

The next prisoner says a few hurried words in Vietnamese as the sergeant stands over him. When the sergeant kicks his feet, the prisoner closes his eyes. A bullet shakes his head.

"It's murder!" I hiss to the man at my side.

"They cut off Sergeant Rocci's cock and stuck it in his mouth. And the same with five of his men," the voice says. "After they spent the night slowly shoving knives into their guts. If you had been here to hear the screams—they screamed all night. This morning they were all dead, all gagged with their cocks. This isn't murder; it's justice."

Another head bounces off the ground. The shock wave hits my body.

"They sent us to pick up twenty-one *prisoners,*" I plead.

"You'll get 'em. They'll just be dead, is all."

The sergeant moves down the line, stopping prisoners who try to escape. The line of men grows longer than it had been, and the sergeant grows distant. His face glows red and the heads bounce. And then he looks up at me. I jump out of the chair and get a drink.

I decided we should take a weekend trip to New Orleans with friends, Ray Welch and his wife. I felt excited about the trip, thought it would be the break I needed—it would distract me from my memories. Hadn't been away from the post except to go to my sister's wedding in Florida one weekend without Patience. My sister, Susan, asked me to wear my dress blues with medals. For Susan, I put on the bellhop uniform and medals. Drunk asked me, where was my flag? Loud. People all looked at the geek Army guy—one of the guys losing the war. I walked away. Now, though, I'll be with Patience and my friend, Ray; and we won't wear Army stuff.

Missed the plane to New Orleans Friday night. Spent the night in a cheap Fort Worth hotel, laughing and drinking. Caught a plane the next morning, checked into a medium-priced (dumpy) hotel. The fun of the previous night wore thin. Wondered what I was doing in New Orleans. See the sights, Patience said. We got a cab, told the driver to take us to the sights.

Got out at an old park. Feeling bad. Held my breath because I didn't want Ray to see me breathe into a paper bag—too embarrassing. We walked to an ancient graveyard; I dropped back from the others, feeling faint. Squatted, head between knees, on the sidewalk. Patience comforted me. I stood up and walked inside the cemetery. Sank to my knees on the grass, inside cool walls, beside quiet vaults.

Made it to a sidewalk café as if it were a desperate mission. Sucked down whiskey, shaking. Four whiskies later, not shaking. Back to normal, telling funny stories. "Man," I said, "Don't know what that was all about, but I'm feeling fine now." I smiled. Ray and his wife looked relieved.

I needed to snap out of this feeling of depression. I took a Hiller out by myself one Saturday. I flew the riverbed alone, swooping from clifftops to the valley floor and up to the other side. I felt okay in my helicopter.

I autorotated into the same place my student and I had the near-collision. Picked up to a high hover and floated slowly across a grassy ravine to a field, savoring the magic of levitation. No other helicopters were in sight. I put the toe of the left skid on top of a fence post and twirled around it. I practiced keeping the tail into the wind, hard to do smoothly. I turned around and saw a deer, a stag, bounding two hundred yards away, running to the tree line.

Dump nose and pursue. Intercept deer crossing the last clearing before the trees.

Deer veers away, leaping rocks, bushes, and ditches—eyes wide. Fly beside the running deer, alone, unaware of the helicopter strapped to me. Slide in front, facing the deer.

Deer turns. I block.

Deer stops for second, stares at the clamorous, hideous thing chasing it; stumbles backward, spins around to make an escape. No good. I'm there, too.

Deer sags, legs spread out. Chest heaves. Tongue hangs out from exhaustion. I back away, inviting it to run again.

C'mon, run! You asshole!

Deer stares, eyes glazed, immobile.

I have beaten this deer.

I'd been at Wolters for over a year. Coming into the main heliport with my last student of the day, I took the controls after the student came to a hover at the landing pad, because of the traffic. Hundreds of helicopters hovering to their parking spots made hundreds of rotor-wash storms, so the helicopters were tricky to control. The machine wanted to skitter off with every gust. My hands and feet moved the controls automatically, compensating. The Hiller hovered between spinning rotors, jittery, like a thoroughbred being led through a crowd.

Almost to the parking slot, I feel the helicopter tilt backward and immediately push the cyclic forward. Wrong. Not tilting back. I can *see* that, but it still *feels* like we're tilting back. I force myself to concentrate, ignore the feeling, fly reality. But the feeling is unshakable. Which is real? Bad time to experiment with relativity, so I tell the student "You got it" as I hover into the parking spot. Student says, "I got it." Good student. Figures asshole IP is fucking with him again; probably wondering if IP will cut the power while he tries to park. Student sets the Hiller down like a pro.

Drive to the flight surgeon after leaving the student (he got an excellent grade), still dizzy. Flight surgeon impressed. No flying.

They decided to watch me for a month to see if I got dizzy again. The flight commander put me in charge of our pickup truck. I drove it out to the stage fields and helped in the control towers, keeping track of the ships as they checked in, made coffee. Gofer work. I felt horrible. No flying? That's why I joined the Army. I went to the flight surgeon. Told him I felt great, sleeping like a fucking log. He believed me. I was back in the air two weeks after I was grounded.

Two months later it happened again. This time I was cruising straight and level, felt the ship rolling when it was not. My student landed, never knowing his IP was fucked up. This time I was grounded until they could find out what was wrong.

What is wrong? shrink asks. Dunno. Have a real hard time sleeping. Don't sleep.

"Do you have dreams?"

"Patience asks if I'm dreaming when I jump up all night. I dream, but I can't remember them—except one. But I'm never able to tell her this dream. I tell her I don't dream anything."

"What's it about?" shrink asks.

"I'm not sure where I am, but every morning a truck comes—"

"What truck?"

"A truck loaded with dead babies."

"You've seen this—in Vietnam?"

"No. I've seen lots of dead babies, but not loaded in trucks."

"Continue, please."

"The truck comes. I have to open the back door; I know what's out there, but I still go to the door. It's always the same. The driver backs the truck to the door and says, 'How many do you want?' He points to the pile of dead babies. I always gag at the sight. They all look dead, but then I see an eyelid blink in the pile, then another."

"That's it?"

Feeling bad; seeing it. "No. I always answer, 'Two hundred pounds, Jake.' I laugh when I say it. Jake picks up a pitchfork and stabs it into the pile and drops a couple of corpses on a big scale. 'Nearly ten pounds a head,' he says. Inside my head, I'm yelling for him to stop, that the babies aren't dead, but Jake just keeps loading the scale. Each time he stabs a kid, it squirms on the fork, but Jake doesn't notice."

Shrink watches me awhile. "That's the end?"

"Yes."

"What do you think the dream means?"

"I was hoping you'd tell me."

"I'm more interested in what you think it means."

"I don't know."

The shrink sent me to Fort Sam Houston for loony tests. Fort Sam is a big medical post and the Army's burn treatment center. In a hallway I saw many Vietnam veterans, kids with their faces burned off. New pink skin grafts were stretched over stunted noses. The public never saw this—bad for the war effort. I felt terrible; I was whole. Why was I here?

Diagnosis: combat neurosis. They prescribed Valium, so I could not fly. My new medical profile said: *Aviator may not be assigned to duty in combat area.* They were shipping pilots back to Vietnam every day. My new profile was known as the "million-dollar ticket" at Wolters, but I wanted to fly. Without flying, the Army was a drag.

They found out I wrote stories. I told them, yes, I had many rejection slips to prove it. They assigned me to MOI as a platform instructor. I helped write the syllabus and gave lectures about being an IP. I worked with a captain, Robert Giraudo. Just the two of us ran the whole IP ground-school training sessions and had fun doing it. Giraudo eventually made major but turned in his resignation. He said the Army was getting old. Giraudo was okay.

A year later, when they asked me if I was staying (I was getting near the end of my three-year obligation) I said no. The head of the MOI branch thought I was good in MOI and offered me a direct commission as a real officer, a regular Army captain, if I stayed. No.

Out-process. Debrief. Gone. Leave in Volvo packed to brim. Go toward Fort Worth like a Saturday trip, but won't come back for twenty years. See helicopters flying over a butte; blink a lot.

CHAPTER 2

When I'd dropped out of the University of Florida in 1962, I had a grade point average of 1.2. To be readmitted and to resume my major in fine arts, I had to be sponsored by the chairman of the art department, Eugene Grissom. Grissom saw little point in my continuing—who would?—but agreed to sponsor me if I maintained a 3.0 average.

In June 1968 I was once again a college sophomore. I was seven years older than most sophomores. I was married and had a son. I was a veteran of a war still being waged. We moved into a married-student apartment on campus at Schucht Village in Gainesville. I'd gotten a lot of D's and had to take several of my undergraduate classes over—mathematics, history, and English.

When I stood in line at registration, I couldn't believe what silly-simple shit civilians worried about. These people pissed and moaned if they couldn't get a morning class, or if Friday afternoon got busy, or if some crip-course was filled. I had seen grunts infested with intestinal worms, living in swamps, eating crap, dying young, their brains splattered in the mud, their intestines spilled into their laps. Hey! You think *this* is a *problem*?

Every evening, sipping bourbon, I watched the news. Usually they showed a five-minute Vietnam segment: firefight, lots of smoke; wounded grunts, battered and bloody, being loaded onto a Huey.

Looked like my Huey. That film was shot the day before. They were still there, still dying for no good reason, and nobody cared. Die, and get ten seconds on national television; wounded, less.

A machine gun crackled on television.

My gunner is shooting, walking the bullets across the rice paddy to a crowd of people concealing a Viet Cong gunner who's been knocking helicopters out of the sky. I tell him to walk the bullets—give the villagers a chance to run. He does, but they don't run. I see them close-up as the bullets hit. The old woman with black teeth says something to me, then screams. There is no sound. Her wrinkled hand holds a child's smooth arm. The child hangs lifeless and drags the old woman down. She moves slowly, like she is falling through water. The people around her gasp silently and flinch and fall. The machine gun stutters from a distant place. They fall slowly to the ground, bounce, dying and dead. The old woman is saying something, but I can't hear. When I see her lips moving, I realize she is saying, "It's okay. . . ."

Electricity jolts down my spine.

Calm down.

I swallow a gulp of bourbon.

Your war is over.

Fit in.

Wake up. Get out of bed. Waves of fear shoot through my head. Walk to kitchen, eyes swollen slits. Pour three fingers of Old Granddad. Swig that down, watching cars filled with lucky commuters bored senseless on Archer Road. Another Old Granddad. Feel fine now. Arrive at eight o'clock English class with warm whiskey sloshing mercifully through my brain. No one notices. Alcohol is good; it *enables* me to appear normal among normal people.

During my previous student career, my English composition teachers had been myopically interested in grammar. I thought they missed the point—grammar's important, but look what I'm saying. My new English teacher, Yvonne Dell, though interested in grammar, was more interested in my stories.

One story, "Keith's Ridge," is about a teenage kid who sits and stares at grass waving in the breeze a little too long. He starts to see a pattern in the waves, starts to see the pattern as the signs of an invisible entity. When he follows this thing to Keith's Ridge, he is pushed and tugged by strong swirls of wind. He takes the grabbing and pushing as caresses of acceptance right up until he's flung off the cliff. Great story. Dell liked it, asked me if I ever tried to sell anything. I said I'd sent in that one, got a very nice rejection slip. You only tried once? she asked. Yep. I figure these guys know good stuff when they see it. Dell said I should keep trying. I had talent.

I got an A in English—my first in college. I did well in all my classes, finishing my first quarter with a 3.2 average. Grissom was pleased.

My major was fine arts, and within fine arts, I began to specialize in photography. I had won an Army photography contest with one of my prints. I thought photography might be the talent to replace flying. My instructor was Jerry Uelsmann. I'd seen him around when I was here the first time. He was just the photography instructor in 1962; now he was a celebrity in the art world, famous for his surreal pictures. He called his technique "post-visualization," which meant he composed his photographs after collecting many negatives and then combined them in one flawless print. Uelsmann had the highest technical abilities, but that's not what sold his pictures—they're magically arresting images, photographs that Magritte might have made—boulders float over the sea; women are embraced by incandescent spheres. Unlike Uelsmann, I did "now-visualization." I liked putting the picture together in the viewfinder. There is one magic point of view that feels right, makes a picture work, and I was finding them. Uelsmann said he liked my stuff: pictures of empty park benches and abandoned toys, empty houses. He said he liked the emotion in them. I was communicating. I got top grades in his class.

I never used the school's darkrooms to make my prints. I preferred to work alone in the three-by-six-foot closet in our apartment I'd converted into a darkroom. When I came home from classes, I disappeared into this unventilated sweatbox with a bottle of whiskey, and printed photographs. When Patience had people over to visit, I stayed in the closet.

It was getting difficult to concentrate, difficult to see what the point was: these photographs, going to school. Not enough whiskey to make sense of it. Half a quart a day was not enough; was still jumpy; couldn't think; couldn't sleep; was getting worse. Shrink at Wolters had said I could go to the Veterans Administration and get Valium if I needed it. But, he said, "You should be fine after you get out. Being in the Army with the threat of going back to Vietnam is your problem." Wrong. I was out of the Army, couldn't go to Vietnam. Was still nuts. I went to the VA hospital to get Valium. Not so fast; we have procedures here. Had to be evaluated. Evaluation: talk to shrink for two hours.

I kept seeing student demonstrators on campus yelling about soldiers doing the wrong thing going to Vietnam. I got mad. Why, shiny-faced, draft-deferred twerps, are you *sending* them?

Patience was working nights to supplement the $145 a month I got on the GI Bill to go to school. It would've been $125 a month, but I had a wife and kid to support, so I got a twenty-dollar bonus for Jack and Patience. The GI Bill didn't pay for the books, supplies, and the tuition like it did after World War II. (The rate and extent of our benefits was established by World War II veterans who thought we were using rubber bullets and special effects in Vietnam. Getting wounded or killed in this wimpy war just wasn't as serious as it was in World War II.) Patience slept late. I waited for her to get up and make lunch. She made tuna fish salad better than I did, I told her.

Was drinking almost quart a day. Kids showed me marijuana at parties. Made me cough.

End of second quarter, grades dropped. Grissom said I'd better shape up soon. Grissom was right. Grissom was a veteran of World War II; he knew what was going on.

Veterans Administration sent me the results of my evaluation: I was fifty percent disabled for nervousness. I was afraid to tell anyone about my wimp disability. VA sent a check, back pay from the day I left the Army, invited me to come in for treatment:

What did you do in Vietnam?

Flew assault helicopters in the First Cav Division.

Dangerous?

Well, yeah—

How did you get along with your mother?

Huh?

Gave me Valium. Took five, six a day; drank the whiskey; smoked the pot. The Valium calmed me down, but only if I used it with the rest of the drugs.

I kept up my photography. One of the students at Schucht Village, a doctor named Merle Preble, asked me if I would show my pictures at the VA where he did some intern work. I put together a one-man show at the VA hospital library. Not a big deal, this show, but I watched a woman cry at one of my photographs and got a peek at the power of communication.

The leathery cadavers in the dissection lab weren't what I was looking for; they weren't human anymore, just objects kept in tanks of chemicals you studied to see how people are put together. I wanted to see the morgue.

Preble pushed open a heavy metal door, the kind you see on walk-in coolers. Inside the frigid room, feeble lavender light from ultraviolet lamps flickered, barely piercing the gloom. The floor was jammed with gurneys crowded every which way, burdened with bodies covered with strangely hazy glowing sheets. Naked dead people, hunched over inside big plastic bags hung along the wall, seemed to glower at me for staring.

Uelsmann assigned us the theme of death to explore with pictures. I'd seen lots of men slaughtered and it looked painful. I was afraid of it, so I thought this assignment might help me overcome my fear. I photographed myself, whitened with talcum powder, arms clasped on my chest, lying as if in state, so I could see what I would look like in the coffin. Pretty gruesome, but not very real. I asked Preble to get me into the medical school's dissection laboratories and morgue with my camera. He said sure, and we went to the hospital late one night.

"Who are they?" I asked, looking at the people in the bags.

"Regular people. Died in the hospital," Preble said. He looked at me. "You okay?"

"Yeah." I was feeling weak, but I wanted to fight through it.

"Can you photograph in here?" Preble asked. "It's real dark."

I pointed my meter at the wall, at a man in a bag. His arms were together in front of him, his head slumped forward. I could *feel* him decaying. The cold room smelled sweet and stale. Concentrating on my work, I moved inside, squeezing between gurneys. The meter said it was real dark; I would have to use a slow shutter speed. I took a couple of shots of the man. I thought I saw his face move when the shutter clicked. My hand brushed a sheet and I felt heat. I jerked away and looked at Preble. "This one's still warm!"

He nodded, pulled down the sheet. I saw a little girl, about twelve, lying in the death light as though she were asleep. "Want to—"

"No," I said quickly. I was suddenly overcome with the same horrible feeling that I'd had in Vietnam, that I was violating privacy. I had taken one picture of a dead grunt and agonized about it for years. I could hear the people in this room telling me, whispering: This is *private* stuff, Bob. "I think I've seen enough."

Actually, more than enough. I was a wreck for days afterward. I never printed the photographs and got my first C in photography.

Near the end of my third quarter I got a letter from a friend of ours, Frank Aguilera, an anthropology student who was studying a remote country village in Spain to get his Ph.D. Frank said to come see him and his wife, Barbie. The idea that school would get me back on track was proving to be wrong. The graph of my grades was diving southeast. Grissom was disgusted with me. I decided to drop out at the end of the quarter and go to Spain for a while.

Patience was terrified. Just pick up and move to Spain? Now? No!

I told her I had to do something, school sure wasn't working. She eventually agreed. With the money the VA sent me and that which we gathered by selling our car and other belongings, I got together the sum of $1,654, enough to get the three of us to Luxembourg, where I'd buy a used car and drive to Spain. Once there, I figured we could live in Spain on my disability payments of $145 a month. Hell, we might *never* come back.

CHAPTER 3

March *1969*—Luxembourg. Kicking tires at used-car places, I found a brown 1954 Volkswagen, rumpled, ancient; but the engine sounded good. Needed tires, but I thought they'd get us to Spain. By the time we got to France, we had named it the Roach. We drove to the village of Almonaster la Real, Spain, in two days.

Frank and Barbie were happy to see us and we stayed up late talking about the old days at the University of Pennsylvania, where I'd first met them while visiting Patience. Actually, I was visiting Patience's boyfriend, James Elliott, a friend I'd known in Florida. I was a drifter then, a college dropout living in a Chevy panel truck, and they liked me anyway. Patience had introduced me to her friends, who included Frank and Barbie and Bill Smith and Emily Arnold, each couple now married.

When Frank and Barbie asked me about Vietnam, I said the Army really was like *Catch-22* and told them about Mo'Fuck the mongoose who used to fly around with us and earned several air medals. Funny stuff. I didn't want people, even friends, to think I was affected by Vietnam. You ever see a picture of John Wayne having problems after any of *his* wars?

I loved Almonaster la Real. Nothing about it reminded me of anything I'd ever seen before. The place was ancient—Frank showed me records of the village putting in their water system before 1490. The adobe walls of the white buildings were crusted thick with centuries of continuous whitewashing. The stones in many of the narrow streets were the same stones the Romans put there—the wonder of it: imagine, an actual Roman put that very stone right there. The houses were dimly lit with one or two fifteen-watt light bulbs because people had yet to become dependent on electricity. There were only a few televisions in the entire village of four hundred people, one of them at Bar Buenos Aires, where a crowd gathered every night to watch *Mission Impossible* and *I Love Lucy* in Spanish.

That first night, Frank took me to the Casino, a private club at the center of town, which, as far as I could tell, was open to anyone who had money for a drink unless the person was a Gypsy or a woman. He introduced me to the village's busiest entrepreneur, José Garcia Romero (Pepé, for short), who operated two bars, the butane distributorship, and anything else that turned a profit; Pepé's friend Crazy Marcus; José Maria (Maria José's brother), who wanted to do construction work in Germany; Juan Picado, the stonemason; Pepé Hole-in-the-Head, who actually had a nickel-wide crater in his forehead from having a tumor removed; Fernando the incredibly naive teenager; Don Blas, the doctor who could read English but not speak it; and more. They invited me to eat some *tapas* of ancient ham (some hams are twenty years old or more; I actually ate some hundred-year-old ham that had crystallized) and drink some of the region's favorite booze, *aguardiente*, which Frank told me (Frank translated for me because I speak Spanish worse than you do) meant "firewater." Frank warned me about it, which only piqued my professional interest. Pepé poured some crystal-clear *aguardiente* halfway up a small glass and filled the rest with water. When he added water, the *aguardiente* turned milky white. The stuff tasted like licorice, and I really wanted bourbon, but bourbon was unknown here. After the first one, I slugged down the drinks as fast as they served them. Soon I was having fun. I got along fine with the people. They were impressed at how badly I spoke Spanish and how much I could drink. When Frank and I left, I was staggering drunk. When we got back to Frank's place, I walked through his house, out onto the back veranda, and puked over the railing.

In a few weeks, my friends at Almonaster la Real learned to understand my version of Spanish. I could follow their conversations pretty well, but couldn't say much back without a lot of pantomiming and multiple-choice guessing.

Frank and I went to the Casino every night. He was working on his doctoral dissertation, documenting everyday life in the village. I was just there trying to be a Spaniard. Pepé usually tended bar. Men would gather after dinner and swap gossip, brag of adulterous adventures, and spin stories.

Fernando the incredibly naive teenager came in one night and said "I just discovered something you won't believe!" his face bright with wonder. We thought he'd discovered gold, found a diamond, won the lottery or something. He got everybody's attention and explained to us his discovery: if you hold your dick just so, said Fernando, and then rub your hand up and down, like this, it will get real hard and then, if you *keep* doing it, you will feel a very wonderful feeling, he said, a feeling so good it's impossible to describe! It will make your eyes pop! People looked around, the Spaniards shrugging at Frank and me, hoping we wouldn't make generalizations of the Spanish based on Fernando, and then everybody burst out laughing. We bought Fernando drinks and said he'd discovered a mighty fine thing all right.

The villagers were also very fond of tricks, what I call after-dinner magic. Pepé had a trick. He would invite the crowd to arrange all the dominoes in the box on the bar in a legal array—only matching numbers touching each other—while he was out of the room. When someone shouted that we'd finished, he'd call out the beginning and ending domino faces of the chain. It was a terrific mind-reading routine, a simple trick that I never figured out until Pepé told me: he took one of the dominoes with him. The two faces of that piece would necessarily be the two ending faces of the domino chain we'd constructed because of the way domino sets are made.

Pepé's best, though, was this: he swiped a fly out of the air and put it into a glass filled with water. He turned the glass upside down on his palm and the fly floated up to the bottom of the glass.

"The fly is drowning," he said with the voice of a man twice his size, looking sad, his wiseass expression shining through.

"That's a fact," I said, watching the fly struggling, trying to claw through the glass, moving slower and slower.

When the fly stopped struggling, Pepé said, "Poor fly. Drowned while minding his own business. I feel terrible at the brutal things I can do."

Everyone laughed. Pepé turned the glass right side up. When the fly floated to the top, he touched it with his finger and the sopping fly stuck to it. He put the fly on the bar top, where it lay in a little puddle of water. Pepé shook his head sadly and stared at the tiny corpse. *"Pobrecito."* He shrugged and tapped an ash from his cigarette onto it. "At least I can give it a proper burial, eh?"

"Yes, you owe him that!" someone who'd seen the trick insisted.

Pepé nodded. "More, please. More ashes for the fly."

We all flicked ashes on the fly until a little gray burial mound heaped over it.

The fly buried, Pepé suggested we fill up our glasses and drink a toast to the fallen aviator. We all did. "You know," Pepé said, "I feel terrible about this. If it were in my power, I would take back what I've done. I would restore life to this innocent bug." Pepé looked seriously into the distance as if communing with God. His face brightened suddenly and he said, "I will!" He bent down and put his face close to the miniature grave and gently blew away the ashes a little at a time. "Come, little one; come back to life." The fly's wings rustled in Pepé's breath. He picked it up by one wing, set it on his palm, and softly blew air at it for a few minutes. Everyone who hadn't seen this routine stared, amazed. It moved, by God! It stood up, Jesus! It cleaned itself for a few seconds, buzzed its wings experimentally, and flew away.

When the Casino closed at about two in the morning, Frank and I often walked with Pepé back to his place on the road at the entrance to the village. Pepé had his own little open-air bar there, which his wife, Incarna, usually handled while he tended the Casino. Frank and I got into an argument one night on the way to Pepé's and lingered outside the Casino, yelling about something. It was one of those arguments that no one can remember the next day. The local cop, Rudolfo, and a Guardia came over to us, smiling. I had grown accustomed to the Guardia Civil, the state police, who seemed to be everywhere, though at first I was wary of them. They looked menacing in their long green capes and patent leather hats. They packed Walther 9mm pistols and sawed-off shotguns under the capes. The Guardia Civil had the power of summary justice, meaning they could blow you away with impunity if you fucked up and called Franco a queer. They didn't do it often, but they could. The Guardia joined us as we argued while at the same time tactfully moving us to the edge of town.

Standing near a streetlight on the main road, I saw the Guardia's pistol peeking out from his cape and asked him what kind it was, noticing I had no trouble speaking Spanish when I was drunk enough. He smiled, pulled it out of his holster, and held it up. "A Walther PPK," he said.

"Standard issue?" I said, reaching out and snatching it from him. It got very quiet as I inspected the Guardia's pistol. Rudolfo stared at me, his eyes wide. "Robert," he said, "you should not grab a Guardia's gun. It . . . it is not polite."

"Huh?" I looked at the Guardia and saw the worried look on his face. I still didn't understand my transgression, but I handed back his pistol saying, "Nice piece. Same one James Bond uses."

On the way back to Frank's, he explained to me that I was an asshole who had come "that close" to getting shot.

I didn't just hang out and drink in Almonaster. I wanted to be a writer, and living in Spain, not having to work, was a good time to give it a try. So, in addition to drinking, I worked on a short story about a band of primitives who discover a fundamental method for time travel. When I finished the story, we found out that Bill Smith and his wife, Emmy, were in Portugal. We all decided to go visit for the Fourth of July.

The Smiths had rented a place overlooking the Mediterranean. Bill, a genial, freckle-faced Huckleberry Finn–looking guy who I remembered as a terrific cheater in Monopoly at Penn, was now a writer. That they were staying on the coast in a big house was just how I expected writers to live.

To celebrate the Fourth of July, we had a fireworks war in the house. Girls against boys. We threw firecrackers like grenades at each other. Made a lot of noise, and since the Portuguese (except those who celebrate every day anyway) don't honor our independence, people noticed. When we started a small brush fire (the battle had moved outside), the police arrived. We threw buckets of water, which Jack, who was five and just came up to my waist, pumped out of a cistern, on the flames and put the fire out while Smith, speaking slick Portuguese, convinced the police to leave us alone. The man has a silver tongue.

Before we went back to Spain, I showed Bill my time-travel story. He read it and said it was good; just needed a little rewriting, was all. I took that as a polite way of saying I had some talent, and if I worked at it I might torture the stupid story into something bearable. I figured real writers just sat down and wrote the final draft—rewriting was for amateurs.

Spain. I'm walking along the road with Frank. We see a dog lying on the shoulder. I go to it and it wags its tail slightly, but I can see its back is broken. I'm outraged: these fucking people will just let a dog lie here dying? Where's the owner? Where's the vet? Pepé comes over and says someone has to kill the dog, but no one wants to and the vet is gone. You, Pepé says, have to kill the dog. Me? It's not my dog. No one else will, Pepé says, smiling the way people do when they've stuck someone else with a moral dilemma. I squat by the dog and talk to it and it wags its tail, and I'm feeling sick. I stroke the dog. "Good girl. Good dog. You'll be okay." Someone hands me a sledgehammer. A hammer? That's the best we can do? A fucking hammer? They nod. I'm holding the hammer. Everybody begins to leave. Everybody's gone. I have to kill this dog. I'm talking to the dog, but the dog senses something is up and rolls its eyes nervously, its tail slapping the ground. I say goddammit to myself a hundred times and curse the Spaniards and swing the hammer like a golf club and smash the dog's head right after I said she'd be all right.

Everybody buys me drinks at the Casino, but I'm pissed off; I'm shaking. Fernando comes in and tells me the dog didn't die. I jump up. He quickly adds that someone else finished her off.

The Aguileras were packing up to resume life in the States. Barbie left a month before Frank to get their house ready while Frank finished his research. When Frank left, we stayed. I wasn't ready to go home yet. We rented a small house next to Escopeta's General Store on Ramon y Cajal, an ancient Roman road near the center of town.

I pecked at stories. Patience shopped and learned how to cook Spanish food.

Jack knew everybody and spoke Spanish like a native. I saw him run into Bar Buenos Aires one afternoon while I was there. He didn't see me. His friends stayed in the street, too shy to come in without their parents. Jack—who was allowed by everybody to do anything he wanted—swaggered over to the counter and tapped a *duro*—a Spanish nickel—on top, demanding a *chupa,* a lollipop. His head was a foot lower than the countertop. José Manuel, the owner of the bar, leaned over, grinned, and handed Jack some *chupas* and took the coin. Jack walked outside and gave each of his friends a candy and they ran off together, a regular little mob of street urchins.

Jack accepted Almonaster as home with the aplomb of a five-year-old. When Patience and I went to Morocco, we left him in the village with Escopeta's family, the owners of the grocery. Jack was especially good friends with Escopeta's son, Manolo, but he was in love with Escopeta's teenage daughter, Manole. She spoiled him with attention. When we came back a week later with an English couple we'd befriended on the trip, the village kids, dirty faces, short pants, big smiles, swarmed around the Roach, laughing and yelling. Patience pointed out one of the kids as our son. Our new friends were amazed.

This expatriate stuff was getting old. America was in the news— Neil Armstrong had just landed on the moon (most people thought that was great, but one old sage at the Casino warned that it was all done in a studio, with actors and a model lunar lander). As much as I was immersed in the Spanish culture, I missed the States. That was difficult to accept. I had no respect for the political system that created Vietnam, yet I missed the country and the people. The point of this visit, to forget Vietnam and to recover my sanity, was not working. My writing was getting nowhere because I lacked the faith that I could do it. I was drinking a quart of booze a day.

In October 1969, Patience got a letter saying her father had died. The news came when we both wanted to go home. I phoned my dad and borrowed traveling money. We drove to Lisbon to catch a Yugoslavian freighter home. The Roach, which I'd figured would be dead by now, was still running great. Selling it in Spain meant a lot of paperwork and import taxes. The shipping company said it would cost two hundred dollars to bring it with us. We loaded it on the ship.

The Yugoslavian freighter took two weeks to sail from Lisbon to New York because of bad weather. We were three of the twelve passengers on board. We sailed through storms that sank other freighters, tankers, and seagoing tugs. Waves bashed into the superstructure, crashing against the passengers' portholes. Jack got thrown across the main stateroom, sitting in a giant wooden chair, looking very surprised.

Patience weathered the storm in her bunk, sick. I took photographs, making time exposures of the waves crashing against the portholes. I was sober for the entire trip because the ship only had two kinds of booze: scotch, which I couldn't stand, and some ungodly swill called Slivovitska, a plum brandy that tasted worse than it sounded.

When we were a day out, we all crowded around a portable radio and cheered hearing an American commercial jingle: "Chock Full o' Nuts is the hea-ven-ly coffee . . ." Home.

CHAPTER 4

November 1969—We stayed with my parents in North Palm Beach, Florida. I looked for work while we lived off the modest insurance benefit Patience got from her father.

We were feeling so well off (the insurance money came to three thousand dollars) that we decided to fly to Tampa to visit friends. I rented a Cessna at Palm Beach International Airport, loaded up Patience and Jack, and took off. Hadn't flown in three years. Felt good. Patience was more impressed that I was able to understand the tower gibberish than that I could fly. Flying made her sick, too. Jack sat on my lap and yanked the control yoke around like he was on a twenty-five-cent sidewalk ride. He couldn't see over the top of the console, but he was a natural pilot. Whoop! Zoom! Wow! Patience got sick, nixing Jack's flying lessons for the rest of the trip.

We spent the night in Tampa and went back to the plane early in the morning. I'd parked at a grass-strip airport and the plane was covered in dew. While I wiped the windshield and did the preflight, I had the feeling I was over there. I used to do this every morning, getting my Huey ready for the assaults. I felt myself getting tense.

Got in the plane, cranked up. Did a warm-up where I was parked and then pushed in full throttle. We roared down the grass strip and I lifted off, keeping the plane low. I thought I was in a Huey and that Patience and Jack weren't there. I was taking off at An Khe, heading east toward the pass. I skimmed over the trees at the end of the strip and stayed low among the treetops—hard to hit you when you're in the trees. Patience asked if we weren't a little low and I remembered where I was. I stayed low and flew directly toward a tall tree. She said, "Bob?" I pulled up over the tree, just missing the branches, caught a glimpse of the morning sun, felt myself relax. I climbed to cruising altitude. "Are you okay?" Patience said. I nodded.

I was accepted for a job at Pratt & Whitney to make high-speed movies of jet engines in action—I knew enough about photography to bullshit the head of the project. I also had an opportunity to work for Radiation, an electronics manufacturer, in Palm Bay because a friend of mine who worked there, Bill Willis, knew they needed a phototechnician. Willis, a big blond man, and I grew up together west of Delray Beach, Florida. We shared a common interest in science and technology, and I was in the mood for that. Also, the pay at Radiation was better. I took that job.

I'd never worked in an electronics factory before. They put me on the night shift photographing circuit diagrams with a room-sized process camera and developing the twenty-by-thirty-inch film sheets. The job required some skill, but not so much that I was kept occupied. I soon became bored and started taking two-hour lunch breaks. I would wander around the whole place, seeing how they built integrated circuit chips. I saw the whole process, from actually growing the silicon crystal, slicing it to wafers, sensitizing the wafers with photoresists, doping, photomask exposures, etching, testing, and final cutting. Interesting stuff, but my niche in the process—photomask technician—wasn't very exciting. I think the most interesting project I ever worked on was making microphotographs of a competitor's chip. Electronics companies do this regularly—they buy another company's hot new chip and grind it down, layer by layer, and photograph each layer. With the photos, the engineers can see how the thing works and rip off the design.

As long as the projects changed often and as long as they were challenging, I was interested. But that was rare. Usually I messed around with my own photography experiments or played with the computer. Computers were novel in 1970. We had a Digital PDP-8 that I knew just enough about to be its greatest threat. One night, as I taught myself the octal numbering system by flipping toggles on the computer's front panel and watching all the nifty lights flash, I somehow sent messages to the computer that made it dump the main program—the one we used to create some of the photomask templates. Naturally, I didn't mention this to anyone when I left. When I came to work the next afternoon, the place was a madhouse. Since no one there actually understood the computer, they'd flown in a consultant from New York to straighten things out. Photomask production was stalled. The boss asked me if I knew anything about it. Heck no, Boss. I'm always in the darkroom.

A few weeks later, after reading the technical manuals, I dumped the program and reinstalled it, to see how it was done. That guy from New York made a fortune doing pretty simple stuff.

Driving to work one afternoon, I passed a motorcycle shop that had a sparkling new racy-sexy Honda 750 motorcycle sitting out front. No one in America had ever seen a machine like this before. Four cylinders, four upswept exhaust pipes, great noise, lots of power. *Vaaroom!* I took it for a ride. Low-level flying. I had to have it. A few weeks later, I did.

I had a job and a motorcycle; so why was I so unhappy? One reason was I had no home life. My schedule was weird. I got off work at midnight, drove home on the bike, and sat around until about three or four drinking bourbon and watching late-night television while Patience slept. She'd gotten a job on the day shift at Radiation, soldering stuff onto circuit boards. I slept most of the day away, getting up around noon to go to work three hours later. Patience and I became strangers.

One of the girls who worked in the cafeteria, Mary, used to joke around with me when I ate there. She was funny enough to be cute. When I asked her if she wanted to go for a ride on my bike one night, she said yes. In a few weeks, we were sleeping together. It was automatic—I don't know how these things happen. Sometimes I think I was just along for the ride while my dick did the driving.

Big confession a few weeks later. Patience was very hurt. I watched her cry and knew I should feel something—I wanted to feel something—but I didn't. I kept seeing Mary—I couldn't stop. I even told Patience when I'd be away with Mary—don't wait up. For revenge, Patience drove the Roach to Tampa to see an old boyfriend.

She wrecked the car there. When she got back, she said she'd decided she was packing up Jack and going back to school—with me or without me.

Okay. I wasn't sure about returning to school, but my job seemed like a monotonous path to the grave. Maybe if I had more of a challenge, I'd be interested. I went to my division boss and told him I could run the entire photomask section better than anybody there and that's what I wanted to do. He agreed that I probably could, but I'd only been there six months. I said, okay, I quit.

C H A P T E R   5

September 1970—We loaded a rental truck with all our stuff, including my bike. The plan was that Patience and Jack would drive the truck to the house we'd rented in Gainesville and I would meet them there with the Roach, which was supposed to be out of the repair shop that afternoon. The shop was late getting the Roach ready, and I didn't leave Melbourne until eleven.

I smelled gas, but couldn't find the leak. I drove with the windows open. I woke up lying across the front seats. Dim light glowed in through the windshield.

Too much light. Bad place for a mortar attack.

The Huey is leaking fuel?

Tell the crew chief.

Gasoline? We use jet fuel.

I sat up. The Roach's front bumper was touching the guardrail of an overpass. No damage. I must have been going very slowly as I passed out from the fumes. I got out and watched a car hurtle beneath the overpass. Real close. Walked back to the Roach. The smell of gas was very strong, but there were only fifty miles to go. I got back in and drove with my head stuck out the window. Arrived in Gainesville feeling sick. Before I unloaded our stuff from the truck, I found the leak: the Roach had a sediment bowl just under the fuel tank that I didn't know about. The sediment-bowl gasket leaked and the fumes were being sucked in through the dash.

At this time in my life, about the most important thing to me was my motorcycle. It was an intoxicating machine, a freedom ride. I had to return the rental truck in Ocala and take the Honda back to Melbourne for one more week of work at Radiation. I lashed the bike to the metal tie-down rings inside the truck and left that afternoon. In Ocala, a kid ran out in front of me chasing a ball. I slammed on the brakes in time to miss him. I felt a terrific crash in the back of the truck. Stopped, got out, and opened the doors. My pride-and-joy bike was lying on the deck up against the forward wall. The tie-down rings had ripped out. I lashed the bike upright and returned the truck. When I got the bike off the truck, I could see only minor damage to the front fender. When I got on the road, however, the front forks shook badly as I approached sixty. The shaking got worse as I accelerated, then went away at about eighty. I drove at eighty, thinking I should have hit the kid.

A week later, after a messy good-bye with Mary in which I knew the thing wasn't over because I didn't really have the guts to end it, I left Melbourne.

I was back in school studying photography.

I made pictures, enthusiastically at first, but soon got bored—a familiar pattern. Back from the war (it was still being fought) four years, yet nothing seemed to interest me. I spent a lot of time drinking and staring at television. *Star Trek* would hypnotize me; commercials, too. Fantasies interested me. Television was mind-numbing, which is what I wanted. Patience interrupted now and then. "Bob," she usually said, pointing to Jack standing by my chair, "Jack's been trying to talk to you for twenty minutes." I'd listen to Jack telling me about some skirmish he was having with a neighbor kid for a minute and then, when he left, become absorbed in the tube, no matter what was on. I stayed up until the stations went off the air and the television showed snow. I watched that, too, trying to see things in the randomness. I was trying not to ever have to sleep, to avoid leaping up in a panic.

My idea of fun was to get on my bike at midnight, speeding down country roads at a hundred and thirty. Lying on the gas tank, headlight blazing a tunnel ahead, trees swishing by in a blur, reminding me of flying. Low-level flying. Come back, the house would be still. Air humid. Life stagnant.

I had to turn in a final project for my drawing class. I dragged out my old footlocker from Vietnam, still clearly marked: WO-1 ROBERT C. MASON; W3152420. I took everything out and set it up so the end became the bottom and the lid opened on the side. I drew a picture of myself from a slide of me holding my M-1 carbine, smiling a crazed smile, tacked it on the lid of the footlocker. I stuck my bronze star to the drawing. I put a dozen jagged punji stakes on the bottom of the locker, shoved an old fatigue blouse and a plastic wig stand into the sharp stakes. I put my flight helmet on the wig stand and pulled down the black visor. I stared at this creation for hours, short of breath. I splashed red paint all over the punji stakes; spattered drops onto the drawing.

I had a box of memories that I would bury. That would be part of the whole drawing, the burial. I needed something to get the viewers' attention, something that'd give them a sample jolt of fear. I rigged a wire from the lid to the trigger of a pistol loaded with blanks mounted so it pointed at whoever opened the box. When they open this box, I thought, they won't forget it.

I go to class. Set the box on a table near the rest of the drawings. Wait. A girl asks what's in the box. My drawing. She looks puzzled, shrugs. She is not going to get this. A guy asks the same, he's frail, scared of me because I always wear sunglasses and never talk to anybody. He is going to piss in his pants. Eugene Grissom, the department chairman, comes in to help with the grading. Grissom's a vet. He will get it. Maybe he will also throw me out of school.

I tell my instructor, John O'Connor, I have a question. We go to his office. I tell him the nifty trick with the gun. John's mouth drops open, looks nervous. "I get the idea, Bob. But don't you think it's going to scare the shit out of these people?"

"That's the idea. Scared shitless is the drawing."

John nods for a while. "Okay. Okay. But what if we disconnect the gun and just tell everybody it was rigged to go off? That'll scare them, too."

"You think just knowing it could go off will scare them?"

"Oh, yes. Yes. I believe you'll get a very good reaction, Bob. And I won't have to have a heart attack."

"It's just a blank—"

"The noise, Bob. Inside a building?"

"Oh, yeah. Inside here. Make a helluva bang, eh?" I laugh.

"So will you disconnect the gun?"

"Well, John, what about my grade? I mean, without the booby trap, lots of the idea is just . . . lost."

"No. No way it'll affect your grade, Bob. I promise." I nod, thinking about it. O'Connor begins to breathe regularly.

"Okay. I'll take out the blanks. Then the gun'll just go *snap*. Okay?"

"Fine, Bob. That'll be fine." O'Connor pats my shoulder as we walk back to the grading room. "Bob. Thanks for telling me about this. I mean, I really appreciate it."

"No problem, John."

I got an A for the project.

I created excuses to take off on the bike on weekends. Photographic expeditions, I said.

"Why can't you take pictures in Gainesville?" Patience asked.

"I've already shot Gainesville," I said.

"Oh."

I was driving a friend's car up and down streets in Melbourne Beach, looking for Mary. She told me she had moved, but all I could recall of her address was that she lived near the beach. It was three in the morning. I had a bottle of whiskey next to me and I swigged from that as I cruised up and down streets looking for her car. I stopped in front of a house and stared in the driveway, thinking I saw a Plymouth Valiant. I noticed that headlights were glaring in through the windshield. I realized I was on the wrong side of the road. I heard a car door close, and a man materialized from the glare of the lights. He was a cop. He was carrying a flashlight. He shone it on my face.

"What the hell are you doing?" said the cop.

He wouldn't have appreciated the truth. I held my finger up to my mouth and said "Sssh" while I looked left and right. The cop followed my glances and I shoved the whiskey bottle behind my back.

The cop looked at me. "What?" the cop said quietly.

"You know of any parties going on around here?" I said.

"Parties? At three in the morning. No, I don't. Everybody's asleep."

"Not these people," I said. "It's not really a party, they're selling drugs."

The cop blinked. "Drugs? You're telling me you're trying to buy drugs?"

"Yes," I said. "It's my job." I nodded confidently.

"Oh," the cop said, nodding back. He switched off his flashlight. "Where're you from?"

"Jacksonville office," I said.

"You have an ID?"

"You kidding. Get myself killed?"

"Guess that's true." The cop took his cap off, reset it to a more comfortable position. "Listen, there *is* a place, two blocks up and one to the left. I've seen some pretty scroungy-looking people going in and out of a house there. Has about five cars parked in the yard. Can't miss it."

I grinned, nodded vigorously. "Could be the place," I said. I put the car in gear, looked up at the cop. "Thanks."

The cop smiled. "Hey, anything I can do to help." He turned to go back to his car, stopped, and said, "Be careful."

"Thanks, Officer," I said.

I cruised randomly until dawn glowed faintly in the east. Nobody in Melbourne Beach owned a Plymouth Valiant as far as I could see. I drove over to the beach, parked across the street from a restaurant, and watched the sun rise out of the sea. I took a swig from my bottle. I noticed movement at the restaurant, saw a girl dressed in a housecoat come out of a second-story apartment over the restaurant and get the paper. Then I saw a Plymouth Valiant parked beside the building.

I knocked on the door. The girl I'd seen opened it. She held the top of her housecoat closed with one hand.

"Excuse me," I said. "I'm looking for a friend of mine. You might know her."

"What's her name?" the girl said.

"Mary. She drives a Valiant."

The girl looked at me curiously and said, "Is your name Bob?"

"Yes."

The girl turned and called, "Mary. There's somebody here to see you."

Mary thought I was a hero for finding her. She invited me to bed and gave me a hero's welcome.

A few months later Mary had a problem. She'd lost her job, and she and her son (she was divorced) had no place to stay. Naturally, I offered to find her a place in Gainesville. Patience might not understand, though. Problem solved: Mary said she could leave her son with her parents and I thought I might be able to sneak her to Gainesville, where she could stay with friends and look for a job. When I called home and told Rosemary—a friend who shared the house with us— the plan, Patience had picked up the extension and heard me. When I got home, Patience told me she knew all about it and left immediately.

The next day, I went to Patience and told her I'd give up Mary if she'd come back. She did. I swore I was just her friend now, that Mary was in trouble and needed a place to stay until she got herself organized. That is how my girlfriend came to live in the same house as my wife. Patience tried to be nice. It seemed noble at the time, to *both* of us, to have Mary living with us. What did we know of normal? I was a drunken idiot. Patience figured *that* was normal, too. All this seemed tame compared to what was going on inside my head. Still not sleeping, feeling tired all the time. My shrink at the VA arranged for me to undergo a sleep examination at the hospital.

Living with two women (three, if you include the neutral house-mate, Rosemary) isn't easy. And in this case it was absurd. I had assumed an obligation to take care of Mary, and figured Patience ought to understand and go along with that. Patience became unreasonable: "You have nothing to do around the house except take out the garbage, and look at it!" she yelled one night. "*Maggots* are crawling out of the garbage can! You never do anything around here!"

I sulked (I hated it when she got this way). "That's what *you* say. *Mary* says she thinks I do plenty around the house. That's an *objective* opinion—"

Patience's eyes open wide. "Bob, Mary is your old *girlfriend*—"

"I don't want to argue about it if you have to bring up the past," I said. Patience walked off.

A few nights later, while Mary was confiding her troubles to me in the family room—we held hands, platonically—I saw Patience come into the kitchen. She stopped, frozen. She was trying not to go nuts and die from pain, but I saw it as spying on an innocent meeting of friends. I said, "We can see you there." Patience's face became ashen. She turned and went back to our bedroom.

It was as plain as day that Mary was trying to move in, but I didn't see it. After Mary gave Patience a private triumphal look one night while I had my head on her shoulder, Patience told me Mary had to go. What a nag! But I called a friend and took Mary to stay with him and his wife.

Two weeks later my friend said his wife was getting upset and Mary had to go. Damn, Mary sure needed a lot of help. I brought Mary back. Patience, finally losing her grip, left when we arrived. The next day Patience came back, but only to get her things and to see Jack. Jack was at my sister's, but I wouldn't tell Patience where he was. She started screaming and ran out of the house, hysterical. I couldn't figure out why. She must be crazy.

I went to the sleep study at the hospital. For ten nights, I slept in a small room with wires stuck all over my skull and one attached to my dick. The dick sensor would tell the doctors when I had an erection, something they were interested in knowing. I used to fiddle with the sensor while I waited to fall asleep, imagining them in the morning saying, "Jeez-oh-Pete! This guy had a hundred and twenty-eight erections last night!" At the end of the test, my shrink called me in and said that the trouble was that I did not sleep. He said this without a smile. I stared at the shrink. "I know. That's why I come here all the time."

"Well, now we know you really don't sleep, like you say. You stay in REM all night."

"REM?"

"Rapid eye movement: dream state. You never get into deep sleep."

"That might be why I feel so goddamn tired all the time."

"Yeah," the shrink said. "Not sleeping would account for that."

I think I was supposed to feel better that science had confirmed the obvious. I got mad and said some critical things about the psychological profession as practiced by the VA. When I got home, I figured they'd be coming to scoop me up in a big net, so I sat on the front step slugging down bourbon with a gun stuck in my pants, waiting. They didn't come. Instead they adjusted my medications, giving me different kinds of tranquilizers, but I still didn't sleep.

After the sleep studies, I began to cheat on Mary by sneaking out to see Patience. Patience lived near the university with a girlfriend, and I'd go see her and complain how bad I felt and how I wasn't getting along very well with Mary, and so on. Maybe she'd come back? Are you kidding? She was dating normal people, having fun.

A month later, I intercepted Patience as she walked to a morning class. I took her aside and begged her to come home. We both cried. Patience said, "Not with that girl in the house."

I went home and told Mary she had to go. She left.

Two days later, Mary called. She would not give up so easily. She felt I had cheated her and wanted me back. I went to see her, telling Patience I was visiting Bill Willis, my technician friend in Melbourne. I was going to be firm with Mary, end this thing. The result of that confrontation was that she got pregnant.

I told Patience I was going to New York City to photograph the Village with some friends of mine from the photography class. I arranged a $500 student loan at the bank. On a Friday I drove Mary straight to New York in her car to an abortion clinic in the Village. Sunday, Patience picked me up in Gainesville, where my "friends" had supposedly dropped me off. My affair with Mary was over as far as I was concerned.

I was still in school, in my senior year. When I signed up for my final photography classes, though, my instructor, Todd Walker, said I'd been goofing off, and he had decided to give my space to somebody who'd appreciate it. I panicked. Photography was the only thing I had left. I spent the next two weeks working around the clock producing several projects, all having to do with sequential photography. I did a slide show with sound and black-and-white slides that flickered like an old-time movie. One of the shows had Haysup, the rocking horse I'd built in Texas, sneak up on Jack and kill him, which Jack thought was fun. I also made three photo cubes with eighteen bizarre images of the same doorway on their faces. Each face had scenes like a shark floating in through a door, the door opening to the middle of a sidewalk, a naked girl walking in through the door. Aside from being a legitimate reason to take pictures of naked girls, the idea was to create random story sequences by tossing the cubes. I showed a new project each time the class met, impressing the students and Walker. Walker relented at the end of the semester and allowed me to continue.

In the summer of 1971, we moved to a five-bedroom house near the university and rented three of the bedrooms to three other students to pay the rent. Patience and I were still on shaky ground and it got shakier. We had an argument in which I confessed the abortion. We decided to get a divorce when I graduated (otherwise, I would lose some of my VA benefits—let's not be too fucking nuts). Patience went to visit her mother in Maine. I sent Jack to stay with my parents. When Patience came home, nothing had changed—we were in mourning over our dead relationship. Jack came home with symptoms of our problems: he had a nervous twitch and cleared his throat constantly.

Patience yelled at me a lot, pointing out what a jerk I'd been and still was. She began to see a shrink at the university and one day she came home and instead of yelling said, "I love you. Do you love me?" Her shrink, she later told me, had asked her how I felt—was I sorry? did I love her?—and she had to admit she had no idea. So he said to go home and ask. I did love her, and I was sorry, and that was what she needed to hear. We were on the mend.

After I graduated in December 1971 (the first person in my family's history to get a college degree; as hollow a victory as I've ever won) Mary came to see me. She was on her way to Indiana and wanted me to go with her. With Patience and Jack watching, I walked her out to our backyard and said no. I felt bad watching her cry. It wasn't love; I think it had something to do with honor. I was responsible for at least part of her pain. She called me terrible names, and I thought she was mostly right.

My degree was in art, so I figured I could make a living at it. While Patience worked on her last semester, I started a photography company called Silver Graphics and tried to drum up business. I did one wedding and a few pictures of an architect's model buildings. Then nothing.

I decided to apply for a government job as an aircraft dispatcher, a civilian who inspects aircraft and certifies which ones are flyable and assigns their crews for military reserve units and the National Guard. If there was a position for which I was overqualified and should have no trouble getting, I thought, this was it. Waited around rubbing my hands together; cushy damn government job coming up. Got a letter back saying that my disability (fifty percent service-connected nut) made me ineligible for the job. The envelope had stamped on it: *Don't Forget, Hire the Vet.* I complained: how stressful can such a job be? Sorry, that's our policy. Wrote my senator. Sorry, he answered, I tried, but they say—

My dad, a realtor in south Florida, suggested that I import some of the pocketknives like the ones I'd brought back from Spain; we could sell them by mail. Neither of us knew squat about importing or selling by mail, but since he and a friend were willing to pay my way over and buy the first batch of knives, and since I was broke, why not?

I decided to become an importer.

Back to Almonaster la Real. I had a fairly good time seeing Pepé and the gang again, but I felt awkward and unsure of myself as an importer. After I found the place where they made the knives, I bought a few hundred. I had a week to kill before my plane left, so I drove to Algeciras in a rented car and took the ferry to Tangier.

I liked Tangier. When we visited from Spain, Patience and I had discovered a pension called Hotel Florida, so I went there. The rooms were small and plain, cost two dollars a day. Another two bucks bought meals sent up from the restaurant downstairs. Because the rooms were boring, young people from Germany, Holland, England, Spain, Portugal, France, and Canada sat out in a sort of living room around a big table jabbering away in English. Compared to the Moroccans, we were all from the same neighborhood. We smoked keef, a potent form of marijuana, drank sweet tea, and talked a blue streak.

The population of the Florida changed every night as people came and went. My last night there, I talked to a Canadian girl whom I seemed to know but had never met. I had severe wounds from all the trouble I had generated with my fling with Mary, but I was very lonely. I asked the girl if I could sleep with her, no sex, figuring she'd tell me to buzz off. She said okay; and that is what we did—we were both lonely.

On the ferry back to Spain I met three Canadian girls and hung out with them during the crossing. When we got to Algeciras, I offered them a ride to Seville. The annual *feria* of Seville—a big summer festival in which everybody wears traditional costumes and *caballeros* ride around on horses—was in full swing, so I showed the Canadians around, stopping to listen to mariachi music at the Mexican pavilion and eating steak at the Argentine pavilion.

When I said good-bye, they asked me where I was going. I said Almonaster La Real. What's that? Tiny village in the middle of nowhere. They looked very interested. Want to come? Yeah.

We stopped at Cortegana, a town five miles from Almonaster, at midnight and got two rooms. The next morning I created a sensation in Almonaster by showing up with the girls. The village women (who all knew Patience) were bent out of shape. Me, a married man, and three loose (hitchhiker) girls. Oh!

Pepé thought it was funny. I told him I was taking them to Lisbon. He winked. "What a nice person you are, to go out of your way for these poor girls."

I winked back. There was no way I could convince anyone that I was just lonely and that traveling with the girls was innocent fun. Before we left for Lisbon, I went to see Don Blas, the doctor, and got some drugs for a miserable cold I'd picked up. Doc gave me a bottle of antihistamines. I took two pills and we jumped in the car and left.

I made one stop before Portugal. I had a beer and took another pill. We drove into Portugal around sunset. Going around a turn, fifty miles later, I blacked out. I remember going into the turn, then nothing, then the sight of the sharp ditch rushing at me, crash, then nothing.

It was like one of those mornings when you can't seem to wake up except I had no idea where I was.

I didn't remember any shooting.

I thought this was a quiet LZ.

I heard the girls sobbing behind me and remembered I was in a car. "Bob," one of the girls said, "can you open your door?"

It felt like my eyes were open, but I couldn't see anything. I blinked for a while and saw a ruby glow. I said "Sure" and pulled the door handle and pushed on the door. I passed out.

The car shook. I woke up. Portuguese voices chattered all around us, but I couldn't see anything. The door was yanked open and hands reached in and pulled me out. They held me up and my vision cleared. I watched them pulling the girls out; they had lots of cuts. The hood and the trunk of the car stood straight up, all the glass was broken out. The car was a crumpled mess two hundred feet from the road. "You rolled and flipped all the way," said one of the men. "Can you stand?" I said yes. They let go. I collapsed. When they tried to get me up, I said no, it's okay here. The grass on my cheek felt as soft and smooth as cool silk. I wanted to sleep. They helped us into their cars. One of the girls and I sat in the backseat of a very clean car, bleeding like stuck pigs. We looked at each other. She was covered in blood and scared to death. I'd carried so many bloody people in my helicopter I felt almost at home. I told her she'd be okay.

I had crashed on a simple ground mission to Lisbon, and my passengers had gotten hurt. I had really screwed up. Something was odd about my face. Experimenting with my tongue, I discovered I could stick it through a gash under my lower lip. I could also touch my nose with my tongue because it had moved down.

The Portuguese drove us to an aid station at a small town where a doctor bandaged us and stopped the bleeding. He snapped the loose skin on my face together with nylon staples, which did not hurt a bit. Other than feeling like a criminal because I'd hurt the girls, I felt fine. I noticed that the bystanders watching us on the stretchers looked aghast when the attendants carried us out to three ambulances. When I asked where they were taking us, they said Lisbon. Lisbon? Three hours? I lay in the ambulance, completely free of pain, and knew I was in shock. I had seen grunts lying in the back of my chopper, pale, dying, serene, and now I understood. I felt very sleepy. I might not wake up. I slept.

When I woke the shock had worn off. My chest and pelvis were on fire. I lay on a gurney in a madhouse. People were screaming in Portuguese, white coats whisked by, rushing. The girls were gone. White coats stripped me naked and rolled me into a room and X-rayed me. Then someone I couldn't see rolled the gurney down a dim hallway filled with moaning and crying people and loaded me onto a table against the wall. Pain raged through me. People begged, shrieked, wailed for help all around me. I was engulfed in a chorus of agony. I could not raise my head, but I could roll it to the side. A bandaged man across the hall waved a stump of an arm and just kept saying, "Please. Please." I said, "Okay, they'll be back, don't worry." He said, "Please. Please." I told him this was a hospital, not to worry. He kept pleading. An old woman on a table next to me sobbed and moaned. I ask her what was wrong. She cried louder. I was stoic. I was not a panicky fool like these. Be patient. White coats will be back in a minute.

Hour, wait.

Heard myself moaning. Came naturally, part of the symphony. No one noticed.

Morning. Frosted windows bright. Watched two men twist the sheet around the head and feet of the old woman like she was a carpet going to storage. Dumped her on a gurney and rolled her away. Dead. Died alone, afraid. Mouth dry. Pain like fire. I coughed—fucking cold. Electric pain. Something very wrong with my chest. Couldn't cough. Gurgled.

Evening. Windows dark. Talking along with the others. Couldn't tell what I was saying, but it fit. Delirium? I'd watched grunts mutter while they died. Where was this? Reality? Dream? Had to be some kind of dream. I was talking, but I couldn't understand what I was saying. Happens in dreams. I heard: "English?" coming from a head leaning over me. I blinked. I was not English. I spoke.

"American."

"What are you doing here?" the head said.

"Huh?"

"You look terrible." The head shook its face. "I'll take care of it," the mouth said, walking out of my field of view. Dream was getting detailed as hell.

A few minutes later, two white coats came and put me on a gurney and rolled me into a room. Not a dream. Doctor was sewing up my face. For a hundred stitches, he muttered about how this should have been taken care of as soon as I'd gotten here, but that it was a bedlam of a hospital with many more people than they could care for.

After stitching me up and washing off the blood, they put me in a ward filled with about a fifty men. I had a bed and a promise that someone would come give me something for the pain. A guy in the ward held up a newspaper. "You the American in here?" he asked in Portuguese.

"What are you talking about?" I croaked in Spanish. When you speak Spanish as poorly as I do, it doesn't matter much whether you're talking to a Spaniard or to a Portuguese, either can figure it out.

"American businessman and three Canadian girls? What a scandal, eh?"

The men in the ward laughed knowingly. Brightened their day.

The pain never subsided. Totally exhausted, I could not sleep, not for a minute. This was, I decided, an engineering oversight on the part of God. Pain is certainly useful to warn you that you've damaged yourself or that you are exceeding some biological limit like tying your finger into a knot. But what the fuck good was pain now that the damage was done?

The next evening, a woman doctor gave me a dose of morphine and asked me if I wanted to go to the British hospital, where I would get a little attention. Thank you, yes. And (my, oh, my!) thanks for that morphine.

Four days after the wreck, I called Patience from the British hospital. She was in a panic. She had leapt up out of sleep four days before, sure that I'd been hurt, the same moment I had run off the road. Patience is a psychic. She can tell when I'm cheating and when I have car wrecks. I told her where I was and what was wrong: My face was a mess. My ribs were cracked. Something was wrong with my right hip—I couldn't walk.

My dad flew over and came to the hospital. They said I could leave if I could do a deep knee bend. I did a shaky approximation of one, seeing stars. Fine, the nurse said, you can go. Dad contacted the three girls and offered assistance, but they said they were covered—traveler's insurance. It was the first news I had of them since the accident. They were in another hospital, battered, but more or less okay. I was relieved; ashamed.

I gimped out of the hospital on crutches, feeling faint. Dad had never been to Europe before. He took me to his hotel and then out to dinner. I said I wasn't feeling well enough to eat or even sit up, but he insisted—can't heal if you don't eat and aren't active. Besides, how many times did he find himself in Lisbon, after all? Let's have fun! I sat at a table, my head propped on the heels of my hands, watching him eat, feeling sick. He offered me whiskey; I almost barfed. Water. Only water. That night, I woke up every time my father got up to slug down a drink—full glasses of straight whiskey that would kill most people. Surprised: my dad was a drunk, too.

At the VA hospital in Gainesville, they said my hip socket was fractured. I could either stay in the hospital for a month or stay home, on my back, knees up, immobile. Patience said it would be easier if I was home even though it meant she'd have to nurse me. Patience got a job at a bookstore and took care of me: food, bedpan, the whole bit. I felt like a fool. I fell in love with the nurse.

I got out of bed a month later and spent another six weeks on crutches. When the knives I'd bought in Spain arrived, I drew up an ad for—here comes the result of our painstaking research into how to sell stuff by mail—the Elks magazine. My dad, an Elk, thought that would be a great market and he paid for the ad. We sold thirty knives in two months, which, at four dollars apiece, is bad, even in Nepal.

Patience, who likes to share my interests, tripped over one of my crutches one day while I was making ads for knives and broke her toe.

When I finally got rid of the crutches, I decided to get a job painting apartments because it was there. It paid five dollars an hour, a fortune compared to what I was making as a self-employed knife importer. I made myself a good painter. I got to the apartment complex we painters were painting at seven and slopped paint around the baseboards and stuff till three. After a week, I began to get crazy. My mind screamed, this is it? a college degree and you're fucking painting apartments? After three weeks, in the middle of trimming a doorway, I dumped the brush in the paint bucket and stomped off the job. I could be doing anything on earth besides this.

I decided to make a teepee and we'd live in that. I explained to Patience: Okay. If I can't make enough money, then I can reduce our overhead. Jack thought this was a great idea, but Patience looked at me wistfully. Nope. I've decided to do this. Nothing can stop a good plan; this'll work, I promise. I got a permit to chop down cypress trees on Georgia-Pacific land. I hacked around in the swamps for a week and got together seventeen poles. Got a book on how to build teepees. Set the frame up in our backyard and stared at it proudly. It was thirty feet tall and twenty feet across. I could see there'd be plenty of room for us. Then I saw how much canvas it would take to cover it. Problem: I knew what canvas cost. I just stared at the frame for a while, defeated. Hell of thing: can't even afford to live like an Indian. Patience came out and gently said, "Bob, you know, I don't really want to live in a teepee." She was just trying to be nice. I knew she'd love it, really.

I decided to sell cars. I figured I could do that. I went to each car dealer in Gainesville and told them I wanted to sell cars. The Ford dealer hired me.

Hire is a loose-fitting word when talking about this kind of work. They paid a draw against commissions on your sales. The draw was about $85 a week in 1972 and was designed to keep a salesman alive when his luck was low. You could get your draw for a month or two of no sales, but if you weren't selling after that, they'd fire you.

The car salesman's motto is: If business is slow, make business. Or else.

One day, business was so slow and the weather was so hot and humid, the salesmen were too lethargic and bored to even get up the energy to bullshit. By this time, however, I was the number three salesman out of twenty. I was in my prime, eager to make business when business was slow. I saw a painter outside climbing a ladder. I went out and watched him working for a while.

"You need a new van," I said to the guy on top of the tall ladder. "I mean, I *saw* your van."

The guy looked down at me. I wore a short-sleeved shirt, a tie, and polyester slacks. "I know I need a van. I don't have the money," he said, turning back to his work.

"No money? No problem."

"Huh?"

"You say you have no money, right?"

"That's right."

"No problem. We have some great used telephone company vans. I can arrange a loan for you. All you need is a small down payment."

"How small?"

"Let's see." I calculated, using car-salesman training: We took in a fleet of these junker vans from Southern Bell on trade. Worth maybe a hundred and a half wholesale. Company wanted three. "On a nine-hundred-dollar loan, they'd want a hundred and a half down."

"Don't have it." The guy went back to work. Normally I'd quit screwing with such dismal prospects, but there was absolutely nothing else to do except sit inside and swelter and smoke cigarettes and try to work up some interesting car salesman stories with the other salesmen.

"No problem."

"What do you mean, no problem? I don't have *any* money!"

"You don't have any money, right?"

"That's what I said."

"No problem. We go to a loan company—friend of mine—and borrow the down stroke!"

"You can do that?"

"Why not?"

The guy shook his head, painted a few strokes, while I waited on the sidewalk. He looked down. "If you can do all that, I'll buy the damn thing."

I made enough money to buy the stuff we needed and pay the rent. Plus I had my choice of new cars to drive. I hated it. This was rear echelon, black-market-motherfucker work.

I decided to join the Army Reserves. Maybe I could fly helicopters again. Needed current flying time for a job. If I flew again, I'd be happier, stop drinking so much. Wouldn't need Valium, either. There were no aviation units in Gainesville. The closest one, in Jacksonville, didn't need pilots. I join the Gainesville Army Reserve, planning to transfer later.

The reserve guys were mostly pissed off because they'd joined the reserves to avoid Vietnam; and in 1973 the goddamn war was over but they had another five years to put in. I thought this was funny as hell. Tough break, warriors. My unit was a finance company. They didn't know what to do with a chief warrant officer pilot at first, but they decided to send me to school at Fort Benjamin Harrison, Indiana, to learn how to be a unit personnel technician, UPT. I would be a UPT, if that was what it took to fly again.

For about six weeks, I was once again an active-duty warrant officer. This time, though, I was on an administrative mission, as they called it.

The pay was much better than I'd gotten in combat.

I went to summer camp with the warriors. With all my medals, I looked like Audie Murphy to them. Another unit was at camp, an aviation unit. I went for a visit. The pilots were like me, real people. One asked me if I'd like to try it again.

We got into a Bell Loach (LOH—light observation helicopter). I'd never flown one of these things. I put on a flight helmet for the first time in years. Familiar sound: turbine whines, cries to fly. Rotors blur, whop, whop, whop. The pilot said: "Go ahead. Take it up." I lifted the collective, felt myself floating again. Is there anything as magical? Leaned forward and we skimmed over the ground and I leapt into the sky. I rolled and wheeled through the air, seeing the earth as it is, feeling ecstasy for twenty minutes. God wanted me to fly. Pilot said we had to go back. I nodded. Came back to the grass field. Some of the warriors had come to watch. I flew close to the ground, came to a hover. I sat there floating, not wanting to ever touch the earth again. I turned. Hovered to the parking spot. The ground pulled me down.

CHAPTER 6

M*arch 1974*—I decided to start my own car company while I worked at Ford, buying wrecks and fixing them up to sell for exorbitant prices with my brother-in-law, Bruce. For some stupid reason I've forgotten, we took in a brand-new attorney as a partner and somehow, though we sold cars, Bruce and I never made any money. Since I spent most of my time with our new company, the Ford place got tired of paying me for doing nothing and fired me. In a couple of months, the attorney disappeared with the checkbook.

More bad luck: my sister, Susan, was home when their kerosene heater exploded in their rented house. She and the kids got out, but they lost all their belongings, including the thesis Bruce was working on for his master's degree. Things were not going well.

Strategic withdrawal: Patience and Jack and I moved to the Shack, a run-down house in a low-rent part of town. Wind slipped between the warped clapboards of the Shack as it slowly moldered, listing, back into the earth from which it had come. I felt terrible about it—I was a failure as a provider. Couldn't seem to get money together.

We lived on a tight budget at the Shack. We ate six chickens a week on food stamps. Patience made our own bread. We never bought more than five dollars worth of kerosene at a time for the heater. Heating the breezy Shack was a hopeless task anyway. Patience and I had a feather bed; Jack, now ten years old, slept under twenty pounds of blankets. Luckily, Gainesville is a sunny place in winter and you can get warm during the day.

I sat in the sun a lot, thinking about what to do next.

It was cold. I noticed how warm the sun was. Had an idea. Found some scrap copper tubing under my neighbors' house. The neighbors, Joe Leps and Nikki Ricciutti, were friends, so I grabbed the tubing. I bought two cheap door mirrors and cut them into two-inch strips. I fastened the strips next to one another on a frame. I angled the mirrors so each one reflected light onto the copper tubing that I zigzagged back and forth four times and set above the mirrors. When I aimed the frame at the sun, the mirrors collected the light and focused it on the pipes. I hooked up a garden hose and ran some water through the tubing. Came out steaming. Wanted to do more with solar energy. First needed to collect some of the money that was all around.

Mirrors became important in my life. I didn't have to solve any puzzles like: If a mirror image is switched left and right, why isn't it switched up and down? Mirrors became important because they focused money into my pocket.

Some people Bruce and I knew were importing reproductions of antique English pub mirrors—mirrors with the label designs of whiskey and beer companies on them: Old Uam Var, White Label, O'Connell and Flynn, and so on. They sold these to gift shops for $125 and these guys offered to give us half that for each one we sold. We went to see them unloading the mirrors at a warehouse in Gainesville. I took a close look and saw that the designs were silk-screened on the back of glass, then silver was somehow put on over that and the backing was painted on last.

I decided to sell pub mirrors with Bruce.

We sold many mirrors to people who had too much money.

While we were unloading a new shipment of mirrors from England one day, the English guy importing these beauties by the container load, Mike, asked me—the art major—if I thought I could make one. I thought: in principle, in theory, probably not. I said, "How much is it worth to you?"

"Two thousand to set it up."

"No problem."

I decided to make mirrors.

Mike brought over a smaller mirror from England with a picture of Mickey Mouse on it. When he asked if I thought it would sell, I told him, yeah, but Disney would sue him into the gutter.

"Why not sell them to Disney?" he said.

We went to Disney World and met with a buyer named Tom. Tom loved the mirror and immediately notified somebody in England to sue whoever made it into the gutter. Then he said, how much?

Too much.

Mike and his sales manager, a friendly, freckled man, Don Holmes, and Bruce and I formed a new company. We decided the only way to get the price low enough for Disney was to get a big mirror maker to make them for us. I flew out to see the big-time mirror maker at his California plant with two prototypes I'd made and the separations I'd made them with. I dropped off the stuff at the plant and was told I could pick up the production samples in four days.

I drove up Highway 1 to Carmel, where I knew good old ex-Major Robert Giraudo lived. He and his wife seemed really pleased to see me. Giraudo had built a beautiful circular home in the hills overlooking the Pacific. He was a banker now. He and I shared stories about what we'd been doing since the Army, and then talked about the good old days at Wolters. We both drank, but I drank more. Actually, by this time, I drank so much everyone took it for granted that I showed up at their houses with a drink in my hand. I drove with a glass of bourbon in my lap. I thought this was normal. Giraudo started laughing when I mentioned our daily races home after work at the Army.

"I thought I was going fucking crazy that day!" he said.

The back way out of Wolters was a gravel road that went by a spillway next to a lake. After skirting the spillway, the road went straight to the main highway, about two miles away. Giraudo and I used to race each other through the base to get to the road. The first one to the road won, because there was no place to pass after that. Giraudo drove like a combat pilot, too, and the results were pretty even. One day, Giraudo had cut me off and beaten me to the road. I tailgated him, our game being to attempt to pass each other even though it was impossible; it was a wonderful careening romp. When he went into the turn around the spillway, I sailed over the embankment in the family Volvo, crashed down onto the spillway, and raced across, spraying water like a speedboat. I bounced up the road bank on the other side, lurched onto the road, spinning wheels and throwing gravel. I saw Giraudo slide around the turn in my rearview mirror. His car jerked when he saw me. He tried to catch up, waving his arm wildly out his window, but I sped off. When I walked in the door at home, Giraudo was on the phone. "You son of a bitch! How did you get ahead of me? I couldn't fucking believe it was you. I thought it was somebody else with the same kind of car. I stopped and waited for you, you bastard, but you never came!"

We had a good laugh over that. Giraudo finished the evening claiming that I was doing much more than he with life, me being out doing deals with Disney and all. Well, sure, okay. I didn't feel very good about what I was doing. Actually, I thought it was about the pettiest bullshit I'd ever come up with—Mickey Mouse mirrors? I was doing it for the money. Giraudo, banker with big house in Carmel, thinks I'm doing more with my life?

Woke up the next morning with a hangover and had breakfast with Giraudo, watching hummingbirds feeding on his terrace. We said good-bye.

I drove down Highway 101, which wanders among the steep cliffs right along the seashore from Carmel to Los Angeles. I stopped and bought a gallon of California wine I decided to drink on the way.

Drinking in the morning puts a glow on the day. I enjoyed the view and hummed some tunes. I knew I would have to keep drinking all day to avoid a big letdown, but that was what I did anyway. I wondered occasionally if I was drinking too much—no one I knew, except my father, drank like me—but I figured it was alcohol that was keeping me however sane I was.

Saw a girl hitchhiking and stopped. I was in the mood for company. When she got close to the car, I saw a guy appear from behind some bushes.

"He's my boyfriend," she said. "Do you mind giving us a lift?"

"Why not?" I said. I knew the trick, but I didn't care.

"Thanks." She got into the front seat and scooted next to me. Her boyfriend, a small guy with a Levi jacket and a tight mustache, got in next to her. I got back on the road.

"Where you going?" I said.

"Malibu," the girl said.

"Malibu? Sounds exotic. Hear about Malibu all the time."

"It's very nice. We have an apartment there."

They were superficially friendly, as would be expected of two people conning a ride. The girl smiled and said she wanted to be an actress, but in the meantime, she supported them by being a hooker. She said that casually, like it was just a regular job. I was flexible, so I nodded and said something stupid like "That's nice," or something. The guy smiled—like, I get it wholesale.

I stopped for something to eat, but they said they were conserving their cash and would wait until evening. I bought them hamburgers.

That evening, we pulled into Santa Barbara. I drove to a small hotel and got out. They said they didn't have the money to get a room. I should have said "Really? Too bad" and said good-bye. Instead, I said they were welcome to share my room.

We went to a restaurant around the corner after I said it was my treat. Why did I offer to buy? I guess I wanted them, at least her, to like me. I wanted a hooker to like me. I kept imagining how many guys this girl had let poke her to support her and her parasitic boyfriend. I felt sorry for her.

I was a jovial and generous host at the restaurant. I still had an American Express card, so I told them to order what they wanted. I'd switched to bourbon at nightfall and was having a lot of fun listening to myself talk. They laughed and ate.

In the hotel room, while her boyfriend was in the bathroom, the girl said her boyfriend would take a half-hour walk for thirty bucks, a big discount from her normal fee—me being such a nice schmuck, and all. "Thanks for thinking of me," I said. "I'll just sleep." She nodded and shrugged. They slept together on one side of the queen-size bed, I sat up on the other side, drinking.

We arrived at Malibu the next afternoon. The girl asked me if I wanted to stop and look around. I didn't have to be at the mirror plant until the next morning. I said sure, noticing the guy wince.

They had a one-room apartment in a building right on the beach. I really liked the beach; it reminded me of my childhood in Florida.

The girl asked me if I wanted to stay with them that night, to repay me for my generosity. I looked around their tiny apartment. Where?

"We've only got the floor and some blankets," she said.

I thought I saw a glimmer of actual friendliness in her face and felt a rush of attachment.

"Okay. If it won't put you out. I love the beach at night."

When we walked out on the beach, they lagged behind and the guy was talking and gesturing to the girl, like he was scolding her. I carried a big bottle of wine out on a pier. I leaned over the rail and watched the waves and trash swirl around the pilings.

The guy came up beside me.

"Bob. I know she asked you to stay, but she's changed her mind."

I turned to the guy and looked around. The girl was gone. "Where is she?"

"Back at the apartment. She said she doesn't want you to stay."

"Really? I thought—"

"I don't want you to stay either," the guy said. His eyes narrowed as he watched me take a swig of wine. He shook his head, made a face, and said, "You know, Bob, you're nothing but a drunk."

I swallowed as he turned and left, nodding as I watched him walking down the pier, back to his place. The accusation echoed inside me. A drunk? I'm a drunk? Coming from a pimp, the word *drunk* had special impact. I leaned over the railing and let the bottle fall into the waves.

The next morning I picked up the prototype Disney mirrors and caught a plane home.

Tom the Disney buyer was furious when I got back. He'd gotten a call from the California mirror maker asking how he liked the prototypes. I wasn't too surprised—the guy was just trying to take the account away; it's business. Tom was mad because he thought we were going to make the mirrors. Tom said that unless we made them ourselves, he'd have to buy them from the California guy. Disney mirror business was folding up before my eyes.

Don Holmes called that night. He had a solution. He had a very rich friend at Cape Canaveral who'd back Don and me to set up mirror production. Just Don and me. No room for Mike or Bruce. Don's rich friend had a giant warehouse where we could set up the factory. Yeah, but if I did this, I would be abandoning Bruce. We worked together. We started this company. "The company is *dead*, Bob," Don said. "The Disney deal is going to the California guy if we don't make them." Truth hurts.

I decided to start a mirror company with Don.

I went with him to Cape Canaveral to meet the rich guy, John McLeod.

McLeod was an old, lean, silver-haired hawk who glared and yelled at people. He leaned across his desk and stared at me. He was good, reminded me of some of the Army bullshit—staring into people's eyes to make them nervous. "You can get this thing going for five thousand?" he said, almost shouting.

"Right. I've already got suppliers for all the stuff we need, and I know how to make the mirrors."

"So what would you do if I said okay, here's the five grand?"

"You give me the five thousand today, John, and I'll have a contract from Disney tomorrow."

McLeod smiled. "You can get a purchase order from Disney *tomorrow*?"

"Yes." Maybe.

"Great. A man of action. Do it."

Don and I drove to Orlando the next morning and told Tom about our new backer, and our new company, Mirage Design. Gave him the price he wanted. We left Orlando with a purchase order for twelve hundred mirrors.

McLeod was impressed. He invited us out to dinner with a bunch of his friends and bragged about our Disney deal ("Fucker said he'd get a purchase order from Disney and damned if he didn't!"). He told us we had two rooms at a seaside motel, all expenses paid, while we got our factory organized.

Despite a warning from one of McLeod's former friends at the motel—McLeod says these things, but he exaggerates—we took John at his word and lived it up. We had expensive dinners two nights running and one night I spent two hours on the phone telling friends all over the country I'd made the big time. When next we saw John, he was livid with rage about my phone bill, claimed we were con artists abusing his generosity, and insisted that we sign a contract he'd just had drawn up that turned all the money we made on the first Disney order over to him. He'd pay us two hundred a week to live on. We signed. Without McLeod, we had nothing.

For weeks Patience and I, Don and his wife, Celeste, and Don's brother, Jeff, washed sheets of glass and cut them to size. I made the photo silkscreens. Don and Jeff printed the designs, I silvered the mirrors, Jeff sprayed the backing paint on, Patience and Celeste framed the mirrors and put them into boxes. We were a feverish band of hardworking desperadoes.

The pressure to make the mirrors on time made everybody tense as snakes. Disney insisted on timely delivery; McLeod said we were goofing off. One night, Don and I got into an argument about me being on the phone too much. What? Hey, I'm the brains here. I make the deals—Don grabbed me by the throat. Don's a strong man, but I could feel he wasn't squeezing to kill me, just pissed. I stared at him until he let go. Then I went on a rampage, yelled about asshole ingrates trying to murder me, and broke some mirrors. Everybody started screeching like a tribe of panicked baboons and got it out of our systems. Then we went back to work.

We finished the first batch on time, rented a truck, and delivered them to Orlando.

Don went to New York City looking for cheap frames and met Abe Weiner, a mirror maker from Brooklyn. Weiner was impressed by a Beardsley mirror I'd made. He said that Don and I should come back up and talk to him. He wanted to make decorated mirrors, and we knew how.

I told Don the guy was bullshitting us. Weiner called us a couple of times in Florida. I was still suspicious of his generosity. He was persistent. He asked us to fly up at his expense and talk about it. "Just talk, that's all I ask."

Colonial Mirror, a couple of big buildings near the docks in Brooklyn, was funky compared to the slick California factory I'd seen, but it turned out more mirrors. Abe, a big man with a friendly grin, wearing a business suit, showed us around the place, introducing us to a few of his employees: Blackie, a dark fireplug of a man who ran the loading crews, and Louis, the Puerto Rican watchman and neighborhood "manager" who was eventually knifed across the street in a card game he ran. Abe hired local talent, and his factory was seldom molested.

Abe asked what it would take to get us to move to New York. Don and I had discussed this and had come up with a package we believed would make Abe choke; we'd find out how serious he was. I said, "You make us partners and officers in a subsidiary called Mirage Design. You pay all our moving costs; pay us twenty thousand a year [this was considered pretty good in 1975] and ten percent of the profits." Then I tacked on health insurance and paid vacations. Wham!

Abe had a look on his face to suggest we were a couple of astute entrepreneurs putting the clamps on him. He smiled and said, "I think we can handle that." My heart sank. Should've said, how much you willing to pay? Forgot all my goddamn car-selling training.

A few days later, Abe and his dad, Benjamin Weiner, flew down and inspected our operation. Mr. Weiner, though expressing shock at the crudeness of our makeshift operation, was nevertheless impressed that we actually made the mirrors ourselves. At the airport in Orlando, the Weiners declared we had a deal.

We visited Gainesville before we left Florida, inviting our friends to a restaurant south of town for a party. I partied hard, got too drunk, stumbled into the men's room, and fell down on the tile floor for a nap. When I woke up, I saw a guy drying his hands with a wad of brown paper towels staring down at me, his face screwed up with disgust.

CHAPTER 7

June 1975—Dressed in a three-piece suit, Abe pushed a cart through a department store in Staten Island, loading it with sheets, pillows, plates, silverware—to furnish an apartment he'd gotten for us—commenting on each item's suitability. Don and I weren't allowed to make a choice: Abe knew best. It was funny to see a millionaire worry about such minutiae.

Our new factory, a Colonial Mirror warehouse on Twenty-eighth Street near Fourth Avenue, about four blocks from the docks in Brooklyn, was a shabby building in a run-down neighborhood. Abandoned cars littered the street and the warehouse was surrounded by low, drab apartment buildings. Most of the people in the neighborhood were Hispanics who'd work for the minimum wage, which is one reason why people set up factories in Brooklyn.

Inside there was nothing except some pallets of glass and seventy-five hundred square feet of concrete floor. The place was hot in the summer and cold in the winter. My stomach sank. We were expected to create a mirror factory in this warehouse and fulfill outstanding orders to Disney in just a few weeks. Should I tell them now I didn't know how to create real factories?

I was having terrible hangovers in the mornings. This was new. My mother-in-law, Constance Hartwell, a shrink with alcoholic patients, always said I was doing serious damage to myself with alcohol. Was she right? She'd been sending me vitamin B pills for years with little notes saying they *might* help prevent permanent brain damage, the sweetheart. Okay. I knew normal people who drank wine with their meals. I could be moderate, too. I switched to wine. I drank wine before, during, and after meals until I was drunk enough to fall asleep. Still had hangovers, but not as bad.

Don and I discovered very quickly that we really knew nothing about setting up factories. All we really had was the courage to try doing the things we thought might work.

Patience and I had rented the bottom floor of a two-family house in the Flatbush section of Brooklyn. We gave Jack a key and he took care of himself. Jack was growing up fast. At eleven, he was going to school in the neighborhood and learning to play basketball at the local court. Patience and I were rarely home until dinnertime. We had gotten into a routine of twelve-hour workdays, shorter Saturdays, off Sundays. (Patience and I were together twenty-four hours a day, something many people can't do and stay married. I think our previous debacles brought us closer together.) Our only friends, other than Don and Celeste, were Bill and Emmy Smith, who lived in Manhattan.

We hadn't seen Bill and Emmy since Spain and we'd never met their two young daughters, Nell and Luisa. Emmy invited us over for dinner almost every Saturday. Sometimes we went out to dinner while Jack babysat. I remember those evenings as exciting times in a boring world. Bill was working on a novel about vampire bats, something his new agent had encouraged him to write. He'd written a series of books about a Vatican dectective; a series about a Gypsy dectective, one of which was called *Gypsy in Amber;* and a book called *The Indians Won.* He wasn't making a fortune, but he was making a living. The vampire bat book was his first serious attempt to hit the big time.

At one of our dinners with the Smiths, I met Bill's agent, Knox Burger. Knox was in his fifties then and looked like Gerald Ford. He limped a little from a birth defect and used a cane. Knox struck me as a wry guy and I enjoyed being around him. I asked him one night, "So, Knox, what is it that literary agents do, actually?"

"Bill writes the books. I sell them," Knox said.

Being a neophyte business tycoon, I saw everything in terms of overhead, profit margins, contracts, and advertising. I understood Bill's operation: he worked in a corner of his bedroom (low overhead), he turned blank paper (no breakage) into books (high profit margin), and Knox handled the business side of it (instant business acumen). It appealed to me. My operation cost a fortune to maintain, and my sanity to manage. My product was sickeningly breakable, and of dubious value. I envied Bill.

When we went to Bill's, he'd show me his latest stuff. I liked the vampire bat novel. Bill had asked me how one of his characters could discover, in a maddeningly incremental way, thousands of bats flying toward him. I told him how a device could be made with a bundle of tubes, each tube tuned to a different bat frequency. Bill used it to increase suspense as a horde of bats descended upon the character. Bill was also working on a novel set in Russia and had a map of Moscow taped on the wall behind his typewriter. The Russian book was a pet project he'd been working on for years. He'd even invested in a five-day trip to Moscow to get a feel for things. I read the first chapter several times as Bill made changes. When he wrote an opening with three faceless corpses in a Moscow park, I thought it was a throat grabber.

I told Bill the mirror business was driving me crazy. We'd just had a robbery. One of our trusted employees had hidden in the factory when we closed, loaded up our delivery van with mirrors, and driven it through the goddamn door.

The employees were driving me nuts, I told Bill, and Abe and his dad, I said, were definitely tuned to a different frequency. They took me with them to buy a warehouse because it had a giant overhead crane system they needed to handle pallets of glass. Ben, Abe's father, looked around, grudgingly admitted the building was okay, except for "that thing. That—" he pointed to the crane he was dying to own, "that thing, Abe, it'll cost a fortune to tear that out." Abe nodded sadly. The broker and the owner panicked.

"Tear it out!" they said, seeing a done deal evaporating because of this loopy old man. The broker looked at the owner and back, said, "Maybe we could lower the price a bit—to take care of the removal expense?"

Ben turned around, looking interested. "Maybe. But it would cost twenty thousand to get rid of that . . ." he pointed at the crane again, "thing."

The broker and owner went to the back of the warehouse, had a conference. Abe and Ben whispered and snickered. The broker came back and agreed to knock twenty thousand off the price. Ben said, "Okay, Abie, if *you* want the place, we'll buy it." The broker and owner sagged with relief. On the way back to the office, Abe and his dad giggled like kids. I don't get it. I mean, I *get* it—they saved twenty thousand—but I don't care. These guys are like aliens to me, I said to Bill. I'm learning this stuff, but I hate this business.

"Why don't you get out of it?" Bill said. "You can write. Write about Vietnam."

I can write? Bill thinks I can write? Bill got me fired up at the idea of being a writer. I even set up my typewriter in my bedroom in the heat of inspiration. It was futile. I couldn't get past the first page. My life was making mirrors and trying to sell them.

The mirror business ground on monotonously, a series of problems that, once solved, left me feeling unsatisfied. I had bouts of uncontrollable anger. I broke my hand when I punched our bedroom door.

Anxiety symptons returned. After dinner at a Chinese restaurant, I felt dizzy and confused. I could barely walk when we left and I fell to my knees on the sidewalk outside. My heart was clinking around in my chest like loose change. Patience drove us home. I lay in bed. Patience put her head on my chest and listened. My heart was going: ThumpThumpThump. Thump. Pause. Thump. Pause. Pause. It was like I'd just come back from Vietnam. We lay there in the dark. There was nothing else we could do. This had happened so many times before. It had to be anxiety, but was it? We fell asleep not knowing if one of us would wake up in the morning.

After a year, sales were dismal. When it looked like we were going belly-up, Don threw in the towel and went back to Florida. Patience and I stayed because it was all we had.

I called my childhood friend Bill Willis, the technician who had helped me get the job at Radiation. I asked if he wanted to manage production at the plant so I could work on sales. He'd just quit a job in California and said yes. He flew in and almost immediately I realized I'd made a mistake. Bill was a terrific technician, but a terrible manager. He wanted to do research into all kinds of different ways to make mirrors when what we needed to do was get the ones we had already made out the door faster. He was just doing what he did best; I'd hired him for the wrong job. We argued for two months about doing research until I got the courage to fire him. My delay had only made it worse. Bill had brought his wife, Sarah, from California and they'd gotten an apartment. I arranged for the company to pay his expenses back home. When he left, he shook hands with me and said I'd done the right thing.

A few weeks afterward, my body sent me a painful message, saying that it had developed an extreme dislike of alcohol. What a shock. Alcohol was as much a part of my biology as my blood. The message was a headache so horrible I couldn't see straight when I woke up. I tried working that morning, but words didn't make sense through the pain.

Some employees told me about eight new emergencies. I heard: buzz buzz glock. I felt like puking for hours. By noon I'd gotten so pissed off—booze had let me down—I decided to quit drinking. I had one of my employees take me to a local high school and bought some pot. (That's where he got it. The kids ran a smooth operation there— lookouts in the playground, premeasured marijuana in five-, ten-, and twenty-dollar convenience packs—very entrepreneurial.) I switched to smoking pot after work. It wasn't as strong as booze, but it was less toxic. I began to feel better immediately.

Abe took me to lunch at a stevedore diner on the docks one winter day.

Eddie's Diner, hot and steamy, crowded with dockworkers wearing knit caps and fingerless gloves, was in the corner of a warehouse. You picked up a steel tray at the door and got in the serving line. Abe said, "Stevie, make us a couple of the chef's specials, okay?"

Stevie, a toothless guy with huge, hairy arms, grinned. "You got 'em, Abie." Stevie grabbed two loaves of Italian bread, sliced them in half like he was making a hoagie, and ripped out most of the bread, leaving shells. He flopped the shells on plates and ladled in mealy meatballs, clotty gravy, and big chunks of boiled potatoes. He put the top on each sandwich and squashed it flat with his hands. Gravy and potato chunks oozed out the edges. He plopped them on our trays. "Great, Stevie," Abe said. "This is a complete meal, here." Stevie grinned and said, "Eat one every day the rest of your life, Abie, and you'll live that long."

We walked to a table covered with junk. Abe cleared the table. The sandwich was utterly tasteless, but filling. Abe ate a few bites, put it down, lit up a cigarette, and smiled at me. For the first time since I'd known him, he asked me what I'd done in Vietnam.

Vietnam veterans were in the news: going nuts, killing people.

"I flew slicks."

"What's that?"

"We flew the grunts into battle. We were a crew of four in a Huey helicopter: pilot, copilot, crew chief, and gunner. We flew in flights of four ships, four flights to a company, usually. When we got close to the ground, we usually took heavy machine gun and rifle fire."

"You had armor?"

"Yes. The seats were armored. We had an armored side panel. The bullets, however, were mostly coming from the front during the assaults. You couldn't move during the landings—to try to dodge the bullets or anything. You couldn't duck. You couldn't hide. You couldn't turn around. You had to stay together, on course. Both pilots held the controls in case the other got hit. When the bullets got close, all you could do was tighten your stomach. Sit there. Fly into the bullets."

Abe grimaced. "Damn."

I nodded. "You can do this for a while, but it starts to fuck up your mind. I flew a thousand missions."

Abe leaned back on his chair, puffed some smoke, nodded. "Sounds like a bad time, Bob. I'm sorry you had to go through that."

"Me, too."

Abe smiled. "You know, Bob, the Jews have a tradition. We try to turn misfortune into fortune. It'd be symmetrical, you know, if you could somehow turn it around—turn that bad experience into something good."

I liked the idea, but I couldn't see how making mirrors was part of any "symmetry."

With sheer luck, business got better. A guy called and said he'd seen one of our mirrors that had a vintage Vogue magazine cover showing through the mirror. He wanted to know if I could do the same thing with a record album cover. I said sure.

When the mirrors were shown at the New York gift show, they were a sensation. The booth was swamped. Crowds of buyers actually pushed and shoved each other to order rock and roll mirrors. I couldn't believe it. We had sales; now we had to make lots and lots of mirrors.

I had designed a fifty-foot monster machine that could crank out these mirrors at the rate of about three thousand a day. We'd built the thing to make the Vogue mirrors, but we'd never operated it at capacity. I hired almost everybody in the neighborhood, and the place started cooking. In a few months, we had to operate two shifts to keep up. I was making money. Ben Weiner was smiling.

I celebrated by taking a couple of sailplane lessons in New Jersey.

The instructor wanted to know what my experience was.

"Never had a chopper pilot out here before. Ever fly fixed wing?"

"Some. I learned to fly planes when I was sixteen."

"Well, this sailplane stuff is pretty easy after you get into the sky. The big deal is being towed up by another plane: you know, on the end of a long rope. And when you land, you got this silly one-wheel landing gear; but it works fine."

I nodded.

"Ever do any formation flying?" he asked.

"Lots."

"Well, being towed is flying in formation. You just keep the sailplane at the right position, and you'll have no problem."

I took a few lessons. The guy was right. I could handle the tow just fine. The next weekend, I came back for more. On our first takeoff, I heard a snap and saw the tow line zing ahead. I was about two hundred feet off the ground, over trees. I spotted a clear farm field ahead and aimed for it.

The instructor said, "What are you doing?"

"I'm going to land up there."

"I see what you're up to. But you don't need to go there. You can turn this thing around and land downwind."

I looked down at the trees.

"Go ahead, turn around," the instructor said behind me.

I shrugged. "Okay, it's your plane. I don't think we'll make it."

I banked hard and turned around, set up for a landing. I was amazed.

This thing wasn't sinking at all. If we'd been in a regular plane, we would've already been in the trees. If we'd been in a helicopter, we wouldn't have had time to make the fucking turn. I landed. The guy got out laughing, said I sure knew what I was doing and how about taking it up again, solo.

The instructor towed me up. When I pulled the release at twenty-five hundred feet, I pulled back the stick and swooped up high. Hold it, hold it, stall, flip nose down. I was laughing. Tears flowed. I circled around the airport, cheering, playing in the thermals that pushed me up. A half hour later, I landed on the single wheel, rolled up to the flight line, stopped, balanced the plane level in the breeze for a moment before I let the left wingtip gently touch the ground. Fun.

We were shipping lots of rock and roll mirrors; I was making money, but how long could it last? Album cover mirrors were definitely novelty items and were about ninety percent of our total business. I was worried sick. We didn't have any other prospects.

I was still messing around with mirrors as solar collectors in my spare time. I should mention that in 1976 the new president, Jimmy Carter, had declared that the need to develop alternate sources of energy was the moral equivalent of war. I agreed completely. It was the first rational idea I'd heard from a politician. I got involved, doing experiments with solar energy. After several tries, I built a toy car that ran directly off sunlight, to prove to a dubious engineer friend of mine, Ed Pollitz, that such a thing would work. I tested the car in Prospect Park and drew a crowd of kids who never knew it was pulling itself through the grass with just the power of light.

Solar energy was my big dream: Abe pointed out that that was all it was. He told me the difference between us was that I was a dreamer and he was a doer. I had no problem with that; the world needs dreamers, too. I still thought solar energy should be a Mirage project. I figured if we were making mirrors, why not get into the solar energy business?

I thought of a different approach: an inflatable mirror. Just put two circular sheets of plastic on top of each other, one of them transparent, the other mirrored. Seal the edges and clamp the plastic in a frame. Pump some air between the sheets, and they'd both push out, making convex surfaces. If the transparent side of this arrangement is pointed at the sun, the mirrored side should focus sunlight. Would it actually work? I spent a couple of days at the factory building one.

My prototype was four feet in diameter. A concave glass reflector that size would cost a couple of thousand dollars. My plastic one cost twenty bucks. I mounted the two sheets of plastic between two plywood rings and screwed everything together, sealing it with a bunch of silicone rubber. I put a tire valve in the edge of the frame and pumped it up with a bicycle pump. Looking through the clear plastic, the mirrored plastic formed a perfectly beautiful concave surface (spherical, not parabolic, just fine for concentrating sunlight). I took it outside on Twenty-eighth Street. The afternoon sun was low. I put a soggy piece of cardboard I found in the gutter on a chain-link fence, stood back about twenty feet, and aimed the sizzling beam from my mirror at it. In less than a second, the cardboard poofed into a cloud of smoke and then burst into flames.

Patience and some of the people at the factory saw this test, and I had them sign my drawings as witnesses. I intended to patent this thing, become rich and famous, and contribute something besides decorated mirrors to the world.

I went to a law firm that Ed Pollitz recommended. (Pollitz, after seeing my solar-powered car working, thought I "had savvy.") The patent attorneys were impressed at the simplicity of the idea; the fundamental nature of it reeked of originality. No one had heard of such a thing. I put together a set of drawings and applied. Two weeks later, I got the result of the patent search. Someone had patented the idea nearly a century before it could've been made.

I was so disappointed I gave up. Abe was openly relieved. He'd seen me messing around with toy cars, about five different kinds of glass reflectors, and now this plastic inflatable thing. He claimed I'd been diverted from my real responsibilities dreaming about this solar thing: "Now can we get back to work?"

Had I any brains, I would've applied for a design patent—a patent on the way the mirror was actually made and how it would be used to collect solar energy. But I didn't.

In the midst of a bustling factory pumping out rock and roll mirrors by the thousands, I had a sick feeling in the pit of my stomach that the company was coming apart. A few weeks after the solar mirror debacle, Abe came to see me.

"Bob, this album mirror thing is going great."

"Yeah, Abe, as long as it lasts."

"Don't worry, we'll get more customers." Abe paused, frowned. "Y'know, Bob," he said, shrugging, "Dad thinks that ten percent is way out of line now. He's got a point, too. Who would've thought this would do so well?"

"You want to cut my share?"

Abe nodded. "Five percent?"

"I've dedicated myself to this for over two years and now you want to cut me out?"

"Not out, Bob. You'll still make a goddamn fortune."

I stared at Abe. This was perfect. I had learned enough about business to recognize real talent when I saw it and to know I didn't have it. I'd been feeling terrible about what I was doing. Even moving to a better, rent-free apartment, getting a new company car, a twenty-five percent raise, cash bonuses, none of that helped me feel good about myself. Looking for help, I'd read *Your Erroneous Zones*, by Wayne Dyer. I was impressed by one of the questions in it: "What would you do if you had six months left to live?" The point of the question was that if your answer wasn't what you were doing, then you weren't doing what you—in your heart of hearts—wanted to be doing. I asked a lot of people this question, including Abe. Usually they said they'd go on a big trip, move to Tahiti, kill their worst enemy, or something similarly exotic. When I asked Bill Smith, he said, "I'd work a little faster so I could finish this book." He was the only person I knew who wouldn't change what he was doing. I didn't know if I wanted to be a writer, but I knew I didn't want to make rock and roll mirrors and get ulcers worrying about future sales. Let somebody who's going to live forever put up with this shit. I looked at Abe and said, "Okay. I quit."

CHAPTER 8

April 1978—I decided we'd move to Florida.
I'd visited Florida often while we were in New York, just to get away. Patience usually stayed behind because the factory was like a young child, it couldn't be trusted on its own. On one of my visits in 1977, I heard that some property on the Santa Fe River northwest of Gainesville was going to be sold in ten-acre tracts. We'd dreamed of living in the woods. I flew back to New York, told Patience about it, and she got on a plane that night. Two days later, she came back with a contract for deed on a triangular piece of land with over eight hundred feet of river frontage.

So, when we quit, we had a place to go. Uncleared wild north Florida woods just outside High Springs, but it seemed infinitely superior to the landscape of junked cars and squalor we had lived in.

We had an apartment full of stuff and had to move it ourselves, so we had a giant garage sale to thin it down. As spendthrifts, Patience and I, in two and a half years in New York, had managed to save about three thousand dollars. Rather than wasting money renting a truck and a storage warehouse in Florida, I decided to buy a school bus in New Jersey for fifteen hundred dollars. I brought it to Brooklyn and loaded it up with everything we owned. Bill Smith, who thought I'd finally gotten smart, helped us.

Patience and I figured that when we got to Florida, we could live in the bus while we built a place. Unfortunately, there was no room left. So we drove first to Maine—towing the Roach—and sold our piano to Patience's mother and gave Patience's sister, Vickie, boxes of books. The load lightened; we had space to set up some cots and stretch out. We drove from Maine to Florida in four days.

We arrived at the property on a warm spring morning and drove in as far as we could on our sandy road. The three of us got out and tromped around the woods to scout out a suitable path for a road to the river. The route decided, we worked like mad people, hacking down small trees and clearing brush with an intensity that was more than eagerness. We were obsessed. We wanted the bus to be where we imagined it should be: sitting on the riverbank, *now*. Patience and I hacked; Jack dragged the branches away. Late that afternoon, Patience and I, exhausted as first-day stevedores, drove the bus along our rough path and parked it next to the river. It felt like a victory.

The next morning, I stood on the riverbank and wondered what to do next. We had about a thousand dollars, the school bus, and a mortgage. We would soon be out of money.

Probably the only clever thing I did in New York was to have Abe meet me at my attorney's office on Park Avenue, the same firm I'd used for my patent search, to negotiate a severance contract before I left. We couldn't agree on a contract, but Abe knew I was serious. I left New York without a severance agreement, but I promised I wasn't going to give up.

I called Abe and told him I wanted to come up and finish our business. He said okay and even agreed to have his company pay my way. When I got to New York, Abe surprised me by almost immediately offering to pay me eight hundred a month for two and a half years. For over two years Abe and I had competed in a game for which I had no talent and eventually lost. I guess he liked the way I lost. I agreed to his terms: in return for the money, I would not compete with him. I would've paid *him* to keep me out of the goddamn mirror business.

When I got back to Florida, I felt pretty good. I had some breathing space.

My dad invited us down to his Deerfield Beach condominium. "Now that you're out of the mirror business," Dad said, "you should get into the real estate business." He said he was making tons of money and he'd teach me how to do it. Real estate wasn't for me and I said no, and it really disappointed him. I still needed money to build a place to live, though. Dad gave me the name of a banker who'd lend me three thousand dollars.

When we got back to High Springs, I went to lumberyards and got prices for all the stuff you need to build a house. I sketched the largest cabin that I could build for three thousand dollars, a little thing sixteen by twenty feet. I made the roof steeply pitched so that the attic could be used for living space, too; that would give us about six hundred square feet. It wouldn't be enough for Jack (now fourteen), but he was living in a tent next to the school bus now and it would be a relative improvement if he could move into the bus when we moved into the cabin.

For six months we lived in the woods developing a routine. Jack drove out to the school bus stop each morning and ran home in the afternoons. (He was on the school's cross-country team.) Patience walked out later and got the Roach and often went to the library in town to use their bathroom (the mosquitos were fierce that summer). I'd quit smoking and started jogging.

I cleared trails all over our property, exploring every inch of the land. Our property was triangular, nearly eleven acres of old hardwood forest—live oaks and hickory trees—with dense underbrush between them. When I'd gotten a good idea what the land was like, I decided to build near the center of the triangle on high ground because river land floods occasionally. We figured that eventually we'd build a larger place on pilings next to the river when we could afford it.

I drew up the final building plans for the cabin at the library in Gainesville. I'd never designed or built a house before. When I had a question about what size beam to use, or how the foundation piers should be made, or how many electrical outlets I had to have, I walked across the street to the county's building permit office at the courthouse and asked them.

Six months after we got there, a truck brought us a load of wood, pipes, shingles, and nails and dumped them at a clearing I'd made. I was going to turn it into a cabin.

We couldn't afford to set up a temporary electric pole, so I used hand tools. We started the project thinking that we would all work on it. That lasted only a few hours. I wanted to finish the cabin fast.

I had no conception then about the process being the important thing. I wanted results. My internal voice was scolding me about being a quitter and a loser because I left a good job to live in the woods. And how could I move my family into the boonies? And what the hell do I know about building houses? And on and on until I would go into rages and throw tools into the woods and scare Patience and Jack away. So unless it was absolutely impossible for me to do it myself, they stayed away while I forced building materials into a cabin with the power of sheer anger. While I built the cabin, Patience began writing a book, a fantasy novel. Of the two of us, we expected she would be the first published.

We moved into the cabin before it was finished, a common country habit. People around me were building houses while they lived in them. Another Vietnam vet, John Tillerman, was building a house about a half mile from us. He was some kind of sailor, or something. He moved in before he finished, too. Seemed like a good idea to everybody: dry the place in (meaning that only the roof and exterior walls were finished) and then work on finishing it on weekends. Wrong. Everybody moved their stuff in and that was the end of it. Working on the place created a sawdust–plasterboard–wood chip mess and it was just too much work to move everything out and back in every weekend. I'd built a bench and a table downstairs, and Patience and I slept in the attic, under exposed insulation. Jack moved into the school bus. The windows were unglazed, covered with flaps of clear plastic sheeting stapled to the window frames.

However rustic it was, the cabin did keep the rain out. In winter, we heated the place with a little cast-iron woodstove that worked great. We had plenty of firewood.

We accepted this level of completeness as complete enough and began to wonder what we would do when my severance ran out.

Now that Patience was writing, I'd been thinking about Bill Smith's occupation a lot. I remembered a conversation I'd had with Bill and Knox at lunch one day. I told Knox I wanted to be a writer, and I wanted to use my Vietnam experiences as the basis for a novel. Knox asked me to tell him what I did over there. I talked for an hour. When I'd finished, Knox said I should forget about writing a novel: I should tell the story in my own words.

"A memoir?"

"Yes," Knox said. Bill, sitting beside him, nodded.

"Shit," I said. "Plenty of people had worse things happen to them in Vietnam. Why should anyone care what happened to me?"

"Sure, maybe that's true," Knox said. "But they aren't writing about it. If you write it like you tell it, you might have something."

I decided to write a memoir.

Did I have enough to say to make a book? I sat on the bench in my cabin and started listing the events that were still vivid to me. I labeled them with titles like "One Leg" (about trying to haul some wounded grunts to a hospital only to have them all die) and "The Rifle Range" (a sandy field near Bon Song where we were mortared). I scribbled furiously until I ran out of memories. I counted the list. Two hundred and forty distinct events. Plenty for a book. However, though I remembered the details very clearly, I really didn't know, with any confidence, when they had happened. Vietnam was a confusing time, almost a dream to me. I'd flown thousands of sorties; I'd seen hundreds of firefights—everything blended together. I couldn't recall, for certain, the order of things. I asked Patience if she had the letters I'd sent her from Vietnam.

"Yeah, asshole, I do," she said, laughing.

I'd thrown her box of my Vietnam letters into the street on one of our moves in Gainesville a few years before. Patience saw me do it and told me to get them back. I said I wanted to forget about ever being in Vietnam; it was time to forget. "Fine, forget it. But they're *my* letters." She got the box and kept them.

I opened the envelopes and suddenly traveled back twelve years.

18 Feburary 1966

Dear Patience—

Sometimes, the above greeting stops me cold! Dear, *Dear* Patience I love you so much!

I've flown so many CA's [combat assaults] lately, that it's getting to be commonplace. The rattle of our own machine guns don't even make me start any longer. The return fire still makes me, shall we say, anxious. I haven't taken any hits lately. Today, we went after some wounded troops at an LZ that was under VC mortar attack. They were zeroing-in on the landing pad as we approached, but we escaped (natch).

I'm so very tired of this rot! When we need R&R's the most, they cancel the program for all officers! Gee whiz and heck! It makes me think black thoughts about the army!

This will be extra short tonight.

I love you,

Bob

P.S. Please send some more envelopes.

I felt my face flush. There was nothing literary about my letters to Patience. They were clumsy, flippant, and artless. I seldom talked about what I was doing in them. However, they were enough to fix past events in time for me. I put the 750 pages in chronological order and sorted my list of events to match.

When I got the chronology straight, I decided first to write a few of the scenes to see if anyone wanted to read them. It's one thing to have a story; it's another to put it on paper.

The memories came back as I typed. These weren't my funny war stories. I wrote what I felt then, and the feelings still hurt. The guy in "One Leg" was a grunt whose testicles and a leg were blown off. I had to get him and his four buddies to an aid station fast. I wanted to get them back. I really tried. I felt like I was rushing over trees in the Ia Drang Valley, again; trying to make it to Pleiku, again; hearing my crew chief say the guy died, again. They all died, again. I saw a glint on One Leg's wedding band as they dumped him on a stretcher. Tears came for the first time.

I showed my story to Patience and our friend, Rosemary, who was in the creative writing program at the university. They both cried, which I took to be a good sign. I wrote several more scenes, sixty or seventy pages worth, and discovered I had something to say. These were not smoothly written, publishable vignettes; they were stories with feeling and they affected people. I could smooth them out. What else do you need?

CHAPTER 9

February 1979—I decided I needed a break to put my memories in order. I'd read that there was going to be a total eclipse of the sun in February. The path of totality would cross several western states, one of them Montana. I remembered I had a friend out there, James Elliott, Patience's old boyfriend and a guy I'd known as a kid. I called him up. We hadn't talked for eighteen years, but, on the phone, it seemed that no time had passed; we got along just great. The only subject that still made Elliott's voice change was Patience. Otherwise, things were fine. I told him I wanted to come out to see the eclipse. Was he up to an adventure? Yes, and he would pay my way.

I took the train from Waldo, Florida, to Sandpoint, Idaho.

Elliott met me at the station with his girlfriend, Eva. When we got to his place in the wilds of western Montana, I laughed. His house was virtually a copy of mine. It was four feet longer, but everything else was the same including the A-frame upstairs. We sat in his cabin drinking wine and swapping stories about our childhood that put a glaze on Eva's eyes. Elliott and I took the bottle outside and stumbled around in a genuine Montana blizzard, fell down in the snow, laughed like idiots.

The next day, Elliott, Eva, and I set out in his truck across Montana to rendezvous with the shadow of the moon. We talked about the old days and what we'd done since we split up in New Orleans. I told him I was going to write a book about Vietnam. He smiled dubiously.

We stood on top of a small hill. The light was dim, but not as dim as you'd think with the sun almost completely occluded. I had a piece of exposed X-ray film I used to look at the sun. Even when there was just a sliver of sun left, the light seemed almost normal. Then we saw a shadow approaching from the west. It rushed, flowing over the hills, steady and relentless. It was breathtaking. The wave of darkness hit. Snap! the stars came out. The lights of a little nearby town blinked on. We felt the quiet of sudden darkness. You could only hear the cold breeze rustle among the three of us on that hill. The corona of the sun blazed out from a black disk, a ring of pure energy. I took some pictures of the way the world looked from where we stood. Five minutes later, off in the distance, we saw the light rushing over the mountains, beating back the night. It's things like this that remind me I'm living on a *planet*, spinning around a *star*, somewhere in *space*.

Elliott took the train with me to Minneapolis. I was stopping there to visit Bill Willis. Elliott had known Bill when we were kids, too, and wanted to see him.

Bill had a proper job for his talents now. He worked at Bell and Howell as a technician and made a nice living. How many guys would still be friends with somebody who'd fired them? Bill was one. He took Elliott and me into his apartment, showed us around the Twin Cities, and even stuffed some cash into my pocket before I left, like a mother.

On the trip back, I remember talking to a woman who asked me what I did. I didn't know, so I said "I'm a writer" and nearly choked.

I messed around getting my notes and courage together, and then I began writing my Vietnam memoir. The date was May 17, 1979. (I know this only because Patience keeps a journal.) I decided the book would have twelve chapters, one for each month of my tour (August 1965 through August 1966), and I chose to write the November chapter first—when I was in the battle of Ia Drang Valley in 1965. November was filled with action, and I figured that would be the one to show a publisher.

When I finished, the chapter was thirty pages long. Patience read it and marked it up, saying I should give more details here, clarify this, expand that, shorten this, and so on. Patience is a very talented editor and a real pain in the ass about it. I rewrote it, the first time in my life I ever rewrote anything. When I finished, I had seventy pages. Much better, Patience said, and marked it all up again. I rewrote it again. Good, she said. I sent it off to Knox.

Knox wrote back saying it was powerful stuff, and I ought to keep at it. He said that if I got two hundred pages together, he'd take it around to see if he could sell it. I spent a day experiencing uncontrollable elation. With the exception of flying helicopters, I hadn't done anything that gave me such satisfaction.

Knox had also said, "Have you read any Vietnam books?"

"No. I'm afraid they'd influence me."

"Amateur. Get some. Read them. See how they handled it."

I read *A Rumor of War,* by Philip Caputo. Caputo was a grunt Marine officer in Vietnam the same time I was there. He'd been tried for murder; had a lot of terrible things happen to him that I hadn't experienced. Caputo's book was also intimidating to me because the man wrote so damn well. I wondered if I was up to the task.

I read *The Killing Zone,* by Frederick Downs. Downs's description of himself being blown to shreds at the end of book was electrifying.

I read *If I Die in a Combat Zone,* by Tim O'Brien. O'Brien's book was about his tour as an Army grunt. It was a tough and moving narrative, but I thought I could match his writing skill. *Going After Cacciato,* his Vietnam novel, knocked my socks off when I read it later. He opened my eyes to kinds of writing I'd never thought of.

I read a short story in *Harper's* called "Good Morning to You, Lieutenant," by Larry Heinemann. A Vietnamese girl gets raped and murdered in the story and it *felt* like it. That story pissed me off for days. When I calmed down, I realized that the events were fictional, but the feelings weren't. Heinemann was communicating emotion to me. I wanted to affect people like that. I had to tell people what it *felt* like to be a helicopter pilot in Vietnam.

When I read *Dispatches,* by Michael Herr, I decided that if a *journalist* could make his Vietnam experiences interesting reading, so could I.

It took me until February 1980 to put together a two-hundred-page manuscript with a thirty-page outline of the rest of the book. I couldn't think what to call it, so I sent if off to Knox untitled. A week later, Knox wrote back and said he really was moved by it and would take it around. He warned me not to get my hopes up. The material was good, but it was going to be tough going. In 1980, nobody wanted to publish books about the Vietnam War.

That last bit just went by me. The fact that Knox liked what I'd written was exhilarating in itself. That he was going to try to sell it was a triumph. Just before we left New York, Knox had sold Bill's vampire bat book, *Nightwing,* and the film rights for hundreds of thousands of dollars. It changed Bill's life. He was on the *Today* show, for chrissakes! He'd even gone to the publisher who was giving him crap about not sticking to the outline of his Russian novel and bought the thing back so he could do it *his* way. Wow!

Yes, indeed, I figured it might take a couple of months, but I was definitely on the road to success now. And I was happy.

CHAPTER 10

March 1980—I figured it might take a few weeks to sell a book, so I waited a month to call Knox.

"Knox, I don't mean to bother you, but—"

"Yes, you do."

"I do what?"

"You mean to bother me. Look, Bob, this is a tough sale. Don't hang around waiting on pins and needles. This could take a long time. Why don't you get a job?"

Good advice. The money from my severance was almost gone. I'd decided that I'd finish the Vietnam book if somebody bought it; otherwise, it was just too damn painful to do. Instead of looking for work, I started a book about something fun, something I was fascinated with: robots. Back in 1970 I'd read an article by Marvin Minsky of MIT. He described a little robot they'd built that just wandered around the lab on its own. When its batteries got weak, it'd find its way to a receptacle, plug in, and recharge itself. I thought that was amazing. Minsky also said that the thing, which had a TV camera for an eye, would just loiter around the place, staring at people. One woman in particular, a secretary at the lab, often found herself the object of this mechanical scrutiny and said it was unnerving. Minsky claimed not to know why the little pile of parts did that. I was drawn to artificial intelligence by that article and was reading everything I could find on the subject.

When I decided to write a novel, I figured I'd make the hero a machine.

Eventually I realized it would take more time to write a novel than I had. My Vietnam book was somewhere in limbo. I was not getting rich like I'd imagined. I applied at the local plastic pipe factory as a plastic-pipe-extrusion specialist and was turned down. I read the classifieds every day. I wasn't getting anywhere. Luckily, Elliott called and said he wanted to come down. He wanted to go on a big canoe trip down the Suwannee River.

I'm usually not one to point out personal abnormalities, but I have to say here that Elliott is rich, always was. He'd inherited a comfortable fortune when his dad died and had a steady income from a portfolio of stocks and bonds. On our trip to see Willis, he'd advised me that a good investment to make was in railroad cars. Buy 'em—thirty thou or so—and lease 'em. This was gibberish to me—at any moment, without too much trouble, Patience and I could put our hands on maybe twenty bucks.

So Elliott showed up in a rented car and we all decided to go to our hometown, Delray Beach, and visit my father on the occasion of his sixtieth birthday before we went on our big river adventure. Patience and I stayed with my parents in Deerfield Beach. Elliott stayed with his mother in Delray. It was spooky visiting Delray Beach again. Lots of changes. South Florida had become overgrown with condos built on land that had been covered with sea-grape trees and sand dunes when I was a kid.

When we came back up to High Springs, Elliott and I began to get our gear together for our trip down the Suwannee River.

This would've been a fun trip under normal conditions, but Elliott and I had differences that began to surface and produce tensions. Little things cropped up while we were getting ready to go: Elliott would say let's go out tonight for dinner. We'd think he meant he was buying (he's wealthy and he asked), but he didn't. So we almost get stuck for a check at a restaurant we never would have gone to had we not been invited. We'd have to point this out to Elliott. He wasn't trying to be unthinking or uncaring; it just turned out that way because he didn't, couldn't, understand what it was like to be actually, honest-to-God, poor.

I'd prepared for the river trip by inventing a new way to do it. (My instincts have always been to invent things that can't be patented when

I need money.) I invented a way to connect two canoes together with a platform upon which a tent could be pitched. I made the platform of thin strips of cypress held together with cord woven through the slats. I made it in two sections, each four by eight feet, so they could be rolled up and carried when we had to portage around the shoals at White Springs. Unrolled, tied together, and clamped to the canoe gunwales, we had an eight-foot-square platform sitting across two canoes—something like a catamaran—that allowed us to make the trip comfortably. One of the big problems of long trips down the Suwannee, or any river, is that you're never sure when to stop and pitch a camp unless you know the river. At sunset, you might be next to private property or a swamp; so you start looking for a place early in the day to be sure you have a campsite before dark. With Mason's Unpatented Canoe Raft, that was a worry of the past. Sunset? Not to worry, just keep drifting. We lighted the fire in our hibachi and cooked dinner at sunset. When we got sleepy, and when we fucking well wanted to, we'd just snatch a low branch and tie up for the night. Sometimes beavers would slap water on our tent, letting us know we were trespassers, but most of the time things worked out fine.

Floating down a river is one kind of adventure; it is another adventure to be confined with a childhood friend you haven't seen for almost twenty years while you're doing it. Except for the eclipse, Elliott and I had last been together when we went to California back in 1962. We had fun then, both young, wild, and unattached. He was dating Patience at that time, but she was in Philadelphia. We stayed in California for a year and drove my Chevy panel truck to New Orleans, where we parted company. In the intervening years, I'd gotten married, become a father, spent a year in combat, been a businessman, and was now, at thirty-eight, trying to get my midlife crisis together. Elliott, on the other hand, had lived in Haight-Ashbury and been a genuine hippie flower child until his father died. He'd been married and divorced, had a child, too. Now he was a rancher. He was a rancher like I was a writer: by proclamation. He had a lot of property and maybe a hundred head of cattle. He wore a cowboy hat, cowboy boots, and talked with a drawl like they were filming him in some goddamn movie. I liked this guy, but at the time, on that raft, me broke and him rich, Elliott was tough to deal with. We talked about everything, explored every avenue of mutual interest, only to find we didn't have any mutual interests. Time and experience had changed us too much. We had a commonality of youthful experiences, but it would take more than a river trip to bring us up to date as men.

I have to say that we made that trip in a record-setting nine days. That's one hundred seventy-five miles of winding river in nine days in a floating tent. As far as I know, no one, in a floating tent, has beaten that. When we got out at a town called Suwannee at the end of the river, Elliott and I were barely speaking. I called Patience to pick us up. Elliott and I had a quiet lunch.

He left a few days later, and it's taken until recently for us to talk. We're still working at being friends.

C H A P T E R   1 1

June 1980—Patience was delivering newspapers in a new Volkswagen Rabbit we'd bought with help from her mother—an outright cash grant for a down payment is what it was. Patience left every morning at two and delivered a hundred and twenty papers along a hundred-mile country road, a routine that tortured cars until they broke, and numbed people senseless. She got home at seven or eight, tired, and slept until early afternoon. This went on seven days a week. It was a job for desperate people who couldn't think clearly enough to apply their other talents.

I tried to ignore our situation. I worked on my robot book and worried about my Vietnam book. Knox had sent me a total of five rejection letters from houses like Putnam and Simon & Schuster. They all liked the writing, they said, but none of them thought people wanted to read about Vietnam. That the war was so useless that nobody even wanted to *read* about it. Then, of course, maybe these editors were just brushing me off because I couldn't really write well enough.

I began to lose faith in myself. Until somebody bought something I wrote, I was just *dreaming* about being a writer. Patience was *doing* something to make money for us and I was doing nothing. In October I said, all right, fine, I'll deliver newspapers, too.

The idea was that I could deliver papers at night and still write during the day. But getting that paper route was like falling into quicksand. My nights were almost okay: a hundred miles of speeding down wild country roads in the Roach was a driving challenge. My days were spent recuperating from the trip. I was making enough money to survive, but I couldn't write. The combination of an inverted day and a feeling of trapped desperation took its toll. My anxiety symptoms visited me with renewed vigor. I began to leap up out of bed more often. I was a nervous, cranky guy during the day, and at night I was a sullen and grim person on the route, pushing myself to make it faster, to make it end as soon as I could so I'd have time to think straight, get out of this trap. I drove like a fiend and could beat Patience back home by an hour or so.

I read about Bill Smith, who now called himself Martin Cruz Smith, in *Newsweek*. His Russian book, *Gorky Park*, was an outrageously huge best-seller. He'd become a millionaire. I was really happy for him, but too depressed to call.

I'm driving the last ten miles of my route. It is four in the morning. The moon is flickering through the overhead branches that form a canopy over a lonely road somewhere near the edge of the planet. I come into a turn I know by heart and feel the car do a sickening twist, a mind-bending wrench. I feel my breath burst in surprise as the road, striped and dappled with moonlight, rises up before me like a wall. I jam on the brakes, slide to a stop, and open the door. I have to hang on to the car. I shake my head, trying to snap out of It. But It isn't having any part of being snapped out of. I'm reeling through space, falling into It. I'm dying.

The wall finally flops down, becomes a road again. I am still reeling, sickeningly dizzy, but I crank up the Roach and drive, driving like I used to fly instruments in helicopters. You learn to trust the instruments and not the seat of your pants when you get into bad weather. I am in the midst of a mind-storm.

Somehow I make it home. Patience is still out on her route. Jack is asleep in the bus. I call my Vietnam-veteran neighbor, John Tillerman. Tell him I'm fucked up, dizzy as a loon in a tornado. Just saying that helps, and though he offers to help, I say I can make it to the VA hospital. Leave a note for Patience and Jack.

I get to the VA before dawn, fully expecting to be greeted with cheers for the harrowing thing I've just done, what with driving twenty-five miles as fucked up as I was, and all. Even before dawn, the VA is never caught off guard. They're professional. They wave my complaints aside and tell me to have a seat. I tell them it might be prudent to have a doctor see me before the fucking symptoms go away. We might actually be able to fucking find out what's fucking wrong, but they reaffirm the importance of sitting. One sits in the VA; it is one's fucking duty.

I sit.

By ten o'clock, the dizzy spell has gone. I'm so angry when I see a physician's assistant that tears dribble from my eyes while I snivel about my scary ride through the Valley of Death. She commiserates. Actually, she gets mad and makes a scene with the clerks who have had me sitting out in the waiting area for four hours. But it's too late, and no one ever diagnoses what happened to me that night.

Bad luck comes in bunches, like troupes of sideshow freaks. No longer dizzy, I hit the roads for a few more days before the Roach—the car I bought in Luxembourg twelve years before when it was already fifteen years old—goes rubba-rubba-clunk one night, and dies.

Damn, I have a paper route to route! People depend on me for their news, here. I go to the local Rent-A-Wreck place and rent a wreck—these guys don't lie—that looks bad enough to get you arrested in any decent crime-watch neighborhood.

I forge ahead. The wreck isn't just ugly and loose and dangerous, it sucks down gas faster than I can buy it. It only takes a couple of trips for me to realize I am losing money each day. Frantic calls to mechanics all over Gainesville prove futile. The Roach is dead and only transplants from Germany will bring it back to life.

In an embarrassing panic, I call Elliott in Montana. I tell him the deal, ask him to lend me a couple of thousand to put down on a new car. Elliott is silent for a while. I can hear him swallowing as he composes an answer to a deadbeat friend, a monkey's paw grasping for money—the guy he had nothing in common with, stuck in a tent on a river for two fucking weeks; *that* guy. "Damn, Bob. You caught me right in the middle of fixing my road. Afraid I can't help you, buddy." Sweep, sweep. That hurt. I figure if an old friend who has plenty of bucks won't help me out, then who will?

The idea of going to my parents is just intolerable. They've already muttered a couple of I-told-you-so's recently about trying to be a writer when I could have gone into real estate. I borrowed a thousand from Smith when we first got to Florida and still haven't paid it back. Knox? Well, Knox is my agent, not a small loan company.

I'm standing on my mortgagor's riverbank wondering what the fuck I'm going to do when the rest of the bad luck troupe arrives.

"Mason, I hear your goddamn car broke down," says John Tillerman, who's walked up behind me.

I nod at the river. "You heard right, John."

"Well, I came over to offer you a job."

Job? John has told me he ferries sailboats around for rich people —you know, from their summer homes in Cape Cod to their winter homes in Saint Thomas and stuff—what kind of job can he have for me?

"A sailor job," John says. "Pays good. How does thirty thousand for two weeks' work sound to you?"

It takes my breath away, is how it sounds. Thirty thousand? I could live for three whole, restful years on thirty thousand dollars. I'd have all the time I need to finish my book. It'd change my life; that's how it sounds. But then, I ask what kind of work a sailor can do for two weeks that's worth thirty thousand to anyone.

I already know the answer to that. I just want confirmation. I've been approached by people a few times in the past about flying a plane load or a helicopter load of marijuana into the country. One trip, lotsa money was the common thread of these deals. I've always turned the offers down; never even knew if they were serious offers; didn't want to know. I wasn't against marijuana; I just knew I wasn't cut out to wear stripes and get butt-fucked.

Times change. It feels like an inevitable thing is happening here— like a cosmic gift after so much bad luck. I've just gotten the sixth rejection letter for my book—writing is obviously not making me money. Two weeks on a dangerous mission could save my ass. And hey, I've had professional experience doing dangerous missions—it's what I was *trained* to do. It is right down my alley.

I decide to be a pot smuggler.

Feeling a shot of adrenaline jolt me, I say okay.

John and I walk up to the cabin. Patience is just back from her paper route. I tell her I am sailing to Colombia.

Patience says, "I think that's the dumbest thing I've ever heard of."

I say, yeah, uh-huh, but "John says I'll make thirty thousand for two weeks' work."

Patience's eyebrows rise and she cocks her head and wrinkles her brow and finally she says, "Oh." And nods.

PART TWO

THE
SCAM

CHAPTER 12

November 1980—John Tillerman had been a helicopter door gunner in Vietnam in 1969, had chosen to move to the same woods I had, was also building his own house. We had similar backgrounds and interests when he offered me the smuggling job.

As people, we were quite different. Tillerman was big: six feet tall, 175 pounds; a sturdy man, strong, filled with energy bordering on frenzy. I was medium-sized, medium strength, and lazy. Tillerman set a dizzy pace, racing around making sure everybody was happy, which put some people on edge. He went to the University of Virginia after the war and graduated in 1974 with a major in psychology.

Patience had seen John walking down our road, found out he was a new neighbor, and brought him over to see our place. We told him we were trying to be writers, which seemed to impress him. He said he sailed yachts for a living.

As I got to know John—I'd wander up the quarter-mile sandy path between our properties and watch him and his uncle building his house—I learned that he'd taught himself to sail by building his own small boat and sailing it single-handedly to England and Portugal and back. He seemed to have plenty of money, which, he explained, was the consequence of his ferrying-yachts-for-rich-folks business. He was generous, the kind of person, I think, who'd be generous even if he was actually rich, rather than just flush. He insisted on lending me the money to buy an electric typewriter to replace the manual portable I'd been using, without setting a pay-back date. When we had car breakdowns on the paper route, he'd immediately offer his car or truck.

Tillerman was gone for weeks at a time. When he returned, he'd come down and tell Patience and me about his adventures at sea, describing the kinds of people he had to deal with—always portrayed in his stories as rich, selfish, dumb as stumps—and the perils of sailing. He described hair-raising storms that lasted days. He claimed pirates were boarding yachts in the Caribbean and killing everybody on board just to get boats to sell to drug smugglers. I liked the stories because I liked adventure and I'd always wanted to sail, but John's drinking habit—something I understood very well—often made his tales repetitious and tiresome. I wondered if I was like John when I drank.

But John was a godsend for us, and he set about teaching me the business. The business was smuggling marijuana and only marijuana. He and his friends had considered bringing in cocaine—it's much more compact and profitable—but they decided they couldn't handle the karma (these were sixties veterans, grown-up flower children, graduates of the Carlos Castenada School of the Universe). Marijuana, in their opinion, was harmless. John smuggled pot, but he seldom smoked it, preferring alcohol.

We drove to a marina in Jacksonville to see the *Namaste*, a thirty-six-foot custom-built sailboat based on a Westsail hull. She was a fiberglass double-ender based on a Norwegian lifeboat hull design. The *Namaste* had just been put into the water after being trucked from California.

"See how the cabin is almost flush with the deck?" John said.

"Yeah. That's good?"

"You bet, Bob. Very good. When the waves start coming over this lady, they don't have anything to bash against."

"Good design."

"Yep. They use boats like this in the North Sea, Bob. They know about storms up there." He pointed to a Hunter sailboat which looked posh with lots of varnish and brass and teak. "Piece of junk, Bob. Total waste of money. That boat was *designed* to sit right there, tied up. It's a party boat for people who don't know how to sail."

We hunkered down on the dock and John pointed to the *Namaste's* painted waterline. "See how it's about half a foot out of the water?" John smiled. "They did that in California before they shipped it." He looked around. The closest person was a guy sitting on a deck chair in the Hunter, a hundred feet away. "That's so when we load up with a couple tons of product, the water line looks just right, like we got nothing on board, eh? Empty fucking boat."

I nodded. These guys think of everything.

The *Namaste* didn't *look* seaworthy, however. Its mast and rigging had been removed for the truck ride to Florida. Coiled cable, crumpled tarps, paintbrushes, paint cans, and tools lay scattered on the deck. "It's a mess, Bob. But in a couple weeks you won't recognize her. We got lots to do. We have to step the mast and set up the rigging just to get it sailing, and that's only the beginning. We need to put on the vane gear—"

"Vane gear?"

"Yeah. It's this tricky gizmo from England that steers the boat automatically. Works like a charm. You're going to love it. You like mechanical stuff, I know. No one gets stuck holding the tiller with that thing on the job." He smiled. "Vane gear, new radios, antennas for the fucking radios, depth finder, bonding strip—"

"Bonding strip?"

"It connects everything to the ground side of the electrical system. We'll put a copper strip all around the inside of the hull and make sure all the metal stuff and all the electrical stuff is hooked up to it. It's good in lightning, and it's good for the electrical stuff. That's going to be your job, Bob."

"This smuggling business sounds kind of like work, John."

"That's a fact, Bob. We'll earn our money."

"So, mast, sails, wind vane, and bonding strip. Then we go."

"Nope. Need to clean out the water tanks—water smells like a damn locker-room shower stall; get a canvas dodger—that's like a convertible top that sits over the hatchway, keeps major water out when it gets nasty." John swigged beer. He had a can with him from dawn until he slept. He wiped his mouth with the back of his hand.

"Yep. Need to buy lots of stuff. Tools, spare parts for the engine, nautical charts, food—lots of food. Basically, Bob, what we have here isn't a yacht; it's a yacht kit. You like kits?"

We laughed. John was referring to the struggle we had had putting together an ultralight airplane he'd bought six months before. The plane arrived as a big bundle of wires, tubes, and fabric with an instruction book. The thing was complicated, took us weeks to put together. I refused to fly it because it didn't have what I considered to be proper controls. John flew it, and crashed every time. Disgusted, he later sold it.

"Anyway, most yachts are used like that one." He pointed to the glitzy Hunter. "And they come apart in the first serious storm. I know what boats to use and how to rig 'em so they make it."

After John showed me the *Namaste*, we drove around Jacksonville in his pickup truck buying supplies that John paid for in cash. Getting the boat ready would cost twenty thousand dollars, all cash. He had wads, pounds, stacks of cash. A lot of money flashed around in this business, but I think it was the work itself that John loved the most. "This is free enterprise at its most exciting—one of the last real adventures left, Bob," he said. "I mean, sailing the seas, avoiding the Coast Guard, pirates, making lots of money. This is exciting stuff. How much adventure is there left in the world? Sometimes I think I lived before and I was a pirate or an explorer, something on the high seas; I can feel it. I did this before."

"How much time do pot smugglers get these days?" I asked, surprised, but it sprang from my mouth automatically.

John shrugged. "Two years," he said quietly. "Some people I know did two years."

A jolt shot through me. Could I handle two years in prison? Did I even want to know if I could? Concern for the consequences is natural before dangerous missions, so I quashed the nagging foreboding that I was on a doomed quest. John knew what he was doing.

I had known what I was doing during the assaults in Vietnam; and I believed that was why I survived. But on this mission I had no training. I didn't know anything. I'd never been a smuggler before. I didn't know how to sail, had never even been close to a sailboat. "The odds of being caught," John continued, "are about nothing outta nothing, Bob. Lotsa guys out there doing this; very few caught. Maybe five percent. If that much."

We stayed in Jacksonville, living and working on the *Namaste* during the week, returning to High Springs to visit our wives on weekends. At the marina, John walked to a nearby phone booth at ten o'clock every night and waited five minutes for a phone call from the scam master. The phone rang about every other night. I never heard what was said—didn't want to.

After the forty-foot mast was stepped, John began to rig the boat. He did most of the rigging himself. He was setting the boat up so most of the lines for the sails—halyards and sheets—were controlled from the cockpit so we wouldn't have to go out on deck during storms. John gave me a roll of thick copper tape and told me to attach it to the bulkheads in a continuous circle around the inside of the hull. I worked in the cabin most of the time.

Below decks, the *Namaste* was divided into three compartments. Coming through the hatch from the cockpit, I stepped down a short ladder into the galley, which had a counter we used for navigation plotting and cooking on the starboard side. (The counter was the only tablelike surface on the boat. John had removed a fold-out table from the main cabin because it took up too much room. Bales are bulky.) A gimbaled alcohol stove was mounted next to a counter and small sink directly across the aisle. A low partition and a post separated the galley from the main cabin, which had an upper and lower bunk on the port bulkhead, a cushioned bench along the other. The bow compartment contained the head (a pump-to-flush-toilet), a rope locker, two narrow bunks that met at their heads in the triangular bow space, and the sail closet where spare sails, anchors, and spools of line were kept.

John wanted the bonding strip installed neatly because the *Namaste* would be turned over to a partner after the trip. That partner had put up the money for the boat and the outfitting, and he'd be coming to inspect the boat before we left. I had to thread the copper strip through all the partitions, which meant a lot of tedious cutting and carving to get through the plywood panels and lots of bending and soldering to route the copper ribbon and make it conform to the bulkheads. I spent over a week doing this.

John finished the rigging. The *Namaste* began to look like a sailboat. She was thirty-six feet from the tip of her bowsprit (a spar that projects from the bow) to the stern, and twelve feet wide. John called the mast and sail arrangement a jib-headed cutter. Two forestays (cables that brace the mast) ran from the mast forward. The longest, from which the jib (forward sail) was set, called the jibstay, ran from the masthead fitting to the tip of the bowsprit. The second stay, which held the staysail (the middle sail), was attached fifteen feet behind and parallel to the jibstay. The mainsail boom, hinged to the base of the mast, hung across the cockpit from the mast to the stern, able to swing inside the running backstay, which was anchored to a small stern pulpit. Shrouds (also cables) ran from the top of the mast to each side of the boat and were held away from the mast with spreaders. All the stays and shrouds were anchored to deck fittings called chinplates, with turnbuckles so you could adjust the tension in the cables. Two plastic-coated cables attached to stanchions, looking like a fence, ran from the bow pulpit (a narrow platform with a steel railing that sat on top of the bowsprit) back along each gunwale to the stern pulpit. This fencelike thing is called a safety line. It is the last thing you can grab when you're being washed overboard. John added one cable down the middle of the boat, running parallel to the deck, from the mast forward to the bow pulpit. This cable was a safety line to which you could clip the snap-shackle of a safety harness if you had to be out on deck in a storm.

While I finished the bonding strip, John was out buying brand-new radios: a single-side-band long-distance transceiver, a short-range ship-to-ship transceiver, and a loran navigational receiver. When the bonding strip was in place, I ran wires from the aluminum mast and every major cable and metal part of the boat to the bonding strip. If lightning hit anything, the charge would be channeled into the sea.

I unpacked the radios John had stacked in boxes in the main compartment. John had experience installing marine radios, but the details on these high-tech receivers exceeded his knowledge. I knew nothing about installing this stuff, but I studied the instructions in the boxes and visited marine electronics stores and asked them what do do.

When I worked on the boat, it was just work, but interesting work. Something about boats makes mundane chores more fascinating than the same work on land. I didn't think about what I was doing.

When I was out shopping for wire or paint or caulking or just getting advice, I was constantly aware that I was helping get a sailboat ready for a smuggling trip. I had the childish feeling that everyone I talked to could read my mind—they could see this red neon sign blinking next to me: Smuggler. Blink. Smuggler. It was an eerie feeling, but it was not just paranoia. When people at marinas in Florida see two or three men, who pay for everything in cash, working full-time getting a yacht ready for deep-water sailing, they become suspicious, and it's usually well founded.

During the second week of preparation, we picked up the third member of the sailing team, Bob Ireland, at the Gainesville airport. Bob, who came from Indiana, was my size, with dark hair, and (I found out later) was an accomplished artist. He joked around with John and affected a Spanish accent because John could speak fluent Spanish and loved to hear Ireland massacre the language. Immediately, John decided we had to have nicknames because "two Bobs will make us crazy."

Ireland said, "Me? I'm definitely a Rámon—" He turned to me in the backseat and said, "You? You look like an Ali to me, Bob. Okay?"

"Call me Ali," I said.

"Ali! Ali!" Ireland chanted. Muhammad Ali the huge prizefighter; Bob Mason the 135-pound pencil-neck. We all laughed.

We drove to our woods near High Springs.

John got out a rolled-up nautical chart that night while we sat around his dining-room table.

"The plan, man?" Ireland asked. John moved some plates aside and unrolled the chart.

John smiled, swigged some beer. He spread out the chart and put glasses and ashtrays on the corners because it wanted to roll up. "*Wanting; having*, Rámon." This was John's favorite expression: the smuggler's slogan. "Wanting lots of money; having plan." John picked up a pencil and tapped on the map at Jacksonville. "The plan. We leave Jacksonville when we get the word," John said as he began tracing a route with the pencil. "We sail due east for a while, due east, till we get to deep water, here. Deep water, out past the Bahamas. Then we head southeast to the Virgins. All told, the first leg is about thirteen hundred miles. Thirteen hundred miles. Take maybe ten days, two weeks. About ten days, if we get good winds. Then we'll lay over in

Saint Thomas for a few days before we head south. A few days there, then we head south." I stared at John. Why was he repeating himself so much?

"What's going on in Saint Thomas?" asked Ireland.

"Take on final supplies. Stock up. Top off the fuel tanks, the water tanks, and stock the food lockers—"

"And *la cerveza* locker, sí, Juan?" Ireland laughed.

"Is a bear Catholic, Rámon? The *cerveza* locker? The *cerveza* locker? This ain't gonna be an easy trip, not easy, no, but we're going to be living *good*." John raised a beer and we touched cans. "Living good! Wanting; having! Okay. We reprovision here; we also install the transducer for the depth finder. Have to have a depth finder. I know a beach we can use to keel-haul the boat. We'll keel-haul the thing—"

"What's that?" I asked.

"Basically. Well. It's simple. We get the boat in shallow water at high tide. Then we haul it over on its side; pull it over on its side when the tide goes down so we can get to the bottom of the hull and drill a hole for the transducer—the thing the depth finder uses to send and receive sonar signals."

"Why not do it in Jacksonville?" I asked.

"We're running out of time, Ali. No time. Plus we'd have to haul the boat and I think the people at the marina are getting suspicious. They act suspicious. Besides we have to wait in Saint Thomas for the scam master to bring us some money anyway. We'll have time to kill there."

I nodded, distracted. John was nervous. And seeing the plan on the table suddenly made what had been just talk reality. Before, I'd been a sweaty laborer working on a boat, forgetting, or denying, why I was.

"Okay," John said, tapping the pencil on Saint Thomas. "Okay. Saint Thomas is the last we touch land until we get back, okay? And this Caribbean leg is dangerous," he said, dotting a line between Saint Thomas and Colombia. "We got dangerous shit here. We got pirates out here sniffing for our money and the boat on the way down. We got pirates out here sniffing for our cargo and the boat on the way back." Pirates? Ireland and I look at each other. "Now. Okay. We sail from Saint Thomas, windward across the Caribbean, six hundred and fifty miles directly to the Guarjira Peninsula, and meet up with Ike— that's the code name for the contact—on the coast, near Carrizal, here. About here," he said, making a tiny dot next to the coast. "We load up and beat back across, out through the Annegada Passage through the Virgins. Trade winds are always from the north; have to beat back up; not comfortable; need industrial-grade jockstraps for that part. Now we got fifteen hundred miles of dodging el Coasto Guardo." John smiled. "But that's why we're so far out, off the usual routes. Coast Guard stays closer to land. We curve way out and come back in until we get about here," John said, tapping on a spot about two hundred miles off the coast of South Carolina. "About here, then we turn southwest."

"Whot happy, Juan? We meesing the Florida?"

John laughed. "No. No meesing the Florida, Rámon. No meesing the Florida. No. From here we sail to Charleston. Near Charleston; they haven't decided exactly where, yet."

"Charleston? Why?" Ireland said, dropping his mangled Spanish routine.

"Because that's where we make the drop-off, Rámon. Destination-land. Where we go. The shore team is already there, living in a beach house, checking out the area. They live there now; they fish; they shop; just folks; checking it out." John winked and smiled. "Surprise! We not going where you theenk we go, eh, Rámon?"

Ireland nodded, looking worried.

"Don't worry, Rámon, Spence is there; Mitford; Wheely and Rangey Jane; about fifteen dingers you know. They know what they're doing. They're watching everything: the drop-off point and every approach to it. They'll give us the final clearance before we come in." Ireland smiled, but he was still worried about something.

The spot where John said we'd turn southwest was a hundred miles north of Charleston. "Why so far up before we turn back?" I asked.

"People spot us coming in will think we're cruising down from Cape Fear; think we're a yacht on the way down from New York, maybe. Just on a cruise from New York. No clue we're coming up from Colombia, Ali. Not a clue."

Pretty slick. Except for saying everything twice, I was beginning to think John had his shit together.

"That last leg is over fifteen hundred miles of winter Atlantic. Lotsa nasty weather, amigos. Winter Atlantic weather." John grinned. "Altogether, we're talking about more than a four-thousand-mile cruise, here. Four thousand miles, plus."

"*Madre mío!*" Ireland, reacting to the distance, smiled and then, looking serious, said, "But *why* Charleston? We've always had good luck in Florida."

"Florida's getting hot. Too hot in Florida. Last place they'd expect to see pot coming in is Charleston, Rámon. Nobody goes to Charleston. Who goes to Charleston?"

"Nobody goes to Charleston," Ireland said, smiling.

"Right," John said.

I walked home feeling antsy. Four *thousand* miles in a thirty-six-foot sailboat? Pirates? Coast Guard? The plan seemed okay, but what did I know? What were the odds? I fought back the nagging of my conscience, which claimed I was just not cut out for this stuff. It was just not me. I considered quitting that night, before I got in any deeper, but I'd said I'd go. Plus the alternative was grim: no money, no job, no hopes for either. Besides, I reminded myself, I had felt the same sickening butterflies in Vietnam, just before the assaults. Once you get into action, the doubts vanish. Just suck it up and do the mission. Thirty thousand dollars could last us three years. Three years to get a book published.

Just do the mission.

CHAPTER 13

November 30, 1980—Jacksonville is having a cold snap. It's forty degrees inside the *Namaste*. I'm lying in my bunk in the main cabin. I put my hand out and touch the bulkhead. The hull is just thick fiberglass, cold as steel, clammy. Ireland is asleep in the bottom bunk, John is on deck talking to the partner, Ray, the guy who owns the boat. I can only catch snatches, but I get the gist. Ray is unhappy with how long it's taking, how much it's costing. John is talking, louder, repeating himself. I'm getting depressed.

"Sure," John says. "You sit out there in California while the dingers are busting their nuts putting the fucking boat together. Comes on a truck. Comes in fucking pieces. Yacht-fucking-kit. What do you know about going to sea, Ray?"

Ray says something, but he speaks in a low voice. I met him when he arrived and he acknowledged me as one of the help. He was friendly, but distant. He was a businessman trying to get his ducks in a row. I sympathized.

"Yeah, you sailed. You sailed once," John said. "Somebody else did the work, you were management, along for the ride."

"Along for the ride?" Ray's voice was angry.

"Okay. Okay. Sorry. I exaggerate sometimes—"

"Sometimes?"

Ray talked for a long time, and I drifted off. Did John know what he was doing? Or was Ray just being a nagging boss? I wished we could just get going.

Ray was gone the next morning. John told Bob and me that he had smoothed everything out. Ray was just an asshole worried about his money. "I told him he was going to make a fucking fortune and we were going to make it for him. Asshole." We smiled. It's great fun to hear the boss called names. Ray wasn't *the* boss, but he was part of . . . management.

John took us to a nearby Big Boy restaurant for breakfast. While we ate, he told us we were almost ready. It had taken a month to get this far, but the time was near. I was happy to hear it and nervous as hell.

"We move the *Namaste* today," John said.

"Move her? Why?" Ireland said.

"Guy at the marina knows what we're up to."

"He knows?" I said. "He said so?"

"Didn't say it. I can tell. We move down the river. I figure we can finish up in two, three days."

We sailed about twenty miles down the Saint Johns River to another marina. The *Namaste* sailed beautifully. I couldn't get over how the light breezes could push this twelve-ton boat along at walking speed.

We got a slip at the marina. The autopilot, the vane gear, had just arrived from England. It's called an Aries wind vane and John put me in charge of installing it. I had to drill oblique holes in the rounded stern and attach the mounting hardware. Took a day. When I'd finished, we had this weird-looking contraption hanging off the back of the boat. We christened it Rosalinda, in keeping with the Spanish theme that Ireland had established.

Rosalinda had a plywood vane, about the size of a blade on a ceiling fan, that reached above the deck about four feet. The vertical vane flopped around trying to keep aligned with the wind. When the vane twisted Rosalinda's mechanism, it turned a long rudder that stuck in the water behind the stern. The wind vane's rudder was attached to the tiller with ropes. The idea was that once a course was set, the wind vane would remain stable, pointing into the wind. If the *Namaste* changed course ever so slightly, the wind vane's arm would twist and Rosalinda's rudder would move and pull ropes that tugged the tiller and put her back on course. It was a clever rig.

That night we went to a movie, *The Elephant Man*, about a poor bastard who had a hideously deformed face and body. Afterward, everything disheveled, dirty, deformed, or smelly was preceded with the adjective *elephant*. A messy bunk was an elephant bunk; a tangled knot was an elephant knot; a stale beer was an elephant beer; and, of course, there was elephant underwear.

We drove to a shopping center in John's elephant truck and raided a Publix. We were kids on a shopping spree. I think our high spirits resulted from the relief that something was finally happening. We used to do the same thing in Vietnam—get happy to be doing something, even if the something was going to get some of us killed. We ran up and down the aisles, each of us with two grocery carts, dumping in whole cases of food. We got canned meat, canned beans, canned vegetables. We got fifty pounds of rice. We got ten cases of beer. We got a case of Winstons. We got forty one-gallon plastic bottles of drinking water in case we ran out. We did all this yelling: "Hey, Juan. Needing theese corned beef?"

"Wanting; having," John would yell.

"You like asparagus?"

"Wanting; having."

People could not help noticing us. Probably they thought we were just crazy. It was fun buying all that stuff.

We took hours loading the boat. We packed the beer in the ice chest and buried it under four bags of ice. John said we'd re-ice it just before we left. This was a priority with John. He knew the ice would melt in a couple of days, but he was determined to have cold beer for as long as he could. Ireland and I seldom drank. We were smoking pot.

We pulled up the cushions on the starboard bunk to pack some of the canned food in the lockers there. John pulled out a padded rifle case and took the opportunity to show Ireland the gun he'd bought for the boat. He slid it out of the case—a Winchester .44 magnum lever-action rifle. "Nice," Ireland said. "I guess." Ireland wasn't familiar with guns. He turned to me. "Nice, Bob?"

"Stop a charging rhino in its tracks," I said.

Ireland shrugged, smiled. "Nice."

John stashed the rifle under the other bunk and we stacked boxes of canned food in the locker space, converting the locker into an elephant locker. I noticed two cans of paint and a can of paint thinner and asked if we should throw them away—just take up room. John said we might need the paint in the Virgins.

We got to bed late.

We were ready.

John phoned the boss, but didn't get a go-ahead. Something was fouled up with Ike, our Colombia connection. The next day, December first, the scam master still had us on hold, but John announced that we were leaving on the second anyway. "They'll have it figured out by the time we get there."

Patience and John's wife, Alice, came to the marina in the morning. Patience brought my old flight bag, the same one I'd used in Vietnam. It was appropriate; I used to pack it when we stayed out in the boonies for a month at a time. She'd packed it with most of my clothes: four pairs of Levi's, four sweatshirts, and one change of clean street clothes and loafers—for the drive back home. She showed me a packet of letters, each one dated; she said I should open them on those days. Patience likes to write. She'd also packed my Nikonos camera, a Vietnam talisman I was happy to have with me, my Texas Instruments programmable calculator I'd bought in New York when I was an executive, and my Swiss Army knife that Patience's mother had given me. I had all my best and luckiest things to take with me.

We spent the day sailing the *Namaste* around the Saint Johns River. John showed off his sailing abilities by taking on challenges from other yachts and did really well considering the *Namaste* was such a tub. We practiced tacking, John yelling "Hard a lee!" when he was ready to make the turn, and got used to ducking the big mainboom that swept across the cockpit when we came about. The jib had to be pulled over during the tack, but the staysail was self-tending, swinging across by itself when we came about. During this shakedown cruise, John showed us how his rigging worked. He'd run the halyards and downhauls that controlled the sails, aft through guides on the deck, and into the cockpit, allowing us to control the sails and stay out of the weather. John used the same layout when he did his solo Atlantic crossings.

That afternoon we had a picnic on the boat back at the marina. I couldn't taste the food. Patience was wide-eyed and distracted with nervousness, but she, too, had come to believe this trip was our only option.

Today was our seventeenth wedding anniversary. We went below and made love on the forward bunks—the only compartment with a door.

At sunset John came back after one last call. The scam master, in California, was still undecided about when we should leave. We agreed with John that we should just get the hell out of here and see what happened. People at the marina were getting to know us; asked more and more questions. We were antsy to be moving.

Patience and Alice stood on the dock waving. I could feel a filament of attachment stretching to keep me there on that dock, but it got longer and longer and finally snapped. I waved until Patience was almost invisible, a tiny dark figure against the red sky.

CHAPTER 14

Wind gusts swirled among the buildings, buffeting us from random directions as we motored through the narrow shipping channels that go through Jacksonville. We honked our portable gas horn at a couple of drawbridges to make them raise them so the *Namaste* could get under. John had the weather radio on and we could hear that the seas outside were fifteen feet, winds thirty-five knots and increasing; but it seemed fairly peaceful in the channels that meandered through the city. John set Bob and me running around securing loose equipment. I tied the cabinet door handles together, which seemed unnecessary. I'd been living on the *Namaste* for a month and had become accustomed to her being a level and stable platform. I knew she would heel over in the ocean, but I couldn't imagine her leaning far enough that stuff would fall out of the cabinets.

John asked me to crank up the loran. I went below and opened the electronics cabinet at the back of the counter where the loran was, next to the single-sideband radio—a radio that can communicate over very long distances. I tuned the loran and got a readout. I plotted the readout on our chart and found our position matched reality—Jacksonville inlet, right next to the Mayport Naval Station. I told John it was working fine. The loran was our primary navigational tool. These radios monitor transmissions from a bunch of shore stations and can pinpoint your position to within a hundred feet. They are truly marvels of technology.

We had an outgoing tide. When we hit the mouth of the inlet, the rushing water twisted into huge rolling furrows and the *Namaste* began bucking and yawing in the turbulence.

When we got clear of the inlet, the wind was howling at thirty-five knots. The *Namaste* bucked into huge breakers, shuddering like she'd run aground. The wind shrieked through the stays and shrouds. About two miles offshore, John announced it was time to set sail. Bob and I manned the mainsail and staysail winches under the dodger and John winched the jib halyard beside us. John let the boat weathervane into the wind while we hoisted sail. The empty sails snapped and popped in the gale like big flags, sounding like bullwhips. You could feel the boat quiver with the shocks. It took less than a minute to get the sails up. John shut down the engine and let the *Namaste* fall off the wind. The sails filled and she heeled over, so fast that I thought she was going to be knocked down. The starboard gunwale went underwater and the *Namaste* lurched ahead, crashing through the surf. It was like a roller-coaster ride. John said that cruising with the gunwale underwater was called "putting the rail under." For a neophyte, though, seeing the side of the boat go underwater was alarming.

John showed us how to adjust the sails. When you took up slack, pulled the sails tighter to the boat with the sheets, it was called sheeting in. Let them out, sheeting out. So John watched the sails and the rail and called, "Sheet out." By sheeting out the sails, we took off some of the sideward pressure and got the rail out of the water, on average. The bigger waves crashed across the deck and poured into the cockpit. The sea was a fury of shoving dark shapes and we were in their way. We couldn't see anything in the pitch-black night, just the water within a few feet of the boat that our dim red and green position lights illuminated. Waves crashed across the deck and slammed into the dodger. The dodger was just canvas and the only thing keeping water from cascading down the hatch. John tugged Rosalinda's control lines, clicking the vane ratchet until the *Namaste* came to a course of about a hundred degrees east-southeast. We gave Rosalinda a little cheer as she held the *Namaste* on course against such massive forces.

We were soaking wet, crowded under the dodger. John asked me to check our position on the loran. I went below. Above, in the cockpit, the rolling and wallowing hadn't bothered me. It was difficult below decks. I began to feel nauseous immediately. The loran was on, its power light showed it was on, but the position readout lights were blank. I reset it and punched the readout button. Nothing. I went up and told John, over the howl of the sea, that the loran wasn't telling me shit. Maybe he could get something out of it. He cursed the maker, Texas Instruments, and went below.

The cabin lights coming through the hatch made Ireland's yellow slicker glisten. He cupped a joint against the wind and jutted his chin to the back of the boat. "That Rosalinda. How 'bout that girl?"

I nodded. "Be hell having to man the tiller in weather like this."

"Shit, Ali, manning the tiller is a drag in any kind of weather. You just sit there for hours pushing that stick back and forth to keep the fucking compass on track. I've tried lashing them down to hold a course, but that only works for a few minutes at a time. I'm real glad John insisted on getting her." He blew a kiss at the autopilot. "I loooove you, Rosalinda!"

"Bob," John yelled. We both looked. "I mean, Ali. I can't get anything, either. See what you can do. You know more about electronic shit than I do."

"Me? I've never even seen a loran before."

John nodded. "See what you can do."

As I went below, I saw Ireland lean over the side, barfing. The Namaste was plunging down huge water valleys that put my stomach in my throat and then crashing up the other side with a surge that stretched my scrotum. But I'd been in storms at sea before. My dad and I went through a hurricane in his forty-two-foot fishing boat when I was a kid. I'd spent a month on the USS Croatan on the way to Vietnam. I knew how long I could last before I puked. Below, without the reference of the dim horizon, there were no outside clues as to what was happening. The cabin was a grotesquely tilted room with shifting, unpredictable gravity. One instant I was pressed against the counter, the next I was flung against the stove. The wooden parts of the boat—the cabinets, the bulkheads, and the deck—creaked as the fiberglass hull flexed. I swallowed bile and clung to the chart counter, flipping every switch on the loran. I had it do a self-check, which said everything was okay. Everything was okay except that it wouldn't give a position readout.

I went back up just as I was about to throw up. The wind and the spray washed the sickness away. I told John, "The fucker's broken, John. Maybe when it calms down I can go into the engine compartment and check the antenna connections. That might be the problem."

John nodded. "No problem."

"No problem?" I said.

"Right. The most we'll travel in a day is a hundred miles. This is a very big ocean, Bob. We steer this course for two days anyway. You can get it working tomorrow."

I nodded. Maybe.

Nobody wanted to go below because it made you sick. We'd drawn straws for the watches—or rather, Ireland and I had drawn straws. John wanted the four-to-eight watch so he could catch the sunrise for navigation. Ireland got the twelve-to-four, leaving me with the eight-to-twelve. The watches were four hours on, eight hours off, twice a day. I'd gotten the easy watch: eight to twelve in the morning, eight to twelve at night. We'd stick to that pattern for the whole trip. It was eight o'clock, my watch for another four hours, but John and Ireland stayed in the cockpit.

The wind was picking up. The rail was farther underwater and waves were breaching the cockpit coaming. We sheeted out the sails as far as practical, but the *Namaste* still heeled too far over. John decided that we had to reef the sails. Then Rosalinda broke.

We didn't realize Rosalinda had let go until the *Namaste* came up into the wind and the sails began to flap with thunderous cracks. John jumped onto the tiller and got us back on course. "Ali, you hold her on this course, just off the wind, keep it loose, while Rámon and I reef the sails." I sat back beside the tiller and held on. Waves bashed against my jacket. It took both hands to wrestle the forces shoving the *Namaste* around. John switched on the overhead deck lights and we could see the roiling, thrashing sea all around our bobbing cork of an island. John and Ireland put on safety harnesses—we only had two—and John yelled to me, "If anybody gets washed overboard, Ali, just turn about, sail in a circle. Drop the sails, crank up the engine. Just go in a circle and get the searchlight." He climbed between a safety line stanchion and the dodger and out on the deck. Ireland followed, low like a spider, clutching the mast, sheets, halyards, stays, downhauls, shrouds, rail, anything he could get his hands on. They got to the safety cable and snapped their harness lines to it. I watched them struggling to keep their footing and wondered how you turn sailboats in circles. What happens to the sails when you turn? If I let go of the tiller to let the sails down, where would the *Namaste* go? Do they ever *find* people who go overboard?

I downhauled the staysail and they wrestled with the loose cloth for fifteen minutes, trying to gather it together to lash it to its boom with short pieces of rope called hanks through grommeted holes in the sail called reef points. The staysail secured, they made their way to the mainsail amid crashing waves. When they grabbed hold of the swinging mainsail boom, John made a cranking motion, a signal to let the sail down a little. I let the tiller go, grabbed the mainsail winch, let the halyard out, and pulled the downhaul in. Then I grabbed the tiller and got back on course. John and Ireland, battered by waves, tried ten times at least before they could capture the flapping slack in the sail and gather it up. They tied the folded slack to the boom with hanks put through the reef points. When they finished, the jib was up, the staysail was down, and the mainsail was about half its normal size. John told me to let the boat fall off the wind. I pulled the tiller and the *Namaste* heeled over, but not as far as before. The rail rode out of the water. John and Ireland staggered aft and unhooked their safety lines. As they made their way the last few feet to the cockpit, a wave buried them and rolled up over the dodger. They completely disappeared. Then, when the water receded, I saw them flat on the deck, hanging on to ropes. They got up and with a lot of effort got past the dodger and back into the cockpit.

"What's so hard about that?" John said, laughing, soaked to the skin.

"Dammy. Elephant weather," Ireland said.

We laughed.

We spent an hour tying Rosalinda's broken pulley to the boat with ropes. The patch worked and Rosalinda freed us from having to sit out in the weather. The rest of the night was without emergencies. The only problem was seasickness. John and Ireland were throwing up. John did it on purpose. "No use fighting it, Ali, just let it rip," he said as he leaned over the side. When it was my turn to go below to sleep, I felt myself getting sick as I tried to get to the bunk across the tilted, pitching cabin. I grabbed the bunk, pulled myself in, and the feeling vanished. I had to hang on to the sides of the bunk to stay in, but I soon fell asleep.

It wasn't any calmer the next morning, but at least daylight made the rolling mountains of water through which the *Namaste* plunged visible.

Every so often a particularly monumental wave spewed across the deck and into the dodger. The dodger was amazingly resilient. It just drummed when a wave hit it and bent with the force, shrugged, and sprang back in position. John was right about the dodger. He was also right about the low cabin profile. The waves had very little to hit against—the forward cabin bulkhead was only eighteen inches above the deck. I came to think of the *Namaste* as being very tough, and of John as being a master sailor.

While we sipped hot coffee, we saw a sea gull, sitting in the ferocious water preening itself contentedly while it rose and fell twenty feet with the waves. Anywhere is home to a sea gull.

After coffee, John and I considered making Rosalinda's repairs more permanent, but decided it was just too rough to be messing around trying to drill new holes for the pulley mount. The rope was holding okay; we'd tied it through a drain port in the gunwale and through the ring of one of Rosalinda's pulleys that guided a tiller control line. We'd fix it better when it got calmer. I went below and puzzled with the loran.

During the night I had become more tolerant of the evil motion below decks. It took longer for me to feel sick. I unhooked the hatch ladder and laid it on the deck so I could get to the engine compartment doors. I opened the doors and squeezed in. This engine room was not designed for standing people. It was designed for crawling people. I had to squeeze past the engine on my side. Not *past* it, precisely. Sometimes I was beside it, sometimes on the bulkhead opposite it, sometimes on top of it, depending on the motion of the *Namaste*. I had a flashlight and some tools—pliers in my pocket, a screwdriver in my teeth. I wedged myself against the engine with my head back in the stern, under the cockpit, where the antenna connections were. The loran used a specially isolated section of the stainless steel backstay as an antenna. The antenna lead came through the hull and under the cockpit. The connection looked okay, but I undid it and scraped the wires clean with my knife. I reconnected the lead and wriggled back past the engine. We were on a tack that had the chart counter on the low side, so instead of trying to claw my way to the loran, I lay across the front of the counter. I switched it on, got the ready light, hit the position check. Nothing. Recycled it. Nothing. I got the instruction manual for the thing and went on deck.

They could read my face. "No worky?" Ireland said.

"Nope. Nothing. I can't understand it. Worked fine when we installed it. Worked fine right up until we got into the ocean—"

"Sounds like a loose connection," John said.

"I know. I checked the antenna. It's tight. The radio's getting power. It might be something on the circuit board that's loose, but that's beyond my talents, messing with the circuit board."

John got up and stepped into the hatchway. "We'll have it fixed in the Virgins," he said, and went below. He came back in a minute carrying his sextant. "Want to learn celestial navigation?" He asked us.

On the third day, the storm died. The sky was clear, the wind steady. I sat in one of the lawn chairs we had lashed under the dodger and watched Rosalinda steering. We'd replaced her broken pulley mount and she worked flawlessly—the compass was locked on course.

"Ready?" John said. He sat beside the tiller making a sun shot with the sextant. His body leaned in all directions as he tried to keep himself vertical. He swung the sextant from side to side while he adjusted the micrometer drum that moved the index arm along the arc. I watched the seconds tick on the Casio wristwatch we'd bought as a chronometer. "Mark," John said.

I said, "Eleven thirty-seven, twenty-two seconds."

John nodded. He held the sextant down and read the degrees off the arc scale and the fractional parts of a degree—minutes and seconds—off the micrometer drum. He wrote the measurement—the altitude of the sun above the horizon—and the time I'd called on a pad. "Okay. We need two more to make a good plot. We'll do it again in fifteen minutes."

I nodded, smiling. I felt good. The ocean was beautiful. Steel-blue waves moved past us, looking solid as granite. If it were a movie, and you froze a frame, you'd think you were on a glassy, volcanic, primeval plain that went to infinity. The horizon encircled us; we really were in the center of the universe. The *Namaste* leaned into her trek and, as tubby as she was, cut a fine swath through the sea. She was alive. Creaking wood sounds came from below deck. Wind sang through the stays and shrouds. She paused as the bow pierced the waves, raised herself, and pushed ahead against a cobalt mound, the top of which boiled across her bow. After cresting the wave she rushed down the other side and you could feel the joy of success in the relief of the rigging and the surge of acceleration.

I studied the sails that were capturing the power. They were full, perfect arcs, taut as drumheads and trimmed to perfection—not one wrinkle or tremor. People have spent centuries making up names for the parts of sails. There's the head at the top, the leech at the trailing edge, the clew at the end of the boom, the foot on the boom, the tack at the mast. They call the interior of the sail the luff. To make the whole thing stiffer and less inclined to flap around, they invented yardstick-sized sticks, called battens, and stuffed them into batten pockets they sewed in the leech. I never knew a piece of cloth could be so complicated. These are airfoils, I thought, wings. They just have a lot more names than airplane wings. The *Namaste* is flying just like a plane, except it's flying on its edge.

I'm a pilot. Understanding how wings work is part of my nature. I used to wonder where I'd gotten the desire, the obsession, to fly. The first dreams I can recall were about flying. I was born in 1942; not very likely I'd been an airplane pilot in a previous life. I don't believe in reincarnation, but if I did, I'd have to think I might've been a sailor, or a bird.

Ireland came up from below, where he'd been napping. He had a cup of steaming coffee in his hand. He watched John swinging the sextant and looked at me. *"Buenas* mornings, Ali. We know where the fucky we are?"

"Not yet," I said. "We're—"

"Ready?" John said.

"Ready." I checked the watch.

"Mark."

"Eleven forty-six and thirty-one seconds," I said.

"Now we know, *sí*?" Ireland grinned.

"Yes," I said. "Now we know."

"Where?"

I pointed to the sun and said, "We are north of the sun, in the Atlantic Ocean."

"So." Ireland grinned and nodded. "Elephant navigator."

John came up under the dodger with us. He put the pad down on the ledge next to the hatch. "We've got two shots. You can fix your position with two, but it's better to have three. Four, even. Least one of them is going to be fucked up. Trying to put the sun on the horizon from a pitching deck ain't easy. Wanna try?" He held the sextant out to me.

I went back beside the tiller with the sextant. I'd done this the day before, so I knew the principle. John was right; it's hard to do. The sextant has a small telescopic sight which you look through. On top of the sextant is a small mirror, an index mirror, that reflects the image of the sun onto another mirror, a horizon mirror, and finally into one half of the split image you see when you look through the telescope. The idea is to sight the horizon through the telescope and then adjust the sextant until you see the sun in one side of the split image. When the sun's image is close to the horizon, you adjust the mircrometer knob until the image of the the sun's disk just kisses the horizon. The trouble is the pitching deck makes it nearly impossible to hold the sight steady. I got the sun close to the horizon and then swung the sextant vertically in a small arc, making the image of the sun swing back and forth over the sea. The bottom of the arc of the swing is straight down, something that's otherwise impossible to know on a moving boat. I called, "Ready?"

John said, "Ready."

I swung the sextant and twisted the micrometer knob. I nudged the sun until it just kissed the horizon. Got it. "Mark."

"Twelve oh one, seventeen seconds," John said. I went back under the dodger as he wrote it down. "What'd you get?"

I read the scale. "Seventy-five degrees, thirty minutes, six seconds, give or take a few seconds." John nodded and wrote that down next to the time.

"All right. Now we can calculate." He got the *Air Almanac* from the clutter—books, cigarettes, my camera, a jar of Skippy's, and a box of Ritz crackers—we kept behind the windshield and paged to the date. There's also the *Nautical Almanac*, but John liked this one; they're essentially the same. The *Air Almanac* is a book of tables, updated annually, that show where the sun is for any time of day, relative to Greenwich, England. You have to convert your local time to Greenwich Mean Time and then calculate at what latitude you would have to be to see the sun at the elevation you measured at the time you measured it. It takes a good five minutes to do this by hand, and any small arithmetic errors can put you off by hundreds of miles. I figured I could program my calculator to do most of the math, when I understood how to do it on paper.

When you've got the numbers, you draw an arc with a compass on a universal charting sheet, centered from the guessed position you marked on the sheet. I'm leaving out some nitpicking details, but essentially, where the arcs cross is your location—plus or minus a mile or so. John went below and drew the arcs. He came back up with the charting sheet. The arcs all crossed, but not at one point. The intersections made a triangle big enough for a dime. The space was the margin of error, about two miles, and ours was about as good as it gets on a small boat in a rough sea. "Here," John said, pointing proudly at the chart. "We're here. In this little fucking triangle!" We marked the spot on our map—about two hundred miles off the coast of Florida.

"Ali was right!" Ireland said. "We're north of the sun, in the Atlantic ocean! What instincts, Ali."

I grinned. "Guess I'm a natural navigator."

By late that afternoon, the sea was calming. The winds were still pretty strong and the *Namaste* cruised smartly through the smooth sea at about five or six knots, fast for her. Knots, as I'd discovered reading the sailing books John had brought, meant exactly that. A hundred years before, sailors used to tie regularly spaced knots in a string, put a float on the end of it, and toss the float overboard. As the string played out, the sailors counted the knots that slipped through their fingers for one minute, and that would be how many knots they were going. Knots means nautical miles per hour, and we got it by timing ourselves between one position fix and the next. I wanted to try the counting-knots-on-a-string method, though.

Bob had cooked some chicken and rice on the alcohol stove. We had no designated cook. We took turns at irregular intervals, whenever the mood struck us. I cooked often—something Patience would have been amazed to know—because I enjoyed the challenge of making a meal against the adversity of the rolling and pitching boat. In a real storm it could take hours making a meal, but sailing provides lots of hours.

We sat in the cockpit at sunset and watched the sun sink into the sea. The red glow shimmered, a million flecks of red from a million moving facets on the sea. We checked the time when the top of the sun's disk intersected the horizon, a free sighting we could use. As we ate, sunset became dusk. Night fell. The stars, following Venus's lead, seemed to pop out of the sky. Before we finished eating, a brilliant dome of stars hovered over us. I stood up and looked around. The faint line of the horizon was a circle around us, the edge of a disk, the edge of the world floating in space. I sat down.

"What the hell's that?" Ireland said, pointing west.

John and I looked. A green oblong shape hovered twenty degrees above the horizon.

"Hey," Ireland said, "I don't believe in these things, but what—"

"Yeah," John said. "Look at that. It's moving."

It was growing larger, looking very much like it was approaching us. I watched it, thinking there was something familiar about it. It suddenly moved back, getting smaller.

"Jesus," Ireland said.

"It's not a UFO," I said. "I mean it is—UFO means it's unidentified—but it's not a ship, a spaceship, or anything—"

"Why are you always such a fucking cynic?" John said. "Big, bright green thing, hovering, comes at us, goes back, and you *know* it's not a fucking flying saucer. Why?"

"Because it doesn't act like a spaceship—"

"Oh," John said, turning to Ireland. "Doesn't act like a spaceship, Rámon." Then he turned back to me. "What the hell you talking about?" John said, disgusted.

"She's coming again," said Ireland.

The shape seemed to rush toward us, getting huge. You still couldn't see a surface or a clean edge, but the fact was, it was *something* coming our way. I really *wanted* it to be a spaceship. It dropped lower and seemed to be rushing us at low level, like a fighter on a strafing run. Then it changed course and swooped north, disappearing up among the stars in just seconds. I could feel John and Ireland staring at me.

"Still," I said. "There's something not right about the way it flies."

"Awww," they groaned.

"So *que* is it?" Ireland said.

"I'm not sure. But it started out due west, right over Cape Canaveral."

"It wasn't a fucking rocket, Bob," John said.

"No. But maybe they were testing something. Maybe they let some kind of gas out real high up, to check dispersion or something, I don't know. But it looked like a gas cloud to me. It wasn't moving, it was just getting bigger and smaller—"

"And then it rushed us—" John said, laughing.

"And then it got real big and finally collapsed," I said. "It looked like it shot away, but it would look the same if it was a gas cloud that just shrank to nothing."

"Awww," they groaned.

We were listening to the news on a Miami radio station the next morning when we heard that John Lennon had been murdered. That put us all in a funk, pissed that weirdos like his killer were allowed to live at all; made us wonder at the fact that some people weren't people, they just looked like people. We listened while they played "Imagine."

A while later, we heard that NASA had released some weird green gas in the upper atmosphere over the cape, causing hundreds of UFO sighting reports. Ireland and John looked at me and said, "Awww."

"Elephantshit!" Ireland yelled. "That's what they always say." We laughed.

By noon the winds were dying. The sea was sagging from riotous mountains to gentle dunes. John spent a lot of time trimming the sails, trying to coax as much energy as he could from the little wind that remained. The *Namaste* was doing two knots—a slow walk, and slowing.

"This is sailing," John said. "One minute you're on the verge of being sunk in a fucking storm, don't know whether to shit or go blind, the next minute you're looking for oars."

As the wind died, Rosalinda became less effective. By sunset, Rosalinda's wind vane flopped around uselessly and we steered by hand. Watching bits of seaweed crawl by, John said, "Well, fuck it. Let's crank up the engine. That's what it's for."

We dropped the sails and John started the engine. It ground a bit and finally caught. It was a Cummings thirty-horsepower diesel. The *Namaste* grumbled. I felt she did not like being pushed by a motor, but she cruised ahead anyway, muttering and vibrating. We could feel the breeze in our faces. It was a relief to be moving.

Under power, Rosalinda was completely useless. The relative wind she used as a reference to steer by was always coming from straight ahead, no matter what direction we motored. Rosalinda would just steer us in random directions, so we had to man the tiller during our watches. Sitting beside that big stick for four hours at a time, moving nitpick left, nitpick right, trying to keep the compass on the mark, made you really appreciate autopilots. John said that if he owned this boat, he'd have an electric autopilot installed for when he had to motor.

I woke Ireland at midnight for his watch. I went back on deck and waited by the tiller. So far, this trip was a pleasurable adventure. But I felt a chill when I thought about arriving at Saint Thomas. End of the cruise; beginning of the raid. Saint Thomas was the initial point, as we called it in Vietnam.

We'd drop low over the initial point, twenty of us—twenty helicopters—each carrying eight grunts. We flew at a hundred knots, but the Viet Cong almost always seemed to know our routes and would be there spraying red tracers into the flight. I heard: "Preacher Six, Preacher Red One. Red Two just went down. Two is down." And Preacher Six, Major Rogers, said, "Roger. Mark the coordinates." The pilot called in the coordinates where Red Two lay wrecked and we sped on, dodging palm trees, some of us thinking—me, for one—we were actually dodging the bullets; watching villagers, who we thought we were helping, shooting. Shooting at us.

Ireland came up through the hatch. I jerked, suddenly aware of where I was. I wondered if trying to write about Vietnam was such a good idea after all. Bad memories. So far, on the boat, I was sleeping well. I think the distractions of keeping the *Namaste* under way and the actual physical stress of the work were responsible.

Ireland sat beside me and asked how it was going. I looked at the compass and came right the ten degrees I'd dropped off, plus another five to make up for the loss. Luckily, the *Namaste* was slow. Minor course changes don't mean much to a sailboat motoring at five knots. The engine vibrated my ass, the wake lapped along the hull, the prop wash fanned out behind the stern, glowing faintly with excited phosphorescent sea life being sucked through the propeller. The stars hovered so close I could touch them. Vietnam was so long ago, yet I could *hear* Preacher Six just then. I heard him.

The next morning, the engine quit.

"Fuel?" Ireland asked. "We out of fuel?"

"Naw," John said. "We have fucking two hundred gallons in the tank."

John pumped the throttle lever and pushed the starter button. Groan. Groan. Nothing. "Shit," John said. "It's a brand-new Cummings, goddammit."

Ireland stayed on deck while John and I went below and removed the ladder so we could get to the engine compartment doors. We crawled in with a flashlight and stared at the engine. It was as big as a car engine. It was gray. It had lots of things sticking off it. John reached in and pressed a lever sticking off a mug-sized thing he said was the fuel pump. "Might've lost its prime," he said, pumping the lever. He sat back on the cabin deck, grabbed his beer, and swigged. He yelled, "Give it a try, Rámon"

Groan. Groan. Spit. Growl. The engine chugged to life. We closed the doors, put the ladder back, and went above. John brought a couple of extra beers and Ireland and I lit up a joint. No engine means you drift around helpless for as long as God wants. It was a relief to hear the chugging and feel the vibration beneath our feet.

An hour later we heard: Sputter. Sputter. Sigh. Pop. Quit.

John leaned against the dodger frame and shook his head with his eyes closed. Ireland and I looked at each other and shrugged. The *Namaste* coasted and stopped. No wind. No waves. There were swells, though, probably leftover energy from the storm, and the *Namaste* rolled back and forth sickeningly. John had us raise the sails and pull them taut, to dampen the rolling. Now and then you could feel a whiff of breeze, but the weather vane on the masthead just swung and twirled as the boat rolled.

John and I went below and looked at the engine again. Still very large and gray with lots of things sticking out of it. John pumped the fuel pump again. Ireland cranked. Groan. Chugga. Chugga. Pow. It started, but you could hear the starter grinding; the battery was getting weak.

The engine ran for half an hour. Got it going again. Ran fifteen minutes more. The next time we tried starting it, we got: Chugga. Chugga. Nothing. The battery was so weak from the repeated starting that the engine was barely turning over. We had to fix the engine.

We sat in the cockpit pooling our knowledge of diesel engines. When we were done, you could've put what we knew about these things on a piece of paper with plenty of room left over to write an insurance contract. John had the only real experience among us. He said air must be getting into the fuel pump, causing it to lose its prime. How? "Maybe it gets in at the seal where it's mounted to the engine. Maybe it gets in at some little pinhole in the fuel line. I dunno."

We had a lunch of peanut butter sandwiches and beer. I even drank one. The weather was getting hot—ninety degrees. We were four hundred miles from Saint Thomas, out of the cold latitudes. We took to wearing nothing.

After lunch, John and I crawled back in to the engine and, with much grunting, twisting, wrenching, and knuckle bruising in the tight space, we managed to get the fuel pump off. We brought it up on deck and stared at it. Looked like a fuel pump. Had a diaphragm thingy, here, must be pushed up and down by that cam whatsit, there. Yep. You push the priming lever and it pumps fuel into the pump. John pushed the lever and we saw a few drops of diesel fuel squirt out. Promising, eh? We did the only thing we knew how: we took out all the parts we could get loose, wiped them clean, and put them back in. It was now very clean, like it was before we took it apart. John and I went down and bolted it back on and primed it. Ireland pushed the starter. Groan. Grind. Rumble. Growl.

Yea!

The *Namaste* surged ahead, once again under way. We drank some more beer and told jokes for an hour. Then the engine quit. The breeze died as the *Namaste* stopped. The sun beat down. The sea was listless, stagnant.

John got up. "This is bullshit!" He grabbed a coil of rope, tied one end to the stern pulpit rail, and flung the coil over the stern. The *Namaste* was moving enough that the rope trailed behind. Then John jumped overboard. We watched him splashing around in the water, yelling, laughing. "What we need is a fucking break! C'mon. Cool off!"

Ireland and I jumped in. It was like three naked boys at the old swimming hole, except the water in this swimming hole was almost a mile deep.

When the *Namaste* drifted too far ahead, we'd swim to the line and pull ourselves up to the boat. I got back on board and fetched a diving mask and my camera and went back in. It was exhilarating. When I put the mask on and looked underwater, it felt like I was suspended in space. The crystal-clear water got darker, turning deep blue hundreds of feet down. Somewhere down there was the bottom. I bet this is like being in orbit, in freefall, I thought. Flickering shafts of sunlight pierced the water and converged at infinity. I dove down and within seconds lost track of which way was up. I had a strange urge to keep swimming down, down to where the shifting light beams met. When I stopped swimming, I floated slowly back up. That's where up is in sea-space. Not from where you fall, but to where you float.

The next day, the *Namaste* sat motionless in a vast wasteland. The water was thick with seaweed and trash. The place is called the Sargasso Sea—which we immediately changed to the Elephant Sea—where several currents converge and swirl together, keeping the seaweed in huge mats. It's a unique kind of seaweed called sargassum which is native to sea currents. Branches of the plant are called fronds, inhabited by unique animals like the sargassum frog fish and sea slugs. The seaweed was alive with little fish that looked like they were made of seaweed, little silvery darting ones, and baby jellyfish. They say baby sea turtles live here until they get big enough to survive open water. The trash—six-pack rings, Styrofoam cups, bread bags, light bulbs, bottles, cans—was obscene. We were hundreds of miles from any land, and here was a trash dump that covered many square miles. "It's like the world is a bunch of rednecks," Ireland said.

We waited for wind. I sat below reading the *Air Almanac*. In the back of the book there's a section that describes the process of plotting your position from your sighting—in case you're on a bombing raid and can't remember how to do it and the captain's yelling, "Where the fuck are we?" I read that and worked the sample problems.

I went above with the sextant and made sun shots and plotted our position every hour. We were moving at less than one mile an hour. We had the radio on, listening to an evangelical show from Puerto Rico, the only station we could get clearly. I wanted to hear them pitch the autographed picture of Jesus Christ with eyes that glow in the dark, but they were just asking for money. Ireland was drawing a picture of the *Namaste*. John was reading a Captain Hornblower book (who,

along with Errol Flynn, was one of his heroes). At lunchtime I made
some beans and rice.

After lunch I went below and pulled the ladder away from the engine
hatch and crawled in. I studied this fuel pump thing. You could see
the copper tubing that fed it coming from two places on the fuel tank
above. There were five junctions in the tubing where air could be
leaking in. Or the seal at the pump itself could have an invisible pinhole.
Start with the obvious. I took the pump off and took it on deck. John
and Ireland glanced over as I wiped the seal with a rag. The rubber
gasket was immaculate, but I smeared it with a layer of silicon rubber,
for insurance, and went below and bolted the pump back in place with
the silicon wet. A couple hours later, I suggested we try it again.

The batteries were very low from trying to start the engine for the
last two days, but the engine caught. We had been through this enough
to know not to get crazy about the fact that the fucking engine ran,
so we just sat where we were and waited. She died in less than five
minutes. I nodded. John got back into his book. Ireland drew.

I went back into the engine compartment and stared at the fuel
pump. It was stifling in the small place because of the heat of the day,
and now the engine was hot from its little workout.

So, if you prime the pump full, it works—the engine runs until the
fuel in the pump is gone. I knew the seal was tight; they use silicon
to seal fish tanks. Obviously, the lines feeding the pump must have a
leak. I looked at the tubing. Air could get in at a connection, or in
through a pinhole in the tubing itself. It could be anywhere. There
wasn't a hint of fuel leaking out, so it was so small that only air leaked
in. I took the fuel pump off again and studied the primer pump mechanism. The lever pushed a piston which squeezed out fuel. I pressed
it until all the fuel squirted out. Then it just hissed as it pumped air.
It pumps air. Idea jumped into my brain. What if I put the pump back
on backward? Then when I primed the pump, I'd be pumping air,
under pressure, into the fuel line. Brilliant.

I went below and reversed the connections. I let the pump hang
loose beside the engine. I attached the pump's outlet to the fuel line.
I went into the cabin and got some Joy detergent, put some in a coffee
cup, and mixed it with water. I got a rag and crawled back under the
cockpit, next to the engine. I swabbed the soap mixture on each joint,
one at a time, and pumped the fuel pump. If the problem really was

an air leak, then I should see bubbles at the hole. At the last junction, a T-connector mounted on the engine compartment bulkhead, I saw foam.

"Hey!" I yelled. I was standing inside with my head out the hatch. "I found the fucking problem!"

"No shit?" John said.

"What's it ees, Ali?" Ireland said.

"We got an air leak in a coupling. C'mon." I waved. "C'mon, I'll show you." I was practically giggling. John crawled in with me, and Ireland squatted on the cabin deck. "Watch," I said, pumping the fuel pump.

"Son of a bitch!" John yelled. "That's it! That little fucking leak is all it takes!"

"Right. All we have to do is epoxy the joint, seal it up. That'll fix it. At least well enough to get us cruising again."

"Right," John said, laughing. "We can put on a new fitting in Saint Thomas."

We had lots of epoxy resin. It's used to make repairs on fiberglass boats. John mixed up a few ounces of the stuff and smeared the goo all around the fitting. Nothing would ever leak in that coupling again. I put the fuel pump back on the right way and we went on deck to wait for the epoxy to cure.

John was beside himself with happiness. He drank two beers in quick succession. We were due in Saint Thomas in a week. He'd had a radio message on the single-sideband that we would be met there by the scam master himself, who'd bring us money. The transmission was encoded as usual: it sounded like a transmission between a home office and a freighter. The conversation was mumbo-jumbo about cargo, spare parts we needed, part numbers, and consignment numbers. Lots of numbers. The numbers were the message. John read some part numbers he said we needed that gave the scam master our position. The scam master sent changes to shipping order numbers that included the date and time he was going to meet us in Saint Thomas. So if this fuel-line patch worked, we would be on our way, and maybe even on time.

Near sunset, we figured the epoxy was set. We went below and pecked at the stuff with a screwdriver. Hard as a rock. I primed the fuel pump.

"Okay," John said to Ireland, "give it a crank."

Groan. Kapock. Sigh. The batteries were too weak to turn the engine.

"Goddammy!" Ireland yelled. "It's always fucking something!"

John nodded, and slid out the tool drawer under the chart counter. He dumped a bunch of tools—Snap-On sockets, Vise-Grips, screwdrivers, torque wrenches—on the deck and fished out a long metal rod, bent in two places, with a socket at one end. He fit the socket onto the end of the engine's crankshaft. "Okay. We can start this thing manually. I've done it before."

He held the crank handle steady with his left hand and cranked with his right. He could turn the engine over, but, as strong as John was, it was too slow. A diesel builds up much more compression in its cylinders than does a regular gasoline engine. I grabbed the crank from the other side and together we tried again. Yank, push. Kathunk, kathunk, pow! We were puffing at the effort. It was like trying to spin a top in sand: there's no momentum to it; it's all brute force. Kathunk. Kathunk. Pow! Growl!

John yanked the cranking rod free of the engine and everybody cheered.

After four hours of listening to every little click, clack, pop, belch, and whirr that came out of the engine compartment, we began to relax. The engine ran perfectly. The *Namaste* was under way.

We celebrated that night by breaking out one of the freeze-dried dinners we'd brought. We only had a dozen of them. We got out the pork chops. They looked like cardboard disks, but when you soaked them and boiled them, damned if they didn't turn into genuine pork loin chops. We served up freeze-dried peas and about a gallon of egg noodles. This sailing life is fine.

Ireland woke me up at eight A.M. I blinked at him in the dim morning light coming through the clear hatch in the roof of the cabin. "Where's John?" I asked. He was out of cycle. Bob wakes John; John wakes me; it's the cycle. Ireland shook his head. "John wouldn't wake up." He smiled. "Too much fun, eh?"

"Yeah, but that means you took his watch, Rámon."

He nodded and crawled into his bunk across the cabin.

I sat at the tiller angry as hell. The captain of a boat should never miss his watch. I was looking for perfection here. I was remembering how if one guy in the team fucks up, the team gets wasted. We had assholes like that in the Cav. We had a captain in our company, a guy we called Daisy, who'd always go into the fetal position in his seat during the assaults. He'd hear the pilots yelling on the radios about taking hits, see the tracer bullets, and then he'd squinch down in the seat, pull up his feet, and try to hide behind his chicken-plate (what we called the bulletproof chest armor). You can't fly while you're cowering in the seat. If the other pilot got wounded or killed, nobody would be on the controls. When you let go of the controls of a helicopter, it goes eight directions at once, apeshit wild. That captain didn't seem to understand that if the ship went, he went. He was too overcome with fear to think.

Somehow, I equated that captain's dereliction of duty with John's, and it made me mad. The two men got mixed in my mind until John's missing his watch became a fuckup with life-or-death consequences.

When John came on deck at lunchtime, I told him what I thought.

"John, do you know that Bob had to stand your watch last night?"

John looked at me, suddenly angry. "What about it?"

"What about it? That means he's up eight hours. It means he's likely to fall asleep on watch and we'd never know if we were going to hit a freighter, go off course, or something. That's what."

John glared—probably thinking, you should *never* hire friends. I turned and went below, sat on my bunk, and got out the *Air Almanac* and started reading.

John came down, staggering. He'd already put down a couple of six-packs. He was madder than I'd ever seen him before. He leaned up close to my face and said, "Look, Mason. I'm the captain here. You're the dinger. Don't you ever call me down again." He glared. "You do, and I'll set you straight. Get it?"

I'm not the fighting type. At least not physically—especially not when it comes to getting into it with a guy that can tie me in knots. I'd need a gun to make it even. I looked back at John's face, watched the anger pouring out of him. Part of the anger was from his drinking. I knew about that from my own life as a boozer. Part of it was just embarrassment. I nodded. "Okay, John. I get it." I looked down at my book and saw him turn and climb back up on deck.

I couldn't read what I was looking at. I was mad, getting really jumpy. I needed to know the team knew what the fuck they were doing. I didn't want to trust my life to fucking amateurs. I simmered for a while. I considered jumping ship at Saint Thomas.

Two days later, the wind came back. We saw a huge black wall approaching us all day. On the radio, the Coast Guard talked about a huge storm, and this was it. We had hours to prepare. As the breeze picked up, we shut down the engine and rigged the sails for the approaching tempest.

When it hit, we were ready. The *Namaste* heeled way over. Huge waves crashed over us. But we had been through this drill before. We pitched, wallowed, creaked, and groaned, but the *Namaste* was up to the task and forged ahead. I was beginning to love this boat. She was stalwart.

"What does *Namaste* mean, anyway?" I asked while we huddled under the dodger sharing a can of cold Del Monte beef stew. Rosalinda was back on the job, holding our course to within a degree or two.

"I haven't got the slightest idea," John said. He was friendly, the argument forgotten. He had not missed a watch since.

"Maybe it means 'Pot Smugglers,'" Ireland said. "Coast Guard probably sold this boat to Ray." We laughed.

"I'd like to get a boat like this someday," I said.

"You like this sailing shit, eh?" John said.

"Yeah. Patience and I could fit it out with a couple of desks. Go where we wanted. Write."

"Not me," Ireland said. "When I get my money, I'm going to buy some land. Build a little house. The only sailing I want to do is on a windsurfer. On a lake."

The next day, the storm was past and the wind was strong and steady. The *Namaste* cruised at five knots. I came up on deck and saw John sitting in the cockpit, naked. A plastic bucket by his side, he was lathering himself with Joy. Lemon Joy is the only detergent that makes suds in seawater, so I'm told. The sight made me cringe. I've always had this phobia about letting salt water dry on my skin. I used to spend half my life playing in the surf as a kid in Delray Beach, but we had public showers at the beach to rinse off the salt water. If I didn't rinse off, the drying salt water would tighten my skin and leave a crust of salt that clung to my clothes when I got dressed and made me itch. I scratched the back of my neck. I was risking my life and my freedom on this trip, but getting sticky was my big fear at the moment.

"Hey, Bob," John said as he stood up. "I don't mean to get personal, but you haven't bathed since we left. That swim was it. What's that? Four, five days ago?" He wrinkled his nose. I watched him hold the bucket over his head and rinse himself off with seawater. He tossed the empty bucket overboard and pulled it back in with the rope tied to the handle and repeated the process.

"Yeah, I know. I can't even stand myself," I said.

So when John finished, I stripped off my shorts, got a bucket of water, and gave myself a bath in the cockpit. I rinsed, went below, and dried off with a towel. Then I waited for the stickiness to set in. I put on clean jeans and a T-shirt and went on deck. When I put my hand in one of the pockets, I felt a piece of paper. A note from Patience: "I love you, the Phantom Phantom." I saw she'd drawn a little-girl face with a big smile. I smiled, picturing my phantom. Fifteen minutes later I didn't feel my skin clinging to my clothes. A half hour later, I'd forgotten my revulsion. I felt fresh and clean. Maybe it was the Lemon Joy.

We had two fishing lines out, hooked to lures we'd made from frayed nylon rope. The ends of the lines were tied to short boards we used for reels. The boards were anchored, jammed against the winches, but the lines were held on to the safety lines with clothespins so that if we got a strike, a clothespin would let the line go and we'd know we had something on. The clothespins let go now and then. Usually it was seaweed. I saw a clothespin snap off the railing and grabbed a board. I yelled that we had something and wound the line onto the board, like a kid with a kite. Two hundred feet behind us, a giant tuna leapt out of the water. Really huge: this . . . big. His skin shimmered like a rainbow in the sun. He leapt clear of the water, shuddering with fury, trying to shake the hook. I held on to the board, not winding, just trying to keep hold of it. John and Ireland were running around looking for a gaff hook. When I felt a slack, I wound on more line. John grabbed my camera and took pictures of the fight. About a half hour later, we had a goddamn big tuna whipping around at the stern of the boat and under the boat, swimming in small circles, tangling the line on the prop. We couldn't get him in, so we waited until he got tired and stopped struggling. When we dragged him on board, we saw he was about four feet long, weighed maybe forty pounds. He flopped around on deck while I tried to stab a knife into his brain. Thunk. Thunk. Quiver. Dead. Lots of blood.

"Wow!" Ireland said. "We eaty fishy tonight, no?"

"No shit!" John said.

I felt sad watching the tuna's rainbow skin fade as it died. I said a thank-you to his spirit, something I'd picked up reading about Indians. This was something special here, a life. I was taking a life to nourish my own. I forget that when I order tuna at a restaurant.

Unfortunately, the sea picked up while I cleaned the fish. I'd chopped him into thick steaks—damn big steaks that'd cost you twenty bucks apiece on shore—put the steaks in a pan, basted them with lemon juice and butter, and put them in the stove to broil. The bottom of the gimbaled stove leaned into the aisle because we were sailing with the rail underwater. The *Namaste* pitched and wallowed as the storm picked up. It was a real challenge cooking the steaks, but just the smell of them broiling made it worth the effort. By the time I'd finished, though, both Ireland and John were feeling the sea and didn't want to eat.

I sat under the dodger, on my watch, and ate the best tuna I'd ever tasted. John and Ireland stayed below, weathering their stomachs.

CHAPTER 15

We sighted land at dusk of the fifteenth day. Before it got dark, we could make out El Yunque, a thirty-five-hundred-foot mountain on the west end of Puerto Rico, and across from it, the fifteen-hundred-foot peak of Crown Mountain, which is what Saint Thomas is—a mountain sticking out of the sea. Land lights flickered through the sea air and I wanted to be ashore. I wanted a hot shower. I wanted Patience.

The wind was strong, the sea rough. I noticed that we all walked around on deck as if on land, a big difference from when we started two weeks before. I guess we'd developed what they call sea legs. The *Namaste* closed the distance to Saint Thomas about an hour after we sighted land. John was below checking the charts. Ireland and I joked about island girls and whatnot. We were free of worry. We had nothing to hide, nothing on board anybody wanted. The trip down was like a rich man's cruise. From now on, things would be different. Saint Thomas was the initial point on the sortie to Colombia. That's how I saw it. Part of a mission. With teamwork, timing, strategy, luck, it could work. Just getting to Saint Thomas, through those storms, was impressive to me. The *Namaste* was tough and so were we. Two weeks in a rough sea will tighten up every loose muscle you have. My stomach was steel outside, jelly inside.

John checked his chart and pointed out the channel markers as we motored close to land. He used the spotlight he'd bought for the trip to sight the channel markers. The thing lit up half the world when he switched it on. He said we'd come in on the west side of the island, get out of the wind. The wind diminished to lazy breezes as we sailed into the island's lee. We dropped sail and, with fingers crossed, cranked the engine. Started right up. We cruised into a cove near David Point, far from the lights we'd seen on the north side. Bob went forward and got the anchor ready. When John gave the word, Bob tossed in the anchor. John switched off the engine. The anchor line tightened. The *Namaste* swung around, aligning herself with the breeze. She rocked gently, contented, I thought.

We dragged out the inflatable dingy. Bob pronounced it stressing the *g*. Din-GEE. "Blowing up the din-GEE," he said. "The dingers blow up the din-GEE." Didn't take long: we had a foot-powered air pump. Got the thing inflated and threw it overboard. John said Ireland should stay on board while he and I went ashore to get provisions. He meant he wanted to get some beers. He'd been out for two days. He was sober, joked around less, talked less doublespeak.

We were only a couple of hundred yards off, and it didn't take long to row ashore. John rowed. "Tomorrow we go around to the south side, to the main harbor. I don't like to come in around all those boats at night," he said, stroking.

"There's lots of boats there?"

"You won't believe it."

"What's here?" I said, pointing to the moonlit beach.

"I don't know. Never been this side of the island before. But I think those lights are maybe a marina or something. Maybe they have some cold fucking beer."

"Say, John, do you mean, 'cold *fucking* beer' or '*fucking* cold beer'?" I said, laughing.

"Yes," John said. "That's what I mean: Budweisers with ice sticking to the cans; brew so cold your scrotum will shrivel."

We saw a dock, a big house, but no marina. John rowed up to the beach and we jumped out and pulled the dingy up on dry land. The ground felt like it was moving and I almost fell over. When we let go of the dingy, I stood up with my arms out, like I was balancing on a tightrope. I laughed. "They're right! Sea legs," I said.

We stumbled across the sand and came to the house. I was laughing. I just couldn't get over it. I could not convince my body that I was on land. The ground seemed to pitch and roll, like the sea. I walked stooped over, like I might fall off the earth. The house was a clubhouse, I think. We walked all around it. Nobody there. We walked through the club's landscaped grounds until we came to a gravel road. We stood on the road and looked toward the only lights around, about a quarter mile away. The trouble was, neither of us had thought to bring shoes, and the gravel hurt. "John, you really must want a beer, to go through this torture."

"Ice cold, freeze your nuts off," John said, laughing. "Besides, isn't this fun? Shore leave. Wanting; having."

The lights were at a garage and it was closed. We seemed to be in a part of the island that closed up early. John was pissed, "Dammy! Wanting; but no having?" John was picking up Ireland's manner of speech; so was I. I was saying din-GEE as soon as I heard it. John shrugged and said he'd make up for it tomorrow. We tenderfooted back down the road to our dingy.

There had to be two hundred sailing yachts in Saint Thomas Harbor. I was astounded. Where'd they all come from? What were they doing here?

"Some of them—a *lot* of them—are here for the same reason we are, Bob," John said.

I think he was right. As we threaded our way among the anchored boats, I saw mostly men on board. Mostly three men on each boat, just like ours. They waved, we waved. When we got within six hundred yards of the docks, we found a spot big enough to anchor the *Namaste*. I went forward and dropped anchor at John's command. The *Namaste* settled back against the anchor line. John stood up on the deck and looked at our neighbors. "Good. We're clear all around. When she swings around with the wind, and they swing around with the wind, she won't hit anybody." Glad he thought of that; I sure hadn't.

We put on clean clothes. A note Patience had stuck in the crotch of my underwear said: "Use it and lose it!" The little girl smiled, holding a knife. Damn, Patience, I'm not like that . . . then I remembered she had every reason to believe I was. We flopped the dingy overboard and jumped in. Bob and I decided I'd row in; he'd row back out. As we passed by the boats, we got questions: "Where you from?" "Jacksonville?" "Got some weather, eh?"

We passed a houseboat, or rather a house on floats. It was a rundown two-story shanty. You could see that it was built to be a cheap place to live; there was no fee to anchor off in the harbor. A woman on the front porch was hanging up clothes. "Lots of these people live in the harbor," John said. "See that guy out there with the big windmill on his boat?" I looked and nodded. "He was here last time. Lives there, generates his own electricity with that windmill, distills his own water in a solar still, catches fish to eat; only comes ashore to sniff out women when he gets tired of jerking off. Neat guy, Mason. You have a lot in common with him. Oughta go meet him."

"Yeah," I said. "You make him sound real glamorous, John." Actually, I did want to meet the guy. This was just a tourist stop, wasn't it? I wasn't a pot smuggler yet.

The docks where we tied up the dingy were shared by the Islander, an island-rustic bar and restaurant, and the Harbor View, a large, modern hotel. We blended into the tourist traffic—mostly people sightseeing off cruise ships—looking in the shops that ringed the plaza between the hotel and restaurant. They sold tropical T-shirts, palm frond hats, conch-shell lamps, ice cream—tourist geegaws and whatnots. I was looking for a pair of sandals and a place to develop some slides I'd taken. I found a photo shop and asked the guy where I could use a phone. He said the hotel had pay phones. We found the phones. John and I called our wives; Ireland called his girlfriend.

"I miss you," Patience said.

"Me, too. How's Jack?" Jack thought I was just working as a sailor.

"Oh. He came in second. Cross-country race."

"That's great," I said. I'd seen Jack run in two races. A lot of fathers were at every race. Now one of the fathers was on a pot run. There was one way out of this trip, but Patience hadn't mentioned it. I asked anyway. "Heard anything from Knox?"

"No. That last letter from Norton was it." An editor at Norton had said he thought my manuscript was very well written, BUT: the usual stuff about no one wanting to read about Vietnam.

We didn't talk long. I told her a little about the storms and stuff, said we'd be home in a couple of weeks; I'd call before we left Saint Thomas.

Outside the hotel compound, Saint Thomas was pretty scruffy. We walked along a busy, litter-strewn street to a place John said served great hamburgers. We'd been talking about hamburgers for days. The street reminded me of the crummier neighborhoods in Brooklyn. I was really impressed by this. Saint Thomas was a tropical paradise, yet the citizens buried it in trash. Also, no one smiled. If you tried smiling at someone, you got a sullen stare back.

We got our hamburgers and fries and milk shakes and sat down at a table covered with catsup, pieces of dried onions, relish, and a hundred flies.

"Man, what a dump," I said. "Why's everything so dirty?"

"The people don't give a shit," John said. "They're all on welfare and they're pissed off at those white people living up on the hills." He pointed to a mansion that hung out on a cantilevered deck off the side of Crown Mountain. "They're pissed off at them because they're rich, and if you're a white tourist they're pissed off at you because you're white and, since you're a tourist, probably rich, too."

"Hot dammy!" Ireland said, flicking his eyebrows at the hamburger he held in two hands. "Living good, Juan!" He bit into the hamburger, squishing out catsup, smiling as he chewed.

While we ate, John said we would spend a couple of days getting supplies, and then sail to Thatch Cay, just to the east of Saint Thomas, to keel-haul the boat and install the depth finder. We needed the depth finder because we were going close to shore in Colombia, and the last thing we needed was to be pinned there, waiting for the Colombian navy.

We walked to a grocery store and bought four bags of groceries, six cases of beer, a case of Cruzin rum, and ten cartons of Winstons. We filled a cab with the stuff and drove back to the docks. John had Ireland wait with the supplies while John and I went into a marine supply store and bought a new fitting for the fuel line, plus spares

We loaded up the dingy and rowed back to the *Namaste*.

That afternoon I replaced the fuel-line fitting and then just loafed around the boat watching life in the harbor. Some people sunned themselves on the decks of their boats; others polished brass, painted bright work. Everybody was laid back. I wasn't laid back. I was plagued with doubt, tense with worry. I wondered if I was really able to go through with the scam.

At dusk we rowed back to the docks and went to the Islander.

The Islander was the kind of place they keep dirty on purpose. The ceiling was fishnets tacked to beams with dusty seashells and starfish drooping down in the nets at odd places. A stuffed sailfish nailed to a driftwood plank had cobwebs in his open mouth. We sat at a table on an upstairs balcony, with a good view of the harbor.

It was sunset, and the island was beginning to look good. Lights flickered along the harbor's edge, ringing the dark water like a glittering necklace on velvet. Two hundred yachts basked in a calm harbor. We decided that the *Namaste* was one of the best-looking boats in the basin.

I sipped a beer, my second, and began to think of Saint Thomas as a pretty nice place to be. After a while, you barely noticed the trash and stopped trying to be friendly with the natives. And the weather was terrific. Here it was, the middle of December, yet the breeze was soft and warm, balmy. Perfect weather.

I had a bowl of conch chowder and another beer.

Ireland and I stayed out on the boat the next day, cleaning and making repairs, while John rowed in to phone the scam master and find a place to fix the loran. He'd taken the radio with him.

John came back after lunch. No luck getting the radio fixed. It'd have to be sent to the states for repair—weeks. We could buy a new one on the island, but loran sets cost fifteen hundred dollars, and John told us we were down to less than a thousand. The scam master, the money man, was coming in two days, but John doubted he'd spring for a new radio because John was way over budget already. Who cares? he said. We were doing fine with the sextant and the wristwatch. We were here, weren't we? True enough. We'd crossed thirteen hundred miles of open sea, storms, drifting becalmed, motoring, and we'd hit Saint Thomas dead on without the loran.

John decided we should find a place to haul the *Namaste*.

When we sailed east around Red Hook and north, up the Leeward Pass, I saw scores of beautiful houses set on the hillsides of the island. This seemed to be what Saint Thomas was for: a place to perch one's house and take in the view. And hell, I imagined a mansion owner saying, labor is cheap, if somewhat sullen. Let them make their own fortunes.

It took less than two hours to get to a suitable cove at Thatch Cay. It was high tide, but according to John's tide tables, that was only a foot or so in this area. We dropped sail in a lagoon that looked like it was out of a movie—blue water, white beaches, palms and sea-grape trees crowded right up to the water. We motored slowly, crawling toward the beach. We dropped an anchor off the starboard side when we were within two hundred yards of shore. This would be the anchor we would be pulling against later. We crept toward shore, paying out the anchor line, until we felt the keel bump the sandy bottom. John stopped the engine. We put the anchor line around a winch and pulled ourselves back out a few feet to where we figured the *Namaste*'s keel was hovering just a couple of feet off the bottom. When the tide went out, she'd be almost aground. John didn't want to actually ground her; he was afraid she'd get stuck. We dropped another anchor to keep us where we were.

By the time we got this far, it was getting late. John said that it would take half a day to roll the *Namaste* over and drill the hole for the depth finder. Might as well look around. We rowed the dingy ashore to explore the island.

We splashed through warm, clear water, felt hot sand on our feet. We sat down on the beach and just looked. The sun was low, golden. Coconut palms arched over the sand and crystal-clear waves lapped the white beach. Fiddler crabs scurried through the driftwood and seaweed looking for food, turning cocky and aggressive when they bumped into other fiddlers. I took some pictures. I framed a shot with palms drooping over the water, Ireland and John lying on the dazzling beach, the *Namaste* gleaming white against a cobalt sky. I walked to them and sat down. "Wow!" Ireland said. "This is right out of a cigarette ad. It's perfect. Why don't people live here?"

John agreed. "This is beautiful, no two ways about it. Fucking lovely."

I turned around and stared into the tropical jungle behind us. A hundred feet into the vines and undergrowth, it got very dark. A little spooky. Didn't know what was in the shadows.

When the sun dropped behind the ridge of Saint Thomas Island, we found out why people didn't live here. We were assaulted by swarms of sand flies thick enough to cast shadows. Some people call them no-see-ums, because they're so tiny. They are very tiny bugs, true, but each one packs one helluva bite and they attack by the thousands. These things are goddamn flying piranhas. We jumped into the dingy and splashed back out to the boat. That stopped them for a while, but as soon as it got darker, they swarmed aboard, though not as thick as on shore. We sat around with towels wrapped around our heads, being miserable, while the sand flies fed. Ireland offered the theory that the sand flies used this beautiful tropical island as bait for humans.

At dawn we got to work.

Ireland and I rowed ashore with a big spool of line. We tied one end of the line to a big tree trunk and then rowed the other end back to the *Namaste*. John tied it to the mainsail halyard so that when we cranked the winch on the mast, instead of raising the sail, we'd pull on the two hundred feet of line attached to the tree. The idea was simple: the line from the anchor we dropped as we came in went through a drain port in the gunwale amidships and back to a winch in the cockpit. When we winched in the two lines, the *Namaste* should lean over. And she did, for a while. The problem was that the pulley at the masthead was embedded in the mast, the perfect position for raising and lowering the sail. Now, though, the halyard, pulled way off to the side, was binding against the slot in the masthead. The farther over the *Namaste* leaned, the tighter the line jammed, and the harder it was to crank the winch. When it took two of us, hanging on the handle, to move it an inch, John said there was something wrong. The *Namaste* listed over about forty-five degrees, but we needed another twenty.

I suggested we had two problems: the pulley at the masthead was oriented wrong, and the anchor line was set up wrong.

"What the hell do you know about this?" John said. He was covered in sweat from the effort of winching. He was frustrated. He knew it wasn't working like it was supposed to. He was thinking about it; and now the know-it-all dinger was offering unsolicited criticism again.

"Nothing about this, specifically," I said. "But I can see what you're trying to do, and all we have to do—"

"Look, Bob. We almost got it. Need another push at it, is all. Catch my breath."

"Nope. Won't work," I said, my voice tinged with authority. "When you lower the top of the mast, John, you're raising the keel. What is it? Eight tons of lead? You need to move the point where the anchor line is tied lower, below the center of gravity."

"Lower?" John looked at Ireland, who shrugged. "Where? You can't get any lower than the gunwale."

"It's simple, John," I said too smugly. "You've got it rigged wrong. All we have to do is take the anchor line and run it in the opposite direction. Pull it over the other side and down under the keel. Then when we pull against it, we're pulling from under the keel and the keel's weight helps pull the *Namaste* over. But you still need to—"

"I don't see how that would make a bit of difference." John was plainly irritated. "Let's get back to work."

Ireland and I winched in the mainsail halyard, John winched in the anchor line. The *Namaste* twisted between the two opposing forces until she achieved equilibrium—about forty-five degrees. You could not make her lean another degree. We crawled up the deck and hung over the gunwale. The spot we wanted to install the depth finder was still two feet underwater.

John said we should all get on the mainsail winch. More force was the answer. The three of us hung on the handle, jerking down with all our might. We even made the thick bronze handle bend, but the *Namaste* did not budge.

I got a piece of paper, drew my plan, and showed it to John. I spoke quietly, trying not to sound superior about it. "See, John. Most of the weight of the boat is in the keel, and the way you've got it now, we're trying to raise the keel out of the water. If the keel was touching the bottom, it would work. I know, you don't want to be on the bottom because we might not get her off. Fine. So we have to make her think she's on the bottom. That's what will happen if we run the line under the keel."

John nodded reluctantly. "That'll do it, you think?"

"Yes, if we rerig the masthead pulley, too. It's got way too much friction with the line going the wrong way."

"We'll try moving the anchor line," John said. "We'll see what happens."

"But—"

"We'll rerig the anchor line, Bob," John announced.

Bob and I let out the mainsail line and the *Namaste* was once again standing bolt upright. It was getting close to ten o'clock. I undid the anchor line and Bob swam it under the keel and up on the other side. I pulled it through a guide and into a deck winch and took up the slack.

We winched the top over again. The *Namaste* leaned farther over than before, but as the line left the mast at ever increasing angles, the friction at the masthead increased.

"I didn't think it would work," John said, going below for a beer.

I followed him down. "John," I said as he reached into the cooler. "I know this'll work." I tapped my drawing. "We know your way won't. We can winch on that fucking thing until the line breaks—it's cinched up tight as a knot. It's not going to work and you know it."

"You *know* my way won't work?" John glared at me. "I'm the fucking sailor here, Bob. I've done this before."

"It doesn't matter, John. It's simple physics."

John shook his head angrily. "Physics? Shit. I fucking hate it when goddamn *academics* try to take on the real world."

"I'm not an academic, John. I'm good at this stuff."

"Not an academic? Not an academic? You're a fucking writer."

"Really? Seen any of my books? I was a farm kid, John. Had to invent all kinds of gadgets to get out of doing chores. Then the Army: helicopters—ever seen anything more complicated than a helicopter? Then the mirror business—invented all kinds of machines there. I see what we have to do. That's all."

"That's not all," John said, swigging from his beer. He swallowed and said, "You know what your problem is, Mason?"

"No, John. What is my problem?"

"*You* want to be the fucking *captain*."

I didn't want to be the captain. As it was, I was the worst crewman you could imagine: an argumentative know-it-all sailor on his first trip in a sailboat.

We went on deck and ate some peanut butter sandwiches for lunch. John stared at the island while I explained to Ireland, for John's benefit, my plan. Ireland nodded, but refused to take sides. I asked him if he thought it would work. "Don't know, Ali. I'm just a dinger," he said, looking worried.

After lunch John said, "We could just haul a pulley block up to the masthead with the mainsail halyard. Then we could run the beach line through that pulley and down to one of the winches. That should work."

"That'll work great," I said.

Once the decision was made, things brightened up. Ireland and I rowed back to the beach and untied the line so John could pull in enough slack to make the changes. John put the beach line through a big pulley block he'd found in our spare-parts drawer and hooked the block to the mainsail halyard. By the time we got back, he'd run the beach line through the pulley and wrapped the end around a winch. He was raising the pulley, with the beach line through it, up to the masthead as we climbed aboard.

Ireland and I cranked the beach line through a winch in the cockpit and John winched the anchor line tight next to us. The mast went over, the keel flipped up. The *Namaste* leaned over until the port gunwale went underwater. We got the side of the keel to the surface, probably could've laid the boat flat with the leverage we had.

We spent another hour drilling a two-inch hole in the bottom of the hull. John and Ireland worked outside, sitting in the dingy. Ireland held the dingy against the hull with a line tied to the safety rail while John drilled a hole where he wanted the transducer for the depth finder. When the pilot hole came through, I drilled from inside with a two-inch hole-saw set in a brace. Took about twenty minutes to grind through the hull, which was two inches thick on the bottom. The plug fell out and I could see John and Ireland smiling outside. We set the depth finder's transducer in the hole in a bed of epoxy.

The *Namaste* lay cocked on its side for four hours while the epoxy set. We played with the dingy and skin-dived.

Late in the afternoon, we let the *Namaste* back upright. I ran a wire from the transducer to the depth-finder dial we'd installed next to the compass in the cockpit. We flipped on the power and, sure enough, the thing said two feet. Watching the finder tell us the water was getting deeper as we pulled ourselves out to the anchor was fun.

We anchored out far from shore, out of range of the sand flies, and broiled three big steaks. We toasted our success with beer, told jokes, and yelled insults at the sand flies. It felt like we'd really done something.

The next morning we sailed back to Saint Thomas Basin to finish provisioning the boat. And to meet the scam master.

John brought him out to the *Namaste* in the dingy the day after we got back to the harbor. His name was Dave, and he'd brought his wife, Nancy, with him. They looked just like any other couple on a weekend jaunt. They climbed aboard, to a thoroughly spiffed-up *Namaste*. Ireland and I had been cleaning up the boat all morning. John introduced us and I found out that Dave was a Vietnam vet, too. He'd been a grunt in 1969, earned a Purple Heart. That made me feel a little better. Most grunts I knew were good at keeping cool under pressure. I'd learned, from John, that Dave had made this his mission by pushing out the usual scam master. Dave had put this whole deal together and had a point to prove to the boss—that he was as good as the other scam master. Dave was clawing his way up the corporate ladder.

We talked for a while in the cockpit. Dave was impressed that I'd been a helicopter pilot; loved helicopter pilots because they'd saved his ass a bunch of times.

Nancy pulled from her purse a brown-paper package the size of a thick novel and handed it to John. John tore it open like it was Christmas morning. Inside were twenty-five rubber-banded bundles of money. Twenty-five thousand dollars. They excused Ireland and me while they talked business. Dave had all the codes and times for the pickup and wanted to brief John. Ireland and I went forward, sat against the cabin bulkhead on the foredeck, and smoked pot. "That money isn't for the pot, is it?" I said. "I don't think so," Ireland said. "We're picking up probably a hundred and fifty thousand worth. That's probably just the buyer's fee."

A half hour later, John called us back and said Dave was taking us all out to dinner.

The next morning, John announced this would be our last day in Saint Thomas. We could use the time to tie up loose ends, make our last phone calls. We went ashore. I helped John shop for a box of silicon sealant he wanted to caulk the gunwales with. We'd detected some leakage: the lockers under the bunks were sloshing with water.

I got my slides back from the camera shop and mailed them home.

I called Patience and told her we were ready for the next leg of the trip. She knew what that meant and her voice sounded fearful. So did mine, I guess. I was jumpy, nervous, abrupt. I just wanted to get it over with. "I'll be seeing you in a couple of weeks," I said.

"I love you," she said, her voice breaking. "Be careful."

"I love you, too. Two weeks; maybe three. I'll be home."

We met Ireland back at the dingy. It was five in the afternoon, so we went into the Islander and had some beers. I ordered chowder.

While I was waiting for the food, I spotted somebody I knew. Impossible! I tried to slink down in the chair, but he saw me and walked over. It was Cal Fisher, a guy I went to art school with. He and I had been pretty good friends back then. Patience and I met him and his wife when we lived at married student housing. His daughter, Carol, and Jack had played together. He sat down on the bench next to me and I introduced him to John and Ireland. I could hardly talk. John picked up on my panic and told Cal how we were down here delivering a yacht to some rich dude, taking another one back up. Cal nodded. I could tell by the way he looked at John that he knew what we were really doing. The Islander was crawling with pot smugglers. Even I could tell who they were. We had a lame conversation for a few minutes. He was working in real estate. He got up to leave. He said good-bye to John and Ireland. When I stood up, Cal moved close to me and whispered, "Bob, what are *you* doing here?" He gave me a knowing smile and left.

I thought, what *am* I doing here? I could've gone into real estate, too.

John announced that we were going to have one last party before we left. A fucking tie-one-on party. I said maybe we should be cool, unobtrusive.

Even Ireland thought I was being paranoid. It ended up that I took the dingy back to the boat with the stuff we'd bought and John and Ireland stayed to party. They said they'd come down to the beach, close to the *Namaste,* when they finished, and yell for me to row out and get them. Fine.

I sat in the cockpit of the *Namaste,* alone for the first time in weeks. I watched the boat next to us, a legitimate yacht. I wondered what people did to get that much money legally. We had seen a two-hundred-foot yacht moored by the fuel pumps manned by a crew of twenty sailors, all wearing beige uniforms. One of them told us the owner lived on the boat by himself. A Bell Long Ranger helicopter, painted to match the beige and brown trim of the yacht, perched on the fantail of the boat. Now, how does one man get *that* much money? Just the helicopter cost more than a million dollars. I wasn't jealous; I was just bewildered. I thought I was a pretty smart guy, but making money just seemed to be beyond my talents. These people, the yachts, the big houses, intimidated me. I thought I was getting a taste of what the blacks on the island felt.

I made some tuna fish salad and ate in the cockpit. I lay in a lawn chair, chewing my sandwich, staring at the stars. They weren't as bright in the yacht basin as they were when we were out to sea. Too many lights.

At about ten, I heard hoots and yells in the darkness over at the beach; had to be John and Ireland. I climbed into the dingy and rowed over. I heard a lot of laughing. They were thoroughly drunk. When the dingy got close enough, Ireland jumped in. John leapt, too, but he missed and fell in the water. We pulled him in, sopping, over the side.

John sprawled across the dingy, laughing, having a really good time. Ireland was staring up the beach. "C'mon, Ali, let's go!" he said.

"What's the problem?" I said.

"Aw. This Juan." Ireland sighed. "He started a fight at the bar. Hurt a guy."

"Fucker damn well deserved it!" John yelled. Then he laughed.

Ireland kept staring up the beach, toward the hotel.

"Police?" I said.

"Maybe," Ireland said. "I don't think anybody knows where we went, though. We ran out through the hotel and circled back."

"Jesus," I said. "What a fuckup. Our last night, and you get in a fight?"

"Hey, Ali." John laughed. "Best night to fuck up is the last night."

I stayed awake long after John and Ireland were asleep. This was getting too nutty. He misses his watch. He starts fights. He's too stubborn to admit that he's wrong when he is. Cal Fisher knows what we're up to—how do I know Cal's not a cop? Or knows a cop? How the fuck can we keep making so many mistakes and pull this off?

I'm leaving. Tomorrow. Then a pang of guilt hits me.

Who'll stand my watch?

Who'll stand my watch! Are you kidding? Who cares! You could hire a *chimp* to do what I'm doing. It's not my fucking problem. Tomorrow, I'm calling Patience and telling her to send a plane ticket.

What's she going to use for money?

Borrow it from somebody.

Who? The only guy who'd lend you money is on this boat with you.

Somebody will.

Okay. You quit. Then what? Go home and look for work?

My book. Books. I'm working on two.

Your books are a waste of time. Mental masturbation. Be real. You're no writer. You're as much a writer as Elliott is a fucking rancher. No one's going to buy your book. Can't you read between the lines of those polite fucking rejection letters? You're not a writer; you're not *anything*. You'll be lucky to get a job mowing yards, pumping gas. And then John and Ireland will cruise through High Springs in a few weeks; maybe they'll stop and let you pump gas for them, pockets bulging with cash, saying, Too bad, Bob. They gave us each a fifty-thousand bonus, too. Dammy! Wanting; having. Here, take this—they stuff a couple of twenties in your pocket—little something for you, Bob. Buy some shoes or something, eh? Bye, Bob. They hustle off in new Corvettes, leaving ten dollars' worth of rubber on the road, loose bills fluttering out the windows.

Better poor than poor *and* in jail, I say to the other voice that lives in my head and argues with me. Tomorrow I'm leaving. I'm no fool.

The other voice laughs.

I was grim as death the next morning. John noticed, but thought I was just pissed at him for last night. He said he'd been an asshole. I nodded.

We hauled the anchor and motored over to the fuel pumps to top off. I jumped on the dock while John and Ireland helped the fuel guy get the hose to the *Namaste*'s tank. I wandered over to the two-hundred-foot yacht and stared at the bow. A few chips of paint were missing and silvery metal gleamed through. This was a stainless-steel hull? Two hundred feet of stainless steel cake with a helicopter topping. I hated this man.

Why're you stalling? My bicameral companion said.

I'm going. Just have to say good-bye first. Just pissed at this rich guy. Two hundred feet of—

"What's up, Bob?" John said behind me.

"Nothing."

He must have read my mind. "You know, Bob, this is the point of no return. When we leave here, we won't touch land again until we get home. This is it."

What's he think? I'm scared? I may be leaving, but I'm not scared. "I know. Just woke up feeling shitty, is all. I'm—"

John nodded and went into the dockmaster's office to pay for the diesel fuel. I stared at Ireland, my mouth muttering, "Gonna quit." He shrugged and glanced down at the water. John came out of the office and jumped aboard the *Namaste*. They looked at me, heads cocked. I looked at them.

I walked over to tell them, Sorry, I've had it; I'm quitting this stupid mission. You guys'll need my share for new tires anyway—

I stared at John. I remembered the things he'd done for me, like buying me the typewriter—everyone deserves the right tool, he'd said—lending me his car or truck in the middle of the night and never complaining, lending me money and never mentioning it. I watched Ireland pulling in the bow line. He turned and looked at me expectantly. I could hear him saying, Whaty wrong, Ali? He was hard-working, funny. He was loyal.

An hour later we were under sail, heading for Colombia.

CHAPTER 16

A twenty-knot wind sped us toward the Guarjira Peninsula. It was like being sucked down a whirlpool, faster and faster as we got closer to oblivion.

This was the first time we'd sailed downwind; running with the wind, it's called. John had us attach a pole to the end of the staysail and push it out starboard to catch the wind. We put on a large jib and let it billow out on the opposite side. We sheeted out the mainsail until it was nearly perpendicular to the hull. The *Namaste* fairly flew before the wind. I decided to experiment with the old way of figuring your speed, the knotted string. I tied a knot every fifty feet in a hundred-yard length of twine. I threw one end overboard, tied to a board. I counted seven knots going through my fingers in thirty seconds—three hundred fifty feet in thirty seconds equals seven hundred feet per minute, equals forty-two thousand feet per hour. Divide by six thousand eighty feet—one nautical mile—and it equals just about exactly seven nautical miles per hour. I made sun shots and calculated our speed with modern instruments—seven knots. Those old guys knew what they were doing.

The sea was rough, but since we sailed up the smooth incline of the waves behind the crests, the ride was smooth. John pointed out that coming back, beating against the same sea would be a much different story.

The sky was clear, the sun bright and hot. Saint Thomas is at the twenty-first parallel. Sailing south, almost to the ninth—only nine degrees from the equator—we'd feel the sun from nearly directly overhead. I wondered if we would be able to see the Southern Cross from that latitude. I'd never been this far south before.

Rosalinda steered—her wind vane pointing backward into the wind—while the three of us climbed all over the boat caulking the rails with silicone. There weren't any visible cracks, but we knew it leaked because the lockers under the bunks had flooded in the storms on the way down. We smeared the whole seam where the deck joins the hull from bow to stern. After the caulking job, the three of us sat around in the cockpit—sporting tropical print nylon briefs we'd bought in Saint Thomas—sipping cold beer and enjoying the ride, telling sailing stories.

John told us he and his buddy Mitford had sailed to Saint Thomas on a trial run on the boat he'd just built—the one he used to cross the Atlantic. They saw some people skin-diving from their yacht near Thatch Cay, near where we'd keel-hauled the *Namaste*. "We pull up alongside to say howdy and ahoy," John said. "Their wives, nice-looking ladies, were on the deck of this teak and brass fifty-five-foot motor yacht, sunning themselves in these string bikinis, you know? They smile. The guys are splashing around diving for conch, and when they see us, they climb out of the water and invite us on board for drinks. We drink frozen daiquiris at ten in the morning. We shoot the shit. The women—one's a blond, the other's a brunette—are super friendly. They were in their early forties, you know, horny as hell. The two guys jump back in the water, and Mitford, who's been bragging how he cooks conch, goes in with them. I'm watching them diving and then I feel a hand reach up between my legs and grab my cock!"

"You're shitting," Ireland said, laughing.

"No. I'm serious as a heart attack. The blonde has me by the root and she pulls me down next to her. She's taken off her bikini bottom and she's on her hands and knees, wiggling that thing at me while she's reaching back and squeezing my schlong." John giggles like a kid. So do we. "I say, 'Hey, what about your old man? I mean, he's right fucking there!' She says he's looking for conch. Tonight he'll be so drunk he couldn't get it up with a crane. She's rubbing my dick while she's talking and I've got a hard-on. Then her friend, the brunette, grins at us and goes and sits on the transom and talks to the guys when they surface. She looks back at us and gives us a thumbs-up. She's keeping watch for us! I say, what the hell? and mount this bitch. I'm pumping away fast—you know, before I get caught—and she says, 'Relax, captain, slow down, there's no rush.' No rush? Her old man is twenty feet away blubbering he's found a herd of conch down there. 'He'll be busy for hours,' she says. 'Just got his skin-diving gear. He's like a kid with a new toy.' So I'm fucking her right there in front of her friend, nice and slow as I can, watching her husband splashing around. It was weird."

"C'mon, Juan," Ireland said. "Nobody's that dumb."

"I shit you not. That's the way it happened," John said, crossing his heart. "Then her friend, the lookout? Well, she comes back when I'm finished and says I should go tell Mitford to come up and get his share. I jump in and when Mitford comes up from a dive, I tell him, 'Man, I think you should go get on their boat. That lady has something for you.' He looks up, sees the brunette smiling her biggest, brightest fuck-me smile. He says, 'What? What's she got?' Mitford is *really* into this conch hunt. I say, 'You'll recognize it when you see it.' He shrugs in the water, doesn't know what's going on, climbs on deck. In a minute, my party-punch, the blonde, is sitting on the transom as look-out, cheering on her husband and his dufus friend, glancing over her shoulder now and then to check out the action. You should've seen her smile. Scary how women can be so damn deceptive."

"Didn't these guys ever catch on?" I said.

"Nope. They're soused. We have lunch, drink some more, and re-peat the whole thing that afternoon, switching around, until Mitford and me are too wobbly to wiggle.

"The women say, 'It was wonderful meeting you,' with honey voices, when we're leaving. The guys shake our hands and say, 'Yeah. Let's do it again sometime.' Those two women were grinning like girls. I'll never forget it."

I looked at Ireland. "What'd you think? Elephantshit?"

Ireland made a skeptical face and nodded. "Trying to impress us."

"No!" John said. "It's true. I swear to God! Ask Mitford."

"Yeah?" Ireland said. "Dammy! Why doesn't stuff like that ever happen to me?"

After lunch, John said we were going to remove the toilet from the head. "Thing takes up room," he said. "One extra bale is another fifteen thousand dollars." I went below, got a box of wrenches, and went to the head. I wasn't going to miss the commode; we never used it, used a bucket instead, but it cost over a thousand dollars and it seemed wasteful to just toss it overboard. I got it undone and hauled it on deck. John grabbed it by its pump handle and swung it overboard. Made a big splash. Ireland suggested a possible threat to the world by our actions: "What if some fish hits that handle?" Ireland said. "Gurgle, gurgle, gone. Whole fucking Atlantic, down the drain."

Two dolphins came over and played with the bow. I suppose they were scouts because five minutes after they arrived, a whole herd swam over to us, adults and babies. Nearly fifty dolphins surrounded us, diving and blowing, coming to within three feet of the boat. I'd never been so near these animals. Up close and alive, they're beautiful to see. I went out on the bow pulpit with my camera and watched them dart back and forth in front of the bow. Now and then, one would swim on its side and stare back at me. I took close-ups of dolphins staring at me with their built-in smiles that come from a hundred thousand years of laughing. The whole world, most of it anyway, is home to dolphins. What a life. No mortgages, no traffic jams, always plenty of fresh food swimming around. Get laid whenever you want —if you're a dolphin. They spend more time fucking than people do. The guys have bright red retractable dicks and they fuck on the fly. I saw a couple of the guys roll over and flip me a dick. Same as the finger? Maybe. They're smart enough. They'd developed their language before we figured out that vines were for swinging. I envied them their freedom. A dolphin, gliding effortlessly through the water beneath me, stared me right in the eyes for a while, saying, Yeah that's an interesting thing you're on, but what happens to you when it sinks? You don't look like you can swim too good. You've got weird-looking flippers. Yeah? I said. Well you can't drive a car or fly a plane; don't even know what the hell they are. True, said the dolphin. Do you?

The dolphins stayed with us for half a day and moved off toward the southeast, to wherever they'd been going before they met us. I had the feeling we had been a kind of dolphin tourist attraction, a diversion on a long trip.

At sunset, a cruise ship passed us, coming to within a hundred yards of the *Namaste*. I got out the binoculars and watched a young couple standing at the railing, dressed in their cocktail-hour clothes, holding drinks. The guy waved, the girl looked at us with concern. We must have looked awfully tiny to them. We certainly *felt* tiny. Each of their twenty lifeboats was twice as big as the *Namaste*. The Love-Boaters walked around on their gyro-stabilized, speeding behemoth like they were partying on the front lawn of a country estate—tent pavilions, strings of glittering lights, waiters, guests sipping martinis and chattering about business and sex. We were sailing at seven knots, but the cruise ship passed us like we were anchored. ''Dammy,'' Ireland said. ''How does something that big move that fast?''

The wind held steady and strong for two days before it began to slacken. We slowed to three or four knots in the middle of the Caribbean. Still running with the wind, the relative wind—the breeze we felt—was almost gone. The sun began to fry us. It was difficult to believe that just two weeks earlier we were freezing in Jacksonville. Now we were trying to stay cool wearing swimsuits or nothing. The resulting sunburns made us feel even hotter.

On Christmas day, we made a special meal: noodles, peas, and canned chicken. I read the letter Patience had dated for Christmas:

> . . . and I suppose you found a tree to decorate somewhere in the ocean? Ho, Ho. (Christmas humor) I miss you more than I can stand. I missed you even before you left. This is the second Christmas you've missed. Don't let it happen again! I love you. P.

Yeah. Christmas in Vietnam. Now this. The two events seemed related. Both were in the tropics; both happened while I was on missions I didn't want to be doing. I felt lonely for Patience and Jack. I felt like a failure. If I was any kind of provider, I thought, I wouldn't have to make them put up with brainstorms like this one. I resolved that I'd make up for it after the trip.

The trip was my panacea. Every problem I had was going to be solved with thirty thousand dollars. I'd have time to write; we'd be able to pay off the car; I could add on a small addition to the cabin so Jack would have his own room; we needed a new well. Thirty thousand would cover all that with plenty left over. The scammers kept saying: Wanting; having. I wanted lots of things; I was going to have them; if we could just make this work.

Early the next morning I was alone on watch. I stood on the rail amidships, holding on to a stay, leaning over the sea. Warm water splashed my feet. I was naked, and the sun was already hot on my skin. I was brown now, acclimated. I felt like I was born to live here. It was a glorious feeling, bare sun-browned skin caressed by tropical winds, sprinkled with sea spray. I felt like a dolphin must feel—the sea moved by fast, foaming, and I felt like I was swimming, gliding effortlessly through the water. I was part of it—the water, the sky, everything. It was spiritual. I felt a golden glow flood through me and, suddenly, I had an erection. Like those dolphin guys had the day before—a hard-on for life, I guess. The thing just popped up, jutting out in the breeze, wavering over the sea. A couple of quick strokes was all it took. I watched my froth fall back as the *Namaste* sailed onward. I looked at the spot for a while, expecting to see Venus rising from the sea, standing on a giant clamshell, wrapped in golden hair, her hand postured modestly. She never did. You have to be Zeus to pull that one off.

By the fourth day out of Saint Thomas, John was getting jumpier. He took to scanning the horizon with the binoculars much of the time. He was Captain Ahab looking for Moby Dick. In the afternoon he called out that he saw a ship. As we got closer, we could see it was a three-hundred-foot rusty freighter cruising across our path, sailing northwest. As we watched, though, it changed course abruptly and began coming toward us.

"I don't like that shit," John said. He went below and fetched the Winchester.

When John came back up with the rifle, he levered a round into the chamber. "Who do you think they are?" I asked.

"Don't know. But I don't like the way he changed course all of a sudden. Pirates use boats like that."

Pirates. That got my attention. We stood on deck, hanging on to stays, and stared at the boat coming our way. It was steel, long as a football field. How on earth could you defend yourself against that? One rifle against a steel ship? That's like pissing on a forest fire. "Should we go overboard if they attack?" Ireland asked.

"Wouldn't do any good, Rámon," John said. "They'd either shoot you in the water or just leave you to die."

I see us firing a few ineffectual shots against their hull to warn them off. Ping. Pong. They open up with a fusillade of rifle and automatic weapons fire. We duck below and lie on the deck as the bullets crash through the cabin. Then it's quiet and we know they're alongside, getting a line on us. We feel the *Namaste* bump against their hull. We hear them jump on deck. Footsteps run fore and aft. A shadow appears at the hatch. John blows one of them away as he comes down the ladder. Pow! The guy screams. We hear a loud shout and some angry muttering. There's a long silence. Then we hear the forward hatch opening. We have two entrances to cover and one gun. Then a shotgun pokes in through the cabin skylight above us. I feel weak as it explodes.

Ireland and I looked at each other. The ship now bore down on us, closing the distance between us, fast. I felt the butterflies of fear fluttering in my stomach. I'd gotten shot at a lot in my life. I didn't like it. And out here, no door gunners, no help available, I felt naked. I looked down. I *was* naked. I went below and put on my jeans so I'd at least not be humiliated as well as killed. I came back up and stared at the ship. It was near enough to see that no one had painted it in years. It was solid rust. A bilge pump worked hard, pouring a constant stream of water out the side, just above the waterline. The ship was close enough to see a name on the bow, but there was no name. John might be right.

"Can't we call them and make a deal?" I asked.

"These guys don't make deals, Ali. They don't have to."

"This is about the stupidest thing I've ever seen," I said.

"What do you mean?" John said.

"We come down here. We know there're pirates everywhere. And we have no way to defend ourselves? What kind of plan is that?"

John glared at me and looked back at the freighter. We saw a crewman waving from the bow of the ship. He wasn't waving for us to stop, he was just waving. The ship continued past us without slowing. When we hit its wake, the *Namaste* bucked and we started laughing.

"False alarm," John said.

"I wonder why they did that. Change course all of a sudden." I said.

"They were pirates," Ireland said. "But then they got up close enough to see the awesome Ali and the mean Rámon and the beeg fucking Juan! Scared shitless! Waity, say the pirate *capitan*, too much for us pirate guys. We boogie, find easier pickings up north."

Since he had the gun loaded, John decided to start shooting at stuff in the water. He tossed empty beer cans ahead of the *Namaste* and blasted them with the rifle as they came back past us. We all took turns, killing bottles, cans, anything loose. Blam! Blam! What fun. Bring on those fucking pirates! We shot up about thirty rounds before John put the rifle back in its case and stowed it under his mattress.

While I put our evening meal together, I designed a *real* smuggling sailboat. It had a fifteen-hundred-horsepower turbine engine—like the one in the Huey I used to fly—mounted below deck. My boat had hydrofoils under the hull and a deck-mounted 20mm cannon. When things looked grim, we'd drop sails on my boat, give 'em a few blasts with the cannon for fun, ka-pow! and then we'd kick in the turbine and blast away on the hydrofoils at sixty knots. Fuck you, pirates. Fuck you, Coast Guard.

When we sighted land at sunset on the fifth day, we changed course slightly to keep our distance. Our new concern was the Colombian navy.

We sailed parallel to the west coast of the Guarjira Peninsula, scanning the coast, looking for landmarks with the binoculars. Using landmarks, like a big power plant and a mountain peak we could see on shore and locate on the map, we could triangulate our position.

John began calling our contact. "Ike. Ike. This is Tina. This is Tina. Over," he said. He repeated the message for five minutes. We heard nothing but static.

Two hours later, we saw lights popping to life on the coast as darkness set in. We usually ate about now, but no one was cooking. We passed the binoculars around, looking for trouble in all directions.

John tried the radio again. "Ike. Ike. This is Tina. This is Tina. Over."

"Hello, Tina. This is Ike."

"Son of a bitch!" John said to Ireland and me. "He's there!"

"Glad to hear you," John said. "We're about fifteen miles from rendezvous. Over."

"Roger, Tina. We're ready. Let me know when you're within a mile or so. I'll put the lights on."

"Roger, Ike. What about the yacht club?" John radioed. I didn't know what that meant.

Ike laughed on the radio. "Don't worry about the yacht club, Tina. The regatta's over."

"Roger, Ike. See you in about three. Tina out." John put the microphone down, smiling.

"What's the yacht club? Put what lights on?" I said.

"The 'yacht club' means the Colombian navy. They're not around. And Ike's got a Land Rover on the beach. He'll park it facing the water. When we're closer, he'll turn the lights on."

"Who's this guy, Ike?" I asked. Ireland had gone below.

"He's another Nam vet," John said. "Seem to be a lot of us in this business. Guess we have the proper training."

"Maybe," I said. "I still think most of this mission is based on fucking blind luck."

"You call this luck? We hit our target on the dot. We're right on time. Luck? The damn navy is nowhere to be seen. You call *that* luck?" John shook his head like a guy trying to talk sense to an idiot. "Bob," John said quietly, "we've *done* this before."

He was right. I was arguing from ignorance. "You took care of the navy?"

"Ike did. That's part of his job."

"How'd he do that? How do you take care of a whole navy?"

"You'll be meeting him in a few hours. Why don't you ask him yourself?"

Ireland came up from below with a pot of coffee. We made peanut butter and Ritz cracker sandwiches and ate while we kept a nervous vigil. Ike said he'd taken care of the navy, but people boast.

CHAPTER 17

"Ike, this is Tina. Over," John radioed. According to our plots on the map, we should have been close to the pickup point.

"Hear you, Tina. Do you see me?"

We looked along the dark coast and saw car headlights blaze out through the humid air. It looked like we were about a mile away.

"Roger, Ike. I see you. We'll move in closer."

"Okay, Tina. Just watch your depth; gets shallow quick around here."

We'd already dropped the sails and were motoring. Our wake was alive with glittering phosphorescent sea life emitting an eerie green light a hundred times brighter than we'd seen before. The water around the *Namaste* looked like it was lit by underwater lamps in the hull. The bright green prop wash extended back hundreds of yards. As John stood in the cockpit steering the *Namaste*, I watched the depth finder and Ireland stood out on the bow pulpit checking for obstacles—rocks, logs, canoes. It was a moonless night, but you could see well enough in the starlight to spot large objects if they got close enough.

"Fifty feet," I said.

"Okay. Tell me when it gets to fifteen." The *Namaste* had a six-foot draft.

John steered parallel to the shore until he came abreast of the car lights. He turned toward shore and throttled down to a crawl.

"Looking good," Ike radioed.

Apparently Ike could see us, but we could only see his headlights. When we got closer, I could see flashlights bobbing around the car. The depth finder showed the water getting shallow fast. "Fifteen feet." John put the engine in neutral. We drifted closer.

About two hundred yards offshore, I called out, "Ten feet, closing on eight real fast." John shut down the engine and yelled to Ireland to drop anchor. The anchor hit the water with a green explosion, making an effervescent, iridescent green path to the bottom like a stream of glowing champagne. I went forward with some tools. Ireland and I undid the safety line on the starboard side so it wouldn't get in the way when we loaded the bales.

The *Namaste* tugged against the anchor line and gradually aligned herself with the slow current. We saw the phosphorescent wake of a canoe heading out to us. On the beach we saw flashlights jerking around while the Indians got the load together.

We stood on deck and watched the canoe approach. A dark shape against the eerie glow of the water, it looked like it was floating in space. When the canoe came alongside, we could see that it was a huge dugout, twenty-five feet long and about five feet wide, carved from a mahogany tree. Indians chattered and laughed. The dugout was piled with bales of marijuana. When they reached out and grabbed the *Namaste*, a man jumped on board.

"Hey, John. Long way from home, eh?" the man said.

"Hi, Pete. Good to see you, man!" Ike's name was Pete. John and Pete shook hands.

Pete turned around, called four of the Indians aboard—his cargo crew—and told them in Spanish to start unloading. The four Indians in the canoe tossed bales on deck. We all helped, grabbing the bales as they tossed them aboard. I grabbed one. Weighed about forty or fifty pounds, was cube-shaped, about eighteen inches on a side, wrapped in burlap. The bales varied in size, ranging from thirty pounds to sixty pounds. Pete called out the weights as they came aboard and John wrote them down, keeping a tally of what we loaded. I wrestled a bale to the forward hatch and dumped it below. I saw a dark man smiling up at me. He said, *"Bonita, no?* Beautiful, huh?" I smiled and said yes. In the lights below deck I could see the bales had boldly printed on the sides: PRODUCT OF COLOMBIA.

In ten minutes the first canoe was unloaded and on its way back to shore for more. We could see another canoe drifting toward us on a phosphorescent cloud. I went back to the cockpit. John and Pete were sitting on the lawn chairs talking. "Product of Colombia?" I said. "They print that up for the pot?"

"Naw," Pete said, laughing. "They make the wrappings out of coffee-bean sacks."

"Pete," John said, "this is Bob, a friend of mine. He's a Nam vet, too."

Pete sat in the shadows under the dodger and it was hard to make him out. I saw he was clean-shaven, wore casual tourist-style clothes—short-sleeved shirt, jeans—but I couldn't make out his features well enough to describe.

As the second canoe approached, we heard the paddlers singing a native song. "Happy bunch," I said.

"That's right, Bob," Pete said. "This is a fucking major event for them. This is payday. There'll be big parties all night tonight, my friend."

"This is what they do? I mean, all that they do?"

"You got it. Keeping marijuana illegal in the States is the best thing that ever happened to these people. Life's never been better. They got refrigerators now, TVs, cars, trucks—putting money aside for the kids' educations. They're even buying up the land they used to work for the rich dudes who've been keeping them in poverty for the last couple of centuries. Tell the folks back home to smoke mo' pot." We laughed. The canoe came alongside and I went forward to help. John looked below and yelled to the Indians in Spanish to pack the stuff neater, it was taking up too much space. His Spanish sounded perfect. John and the head Indian jabbered about how to pack it so we could stuff more pot on board. We were going to take on as many bales as we could squeeze into every compartment except the galley. John told Pete we might be able to pack four thousand pounds into the *Namaste*, but it'd be tight. The *Namaste* could carry twice that weight, but marijuana, even compressed in bales, is bulky stuff and volume was the limiting factor.

Bob and I helped the Indians wrestle the bales to the forward hatch. Everybody was having fun. Much kidding, laughing, singing. During the next lull between canoes, I went back to the cockpit.

"John says you take care of the Colombian navy. How do—"

"I don't do shit, Bob." Pete struck a match to light a cigarette. I could see him in the light. His face was lean, smooth, friendly. He had close-cropped hair. He looked like a college kid working on his master's degree in English. "Not a thing. These fuckers do it." He swept his arm toward shore. "Their navy, any navy, has one critical link in its organization. The sailors. Most Colombian sailors are conscripts who come from villages just like this one. These guys just cut them in— pay 'em about what they'd make in a whole year, just to keep the navy out of our way for one night. Never see the Colombian navy during the pickups."

"How they do that?" I said.

"Easy. The sailors are the dingers that do the work, right? They keep the engines running—or not running. The engines don't work when they don't want them to. Sugar accidentally falls into gas tanks, stuff like that. They're very resourceful." Pete laughed. "The only other people they have to buy are the local cops. One of them is on shore right now, working for a little extra pay. These guys and the cop will make a hundred bucks apiece tonight just for an hour's work."

"There's a cop on shore right now, watching this?" I said.

"Yep. Fredrico. Wife has a baby on the way; needs the cash."

"They don't talk?"

"Nope. Shit, Bob. Like I said, this is the best thing that's ever happened to these people. They can't believe we pay serious money for stuff that just pops out of the ground. They smoke pot, too, but it's just a fun weed to them; grows wild, always been free. They say, What the hell. Crazy gringos pay *mucho dinero* for these weeds, who are we to argue?"

An hour later, the *Namaste* was filled from the bow compartment back to the galley, four and five feet deep. The only place we could stand below decks was in the ten square feet next to the stove and navigation counter. The bunks were buried under mounds of variously sized and crookedly packed bales of pot. There was only two feet of crawl space between the cargo and the top of the cabin.

Ireland and I hooked the safety line back up and went back to the cockpit with John and Pete.

John had given Pete the package of money and he was counting it as Ireland and I swung around the dodger. The canoes were all back on shore, and I wondered how Pete was going to get back.

"They're sending a canoe out in a few minutes. They got some stuff for you guys—jugs of fuel, a whole bunch of fresh fruit and vegetables, canned food, stuff like that," he said.

Pete finished counting the money and stuffed it into a canvas knapsack slung from his shoulder. He said to John, "Well, too bad you didn't get a bigger boat, Ace. We have plenty more."

John nodded and looked at the tally sheet. "Yeah," he said. "Thirty-five hundred pounds. Shit, this barge could carry five thousand if we could fit it in, no problem."

I saw a canoe drifting out on a cloud of light from the dark shore. When the Indians pulled up alongside, they began handing us five-gallon, basket-wrapped, corked glass jugs of diesel fuel, bunches of bananas, and cardboard boxes of canned food and fresh fruit. When the canoe had been emptied, Pete jumped in. He said "Have a safe trip" and waved. He sat down in the canoe and we watched him being paddled away. His mission was over; he was home safe. Ours was just beginning.

"Okay, guys," John said. "Let's boogie!"

We cranked up the engine, hauled anchor, and were under way in five minutes.

At midnight we were under sail and clear of the Guarjira Peninsula, out of the glittery water. Apparently the area just off the coast of the peninsula is one of the few places in the world that sees such bright displays of phosphorescent excitement.

We were all awake, sitting under the dodger. The adrenaline rush was still with us and nobody wanted to sleep. It felt like we were in the process of making a speedy getaway. We knew we had two thousand miles to go, but that hadn't sunk in yet.

When we were out of sight of land, John said we should smoke some of the product to see how good it was. Ireland and I cut into a bale and yanked out a handful of the compressed weed. The whole boat reeked of the pungent, stale smell of the stuff. We rolled a joint and smoked it.

"Tastes a little stale, John," Ireland said. John nodded and held a pinch up to his nose. "We gotta make sure this stuff stays dry. Stale pot doesn't get much money."

I sucked down a lungful, held it, and let it out. It wasn't very strong stuff.

"What d'you think?" John asked.

"It's not the kind of stuff I'd buy," I said. "Smokes like New York street weed. Nothing like home-grown."

"Good. That's fine. That's where this stuff is going. What do they know of home-grown in Brooklyn?"

I looked down the hatch at the wall of pot. "What's all this worth? I mean, back in the States."

"Right now we're getting about three-forty a pound, wholesale. What's that? Thirty-five hundred times three-forty—little over a million bucks?"

I shook my head and laughed. This was about as artificial an economy as I could imagine. The scammers buy bales of compressed weeds in Colombia where they give it little value and now they figure it's worth a million dollars? Free enterprise.

"It's ridiculous, isn't it?" I said. "This stuff is basically worthless. I mean, yeah, it's hemp, maybe worth, what? A hundred dollars as rope-making material? A million dollars to you guys? It's obscene."

"Hey," John said. "Who are you to question world economics?" He laughed. "Supply and demand is the name of the game; and the government sets the prices. Life couldn't be better."

"Man," Bob said. "They should just legalize the stuff."

"Wash your mouth out, Rámon. They legalize this stuff and a whole economic sector is put out on the street. I mean, what happens to the importers and all their employees? What happens to those poor villagers? And what about us hardworking smugglers?" John laughed. "Let's see, now; if it was legal, priced what it's worth, your share of the deal would come to about two bucks."

Ireland laughed. "Two bucks? Elephant wages!"

We heard thunder and saw lightning to the east. In a half hour, the storm hit. The *Namaste* leaned into the wind and plunged against the building sea. John was right. Going against the sea was much tougher. Waves as big as the ones we'd cut through smoothly coming down now bashed the bow and washed the decks.

I went below and crawled up on top of the pile of pot and lay down. I slept on a pungent, lumpy, million-dollar bed.

The next morning the storm was gone, but the wind was still strong. Daylight showed what a mess we had below decks. The helter-skelter bales had to be repacked just to give us a couple of level places to lie down. The stale marijuana smell, which had been overpowering the night before, was now barely noticeable as we got used to it. I smelled something else, a faint odor of fuel. Maybe gasoline? I made some coffee and went on deck. A light rain drumbed the dodger. I saw a bird sitting on the safety line. Looked like a heron, a freshwater bird. What was he doing a hundred miles away from land?

"Probably got blown out during the storm last night," John said. "I've seen it before."

I leaned out of the dodger and the bird flew fifty yards away, paralleling us.

"The poor bastard can't fly back home," John said. "And he can't land in the water like a gull—soak up and sink like a feather duster. He's fucked."

We watched the bird flying for half an hour. He was getting tired, flying lower and lower. Finally he flew back to the boat and landed on the starboard safety line, jerked back and forth to get his balance, cocked his head, and eyed us suspiciously.

Ireland came up, singing, "I'm Popeye the sailor man—" John and I shushed him. "Quiet, Rámon," John said. He nodded to our mascot, hunched over on the safety line, dripping wet in the rain. "Dumb bird will fly out and drown."

"Dammy," Ireland said, looking at the bird with concern on his face. "Maybe we should catch it and let it go when we get near the Virgins."

John nodded skeptically. "Help yourself."

Ireland spent a half hour stalking the heron while the bird watched every move he made. When Ireland got too close, it launched itself back over the sea and fluttered weakly nearby.

The sky cleared and we beat north through rough seas, the wind whistling through the *Namaste*'s rigging. The heron spent the day flying out, almost out of sight, looking for home, and returning, more exhausted each time, to his perch on the safety line. He'd rest for an hour and repeat the search for his flock. It was depressing. I made an entry in my notebook about, if the bird could think, how easy it would be for him to just decide to sit on the deck and wait until we got close to land and fly ashore. But then, he'd never see home again that way, either.

The next morning the heron was gone. Now and then we saw birds flying around, but they were gulls. The heron was fish food. At sunset we saw another storm approaching. A nasty one. We had to reef the sails. Spent the night wondering if the *Namaste* was coming apart. Had to go out and tighten a loose turnbuckle on the port shroud. The cable had stretched.

I woke up with a headache. The *Namaste* was being tossed extra hard; how could the storm get any worse? I felt nauseous. The gasoline smell, or something petroleum, volatile, was really strong. We figured it was spilled fuel from trying to top off the fuel tank from glass jugs on a rocking boat. But diesel fuel smells like kerosene. I'd had lots of experience with solvents in the silk-screen process when I made mirrors, and the smell was familiar. I hate solvents. I went above with John and Ireland under the dodger.

"We've got to find where those fumes are coming from, John. It's getting real bad," I said. "That stuff will eat your brains out."

"I know," John said. "I've smelled this stuff before, but I can't place it. We'll find it."

We went below. Just the minute or so I'd spent on deck was enough fresh air to flush out my lungs.The chemical stench below was overpowering, sickening. We couldn't open the overhead cabin vent because waves were bashing over the decks. Ireland and I crawled all over the load sniffing like bloodhounds. The odor was equally strong wherever we looked. Somewhere, under thirty-five hundred pounds of marijuana, was the source of the gas that was poisoning us.

We spent a couple of hours moving bales from the left side of the cabin, stuffing them forward and to the right, to get to the locker under the bunk on the port side. It was slow and heavy work in a stifling, cramped, rolling space. We'd shove a bale up to the top of the pile and it'd roll back when the *Namaste* lurched. Eventually we uncovered the locker. Ireland and I pried up the cover. Seawater sloshed over some spare ropes and tools, but we didn't see anything that could be the source of the gas. Disgusted, we took a break under the dodger.

"That stuff makes me see spots," Ireland said. He lit a cigarette and sucked deeply. "Ah. That's better!"

An hour later, we wrestled all the bales back to the port side and burrowed our way down to the starboard locker. We could get to the latch, but there were still too many bales wedging it shut. Took another hour to shift the load clear. We pried up the locker cover. This was the low side of the boat, and the water was deep in the locker. Apparently the silicon caulking had missed the real leaks. We saw the problem: paint cans. The seawater had eaten through the three steel gallon cans of paint and a gallon of paint thinner that everybody'd forgotten about. The paint and solvent were sloshing around in the water, raising an invisible cloud of noxious gas.

Overcome by the fresh blast of fumes, we ran out under the dodger to get fresh air. It was maddening. If we weren't in this storm, we'd be able to open some hatches and vent some of the gas away, but the storm was worse than ever. Waves crashed onto the dodger. We were taking water through the overhead cabin vent, and it was screwed down tight. We tried to talk the problem away. Maybe we could just live out under the dodger for a few days? That was nuts; must be the gas. We shrugged and went below.

We formed a bucket brigade, scooped up the foul goo in pans, and passed them back to John to pour overboard. I could see stars in my eyes; my head throbbed. We got most of the slop out and began passing up coils of rope saturated with the shit, which John threw overboard. We passed up two boxes of rusted, paint-covered tools and John stashed them in the cockpit. Then Ireland and I wiped the locker clean with rags. By sunset the locker was clear and the bales repacked. We were so exhausted and sick, we just drank coffee for dinner. We sat around, groggy and stupid, and stared at the waves crashing over us. This smuggling racket was getting to be very much like real work.

On the morning of the fifth day since we made the pickup, I was alone, standing on the deck next to the cockpit with my arms folded, relishing the sea legs I'd acquired. The sky was clear. The *Namaste* was pitching, waves were washing across the deck, but I was able to keep my balance without thinking about it. I stood there, the wind rushing through my hair, taking deep breaths, flushing out the nagging residue of the previous night, savoring the moment, when I saw land. I called down the hatch for John.

"Puerto Rico," John said. "We have to head farther east, stay away from land." He pulled Rosalinda's lines and the boat headed off on a course parallel to the coast. We were ten miles out, and John was worried that the Coast Guard might see us and want to investigate. Coming down we hadn't worried about the Coast Guard; we were just another yacht then. Now we were a nice prize for a Coast Guard cutter's crew. We would definitely make their day.

That night we kept in sight of the land lights from Puerto Rico and then Saint Croix, working our way toward the Anegada Passage between Virgin Gorda and Sombrero Island.

A huge Lykes freighter came within a mile of us and John hailed it on the radio, requesting a position check. Their loran worked. The radio operator told us our position. John checked the chart. We would make the passage by dawn, if we didn't get stopped.

CHAPTER 18

The sea changed when we sailed through the passage, as though we had entered a different land. The difference was more a coincidence of weather than a geographical change. The wind was dying, and the Atlantic was filled with huge swells instead of the choppy seas of the Caribbean. We felt good. Not only was it New Year's Eve 1981, but we'd gotten across the Caribbean, past the pirates, into the Atlantic. The Caribbean was small, constraining—hell, it had only taken us five days to cross. The Atlantic was wide-open territory—home country, it seemed. We headed due north, away from all land, far away from the usual traffic, and, we hoped, far away from the Coast Guard. That night we broke out a bottle of Cruzin rum and had a party. It was the first hard stuff I'd drunk in four years. Two drinks made me stagger. I was reminded of earlier days and I didn't like it.

I wasn't living without aids on this trip—I just wasn't drinking. I was smoking pot every day. Marijuana made me feel comfortably lazy. It was meditative, relaxing. It was a crutch, but I still needed one. So far, it was working. The physical exertion on the trip and not drinking were actually making me fitter than I'd been in years. I was sleeping better at sea than I ever had on land. I could really get into this sailing life if Patience could overcome her seasickness.

The radio traffic between us and the scam master was now a daily routine. Management wanted to know where we were every day. The calls usually came at night, when the reception on the single-sideband radio was best. John and the scam master, Dave, traded part numbers and other ersatz figures in the coded conversations. John estimated that we'd be arriving at the drop-off point in two weeks, somewhere around the fifteenth of January. I couldn't get used to how long things took on a sailboat. In Vietnam, I used to give ETAs (estimated time of arrival) like, I'll be over your position in thirty-five minutes. Sometimes I'd have ETAs of three hours on long flights from An Khe, in the boonies, to Saigon, say. Two *weeks*? Sailing is slow. Baseball is faster.

The first week on the Atlantic was uneventful. The sea was beautiful and shipping was scarce. The *Namaste* cut through the smooth sea unhindered, making six and seven knots. I spent most of my time sitting against the cabin on the foredeck writing in my notebook. Memories of what I'd done in Vietnam came to me at odd moments and I'd write them down. Something I'd seen or smelled or heard jogged the memory into existence. This phenomenon really fascinates me. How is it that you can know you know something if you can't remember it? It would seem you either know it or you don't. An example given to show how great a computer the brain is, is this question: What is the population of Nepal? You will probably, unless you live there or know the example, say you don't know. The question is, then, how did you know so fast that you didn't know it? A standard business computer, given the same question, cannot know it doesn't know the answer until it has done an exhaustive search of its data base. Somehow, people know they don't know something right away. I was reading about future technologies that would allow computer memories to more closely match the architecture of brains and be capable of knowing what they know very fast. These new kinds of computers wouldn't be programmed, they'd learn. They were to be electronic rather than biological brains. This proposed system was called neural networking, which meant that the construction of the electronic brain was patterned after the neural patterns of our own brains. I decided that the robot I was building for my novel would use this technology.

I wrote down ideas about my robot. I jotted down short titles for the things I remembered about Vietnam. My brain ran a search while I was crewing a sailboat smuggling thirty-five hundred pounds of marijuana into the United States.

I wrote, "Daisy gets the Distinguished Flying Cross."

Captain Daisy, the chicken pilot who hid behind his armor during the assaults, was also the awards officer. They'd lined us up for the monthly awards ceremony. We stood in vague ranks wearing loose jungle fatigues, shifting around like squirmy kids. Pilots hate formations more than shiny boots.

We all got air medals. You got one for every twenty-five hours of combat flight time you logged, the same as did the pilots in World War II. I had five or six by now. Got another one. Then the major and the executive officer got to Daisy. The major started reading his citation, and as he got into it, we started looking at one another. This was not going to be a fucking air medal.

Tom Schall, Daisy's usual copilot, said, "I was with him on that flight. Fucker disappeared behind his chicken-plate." The executive officer looked up and glowered. Schall just glared back. Schall wasn't afraid of anyone, especially the exec. Besides, assault pilots could do just about anything they wanted; they needed us. The major read on about how Daisy had flown a lone ship into LZ X-ray during the battle of Ia Drang Valley. He flew against a hail of bullets, the major read. He picked up some wounded grunts and saved their lives. What? We'd all been there. No one knew what the major was talking about. Daisy's own copilot didn't know what the major was talking about. Everybody knew Daisy hid behind his chicken-plate when the bullets started flying.

When the major finished and we saw he was actually going to pin the DFC on Daisy's chest, the highest award for valor in the air, the formation broke ranks. Everybody just walked off, muttering nastily. The exec officer yelled, ordered us to come back. Nobody did.

During our second week in the Atlantic it began to get cold. We were back in the northern latitudes and the balmy tropics were just memories. Each day we put on more clothes: from bathing suits to shirts and jeans to sweaters and then insulated jackets. I was no longer able to sit out front and write. I hung around under the dodger instead. As it got colder, the sea grew rougher. The skies were overcast most of the time, making sighting the sun for navigation impossible. We sailed for days at a time without knowing our position.

Days blended together. Each morning looked the same as the morning before. For as far as we could see, all around us, was the horizon. Every day it was the same horizon. Sailing out of sight of land reinforces the fact that we live on a ball in space. You can see the curvature of the earth. At night, if it was clear, the stars looked like they were sitting right there next to me and it seemed that we weren't moving at all. South Sea islanders believed, as they traveled across hundreds of miles of open sea, that the boat wasn't going anywhere. Their destination would come to them if they made the right moves. Sitting on the edge of space, alone with the stars, it was easy for me to see where that idea came from.

As we got closer to the States, we got jumpy. Bob dropped his Spanish routine. John was drinking heavily. I smoked pot, made notes in my journal, invented ever more efficient programs to run on my calculator to automate navigation calculations.

We were in common shipping lanes now. We saw as many as half a dozen ships every day, any one of which could've been a Coast Guard cutter. I began to think that the chances of sneaking past the Coast Guard were slight. We could hear the Coast Guard on the radio, talking to the freighters, asking them if they'd seen any unusual traffic. Small sailboats in the winter Atlantic are unusual traffic. We kept our binoculars glued on every ship we saw appear on the horizon, breathing sighs of relief when we didn't see the big red hash stripe the Coast Guard had painted on its ships. The vigil was making us tense as snakes.

As my anxiety rose, I became more critical of John's plan. One of my objections to his return strategy, one that I reminded him of constantly, was that he insisted we sail without our radar reflector or running lights. I argued that the radar on the Coast Guard ships could pick up the *Namaste* without the reflector (a skeletal metal ball made with three intersecting metal disks which showed up as a very bright spot on radar), but when we *were* spotted on radar, our radar print wouldn't show the telltale bright reflection of a radar reflector on their screens. That would look suspicious as hell. Every ship at sea has radar reflectors to avoid collisions, especially little boats like ours. And, I added, at night they would see us on radar and would not only see no reflector signal, but also would see no running lights when someone looked in our direction, which would make us look doubly suspicious. I said we should look as normal as possible, just like we had on the way down. John said we should try to stay invisible—why didn't I stop going on and on about it? It always worked before.

Four days from our ETA, we ran out of dry clothes. Endless storms had soaked all our clothes, and we couldn't get them dry. Sitting on deck during four-hour watches was painful. No one except the man on watch came on deck. The cold wind blowing through our damp clothing chilled us to the bone. My feet got numb inside my deck boots because they'd gotten soaked when I went out to reef the jib one night and never did dry out. My notebook began to swell with schemes about moving back to the tropics if I survived this mission. I could operate a resort; I could run charter sailboats; I could live on a goddamn tropical island and eat sand flies if I had to. I never wanted to be cold again in my life.

Two days to drop-off, we started picking up stateside radio stations. We tried using them for navigation because we hadn't had a decent sun shot for days. John had a portable radio with a rotating antenna which we could swing back and forth and get an azimuth to a broadcast source. Using the directions to several radio stations, we could get a rough triangulation of our position. When Dave called, John gave our position, said we'd be able to make the drop-off sometime between eight and eleven on the evening of the fifteenth. You could hear the excitement in Dave's voice as he pretended to be the dispatcher of some shipping company. The shore team had been waiting for this day for over two months. Hearing Dave's excitement made us feel good, made us feel confident that the shore team had their act together.

The two-thousand-mile trip from Colombia had been too long, too stormy, and too cold. We were weary. We were hypervigilant, filled with anxiety about being caught after coming so far. If we were caught, the scam master (probably not Dave, since this was his scam-mastering debut) would just get another sailboat and crew it with three equally adventurous fools. Us? We'd be in jail.

As we got to within two hundred miles of the drop-off, Dave told John where they'd decided was the best place to make the delivery.

Twenty miles north of Charleston. "Five-Fathom Creek," John said. Ireland had come down from his watch to try to warm up next to the feeble alcohol stove. John had a chart out on the counter. "Here," John continued, pointing to the map. "We come in at this little bay at Santee Point near McClellanville." He traced the canal with one point of a divider. "This canal cuts over to the inland waterway. The drop-off point is here," he said, tapping a spot marked as marsh on the map. Ireland and I looked at the place at the end of a tiny tributary of Five-Fathom Creek and nodded. It certainly looked remote enough to unload a boatload of marijuana without attracting attention.

"I thought we were going in through the port at Charleston," Ireland said.

"We thought about it," John said. "This is safer. The only traffic here is shrimpers early in the morning. We come in at night, nobody around."

"Yeah, but that makes us even more obvious," I said.

"Dave's had people out on the creek every night we've been gone, Ali. Nobody's there. Just shrimpers leaving at dawn. This is the perfect spot," John said.

Fine. What did I know? If we got to the creek, I guessed we'd have made it. I nodded.

"Okay. Now we start getting rid of anything that'd prove we've been to Colombia. Any leftover cans of food, the fuel bottles, all our charts. Everything goes."

We topped off the *Namaste*'s tank with fuel from the glass bottles, threw the empties overboard, and tossed the remaining full bottles of diesel fuel after them. Ireland and I gathered all the leftover Spanish-labeled cans of food the Indians had given us and threw them overboard while John got reams of nautical charts and universal plotting sheets and tossed them into the sea, where they lay like a trail of pale lily pads going to the horizon. In a few hours, there was nothing on the boat that could be used as evidence we'd been to Colombia— unless of course, you happened to notice the five-foot-deep cargo of marijuana in bales labeled PRODUCT OF COLOMBIA.

We had plans if we were spotted. "If it looks like they want to stop us," John said, "we dump the bales."

"The three of us wrestle up seventy-some bales of pot and dump them before a cutter gets to us?" I said.

John was used to this. He'd had forty days of criticism from me. He shook his head sadly. I bet I'd never get another job offer to smuggle pot. "We try, Ali. Besides, we ain't gonna get caught."

This part of the mission required dumb luck and blind faith.

On the evening of the fifteenth, our ETA, we hit fog. We'd all been up for thirty hours straight because we figured we'd be sighting land any damn second. We were nervous with anticipation, squinting out over the gray sea for hours, looking for land and the law, and now we were blind. We were on a course John plotted using the azimuths from radio stations we'd gotten from his radio. The azimuths were crude. When you rotated the antenna to get the direction to a radio station, determining the point of maximum signal strength was an art, subject to errors of five to ten degrees. Our plots, made every half hour, often differed by twenty or thirty miles. Now was when we needed the loran. I turned it on and watched the lights blink very nicely and then show us a position of: blank. The loran thought we were nowhere on earth. I wanted to set the chairman of Texas Instruments adrift in a boat equipped with this loran.

When we figured we must be within ten miles of the coast, we still couldn't see a thing. This was bad. We were depending on sighting lights from which we could make an accurate plot. It's pretty easy to hit *somewhere* on the entire East Coast of the United States when you're sailing west, but that wasn't good enough. Navigating to the rocky and shallow entrance to Five-Fathom Creek would be difficult under ideal conditions.

John tried using the depth finder to plot our position. He had very accurate depth charts for the region. He'd kept the local charts, even had one marked with course lines and notes that showed we'd sailed down from Maine. If we could match up our depth finder readings with those printed on the charts, we'd have some idea where we were. Unfortunately, the bottom in this area was fairly flat. We could only guess that we were somewhere in a circle about twenty miles in diameter, probably near the United States.

At eight o'clock Ireland called us on deck. He'd spotted some lights. John and I went up. There they were, lights. Good old USA lights. The joy of sighting home was tempered by the fact that we were, at the moment, not welcome.

The lights were confusing. As the fog lifted, we could see shore lights for miles north and south. Where were we? John estimated our position by guessing what the lights were, and sailed to where we should be going from where he thought we were. This is hard to do, even flying.

I got lost one night in a helicopter during flight school in Alabama. I flew from one group of town lights to another, all over southern Alabama, running low on fuel, and never could figure which was which until I happened to bump into Fort Rucker, which was where I was going. If I hadn't lucked out, though, people at the heliport could've found me on radar and told me where I was. I, like most of my fellow students, would've found violent death preferable to the humiliation of admitting I was lost—but help *was* available.

Help was not available now. At ten o'clock, after identifying a couple of unmistakable television towers and using them to plot our position, we discovered our guesses were wrong. We were way off course: twenty miles too far north. John turned back out to sea and then paralleled the coast, heading south. He called Dave and told them we'd be late.

"How late?"

"I figure we'll see you by two or three."

"Two or three!" Dave said. I was standing next to the stove, shivering, listening to Dave's dismay.

"Yeah, best I can figure," John said. "Two or three. Had some problems. Ran into some fog out here."

"Maybe we should reschedule the . . . shipment," Dave said. "We're getting real close to seeing daylight, and you know how the unions are."

John put down the mike. "Shit! He wants us to come in tomorrow night. He doesn't want to be unloading the boat in daylight."

"I think he's making sense, John," I said.

"Bullshit. We're here. We made it past the Coast Guard. You want to go back out and cruise around for a day and give those guys another chance?"

I shook my head. "You want to know what I'd do?"

"Do I have a choice?" John said. He was looking very nervous, very agitated. He was out of booze and there was nothing worse than trying to sneak a million dollars worth of pot past the Coast Guard *and* put up with Mason when what you really needed was a goddamn stiff drink and *no* advice. But no, Mason had yet another two cents worth. Shit (I read John's mind), Mason is a goddamn gold mine of ideas. I have the fucking mother lode of opinions about anything on earth, right here in front of me. He shook his head and nodded. "Okay. *What* would you do?"

"I'd wait until morning. I'd go back out into the fog, just make a lazy trip south toward Charleston. Then in full daylight, I'd just balls-it-out, sail right into the main harbor there. Blend in with the other fools out sailing in this fucking weather. There've got to be some. We sail in, hang out on deck, and wave at our fellow yachtsmen. Our waterline looks normal; we look empty. We're just another sailboat. They'd have no reason to be suspicious; there's no sign we've got this shitload of pot on board."

John said, "Then what?"

"Well, then I'd anchor out wherever the other yachts do and wait until night. Then we motor up the Intracoastal Waterway to the same place Dave's picked out—just come in from the opposite direction." I looked at John. He was considering it. "What d'you think?"

He nodded his head slightly, distracted, working on it. I could tell it violated his notion of smuggling, which was to stay invisible. I agreed; I just figured invisibility could be achieved more realistically by cam-ouflage. "Nope," John said finally. "I have a bad feeling about that. I trust my guts, Bob. We go. We go in now."

"Dave said we're too close to dawn," I said.

"Fuck Dave."

I put my hands up against the stove and tried to thaw them out. I felt my whole body getting cold to my core. I had on a sweater and two jackets, but I was shivering. John picked up the microphone and called. "We're coming in."

There was a long silence. "You figure you can make it by two? Three, at the latest?" Dave said.

"I'm positive," John said.

"Okay," Dave said, his voice filled with doubt. "We'll be ready. It's all clear."

We heard Ireland yelling and went on deck. He was pointing at a buoy. John had him steer toward it and went below and got our brilliant, half-million-candle-power floodlight. As we sailed past, we got the number. John found the buoy on the chart and for the first time in days we had an absolute fix on where we where. John drew a line on his chart, from the buoy to Santee Point, at the entrance of Five-Fathom Creek. We changed course. We were closer than we'd thought, and it looked like we might actually make it by two.

Five miles away from Santee Point, the wind dropped off, becoming too variable and too weak for sailing. John elected to drop sail and motor the rest of the way. I watched him push the starter with anticipation. Everything depended on that engine. Grind. Grind. Growl. The exhaust burbled out from under the stern. John engaged the propeller and the *Namaste* grumbled ahead. I breathed a sigh of relief that puffed out as a cloud in the frigid air and joined Ireland on the foredeck.

Ireland and I let down all the sails, rolled them up, and tied them with hanks. We made a neat job of it. We wanted the shore team to be impressed at what professional sailors we were. Look, guys. Forty-four days at sea and we're still cooler than you'll ever be if you live to be a hundred. Even with the heat of the effort, Ireland and I were shivering by the time we got back to the cockpit. A local radio station said it was thirty-eight degrees, but out on the water it seemed much colder than that. Ireland and I went below to warm up while John piloted.

We hugged the stove.

"You looking worried, Ali," Ireland said. "You don't like the plan?"

"You don't look so confident yourself," I said. "I guess the plan's okay. What the fuck do I know about this business? I just have a bad feeling about it, is all. My guts tell me it's a wrong move."

"It'll be fine," Ireland said. "Twenty of our people are just a few miles away. They've got it covered. We get to that fucking creek, Ali, we got it made."

I smiled. "You should know better'n me. But I guarantee I'll never do this again, Bob. Too many things can go wrong."

Ireland nodded. "Me neither. This is my last trip."

John called us.

He was pointing ahead. "See that light?"

"Yeah," I said. A light blinked on top of a channel marker.

"That's it. That's Santee Point." John started laughing. "If those motherfuckers want to catch us, they'd better do it in five minutes, 'cause we're outta here." He cupped his hands by his mouth and yelled to the world, "We're fucking history!"

We motored past Santee Point and into the mouth of Five-Fathom Creek at one-thirty. According to John's chart, it would take us another two hours to get to the pickup point. I watched the Atlantic disappear into the mist behind us. I heard the waves washing the rocks at Santee Point as a farewell salute. The sea had been my home for six weeks. It was powerful, vast. The sea had put my life in perspective. I missed it as land surrounded us. Someday, I promised, I'll be back.

A mile into the creek, it narrowed to about a hundred feet. The chart showed that it got narrower. The sides of the creek were berms raised when they dredged the creek through the surrounding marsh. Stars twinkled overhead. They were stars in the sky again; not stars floating next to the planet. The chill of the night entered my bones and I shivered. My breath puffed out in clouds. The only sound was the chuffle-gurgle of the engine. John had Ireland stand out on the deck with the blazing floodlight scanning the side of the channel so he could steer. The light, which seemed adequate at sea, was now overkill, lighting up the night like a flare.

"John, people can see that fucking light for miles."

"What do you want? You want us to run aground?"

"If you just let your eyes get used to the dark, you can see," I said. "I can see the damn banks without the thing."

"I'm not taking any chances. We run aground now, Bob, we're really fucked."

John knows what he's doing, I thought. We're both listening to our guts. John knows what he's doing. I'm just jumpy. He's right, the trip's almost over. We got past the Coast Guard, the shore team's cleared the creek. We're home free. I'll see Patience tomorrow with thirty thousand in my pockets—a successful hunter home with a bountiful catch. It'll be great. Happiness is warm money. Then why am I feeling so damn depressed? Maybe I'm just tired. Up thirty-six hours straight. Tired makes you stupid, jumpy over nothing. I used to make terrible landings, made dumb decisions in Vietnam when I got tired. Tired can kill you.

I stood next to John watching the floodlight scanning the banks. "How long before we get there?"

"Hour and a half," John said.

"Okay. I'm going below to catch a nap."

"A nap? Now? You can sleep now?"

"Yeah. I used to do it in Nam. You know, between flights. I want to be alert when we get there. There's nothing for me to do now, right?"

John shook his head. "No. We're just driving home, Bob."

I stepped into the hatch. "Wake me when you need me."

John nodded.

I crawled on top of the marijuana and wrapped myself in two blankets. I was tired, but that wasn't why I was trying to sleep. I was trying to sleep to get away from the foreboding of doom I was feeling. I couldn't shake it. Something was wrong with this move. I didn't know what. It might just be I needed some rest. Needed rest.

Patience and I are standing on the balcony of our new house. She's happy, beaming like she does, looking like the little drawing she puts on her notes. We can see the river from the deck that comes out from the bedroom. She has a table and two chairs on the balcony. I sit down and put my foot on the railing. Patience pours steaming coffee into two mugs. "I love you," she says. "You built me a beautiful home, and you did it by writing. I'm so proud of you. I'm so glad you decided not to go on that stupid trip." She smiles at me. "See? See, asshole, I was right. I knew they'd buy your book."

"I knew it, too, Patience."

"You knew they'd buy your book?"

"No, I knew you were right about the trip. I don't think I could've gone through with it anyway. It's just too damn chancy. They make it by luck and they think it's because they're clever. Someday, they'll wake up."

CHAPTER 19

"Ali! Wake up!" I heard Ireland, felt him shaking my arm. I figured it was time for my watch, then remembered we were probably ready to unload. My adrenaline shot up and I was wide awake. I could barely see Ireland, but I could see the look of panic on his face in the dim light.

"Call Dave!" he said.

"What?"

"Call Dave. Call Dave." Ireland's head jerked toward the hatch. I saw lights wavering across the cockpit. Shore team? Wasn't Dave with the shore team?

"Call Dave. Tell him we're busted! We're busted!"

He turned and climbed up onto the deck.

I could barely breathe. This was no joke. He wasn't screwing around with me. Ireland wasn't that good an actor. I climbed down from the marijuana and grabbed the radio mike. I heard a strange voice outside say, "Customs. May we come aboard?" I heard John, trying to seem as calm and as matter-of-fact as possible, say, "Sure, why not?" A shadow moved in the lights above. I peeked up the hatch and saw a man—a man climbing aboard. My heart dropped into my stomach. I felt weak. I put the mike to my mouth and clicked the switch. "Dave. Dave. We're busted. We're busted." I heard his reply overwhelmed with electonic noise. Must be pretty far away. I heard Dave saying, "*Crackle*. Say. *Sssssssst* . . . repeat . . . *rreeeeep* . . . what?"

I repeated the message and put the mike back on its hook. I had to fumble for the hook in the dark, but this was important. If I left the mike loose, it'd fall off the counter and maybe break the cord. As I climbed up the hatch ladder, I heard Dave's garbled reply coming from the radio. I couldn't make it out. Probably he still doesn't know what the fuck was going on, probably never did.

Two men dressed in blue jackets stood by John. One of them held a flashlight pointed at John's face. The other guy was sniffing. We couldn't smell the pot anymore, but they probably couldn't miss it. In the water next to the *Namaste*, I saw a small skiff with a man wearing a matching blue jacket operating the outboard motor, keeping up with us as the *Namaste* idled serenely down the creek, her engine chuffling softly. The *Namaste* only dealt with problems of the sea, but I felt a little let down that she ignored our plight—at least the engine could quit, couldn't it? I stood in front of the hatch to block the Customs agent's view. The man flashed his wallet. I saw the glint of a badge. "U.S. Customs," said the man. "We'd like to see your identity papers."

"We're Americans," John said.

The Customs agent nodded. "I'm sure," he said. "But it looks to us like you're coming from beyond the three-mile limit. We saw your light for miles. We have to check your IDs. Do you have driver's licenses? Passports?"

John nodded and looked at me. All our stuff was down below in a nifty waterproof bag we'd bought at Brasington's Trail Shop in Gainesville. "Yeah. We do. Stuff's down below. I'll go get it." John turned and walked toward me. Nice try—he figured the agent might just stay where he was until John came back up with our identification. The agent followed him to the hatch. My heart stopped beating. My nuts dropped off. I stepped aside. The agent stood beside me and watched John climb down to the counter and lean across it to get the waterproof bag we'd stuffed in the rack where we kept some books. He flashed his light inside. "Need a light?" the agent said.

"No," John snapped. "I can see fine."

"No bother," the agent said. His light flashed from the counter and illuminated a burlap bale. The agent turned to me and grinned. "Have a little extra? Something to declare?"

I didn't answer. The agent said, "Roger. Come take a look."

The other agent came over and saw the marijuana. "My, oh, my. What do we have here?"

The first agent called to the man in the boat. "Sam, call the state police, Coast Guard, local sheriff. Believe we have a little importation violation here."

"They have pot?" the man called back.

"Oh, yes." The agent laughed. "Lots of it."

I heard the guy in the boat, Sam, his voice tinged with glee, as he called every cop within fifty miles. The first agent had gone down below and stood beside John, looking at our papers. The agent nodded, calm and businesslike, as John showed him our passports and the faked ship's papers that said the *Namaste* was a leased sailboat.

"Ali," Ireland called. He was standing in the cockpit, holding the tiller. "Would you steer? I'm not too good at it."

I nodded and went back to the tiller.

I steered along the channel without lights. I could see the banks just fine. The agent in the boat tied his bowline to our safety line and climbed aboard. He ducked his head into the hatch, whistled, and said, "Everybody's on the way, Chuck."

Chuck. The head guy was Chuck. Then there was Rog and Sam. Three guys out working late. Or early. I checked my watch. Three-thirty. The *Namaste*'s engine chugged gently as we motored up the creek. I could see some buildings about two hundred yards ahead. Sam walked back to me. "Hi," Sam said, smiling a really big smile. I nodded. He said, "See that wharf up ahead?"

I nodded. A scruffy shrimp boat was tied up next to a dock. The dock was about twelve feet above the water. The tide was out. There were a couple of buildings about fifty feet behind the docks.

"Good. Pull up there, okay?"

"Okay."

I steered toward the dock. When we were about a hundred feet away, I put the engine in neutral and drifted. "Where you guys coming from?" Sam said. "Colombia?"

"We never left the three-mile limit," I said.

"Oh." Sam nodded. "Unloaded from a mother ship, I guess."

The dock was coming up and I suddenly realized I'd never handled the *Namaste* under power. All I knew how to do was sail across thousands of miles of stormy seas; I didn't know how to dock.

"John," I called. I saw him and Chuck look up. "I don't know how to do this. You'd better handle it."

Chuck nodded to John.

John looked grim; the weight of the bust had broken his indomitable spirit. He came up and took the tiller like a zombie. He muttered, "I'm sorry, Bob. I'm really sorry." I nodded and stood on the deck next to the cockpit. I looked up and down the creek. Not a sign of our shore team. They said they'd be here, in a skiff. Must have seen the intercept, boogied. Thought about that for a while. No. They couldn't have been around; they would've warned us.

John put the engine in reverse and salvaged my rotten approach. Moving like automatons, Ireland and I went fore and aft and tossed our bow and stern lines up over the piers, pulled in the lines, and tied us off. We were numb, working in a dream state—at least I was. John cut the engine and put a bumper between the *Namaste* and the dock so she wouldn't get marred.

Sam came to me and asked me to turn around. I stared at the nylon thing he held in his hand. "Cuffs," he said.

"I thought they were steel," I said.

"Naw. Everything's plastic nowadays. Want to turn around? I have to put these on. Regulations."

I nodded and turned around. Sam put my wrists together and cinched the nylon handcuffs tight. I watched John and Ireland being cuffed.

"Elephant luck, eh, Bob?" I said quietly.

Ireland nodded, looking forlorn, dumbfounded.

We all stood on the rear deck and stared at the dock twelve feet above the water. There was no ladder. Chuck, Rog, Sam, John, Ireland, and I stood there thinking about how we were going to get off the boat. We saw blue lights swinging through the morning mist. In a minute we saw a cop peek over the edge of the dock. "Damn," he said. "Tide's real low, ain't it?"

"Yeah," Chuck said. "Give us a hand. You got help up there?"

Another cop joined the first one and looked down on us, grinning. "Shit yeah," said the second cop. "And a bunch on the way."

The smiley cop lay on the dock and reached down to help Chuck up. They pulled Rog up next, leaving Sam with us. By now there were about six cops standing on the dock, stomping their feet against the cold, lighting cigarettes, shooting the shit.

It was hard for them to get us up because we couldn't grab anything to help. I said to Sam that they should've waited until we got on the dock to cuff us. Sam said I was right, but the cuffs couldn't be unlocked, they had to be cut. Finally somebody agreed with me. Two cops grabbed me under my arms and Sam held his hands together like a stirrup. "Here," he said, "use this."

I put my foot in his hands and stood up. The two cops caught me under my arms and flopped me up on the dock the way we'd brought in my tuna. I rolled over and stood up. A cop pointed to a spot on the boards under a lamp nailed to a post and said, "Have a seat. Right there."

I sat.

John and Ireland sat across from me. We looked at one another, eyes vacant, saying nothing.

The cops had found a ladder somewhere and tied it to the dock. They were scurrying up and down the ladder, checking out the boat. I could hear them laughing.

The cuffs were cutting into my wrists. Handcuffs? I wondered what Patience and Jack would think if they could see me now.

"You are advised that anything you may say may be used as evidence against you. You have the right to remain silent. You have the right to an attorney to be present during questioning," the cop said. He added, shaking his head sadly, "You're in big trouble, Mr. Mason." The cop was a detective from the South Carolina State Police. Three other plainclothes cops sat around the table, staring. Yes. I was in big trouble. I nodded. My hands were crammed behind me, numb. I leaned against the back of the chair, but I couldn't feel it with my fingers. We sat at a table in an office. The owner of the docks had come and unlocked the building so the cops would have a place to do some preliminary interrogation. They'd taken us into the office one at a time. John and Ireland had already been here. I wondered what they'd said.

"We know you were just a crew member," said the detective. "Your buddy, Tillerman, said he was the captain; said you and Ireland were crew."

I nodded. John had said that if we were caught, he'd tell them he was the captain. He wanted the responsibility. He figured it came with the job.

"You mind speaking up, Mr. Mason? We have to tape this."

"Yeah. That's right."

"What's right?"

"Tillerman was the captain."

"Okay. Now." The cop looked at his notebook. "Where'd you get the pot?"

I looked at the cop. "I don't know."

"Who's your boss?"

"I told you. Tillerman was the captain."

"I don't mean him. Who's he working for? Who's the real boss?"

"I don't know."

The cop nodded, screwed his mouth up grimly, and leaned across the table. "Look, Mr. Mason. You're in deep-shit trouble here. You're looking at twenty-five years in prison. You know that?"

"Twenty-five years?"

"That's right. Now, if I were you, I'd cooperate with us. We can't guarantee anything, but we can tell the judge you cooperated. Could help you."

I nodded.

"So where did you get the pot?"

"Look," I said, "I don't want you to get the wrong impression, sir. I really do want to cooperate with you. I don't know much about this kind of thing, but I think it would be smart for me to have an attorney here."

"Don't be stupid, Mason!" the cop yelled. "You won't have this opportunity again. This is your chance to help us out—and help yourself. Do it and I know it'll be easier for you. Where's the rest of the people—the shore team?"

Good question. Probably they were still trying to figure out what happened. I could see the shore team, Dave, Mitford, Wheely, Rangy Jane, all twenty of them, each of them fumbling around trying to find their asses with both hands and missing. "Like I said, I will definitely help you gentlemen. Just as soon as I have an attorney with me."

The cop slapped the table. "That's about the dumbest thing you could say, Mason. Now the judge'll know you were uncooperative when you were arrested. We got you on tape. Goes into the arrest report. Makes you look bad, Mason. He'll know you're protecting criminals. And for what? Don't you think for one minute we won't find them, your buddies. We have a hundred men out there right now. We'll find them. We'll get them anyway, so you have nothing to lose, everything to gain. Where are they, these shore guys?"

I stared at the cop. I had no reason to protect Dave and the band of idiots who were supposed to have the creek under control, who were supposed to clear it for us. All it would've taken was a simple radio call, tell us the creek was being watched. No. Their last transmission said everything was clear. John had asked; I heard him when we got to the creek.

"Absolutely. All clear," Dave had said.

I looked at the head cop, at the three other cops. Everybody was looking as mean and as grim as they could look, like cops are supposed to look when they're trying to scare the shit out of you. They were all staring at me like I was on my way to death row. I felt like I was on my way to death row.

There was something more important than saving my ass. There was this thing: loyalty. I did the same thing in Vietnam. We were wrong to be there, but I fought the fight. It's loyalty to the side you're on. You pick sides, you play the game the best way you know how. When your team fumbles the ball, well, that's the way it goes. Maybe you work it out after the game. You do nothing to help the other side. "You have my statement on your tape machine, sir."

The cop shook his head. "Okay, Mason," he said quietly. "You'll never be able to say I didn't give you a chance. You live with that?"

"I'll have to."

The cop stood up. "Okay. Let's go."

I stood up and walked out to the waiting room where John and Ireland and Chuck and Sam waited. They told me to sit in a chair across from John and Ireland. I sat. The cops went back into the office. I said, "Uh, Chuck."

"Yeah, Robert?"

"Bob. Just call me Bob," I said. "Look, Chuck. This fucking plastic piece of shit handcuff you snapped on me is killing my hands. I can't feel a thing."

Chuck look concerned, nodded, and came over. I stood up and he looked behind me. I felt him tug the cuffs. "Is a little tight." He said to Sam, "You got another cuff, Sam?"

"That was it, Chuck," Sam said, shrugging.

Chuck nodded and said to me, "That was it, Bob."

"Can't you just cut the fucking thing off? I mean, where am I going to go, Chuck? I don't think I deserve to lose my hands over this, do you?"

Chuck shook his head, seemed to be thinking. "Just a minute." He went into the office where the state cops were talking cop strategy, working the phones, radioing messages to search teams and stuff. A minute later he came out with a new plastic cuff. "They had a spare," he said, smiling. He fished a pocketknife out of his pants. "Turn around, I'll fix you up."

Chuck cut off my cuffs and let me rub my hands together. They were blue, swollen, numb as dead flesh. After a while I could feel them tingle. I put my hands back behind me and Chuck put on the new cuffs and cinched them up loose enough so they didn't cut my circulation, but tight enough so I couldn't get them off. "Thanks, Chuck," I said.

"No problem, Bob."

I sat down and stared at the posters on the wall. There was going to be some kind of county fair in McClellanville in a couple of weeks. The Clyde Beatty Circus was coming. A big tiger jumped through a flaming hoop. On the other wall was an OSHA safety poster with diagrams showing you that you should not bend over to lift heavy objects; you should squat down, use your legs. Most industrial back injuries, the poster said, are caused by workers using improper lifting techniques. An electric clock over the secretary's desk said it was five o'clock in the morning. Funny, I wasn't the least bit tired. Guess it was the nap. I stared at the carpet. What a dingy color, brown with yellow speckles. Probably it was supposed to not show dirt. Nice. You could puke on this carpet and never know it.

"Okay, Chuck," the state cop said to the Sam and Chuck from the doorway of the office. "You guys can go. The feds want us to take them to Charleston. Boss just said he wants you to know he thinks you and your boys did a great job, Chuck."

Sam and Chuck smiled. "Hey, it was nothing. All in a day's work," Chuck said. "See you at the trial." Chuck and Sam said good-bye to the cops and to us and left. Friendly guys. I could see the dim glow of dawn outside when they went through the door.

"Okay, let's go," the cop said. John and Ireland and I stood up.

One cop held each of us by the arm and they escorted us outside. They led Ireland and John to separate police cars. My cop, a quiet guy who'd been at my interrogation, took me to his car, an unmarked Ford LTD. He opened the passenger door, told me to get in. I sat down on the front seat with my arms wedged behind me. He closed the door and walked around the front of the car, watching me the whole time, like I might gnaw my way through the door with my teeth. He got in behind the wheel.

The cop was silent until we hit the main highway. "You seem like a well-educated guy," the cop said. "I'd've thought you'd be smart enough to cooperate with us. They had to say they can't *guarantee* you anything. But I know they'd go easy on you if you told me where you guys came from, who's on the shore team. They'd be extra-special glad if you told them who you work for."

"That's why we're in separate cars? Give us our last chance to confess?"

"Yeah. That and to prevent you from cooking up a story together."

I nodded as we joined a stream of commuter traffic. "Yeah. I guess if you left us alone we'd be able to come up with some real clever story—explain away all that fucking pot, all right."

The cop laughed.

It was almost six-thirty. The highway was packed with commuters on their way to work. The cars moved in slow clots along an artery to the city. I stared into the cars we passed, looking at the people. We stayed beside one guy so long, I got to know him. He looked drowsy, tired, pissed off. He sipped coffee from an insulated plastic mug with a picture of Yogi Bear on it.

I read this man's mind. He was thinking: What am I doing wrong? I don't think I can make it through another goddamn day. If shit-for-brains says one more thing about my expenses, I'll tell him to stuff it. I will. He nods. His mind drifts home: What's eating Margaret? I can't figure it out. What does she do all day? The boys are turning into fucking monsters. She's turning into a surly slob. She always used to keep the place clean, kept herself looking nice, smiled now and then. He shakes his head, sips from Yogi. Can't figure it out. I do my part. I put up with shit-for-brains for what they pay sewer workers in New York. I mow the yard every Saturday. I take out the garbage Tuesdays and Thursdays. What more does she want? The commuter shakes his head and smiles a cynical smile. On tap for regional manager, my ass. Shit-for-brains keeps saying that so I won't quit. Sure, you bet. The chances of me getting sales manager over his dimwit brother-in-law are the same as me sprouting another dick.

That's what the commuter was thinking.

The cop said, "You know, I feel sorry for you, Mason."

Funny. So did I.

We left the commuter behind. The early morning sun washed his grim face in gold. I nodded at him, telling him not to worry so much; things could be worse. Start your own business; tell Margaret you love her; take the monsters camping. But he didn't notice me. His mind was working on so many problems he probably didn't see the road.

I wanted very much to be that commuter.

PART THREE

THE
PAYOFF

CHAPTER 20

"**B**end over," the marshal said.

The state cop who'd driven me in smiled awkwardly. The head cop behind the desk shot an embarrassed grin at the Treasury agent standing beside him. Somebody's got to do it.

Humiliation is the tool of choice in basic training. Once, when I didn't move fast enough in the run-fall-in-the-dirt-crawl-and-kill-the-enemy lessons, a sergeant made me grab my crotch.

"What do you feel there, Private?" the sergeant yelled.

"Balls, sir!"

"I don't believe it! You have balls, Private?"

"Yessir," I yelled.

"You aren't a pussy?"

"No, sir!"

"Let me hear it, then!"

"I am not a pussy, sir!"

"What?"

"I am not a pussy, sir!"

I wasn't humiliated that men made me drop my pants (Army training is good for something). I was humiliated that I'd gotten caught. There was nothing these guys could do to make me feel worse.

I dropped my pants on the floor, pulled down my underwear, and bent over. "Spread your cheeks," said the marshal. I reached back and pulled my buttocks apart. I looked at the man behind the desk, the man in charge. He looked down at his desktop. The room was silent as the marshal checked me out. I think this was a kind of staring match: the marshal stared at me, and I, I presume, stared back. I think I was supposed to break down with embarrassment and tell them what they wanted to know. Moments later, the marshal said "He's clean" to the man behind the desk.

I stood up and faced the cop behind the desk.

"You can pull your pants back on, Mr. Mason," he said. He pulled a cord, opened the venetian blinds behind him as I pulled up my pants. The ten o'clock sun was blazing down on a parking lot. We were in a government building near the federal court building in Charleston. A woman, dressed in the kind of professional clothes for women designed to mimic men's suits, was leaning into her car to put her briefcase down. I zipped my fly.

"Have a seat," the man said, nodding toward a chair in front of his desk.

I nodded and sat down. The guy looked at papers on his desk. He and the rest of the cops were dressed in business suits. I was wearing salt-stained, stiff, smelly jeans, two crusty shirts, and a pair of damp running shoes. I hadn't washed for days. The freezing weather had made bathing impossible. I needed a shave.

"Says here you refused to cooperate with the arresting officers," the head cop behind the desk said, looking up from the papers.

"I didn't refuse," I said. "I told them I wanted to cooperate. I still do. I just think I'd be smart to have an attorney with me when I do."

"Bullshit!" said the Treasury agent, standing up to hover over me. "You don't want to help us. You're protecting your friends. You're a lowlife drug smuggler; and now, when we give you a chance to prove you have a conscience, you continue breaking the law by protecting other criminals."

"All I know is that the three of us were definitely on the *Namaste*. I have no idea where anybody else was. That's the truth." And it was, technically. I did know where the shore team was *supposed* to be, but that's all I knew. Where were they actually? I hadn't a clue.

"Okay," said the head cop. "Let's say that's true. Tell us *who* was in the shore team."

"I don't know. I was just a crew member. Nobody told me anything."

The Treasury guy nodded. He looked frustrated. I presumed he'd heard this before; they'd already interviewed John and Ireland. "How did you get the money to the Colombians?"

"I don't—"

"Give us a break, Mason!" the Treasury agent yelled. "You know plenty. You know enough to help us. Do you realize how much money is being sent to these countries by guys like you? Do you?"

I shook my head.

"Millions of dollars every day. It's a disaster. U.S. currency is being drained from circulation and poured into the pockets of organized crime."

I felt the urge to tell him that if we didn't have such ridiculous drug laws, this weed we now pay millions for would be effectively worthless and nobody'd be smuggling it; or if they let American farmers grow it, we could tax it and keep the profits here. The law and drug smugglers have one thing in common: neither wants marijuana legalized. But this wasn't an after-dinner political debate. This was a routine post-arrest interrogation. These guys had probably tried pot themselves; they probably thought the laws were stupid, too. They were just doing their jobs. "That's a shame," I said.

The Treasury guy glared at me and turned to the head cop and shrugged. The head cop looked at me and then at the marshal and the state cop, the same guy who'd brought me here. Everybody was shrugging, saying, Well, we tried. It isn't like the old days, you know, when they could beat the shit out of you and you *would* talk. Now they can only try to scare you. Anything you say without an attorney is a gift for the law. The head cop looked at me and said, "Mr. Mason, you're going on trial soon. Now, unless you change your attitude, I will report in your arrest record that you were totally uncooperative. You will be charged with smuggling marijuana, possession of marijuana, and possession of marijuana with the intent to distribute marijuana. Three major felonies. You're looking at forty years, and that's just the federal charges. The state wants you, too, for all the same charges." The cop stared at me for a second. "You sure you want your record to show that you are unrepentant, uncooperative?"

"You can do what you want. It's your record. I'm not talking about this without an attorney. I can't believe you don't understand that. I've never been in this much trouble in my whole life. I'm amazed you think I should just spill my guts without legal counsel. You'd demand to have an attorney present if you were sitting here."

The cop nodded slightly and said, "You can go." He looked at the cop who'd brought me in. "Okay, Fred. Take him to the holding tank."

Fred nodded and I walked to the door. He opened it and I walked out into a hallway. Fred pointed ahead and we walked.

"Man, you really stink of marijuana," Fred said.

"Wow," I said. "I wonder how that happened."

Fred laughed. Just a regular guy.

Fred drove me a couple of blocks to the federal court building. We walked in the front door, Fred dressed for work, me dressed like a street bum who'd been sleeping in these reeking clothes for two weeks. We walked by some people getting their mail at the first-floor post office and climbed the stairs to the third floor. Fred escorted me down the hall to a cage set off the hallway like a coffee-break room except with bars on the door. John and Ireland sat on benches inside the cage.

They looked terrible. No wonder people think criminals are a dirty bunch. If I hadn't known them, they would've made me nervous.

A deputy came up to us and Fred told him to let me in.

As soon as the door closed, John asked Fred, "Do you smoke?"

"Naw," Fred said.

"Damn. I got to have a cigarette, man." John jerked his head toward me. "Bob, too."

I nodded.

Fred shrugged. "Okay, give me some money and I'll buy you some."

John jammed his hand into his pocket and immediately laughed. "Nice joke—ah, what is your name, anyway?"

"Fred."

"Funny, Fred. You guys took all our money."

Fred smiled. "Okay, I'll lend you a couple of bucks. I mean, I can see you're a trustworthy bunch." He turned and walked away.

John and I chain-smoked a pack of Salems, the brand Fred figured everybody smoked. Ireland sat slumped on a bench, trying to nap. He'd been complaining about his stomach.

I sat next to Ireland, tired but not even a little sleepy, watching John pace back and forth in the eight-by-eight-foot cell.

"So what did you tell them?" John asked.

"I told them Bob and I were crew members on the boat, you were the captain."

"That's it? I mean, you tell them where we came from, anything like that?"

"Nope. Nothing else."

He turned to Ireland. "You didn't say anything, right?"

Ireland grimaced and clutched his stomach with both hands. "No, man."

"Good," John said.

"Yeah. Great, John," I said. "We have them exactly where we want them, eh? I mean, the only evidence they have on us is a fucking boatload of marijuana."

"It could be worse," John said, without much conviction.

"Shouldn't we be getting a lawyer?" I said.

"The team's probably figured it out by now," John said. "We'll be contacted."

I nodded. Right, the team. The same idiots who spent six weeks watching that canal, *except* for the night we came in. That team.

I was too tired to argue anymore. The whole thing was a dream. I sat back against the wall and smoked a Salem. There was nothing to do but wait and watch the process we'd triggered when we bumped into the Customs boat. A whole crew of people trained in the disposition of captured criminals were now hard at work, and they did this every day. It was something to watch, a distraction from the despair I felt.

An hour later, two deputies came to the door and said we had a hearing with the magistrate. We left the cell and followed one deputy down the hall, trailed by another.

A sign on the door said ROBERT CARR, U.S. MAGISTRATE. We went inside. DEA Agent Cook, who'd been at the scene of the arrest, was sitting against the wall near the magistrate's desk. The magistrate offered us the three chairs in front of the desk. A stenographer, a woman, nodded curtly to us when the magistrate indicated she would be taking notes of the meeting. We sat.

"Gentlemen, a federal grand jury has just indicted you. The crimes you are charged with are possession of a controlled substance, marijuana; possession of a controlled substance, marijuana, with the intention to distribute a controlled substance; and the illegal importation of a controlled substance, marijuana." The magistrate looked at us. "Each one of you is charged with the commission of all three of these crimes."

I nodded dumbly, noticing that John and Ireland did the same. I wanted to ask how one crime could become three. And how if you multiply three crimes times three people, you now have nine crimes; and is that actually true? I mean—

"I'll be setting bond for you men," said the magistrate. "And I need some information to help me decide how much they'll be." He picked up a scratch pad and a pencil and asked John, "Your name?"

"John Tillerman."

"Address?"

"P.O. box—"

"You have a street address?"

"One mile off state road 343, three miles south of High Springs, Florida."

"Country place?" the magistrate said, his brow raised.

"Yeah, I like the country," John said.

The magistrate nodded and asked, "What kind of work do you do, Mr. Tillerman?"

"I'm a carpenter," John said.

"I see," the magistrate said, making a note. "And who do you work for?"

"I'm self-employed."

"Okay. And your approximate annual income from this line of work?"

And so on. The magistrate was taking what amounted to a credit application. He asked John all the usual questions: marriage status (married); education (college degree), references, and so on. I began to nod off from fatigue and boredom. Then I heard the magistrate ask, "And your name, sir?" I looked up to see that he was talking to me.

"Bob Mason," I said.

"Robert Mason?"

"Yes. Robert Caverly Mason."

"Caverly? That's unusual."

"It's Scottish."

"Hmm." The magistrate nodded. He then asked me the same set of questions. When he asked me what my profession was, I said, "I'm a writer." It just popped out of my mouth.

"Really?" the magistrate said. "What sort of writing do you do?"

"I'm writing a book about being a helicopter pilot in Vietnam."

"Really? Who's the publisher?"

"Well, I don't have a publisher yet. It, the manuscript, is in New York now. My agent's trying to sell it."

"Oh," the magistrate said, clearly disappointed. Nearly everyone is interested in writers, but not so much interested in writers who are not published. Almost everybody knows an unpublished writer. In New York, where publishers collect tons of unsolicited manuscripts, they will tell you that it seems like almost everyone in America is an unpublished writer trying to get published. I kept asking myself angrily why I'd said I was a writer. I guess I was trying to impress someone at the lowest moment of my life: Hey, I have a manuscript; I have an agent; I've been to New York City.

"So, Mr. Mason, while you are waiting to sell a book, what do you do for a living?"

"My wife and I run rural paper routes for the Gainesville *Sun*."

"And about how much do you make doing that?"

I couldn't tell him the truth. It was just too dismal. Sure, I was dead meat on a hook, I was a captured crook, but I had my pride. I was not going to admit to this guy—who made sixty-five thousand a year—that Patience and I would, if I were working, bring in about twelve thousand a year. "Twenty thousand," I said.

The magistrate cocked his head. Too much to believe. "Twenty thousand between the two of us," I added.

"Oh," said the magistrate, and marked it down on his pad. He asked me the rest of the questions and then did the same for Ireland.

When he'd gotten the personal information, he began asking DEA Agent Cook, as one of the arresting officers, questions about our crime. "Were there weapons involved in this crime, Agent Cook?"

"No, sir," Agent Cook said. "We found a Winchester forty-four magnum, lever-action rifle on their boat. It was unloaded and stored in a case. We presume it was used as a shark gun." That was true, and it was also incredibly fair of Agent Cook not to imply that the gun was part of our crime, considering it would've been easy to do so and would've added much to the seriousness of our charges. Who'd believe otherwise?

The magistrate nodded. "And approximately how much marijuana did you find on their boat?"

"Approximately three thousand pounds, sir."

The magistrate nodded, looking over his glasses at us. It sounded like an awful lot, but it was also five hundred pounds short of what we thought we'd brought in. John and I glanced at each other.

"And what do you estimate is the value of that amount of marijuana?" the magistrate asked.

"At present street prices, we estimate that amount of marijuana is worth about two point four million dollars," Agent Cook said.

The room was quiet for a moment. The stenographer looked up at us. When people start talking about millions of dollars, it attracts attention.

"Okay, gentlemen," the magistrate said. "I have what I need in order to establish bonds for you. It'll take my office a few days to check your backgrounds. I'm sure you understand?" He waited until we had all three nodded that was obviously the case. "Good. Then I will have a deputy take you to the Charleston County Jail, where you will be held until I've made my decision. Thank you for your cooperation."

We waited in the holding tank down the hall while the federal deputies got the transportation details arranged. We asked for food, but they said we'd get lunch at the jail. A secretary from an office a couple of doors away brought us three cups of coffee on a plastic tray.

"You the pot smugglers?" she asked as she handed us the Styrofoam cups through the bars.

"Yeah," John said. "That's us."

She let the tray drop beside her skirt, smiled, and shook her head. "Business isn't so good today?"

"Not so good," John said.

She watched until we sipped from the cups she'd brought and then smiled and went back to her office, a room like ours except it had no graffiti on the walls and no bars on the door.

An hour later, two deputies, one white and one black, let us out of the cell and escorted us to the elevator. They took us to the basement, where they fitted us with chains. They put fat leather belts on our waists which had metal rings on them through which they threaded long chains so we were chained together. If we made a break for it, we would look like three handcuffed mountain climbers in a rush.

"What's this?" John said. "We've been walking around this place all day with no cuffs, no nothing. Why you chaining us now?"

"Regulations," the black deputy said. "I got no choice."

The white deputy opened the door and we walked out, trailing each other. They guided us to a big Ford and let us in the backseat.

It was about two in the afternoon as the Ford drove up a ramp onto an expressway. The sun was bright, the air chilled. We drove along the expressway. The sun hit my face, feeling pleasant. The people in the passing cars seemed so different now. They, any of them, could, on a whim, just turn off at the next exit, go anywhere they wanted to go. They were free.

The black deputy apparently got a lot of complaints about the chains. "I had to transport this guy once, a farmer," the deputy said. "He was in jail for making his own liquor. Judge let him out of jail temporarily to go harvest his tobacco crop, you know?"

"They let people out of jail to do that?" Ireland said.

"Yeah, they can. This judge did. Anyway, this old boy had been home for over a month, the harvest was over, and the judge said I should go fetch him back to jail. So we, Billy, here," he said, nodding to the white deputy next to him, "Billy and me, we go out to the sticks to this guy's house. Damned if he wasn't waiting for us, all cleaned up and ready to go; been out there for a month, could've just took off. His wife is saying good-bye; his kids are crying. Then I tell him I have to put on the cuffs. Damned if he didn't get crazy! He says, 'What? I been out here by myself, trustworthy as you fucking please, and you want to put me in chains?' And I say, 'C'mon, now. This is just regulations. If it was up to me, I wouldn't do it, you know?' Well, the guy just didn't understand it, the regulations, you know. Took it personal. He proceeded to get real loud and nasty and me and Billy had to draw our guns. By then he had worked himself into such a state that made him even madder. He got started looking like he was going to hit us, and we ended up having to shoot the guy."

"You *shot* him?" John said.

"Had to. He woulda taken off. Didn't kill him or nothing. Just wounded him, you know?" The deputy nodded to himself behind the wheel. "Just the same, it was nasty business. I didn't feel good about hurting that dumb redneck. Plus, he got more time for attempted escape. Nasty business. I'm looking forward to retiring this coming year."

Nobody said anything for a while. I watched a family packed in a station wagon pass us. A boy in the back stared at me curiously. I looked away, at the back of the deputy's head. "Where you going? When you retire?" I said.

"Miami. Have a kid down there. Owns a bar. Thought I'd join him in my afternoon years," the deputy said. "Ever been to Miami?"

"Yes," I said.

"Nice, ain't it?"

"It's the pits. I'd give anything to be there right now."

The two deputies laughed while we drove onto an off ramp to a highway. We were twenty minutes from Charleston, in the country. In the distance we could see a complex of low beige buildings surrounded by chain-link fences topped with coils of barbed wire. "That's the Charleston County Jail, boys," the deputy said.

Twelve hours after we'd been caught in Five-Fathom Creek, we were standing in the receiving area of the Charleston County Jail. We were tired and utterly defeated. John was not cracking jokes. Ireland looked terrible, kept complaining that his stomach was getting worse. I just watched, dazed, as they unlocked the chains, pulled them through the rings on our belts. They unfastened our belts and pointed to a black guy standing in the hall. "Follow him," the white deputy said.

We followed the black clerk into a room and gave him our watches and wallets, which he put into manila envelopes and labeled with a felt-tip pen. Then he fingerprinted us. When he finished, he told us to wait outside in the hallway.

We stood against the wall and watched the cops coming and going at the main entrance. A woman behind a tall desk talked on a radio and answered the phone. Guards walked in and nodded at us vaguely as they walked by. All this coming and going inside a county jail was kind of interesting if you'd never seen it before. It was a testimony to our fatigue that it took us fifteen minutes to realize that we could just walk out the door.

"Nobody's watching the damn door!" John hissed.

I stared at the door and watched a guard walk out unnoticed. The woman was talking on the phone and didn't press a buzzer to unlock the door; the door was just open. Now and then, somebody would look at us, but since we were dressed in our sailing clothes, we just looked like run-of-the-mill American deadbeats, possibly homeless, certainly not prisoners. We were invisible as far as people trained to watch people dressed as prisoners were concerned.

"We could just walk out of here," I said.

John laughed. "I know! It's unbelievable!"

Ireland looked at us, grimacing. He said his stomach was twisting up in knots. His suntanned skin had paled and he winced when he said, "They want us to walk out; then they shoot us."

"Naw," John said. "They're not that smart. These people are just working. They don't give a shit about us." He walked toward the door.

I followed, wondering just how far we could get, but John veered from the door and walked up to the woman behind the tall desk. We stood about ten feet from the glass doors to freedom, staring at the woman. She looked up, smiled, and said "May I help you?" with a look of faint surprise on her face from, I believe, our general haggard appearance.

"Maybe," John said. He looked at me and back at the woman. "We're prisoners. Checking in."

The woman grinned, leaned back ready for a big laugh, then snapped forward, assuming the posture of open-mouthed incredulity. "Excuse me?" she said.

"We're prisoners," John said. "Guy told us to wait here, but it's been a half hour."

The woman was nodding as John spoke, but she was distracted, looking everywhere for a guard. One came up behind us and got in line, waiting his turn.

"Johnson," the woman blurted to the guard. "These men are prisoners."

Johnson jerked out of a daydream stupor, which people who work in places like this develop as a survival skill, and stared at us like we'd just stepped off a spaceship.

"Prisoners?"

"Yessir," I said. "Guy told us to wait—"

"What guy?"

I pointed to the room where we had checked our stuff.

"Goddammit," Johnson said. He leaned close to the woman and said, "Call Willy and tell him to get his ass back to work!"

The woman nodded quickly and punched a phone button. Meanwhile, Johnson escorted us down the hall that led into the depths of the Charleston County Jail.

Everything was made of poured concrete in this jail. The floors, the walls—no bricks. They'd painted the floors gray and the walls pale green in keeping with the building's spirit of dull utility.

Johnson stopped at a door marked CLOTHING ROOM and opened it. Inside the small room, floor-to-ceiling shelves were filled with what can only be described as rags—blue and gray tattered pants and shirts. Johnson handed us each a net laundry bag. "Take off your civvies and put everything in the bag," he said.

Johnson waited impatiently by the door as we stripped. Another guard stopped at the doorway. "Thought you went home."

"Thought so, too," Johnson said.

I wanted to ask Johnson if he meant for us to turn in our underwear, too, but he was busy. So I just stood there in my Jockeys and waited. I wasn't in a big hurry. I saw myself in a detached way, standing nearly naked in a place where they kept men in cages. I thought I should feel something. Fear or nervousness, something. I felt numb.

"What happened?" said the guard.

"Fucking Willy had these guys standing around next to the goddamn front door."

"We supposed to put our underwear in the bag, too?" John asked me.

"I dunno—"

"Yeah. Everything goes in the bag," Johnson said.

"Standing by the door?" the guard said, smiling like he was going to pop.

"Yeah," Johnson said. "That damn nig—" He paused and looked up and down the hallway. "That damn nigger is about spacey as they come," Johnson said.

The guard laughed. He seemed to be looking at me, so I smiled back. I knew Willy was spacey, too. Willy didn't allow me to keep my toothbrush when we checked in—I had it in my jacket pocket—but said they'd give me another one. That's pretty spacey, isn't it? A tooth-brush is a toothbrush—isn't it? The guard saw me smiling and glanced at Johnson and nodded at me. Johnson turned around and saw the three of us standing naked, holding three laundry bags of stinking clothes. He jerked his head to the shelves. "Grab yourselves a set of clothes. You get one shirt, one pair of pants, pair of socks." We nodded.

"Somebody'd been up shit creek if these boys had've taken off," Johnson said to the guard. "And you can just damn well bet I'd be the one without the paddle."

"I know it," the guard said. "Jenkins has a hair up his ass when it comes to you, Roy. What'd you ever do to that man?"

I couldn't find any pants that weren't torn to literal shreds, and I was getting pissed about it. This is America, isn't it? "Look at this shit," I said to John. "These are fucking rags."

"They're what you get, boy," Johnson said, irritated. "Get that shit on and let's get out of here."

I pulled on the most intact pair of pants I could find and rooted around the shelves for a shirt.

"The fucker had to come down and catch me one night when I was looped at the Alibi," Johnson said. "Ever since, he's been giving me shit for it."

The guard shook his head, grinning at Johnson's wild ways.

I found a shirt which had two buttons and put it on. I was trying to find some socks. The guard checked the hallway and said, "Yeah. Jenkins can be a real ball-buster about drinking," he said.

We were all three properly dressed prisoners now, standing there in tattered blue uniforms that had been worn by hundreds of men over the last ten years or so, standing in socks, holding our bags of civilian clothes, waiting for Johnson to tell us what to do next before we dropped from exhaustion. "You got that right. I'm thinking I'll transfer to state—" Johnson stopped when he saw the guard looking at us. He turned around. "All right. Put your bags over on that shelf. Grab a blanket and let's get out of here," Johnson said, pointing to a stack of gray woolen blankets on the floor. I'd missed them; thought they were cleaning rags. We each stashed our gear on the shelf and grabbed an armload of ragged blanket and clutched it to our chests. "Do we get shoes?" John asked.

Johnson shook his head like that was the dumbest question he'd ever heard in his entire life. "Naw. We're out. They'll give you some when you get to your cell block."

"Well, Roy," said the guard, "got to get moving. I'm taking the better half out tonight. Her birthday."

Johnson nodded. "Okay, Henry. See you tomorrow."

We followed Roy Johnson down the hall to a big steel door where he waved to somebody through the wire-embedded glass windows. He was signaling a guard who stood in a boxlike pavilion in the middle of the hub that was the central intersection of this jail. From that pavilion, a guard could watch all six wings. The door opened. We walked into the hub. The door closed.

We followed Johnson down a hallway. Inmates began hooting at us as we walked by. We looked pretty silly, dressed in our rags, and they had a terrific time letting us know that. There is only one thing lower than a prisoner in jail, and that is a new prisoner in the same jail. I noticed that the prisoners were dressed in fairly neat clothes and even had shoes. So this junk they gave us was probably just part of some initiation process.

"Hey, assholes," somebody yelled. "Welcome to Charleston!" Hoots of laughter.

Johnson stopped at another big metal door and pushed a buzzer. A pair of eyes peeked through a small barred window. We heard the door click, watched it open. A black guard shook his head and said "I don't know where they expect we're gonna put these fuckers" and made a sour expression.

"Always room for one more in the federal wing, Porter," Johnson said, laughing. We walked in through the door as the guard, Porter, waved us inside. On the other side of the door, we waited while he slammed the big door shut, watching Johnson's face disappear in the narrowing gap. I had the strange feeling that I missed Johnson already. We'd known him longer than anyone else here. We were newborn jailbirds, and just naturally took to the first face we saw.

Porter, our new guard, motioned for us to move down the hall. One side of the hall had windows every ten feet that looked out onto a weedy chain-link-fenced exercise yard. The other side was a wall of steel bars. Four feet behind the bars, across a sort of open-air hallway, there were more steel bars with doors every eight feet, doors to dark cages with men glowering in them. Farther down the hallway, a television sitting on a wheeled stand blared into a large barred room filled with men and gray metal tables. About thirty men, dressed in the same kind of rags we wore, were sitting or lying on the tables. The guard stopped at the TV, which was beyond arm's reach of the prisoners, and switched the channel abruptly. Men yelled and booed behind the bars. One guy said, "Hey, Porter. There's nothing on that fucking channel."

"Shut the fuck up," Porter said. "I said you watch channel four. That's what you watch." He pushed the television farther away from the bars. "How you changing the channel, anyway?"

"Fuck you Porter," somebody said. Porter seemed not to notice and put a key in a lock on the door of the barred dayroom and opened it. He looked at us watching him. I think we had the sort of looks on our faces that said, You mean, go in there? Us? "C'mon," Porter said. "Get in there. Let's go."

We walked inside.

Porter locked the door behind us.

We stood just inside the room, each clutching a blanket against his chest, staring at the men.

The men stared at us. They were mostly black men. With our deep suntans from forty-four days of sailing, we were still lily-whites. Lily-white motherfuckers, as one man near the shower stall at the back of the room muttered. One of them, a big black guy who sat on the table nearest us, said, "What you want? Somebody to show you your fucking room?"

"Yeah," John said, stepping forward. "Where we supposed to sleep?"

The black guy studied John quickly, probably checking his size and the general condition of his muscles. John was in great shape, as well as big, and the guy was impressed. He smiled a little and pointed over his shoulder. "Down the hall."

"Any particular room?" John said.

"Naw. Take your pick," the guy said. "Life's good in the federal wing. You can do anything you want here." He laughed. The half dozen men sitting on the table nearest the television in the hall, which was flickering, blaring about using Tide for your laundry, laughed.

We walked out of the large dayroom and into the barred hallway.

We checked out the cells, looking for a home. They were all filled with black men who just stared at us, not saying anything, not looking friendly. The third cell had three white guys in it, and we went in.

We stood there watching the men, waiting for something to happen. There were eight bunks—steel shelves hung out from the walls on chains with thin pads on them, four on each side. The space between the bunks was about four feet. At the back of the cell, between the two bottom bunks, the builders had crammed in a lidless and seatless commode. A white guy lying on the top bunk near the door reading a book said, "You got your choice of those two next to the shitter and the one over there," pointing to the top bunk at the back. He turned a page and resumed reading.

We looked at each other and shrugged. Ireland collapsed onto a bottom bunk and hugged his blanket. I threw my blanket on the shelf across from Ireland. John threw his blanket on the top bunk. While Ireland groaned, John and I went back to the dayroom.

A dreamy-eyed, loopy young redneck told us that you just went to the bars and screamed out what you wanted when we asked him how you got to a phone or wanted medical attention.

"Who's listening? When you yell?" I said.

"I dunno," the loopy redneck said. "They hear you. Speaker talks back."

John walked to the bars and yelled, "Hey. We want to make phone calls."

Loopy came over to John and said, "They got one here." He pointed to a phone on a table. "Local calls only, though."

John nodded. "Thanks. I don't know anybody around here."

Loopy nodded and wandered off to sit with the guys watching the television through the bars.

"Hey!" John yelled into the hallway, his hands cupped to his mouth. "We want to make phone calls."

"Who wants to make phone calls?" a metallic voice said.

"Tillerman and Mason."

"Wait," the voice said.

"And Bob Ireland needs to see a doctor," John yelled.

No answer.

"Hey!" Loopy called. "This you guys?"

John and I looked over at Loopy. He was pointing to the television.

Me with my trusty Hiller, 1967.

The day I left for Vietnam,
August 1965.

Feasting in "Happy Valley,"
October 1965.

May 1966, after nine months in the Cav.

The day I got back from Vietnam.

With Patience and eight-year-old Jack on a camping trip in 1972.

This is Patience at the pump in 1978. We were living in the school bus.

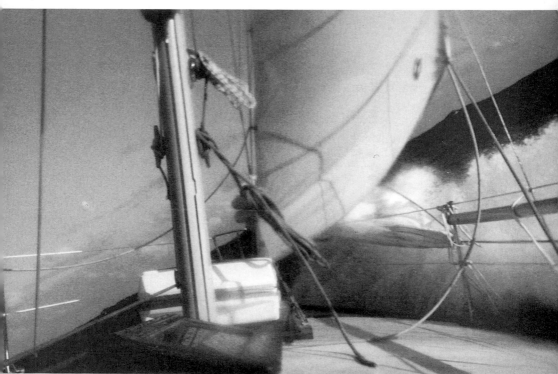

The *Namaste* handled storms well but needed constant maintenance.

At Eglin Prison, August 1983, my home for the next two years.

You couldn't see the picture unless you were nearly directly in front of the TV because you couldn't see through the closely spaced bars at an angle. I walked over while John yelled, "Hey! Can you hear me? Ireland needs to see a doctor!"

I saw the *Namaste* on television. She was moored among a bunch of other yachts at some marina in Charleston. Men wearing blue jackets were wrestling big bales of marijuana out of her and loading them into a van. The announcer said this was one of the biggest marijuana hauls in local history, three thousand pounds worth over two million dollars. "Wow!" Loopy said. "You guys are big-time!"

The big black guy seemed to agree. "Motherfucker!" he said, grinning. "You boys are in some serious fucking trouble!" I could see the respect shining in his eyes.

The drug-bust story ended and the television cut to a picture of a skinny, eerie-looking blond guy wearing glasses thick enough to be paperweights. The picture switched, showing chalked outlines of where bodies had been, zooming in on puddles of sticky blood on the floor of some stockroom while a voice-over said that this guy had killed his boss and co-worker at the Piggly Wiggly food store somewhere in Charleston. He was the Piggly Wiggly murderer. He'd shot his boss and his friend for their paychecks. A seriously dangerous, but stupid, guy.

"Hey!" John yelled into the hallway. "Where the *fuck* is anybody?"

"What's wrong with Ireland?" the voice from the speaker said.

"Something's bad wrong with his stomach," John yelled.

"Wait," the voice said.

We waited, sitting on one of the tables. In a couple of minutes we heard the door down the hall open. Suddenly all the guys who were lurking in their cells swarmed into the dayroom. Everybody was chattering, looking happy. Something was up.

"Chow time," Loopy said. Loopy had taken to hanging out around John and me, telling us what was what around here.

Two prisoners, trustees dressed in new blue uniforms, pushed a food cart up to the door. They began clanging down compartmented steel food trays on a shelf that stuck through the bars. The trays had stuff in them, sloppy, weird-looking kinds of stuff. I got one and looked at it: soupy rice sloshed around in a corner of the tray, a hot dog rolled around in the main compartment, and a dollop of turnip greens sat as an island in pale green juice next to a slice of wet white bread. When they'd delivered the trays, they began to ladle out Kool-Aid into plastic coffee cups you were supposed to have. Loopy, who was sitting across the table from me, said we could wash out one of the extra ones sitting back in the corner. I passed.

I made a sandwich of the hot dog and bread and ate. The hot dog was cold and rubbery. "This is terrible," I said to Loopy.

"Yeah," Loopy said, chewing eagerly while he nodded. "But they bring it regular."

After dinner Porter took me out the big door and down the hall to a phone hung on the wall. He stood about ten feet away while I made a collect call home.

Jack answered.

"Dad?"

I swallowed. Hearing my son call me that was about as much as I could take. Tears started to well in my eyes and I got mad at myself and blinked them back. I looked up to see if Porter was watching, but he wasn't.

"Yeah," I said. "It's me, Jack. Mom around?" My question ended in such a high pitch, my voice cracked. I coughed.

"No, Dad, she went to the store. You want me to have her call you when she gets back? Where are you anyway?"

"I'm—" I had to compose myself again. "I'm in Charleston."

"Charleston? You coming home?"

"Yes. I'm coming home in a few days. Listen, Jack. Tell Mom I'll call back later, maybe an hour. She'll be home in an hour?"

"Sure," Jack said. "Wow. She's sure going to be glad to know you're back, Dad."

"Yeah?" I said. "Well, okay. I'll call back soon. See you soon, Jack."

"Okay. Bye, Dad."

I walked to Porter and said, "I couldn't get who I wanted. Can I come back in an hour?"

"Sure," Porter said. "Just let 'em know in the wing."

"You mean that fucking screaming and yelling communications system you have?"

"Yeah. Intercom system," Porter said indignantly.

Back at the cell, I lay on my shelf and wished I could sleep. They'd finally come for Ireland and led him off bent over double. They said they'd take him to a hospital if they had to. I wanted to sleep to escape. But I couldn't. I'd gone beyond the point of no return, and probably I'd never be able to sleep again. I got up and found John in the dayroom. He was smoking a cigarette. "Where'd you get that?" I said.

"Loopy," John said.

"Hey, Loopy," I said. Loopy, who'd accepted this name without complaint, looked over at me, grinning. He pointed over his shoulder with his thumb at two guys holding a long tube they'd made from rolled-up newspapers. They'd carved a two-pronged fork out of a bar of soap and fitted that on the end of their four-foot paper pole. They were now slipping it out through the bars toward the television. "Yeah?" Loopy said.

"Can I borrow a smoke?"

Loopy bent his neck side to side, a limpy, goofy gesture that didn't mean yes or no. It meant maybe. "I dunno, I only got a couple left, Bob."

"I'll be getting some money, Loopy. I'll buy you a whole pack if you give me a cigarette."

Loopy nodded and I walked over beside him while he fished a pack of Winstons out of his shirt pocket. The guy with the paper stick fitted the soap bar over the tuner knob and twisted it. It had taken them a couple of hours to make this thing, and it was a pretty clever rig. The channel changed and everybody cheered. They flipped through the channels until they got to *Love Boat,* a show they all wanted to see. As the guy started pulling the stick back inside, it was suddenly yanked out of his hands.

"Got it!" Porter yelled. He swaggered into view, holding the stick. He'd been hiding up against the wall in the hallway, out of sight. "I told you, I pick what you see around here." Porter nodded sternly and broke the paper stick over his knee and stomped the soap bar to crumbs. He turned around and switched the channel back to channel four. I never figured out why Porter cared what channel we watched or why he preferred channel four. Life is filled with mysteries like Porter.

I followed Porter along the bars as he walked down the hallway to the door. "Porter," I said. "I'd like to make that call now."

"You got to ask the man," Porter said.

"The man?"

"Yeah, you got to ask them," he said, waving at the hallway in general.

"You mean I have to yell at some people I can't see when I can just ask you?"

"Yeah. That's the rules."

I stood there, hanging on to the bars, watching Porter walk through the door. This guy was serious. I yelled, "Hey! Hey, somebody. Mason wants to make a phone call!"

No answer. They never answered until you yelled for a long while. If they answered right away, then everybody'd be asking them for God knows what. I yelled two more times, louder each time.

"You just made a phone call."

"I didn't get who I wanted to get," I shouted.

"That's not my fault," said the voice.

"Look," I said. "Nobody in my family even knows I'm in jail. When I called before, it was my son. I want to talk to my wife."

"What?"

I could see this nitwit, sitting in some room somewhere with a microphone in front of him, bored out of his skull, snickering at what was probably the most interesting thing that would happen to him tonight, maybe this whole week.

"Look," I shouted, "I'm allowed to make a phone call, and I want to make it now. It's my right."

No answer. I was about ready to yell again when the voice said, "Okay. Wait." I guess he got tired of the game.

I went back to the table and sat next to John. "This is fucked, John. When do we see a damn lawyer?"

"The team's on it, Bob," John said. "I'm sure of it. They won't let us down."

Right. The team. How could I have forgotten? I turned to Loopy. "Loopy. Give me a cigarette."

Loopy shook his head. "You guys got no money," Loopy said. "And I've got almost no cigarettes left."

I stared at Loopy. "We're going to get money, Loopy. Tonight. Didn't you see our boat on TV? Two million dollars' worth of pot? We're big-time smugglers. We're fucking rich, Loopy. Give me a fucking cigarette."

Loopy did his side-to-side, twisting, nodding thing with his head that made you wonder if he had normal connections between his shoulders and his skull and said "I guess" and handed me his pack.

I lit up a cigarette and watched the stick-maker rolling up more newspaper. His buddy was carving another bar of soap with a plastic knife.

We heard the door open and I got up figuring it was Porter coming to take me to the phone, but it was Porter bringing in a new prisoner. Porter opened the door and this scrawny short blond guy with thick glasses stepped in and stared at us. Everybody was quiet because they all recognized him. This was the Piggly Wiggly murderer, for chrissakes. The guy shifted his eyes back and forth, magnified behind thick optics, giving him a nervous, owly look. He frowned and marched directly to a table at the back of the dayroom. Everybody at the table got up and left. The Piggly Wiggly murderer sat down with his back to the wall and stared at us. Everybody in the room stared back. Even the guy making the channel-changing stick stopped working to stare at this guy. Here he was, a guy who just a few hours ago blew away his boss and his friend to get their paychecks. The big question on most people's minds was, how did he plan to cash the checks? This guy was so stupid it took your breath away.

I was staring at the Piggly Wiggly murderer when I heard Porter call me. I could make that phone call now.

"**P**atience?" I said.

"Are you okay?"

I was blinking fast, trying to hold on. "Patience. I want you to know that if you decide to divorce me, I really do understand. I mean, they said I might get twenty-five years."

"Then I'll wait twenty-five years," Patience said. Her voice had the fire in it I'd come to respect when we ran our business together in Brooklyn. She'd been kind of shy when we first got to Brooklyn, but by the time we left she could take care of herself and keep fifty employees jumping, too. New York will do that to a person. "I'll get you out," she said. "I'll find out who to call." I nodded and croaked out "I love you" and said good-bye.

I walked along with Porter, feeling broken, back to the federal wing. I'd had it. Too much bad stuff for too long. How would we ever get through this? When Porter led me through the door, he noticed tears in my eyes. "My, my," Porter said. "Your woman musta been real mad, eh?"

I didn't answer. I walked into my cell and lay down on my shelf and pulled the ragged blanket up around my head. It is one thing to jeopardize yourself by taking risks, another to hurt other people in the process. I'd gone too far. I'd hurt Patience and Jack, my family, my friends. This pain was more than I'd felt in my life. Under the shroud of my blanket, I cried.

Two hours later, about seven that night, Porter told us our attorney had come.

John and I followed Porter along the hallway. Walking past an intersecting hallway, we saw Ireland, doubled up in pain, lying on the bare concrete floor. "Wait a minute, Porter," John said.

"C'mon," Porter said. "Keep moving."

"That's Ireland, our codefendant, Porter. He's supposed to be in the infirmary, not lying on your stinking floor," John said.

"The infirmary's too crowded right now," Porter said. "They'll take care of him."

John looked grief-stricken. As captain, his mission had failed, and now the enemy was mistreating one of his men. It was a heavy blow. Porter opened a door and told us to go inside.

The small room was filled with a table and four chairs. It was, however, a clean oasis in a filthy prison. There was a carpet on the floor and the walls were painted white. A man got up from the table, smiled at us, and said, "Dan Bowling. I'm your attorney."

Bowling looked the part. He wore a tweed jacket over a sweater, a silk tie, tan wool slacks, and brown loafers. He told us he had graduated from Harvard Law School five years before, and his specialty had become drug cases. "I guess it's because I'm the young attorney in the Charleston gang. Anyway, I get most of the referrals when we have a bust around here."

Bowling told us our friends, meaning the team, had hired him, through another attorney, that afternoon, and he knew most of the details of the case by talking to the DEA. "You guys were caught with your pants down, that's a fact," Bowling said, laughing. "But you were caught by Customs agents, and that may be illegal search and seizure."

"Why?" I asked.

"Because only the Coast Guard can stop people in U.S. waters without just cause. They can stop you to inspect your boat for safety items and stuff. If the Customs people had seen you coming in from beyond the three-mile limit, then they could have stopped you. But they didn't spot you until you were in the channel."

"You think that can get us off?" John said.

"Naw. It just means we have a point to argue. We'll make a motion that the marijuana, the evidence, was illegally obtained. If that works, they could still try you for the crime of smuggling and possession, but they wouldn't be able to use the pot as evidence." Bowling laughed. He clearly enjoyed his work. "Makes it tough for the prosecutors. Of course, the judge'll never rule in our favor, but the threat might help. Might be able to negotiate something with it."

"What about the missing five hundred pounds of pot?" I said.

"What?" Bowling said.

"Well, we had thirty-five hundred pounds on board. They claim we had three thousand."

Bowling shrugged. "Well, two things: can you prove you had that much and do you want to increase the severity of your crime by doing so?"

"The count was an estimate," John said. "We can't prove how much we had."

"Nor would you want to," Bowling said. "Let it be, gents."

We talked for about a half hour. John told Bowling about Ireland, wanted to know if he could get him taken care of. Bowling said he'd look into it. John said, "Great. And can you lend us ten bucks?"

Bowling smiled, got a bill out of his pocket, and handed it to John. "What're you going to buy here?"

"Cigarettes, candy, coffee," John said. "This place is the pits. They serve actual swill for meals. And look what they give us to wear."

"Hey, boys," Bowling said, "you guys are in jail in Charleston County, South Carolina. What do you expect?"

"How long?" John said.

"I'll have you out in four, five days. No problem."

They took Bob to a local hospital. He had a bad intestinal infection and stayed there overnight. When he came back the next night, he was pale but smiling. John and I gave him a box of instant-coffee packets we'd bought.

That night, at one in the morning, I woke up because somebody was pounding my shoulder. I looked up and saw a big black man, the guy we first met, leaning over me. He said, "Hey. You got any cigarettes?"

I fished out my pack from my pants pocket and handed it to the guy. He took about half the pack and returned the rest. "Light?" I handed him a book of matches and watched the flame light up his face. He was enjoying this. He threw me the matches and walked out of our cell.

We settled into a routine for the next few days. Time was measured by the passage of meals. Breakfast was usually watery grits, an egg, white toast. Lunch was often cold cuts and two slices of white bread. Dinner was invariably rice with some kind of meat: a hot dog, a hamburger patty, a piece of chicken. Between meals, I read. They had a short shelf of books including about ten Horatio Hornblower novels. I'd never read them, so I did now. I read every waking moment so I wouldn't have to think about being in a cage.

Two days later we were taken out of our cell, given our old clothes, which now really smelled like street garbage, and driven back to the courthouse to see the magistrate.

The magistrate set our bonds at one hundred and fifty thousand dollars each. Bowling objected, jumped up and said that the state of South Carolina had set our bonds for these same crimes at ten thousand dollars. A hundred and fifty thousand, Your Honor? As our hired advocate, Bowling put on a great show, turned to us and pointed out what nice-guys-gone-wrong we were (white, college-educated, middle class). The magistrate sighed, agreed to reduce our bonds to only seventy-five thousand each.

Seventy-five thousand dollars was much more money than I could understand. Bowling, in a private meeting at the courthouse, said that our friends wanted us to try to come up with the money ourselves because it would look bad if we just handed over that kind of cash. "They'd think you were part of some big organized crime syndicate or something."

"Organized? Nobody'd ever accuse us of that if they knew these assholes," I said.

So I called Patience and told her to try to raise money on our property. That was just wishful thinking. It was possible our ten acres were worth that much, but we owed over half that on our mortgage. The house—or rather, the unfinished cabin—was worth maybe ten thousand. Patience called my father.

Dad had come to my rescue when I had my car wreck in Portugal, and now he came through again. He agreed to guarantee my bond by putting up his condominium as security.

Bowling came to see us every day. One day he brought a document the government wanted us to sign, an inventory of the property confiscated on the *Namaste*. The list was surprising for the things not listed.

"Hey," John said, "half the stuff we had with us isn't even on here."

Bowling shrugged. "They'll insist it wasn't there."

"They can do that?"

"Sure. Who do you think the judge'll believe? You or them?"

The loran wasn't listed, which was fine with me. I wished them a long trip in bad weather with that loran. Any of the boat's stuff was fair game, I figured. But these guys had taken my shoes, my knife, my calculator, my notebook, and my camera, none of which was on the list. "I don't care about anything they got," I told Bowling, "except for my notebook and my camera."

"What's so special about them?"

"The notebook is important. I was making notes for my books."

"Yeah?" Bowling said. "You're a writer?"

"Yeah. When I'm not smuggling, I try writing."

Bowling laughed. "And the camera?"

"I had that during my whole tour in Vietnam. It's a good-luck charm. I have to have it back."

Bowling nodded. "I'll check on it."

"And we just ignore that they took all our stuff?" John said.

"That's right," Bowling said. "You start making noises about them stealing your personal stuff, and they'll be all over you like stink on shit. Let it be."

Let it be. Play the game nicely and maybe they won't play hardball.

Captain Horatio Hornblower was blasting the living shit out of a native village on some foreign shore with cannon fire from his ship when Porter yelled, "Mason."

"Yo." I never said "Yo" to anybody before I became a criminal.

"Cop here to take you to the courthouse."

John said, "What about Tillerman and Ireland?"

Porter shook his head.

I got up, breathless. Was it possible? Was I actually getting out of here?

Porter waited while I put my clothes back on for the second time and escorted me up to the reception area. The black deputy who had brought us here was waiting for me by the front door.

"Hello, Mason," he said, wrinkling his nose. "Well, you got a shave, but you still smell like shit."

I nodded. The deputy got out his handcuffs and cuffed me before we walked out to the car. Just regulations, he reminded me.

We said nothing during the twenty-minute ride to town.

A woman on the elevator at the courthouse glanced at me once on the ride up to the third floor. She quickly looked away. I was a stinking, handcuffed beast.

The elevator door opened and the first person I saw was my father. He stood in the hall smiling widely when he saw me. I couldn't move my face for fear I would burst into tears and humilate myself and him. I was in shock. I followed the deputy and just stared at my dad when we walked by him. His face dropped when he saw the grief on mine.

The magistrate said the deputy could take off my cuffs. I sat down while he explained that my dad had put up his apartment for my bail and what that meant. If I broke any of the provisions of my bail, the government would sieze my parents' property. Did I understand?

I nodded.

Would I agree to the restrictions of the bail? No travel outside my county without direct permission from him?

I said yes.

"Okay," he said. "The police will take you back to the jail so you can be processed out."

"Back to jail?" I said.

"Yes. To be outprocessed."

"Oh."

The deputy had to do something else, and while I waited for another cop, they put me in the holding cell down the hall. I paced around the cell for an hour, pissed off. I was technically free—why was I locked up?

Fred, the state cop I had met the night of the bust, came down the hall with a deputy. The deputy unlocked the door and Fred said, "Come on, Mason. I'll take you back to jail."

Fred cuffed me, for the sake of the deputy, but took the cuffs off when he stopped at a light a few blocks from the courthouse. "Seems silly to have you cuffed when you're a free man, don't you think?"

"Yes. Thanks." I reached into my shirt pocket and got a cigarette.

"How you feeling?" Fred said.

"Like I've been beaten to a pulp."

"Nobody hit you, did they?"

"No," I said. "These beatings are strictly self-inflicted."

I didn't have to go back to the cell. I just signed out. They gave me my wallet and my watch and my toothbrush. I walked out the glass doors. Nobody even noticed. Law: you are a crook and have to stay inside. Now you are a crook on bail: you may leave. The sun was setting. I looked up and saw my dad waving from a cab. I walked over and got in.

"I've got to catch a plane back to Fort Lauderdale," Dad said. "You want to ride along?"

"Sure. I'll have the cab take me to the bus station," I said.

We drove to the airport. I chattered like a machine gun, telling Dad about the bust and how Dave had fucked up and on and on with an intensity arising from the relief of release, I guess. Dad nodded, but didn't say anything. When I saw the airport signs, I said, "Well. I guess this is about the dumbest thing I've ever done."

My father looked at me, nodding grimly. "I'll say."

When he got out at the airport, I got out with him to say good-bye and to thank him for doing so much for me. I tried to hug him, something that is not done in my family. But he couldn't. As he walked into the airport, I said, "Thanks, Dad."

He nodded and smiled and disappeared into the airport lobby.

The cabby took me to the Charleston Greyhound bus stop at six. The clerk said the next bus to Jacksonville was leaving at eleven. I sat in the waiting room for five hours, feeling miserable. I was coming down with something. Maybe the flu. I had a fever, congestion, a cough. I wanted to sleep, but there's nothing in a Greyhound bus station but chairs.

At three in the morning, I was in Jacksonville waiting for a bus to take me to Gainesville.

At seven, I got off the bus in downtown Gainesville and saw Patience waiting outside the station. Her face lit up when she saw me.

She ran to me and we hugged. "Sorry I'm late," I said.

CHAPTER 21

I was knocked out of commission for a week with the flu. I believe now that it was my body's reaction to the stress.

One by one, our friends learned I had been arrested in South Carolina. They were amazed. I just didn't look like a smuggler, they said. I reminded them that murderers look normal, too, just to put their thoughts in perspective.

Patience wanted to quit the paper route because it was destroying the new Rabbit. We couldn't, that was our only income. We sold the school bus for $750, which kept us alive for another month.

Jack seemed unaffected when I sold the bus, his room. He was quite stoic. Patience had said he was shocked when she told him I'd been arrested. When I got home, he was reassuring and laughed at my stories of life in a county jail. He was protecting us, I believe. He didn't want us to feel any worse than we did.

I had a real problem concentrating. In the mornings I worked on my robot book because I believed, or hoped, that I could write and if I kept at it, I would eventually succeed. When I began to lose this conviction, Patience would remind me. If someone is working to support you by running a paper route and encourages you to stay home and plink on a typewriter, how can you not be a believer?

One afternoon my agent, Knox, called.

"Guess what?" Knox said. He sounded happy. He didn't know I'd been arrested.

"What?" I said.

"I just sold *Chickenhawk* to Viking. What d'you think of that?"

My heart jumped. The title was strange to hear. I'd sent the manuscript in untitled. A week later, I'd found the basis for the title in the manuscript. It came from a conversation I'd written between Jerry Towler and me in Vietnam about the contrast between being afraid to get into the battles and how you felt when you finally got into them. A chicken before the battle. A hawk during the battle. Chickenhawk. Somebody bought my book? "What?"

"I said I just sold your book to Viking!"

"I'll be a son of a bitch!" I yelled.

We laughed together on the phone for a while. This was really coming from behind. Knox had been trying to sell my manuscript for over nine months. I'd given up and put my energy into the robot book. Now what?

"You finish it," Knox said. "Your editor is a guy named Gerald Howard. He thinks a December deadline is about right. That okay with you?"

"Sure. I've got part one finished. Two to go. I think I can do it."

"Great," Knox said. "They're not paying you a whole hell of a lot for this, Bob. The advance, I mean. You're a complete unknown, and they don't even know if you can finish the book."

"I understand. I don't care how much they pay."

"Well, the advance is seventy-five hundred total. They'll pay you twenty-five hundred now, for the first part, and twenty-five hundred for each of the two parts you owe them upon delivery and acceptance."

I was quiet for a while and said, "Knox. Something's happened you should know about."

"What?"

"I got in trouble a few weeks ago. Big trouble."

"What kind of trouble?"

"I was arrested on a sailboat loaded with marijuana. Three thousand pounds of marijuana."

"Jesus, Bob. When you fuck up, you don't mess around, do you?"

"Yeah, I don't like to do things halfway. Do you think I should tell them? Viking?"

"Ah," Knox said, thinking. "Why don't we just not mention it for a while? When do you go to trial?"

"Sometime in March."

"Any chance you can get off?"

"Our lawyer says we'll lose the trial, but we might win the appeal. Might work, he claims. I think not."

"I'm really sorry, Bob," Knox said. He wasn't angry. He was concerned. We talked for a while, said good-bye. I hung up. I'm not a very excitable person, but I found that I was not able to stand still. I was overcome with joy. I began to jump up and down on the floor. Our dog, Chocolate, began to bark and dance around with me. Patience was working, Jack was in school. I jumped, hopped, and pirouetted all over the cabin. An hour later, I had found my copy of the manuscript buried in a cardboard box. I dusted it off and began reading it to see where I was.

Knox sent a thousand dollars as an advance on my advance.

Our trial was set for March. Bowling's strategy was to have a bench trial—because, he said, we would lose a jury trial anyway—and then appeal the decision. It wasn't what I had in mind. I imagined a jury listening to my background and seeing what led to my decision to get on the boat. Bowling said it would be pointless, that the jury had to follow the law: we were caught red-handed, the law said we were guilty as hell. I know now that a jury doesn't have to rule against you simply because you broke the law; they can free you, declare you innocent against all evidence to the contrary, if they believe circumstances ameliorate your actions. Peer review is the cornerstone of the American legal system. I didn't understand this then, and even if I had, I'd probably go with the team again. I was, after all, guilty. This was to be a team play, and I was one of the team.

I developed writing habits dictated by my environment. By noon, the attic was unbearable. We had insulation in the roof, but it wasn't sealed off with plasterboard, so the heat eventually seeped past the insulation and into the attic space, which was our bedroom and my office. I wrote on a glass tabletop set on plastic milk crates. Abe Weiner had given me the tabletop when I left Brooklyn. I sat on an old telephone operator's chair, which I'd assumed would be comfortable because telephone operators sit all day. I was wrong. They say women have more padding. I wouldn't know, but the chair made my ass numb in a couple of hours. I had written Knox that if he sold my manuscript, I was going to buy a new chair, but I didn't. I wrote for three hours in the morning and reviewed what I wrote in the afternoon, down-stairs.

When Patience came home around five, she'd immediately sit down and want to see what I had written that day.

"How'd it go today?" Patience'd ask.

"Shitty. I just can't seem to make it come out the way I think it."

"That must be tough," she'd say, and read the two or three pages and almost always say, "I can't believe you. This is terrific, Bob. This is going to be an important book."

I'd shrug this off in the cabin and go outside and grin. Without Patience's feedback and encouragement, I don't know what I would have done. Writing is real work with no immediate reward. The process seems ineffectual—you type all day and you're not a penny ahead for it. Patience goes to work and brings back money. I work for hours and all I have to show for it is two or three pages added to the stack. Maybe when I actually got some money for it—

When I got the contract from Viking and the first check, I finally believed I'd actually sold a book. My writing went easier because this book was sold. This was real. I took Patience and Jack out to dinner the day I got the check. It was a proud moment.

Now all I had to do was finish the book.

And get through the trial.

CHAPTER 22

"**A**ll rise. The Fifth District Federal Court is now in session. The Honorable Judge Solomon Blatt, Jr., presiding."

We'd met Judge Blatt earlier, when he had us come in to make sure we wanted to have a bench trial and that we wanted it together. He believed there were sufficient differences in our backgrounds and our involvement to warrant separate trials. We agreed to stand as a team. This was the solidarity of ignorant, self-perceived heroes, represented by a lawyer who was being paid by people whose interests were different.

Sol Blatt, Jr., then got on with it.

They called as witnesses the three Customs agents, who tried to make a case that they knew we'd come in from beyond U.S. territorial waters because our searchlight was so bright. However, the differences between the three men's testimonies was so great that Bowling easily discredited this theory.

The one piece of evidence that proved that we'd actually come in from abroad was a single universal plotting chart they'd found on the boat, one we missed throwing away. We knew the prosecution had this, but at the last moment the government changed prosecutors. The new prosecutor didn't know what they had or he didn't understand what it meant—it was just a piece of paper with pencil lines drawn on it. So far, there wasn't proof we were smugglers. Not that it made much difference. Possession and distribution charges were enough to send us to jail for a long time.

The Customs agents said that the reason they stopped us was they'd heard there was a mother ship coming in that night, and it might be serviced by sailboats. It was a rumor they'd heard.

Bowling made a case for illegal search and seizure based on the fact that there was nothing suspicious about the appearance of our boat— the lights were right, the waterline was right—and there was no evidence we were coming in from international waters. He moved that the case be dismissed on these grounds. The judge decided not to so decide.

Then the prosecution called one of the state cops to the stand. That cop told the judge we had sailed from Jacksonville on December 2, 1980, picked up the marijuana in Colombia, and spent a total of forty-four days on the trip. We were, indeed, smugglers.

John and I looked at each other. How'd they get that?

Then we heard them call Ireland to the stand.

He walked up to be sworn in, his shoulders sagging. Suddenly Ireland's sad looks before the trial made more sense. He'd talked during the postarrest questioning.

Ireland sat down. He glanced at John and me with a look of dread. He confirmed the cop's testimony, said we'd sailed to Colombia and picked up the marijuana.

Bowling then pointed out a rule of law that baffles me to this day. The rule states that if one of a group of defendants admits to committing a crime, his testimony cannot be used against the other defendants. I don't know why this is. I don't understand law. But it's true. The judge agreed. He announced that Ireland's testimony could not be used against defendants Mason and Tillerman, only against defendant Ireland.

The cops in the back of the courthouse groaned. They needn't have. Everything was going their way.

There wasn't much to this case. We were on a boat loaded with marijuana. They caught us. Our only defense was that they may have caught us illegally. The judge declared a recess until after lunch.

We ate at a restaurant near the courthouse. Dan Bowling bought, he being the only person with enough money. He said things were going fine.

"Fine?" I said. "We're going to be found guilty."

"Of course you are," Bowling said. "You *are* guilty. Now all we have to do is wait until sentencing and then appeal the case."

"You think we have a chance in hell?" John asked.

"Hell if I know. I know it's your only chance."

Ireland sat quietly with his girlfriend, Donna. He wouldn't look John or me in the eye. I wanted to tell him I understood. Shit, he'd been up for three days, he'd been sick, they'd put the pressure on. The only thing he neglected, I thought, was going ahead and telling them where Dave and the gang lived. I mean, as long as he was going to talk, why not stick it to Dave? As it was, the only person he hurt was himself.

It only took a half hour for Blatt to finish up after lunch.

Guilty.

John and I were guilty of possession and possession with the intent to distribute. Ireland was guilty of smuggling an illegal substance, possession, and possession with the intent to distribute. It made sense. Everyone knew we were all three on the same boat, but only Ireland was the smuggler. Law is fun.

It didn't hit too hard. We knew we were guilty. And the way Bowling had described it, we seemed to be right on track with some incredibly clever Harvard lawyer trick. Shit, we had the government right where we wanted them. Blatt said we could continue on our bonds and come back in August for sentencing.

I wrote every morning and carried a notebook around with me wherever I went, scribbling notes when I remembered something that I had to put in the book. I wanted to deliver the second part of the manuscript before I was sentenced in August so if Judge Blatt let me go to New York, my editor would have seen it. Patience and I wanted to continue on from Charleston after sentencing, drive to New York on our way to her mother's cabin in Maine.

While I was writing the second part of the book, I wanted to talk to somebody else who was in Vietnam with me. I missed Jerry Towler. He and I had flown together most of our tours. I wrote him a letter and sent it to the Pentagon, requesting that they forward it.

Tension was tearing me apart. My nightly jump-ups were back as severe as ever. I'd leap awake with a pulse rate of 140 or more two or three times a night. The idea that I was actually going to go to jail made me feel sick. I went to the Veterans Administration and asked for help. They gave me Valium and enrolled me in a biofeedback program that was designed to teach me relaxation techniques.

My life was writing and thinking about Vietnam while trying desperately to achieve peace of mind. I began to read books on metaphysics, philosophy, Zen, in my quest for mental peace. I discovered Alan Watts's books. *The Book* was very good, and I systematically read almost everything Watts had written. I loved concepts like: "When you die, you will wake and realize you were never born." Great stuff. Just try applying it to daily life. Zen was more appealing. I discovered some peace through meditation. I also discovered a different way of looking at reality which I still find useful. It was a revelation to me that Zen was just "direct pointing," looking at yourself, your surroundings, the universe for what they really were—illusions, interpretations of sensory input inside your own head. I liked that. Then I worried *who* was doing the interpretations and what *was* who? However, I was thinking. The problem gave life an interesting perspective and helped to divert my thoughts from my troubles.

I finished the second part of my book before we went to Charleston. I called it "Swave and Deboner" because that's how the combat helicopter pilots referred to themselves in Vietnam. We lived in the mud, in tents, like any other grunt, but aviation was supposed to be glamorous. Suave and debonair.

Sentencing was very tough on us because our families came to testify as character witnesses. We waited in the hallway outside the courtroom until we were two hours past our scheduled appearance. John and I had told Ireland we understood, held no grudge, but he was sheepish around us. He really harbored a lot of guilt about talking to the police.

When we finally got in the courtroom, the judge was just finishing up a previous defendant. This guy had been caught smuggling pot for the third time. Blatt listened to a tearful and extended plea from the man's wife and promptly sentenced him to five years in a penitentiary. The guy started yelling at Blatt and had to be dragged from the courtroom in handcuffs.

Blatt apologized to us for the delay and announced a recess until after lunch. My mother-in-law, Constance Hartwell, and my father had flown in on my behalf, and worried that their planes were leaving soon.

I sat in a restaurant across from my mother-in-law and my father. I couldn't eat. My mind roiled with excuses that I thought should be heard. I kept saying that pot shouldn't be illegal in the first place. My mother-in-law said, "But it is, Bob."

She was right. And before they'd finished eating, I'd managed to recognize that even if marijuana was legal, I still would've been guilty of illegal trafficking of a controlled substance. People still go to jail for smuggling alcohol and cigarettes. So when I went back to the courtroom, it was with the hope that Judge Sol Blatt, Jr., would somehow read my mind, see my fear and regret, take pity on my racked and bruised soul, and, in light of all this, not throw me into prison. Maybe he'd make me do work in my community for a few years. What I wanted was just one damn break from the government, please.

When the court reconvened, the judge asked us each to come forward with our character witnesses.

John's father humbled himself before the judge and told him his son was a veteran of Vietnam, and he was sure this was an isolated mistake. Couldn't he give him a break?

My mother-in-law and my father did the same thing. And then Patience stood before Blatt and said, her voice trembling, "Your Honor. My husband didn't want to do this. He thought he had to do it to provide for his family. I know him to be an honorable man who has made this one mistake." Her voice cracked. I looked over. Tears ran down her cheeks as she said, "He's sorry, Your Honor."

Blatt wanted to know what I had to say. My head buzzed. I had a lot to say. I wanted to go through this whole thing more carefully. I wanted people to know my motives, my troubled thoughts, I wanted people that were deciding my fate to know *me*. I stared at Sol Blatt, Jr. His face showed he was unhappy, too. I saw also that he was braced to deliver justice, even if it was painful to him, too. I said, simply, hopelessly, "I'm sorry I made the trip, Your Honor."

When we finished, my father and my mother-in-law excused themselves because they both had to catch flights back home. We went back to our seats.

Blatt then made a short speech about how he hated to see the effects of the drug culture on people like us. He said that he, too, was a combat veteran, World War II, and he felt a strong empathy toward John and me. He added that, from the facts of the case, it was obvious that we were rank amateurs.

I felt my pulse racing in my temples. I was afraid I'd pass out, I was so excited. This was one of those long preambles that leads to the big word: *But*. Finally Blatt said that despite all this, we had indeed done the deed. And he was not going to let people smuggle drugs into South Carolina and get away with it.

He read the sentences. John Tillerman, the captain of the boat—seven years in a minimum-security federal prison. Robert Ireland, the only defendant convicted of smuggling—six years at a minimum-security federal prison. Robert Mason, agreed to be a minor figure in the crime, Blatt's most lenient sentence—five years in the minimum-security prison closest to my home.

Five years.

I knew of murderers who'd gotten less. I knew of rapists who'd gotten less. In Miami and New York, they give people suspended sentences for similar crimes. First offense? Five years?

Bowling immediately stood up and said we were going to appeal the case on the grounds that the government illegally stopped and searched us. Blatt said fine, good luck. Bowling asked that we be allowed to remain free on our bonds. Blatt agreed. Bowling asked if Patience and I could travel to Maine to vacation and work.

"What kind of work?" Blatt asked.

"Your Honor, Mr. Mason has sold a book he's writing about his experiences in Vietnam."

"Really? I'd like to read that." Blatt looked at me. "When does it come out?" The man had just sentenced me to prison and now we were making small talk?

"Ah, I don't know, Your Honor. I haven't finished it."

"Fine. I'm sure I'll hear about it. Yes, you have my permission to go to Maine. Good luck, Mr. Mason."

In the hallway outside the courtroom, we asked Bowling what these sentences meant. How long would we actually stay in jail?

"Normally," Bowling said, "you can figure serving about a third of the sentence. Two, two and a half years, I'd guess."

"What about the appeal? How long will that take?"

"Months. Maybe a year."

"What do we do while we're waiting?"

"Anything you want—as long as you don't violate your bail."

Bowling said he had something for me at his office. Patience and I stopped there on the way out of town. He led me into his office and pulled my camera out of his desk drawer. "Just showed up," he said. "Imagine that." I thanked him. Some cops might be crooks, too, but at least they respected a man's talismans. Besides, it was an old camera. My notebook, however, was gone for good.

By three in the afternoon, Patience and I were on the highway headed for New York City.

I was giddy with happiness, chattering away like a hyperactive kid while Patience drove. Jack had stayed home, busy with his job and his girlfriend, Wallie. I guess I was in shock. We stopped at a motel after dark. I called my mother and told her the verdict. She became hysterical, shrieking things about Patience being the cause of it all. She was in the midst of saying a lot of nasty things I knew she really didn't mean when I hung up. I was a mother's innocent son. I told Patience: "It's great practice in realizing that words are only sound waves."

The next morning I was no longer chattering and happy; I was quiet and morose. We picked up a Charleston paper and saw a small write-up about our conviction. We wondered if the Florida papers would mention it.

We spent one more night on the road so we'd get to the city in the morning. I'd called Knox and told him we were coming.

We drove through Brooklyn, took a ride around the old mirror factory. It was just a warehouse again. Mirage was closed.

Knox's office was in Greenwich Village. We got to his place around ten. His wife, Kitty Sprague, let us in. Knox beamed and said, "Author, author." I smiled, but after the reality of the sentencing, being an author just paled to insignificance. "Thanks, Knox. By the way, I just got sentenced to five years in prison. You think you could lend me three hundred bucks?"

"You're broke?" Knox asked.

"Yep. Twenty-five hundred doesn't last as long as it used to."

"Where you going from here?"

"Thought I'd go meet my editor at Viking and then Patience and I are going to Maine."

"You going to work up there or are you going to fuck off?"

"No time to fuck off. I can work there as well as anywhere."

Patience parked near a fire hydrant on a side street in the middle of New York City and waited for me. I walked into a huge building on Madison Avenue and took the elevator up to the Viking Penguin floors. While I waited in the reception area, I felt a lot like a poor relation visiting a rich uncle. After a minute, Gerald Howard came out. He was a young guy, younger than he'd sounded on the phone. He still didn't know about my arrest and he looked to me then like someone who'd turn pale if he knew he was talking to a convicted felon. We went to his office.

We chatted. Gerald sat in front of a window overlooking the city. I could see a corner of Central Park in the distance. The differences between our worlds were profound, but we had an overlapping interest—*Chickenhawk*. By some strange process that I still don't understand, my manuscript came to be read by someone who liked it and could do something about publishing it. Gerald Howard was the right man at the right time. He was a young editor in the Penguin paperback division, and he wanted to be a hardback editor for Viking. This was to be Howard's first hardback book. He had just gotten the second part of my book a couple of days before and had already read it. I was relieved to hear him say it stood up to the first part, was even, in fact, better.

While Howard talked, I was distracted and made poor conversation. The fact that I'd just been sentenced to prison wouldn't leave me. I kept thinking about Patience waiting downstairs, and felt conscious of the time. I told Gerry, as he insisted I call him, that I was happy he liked my book, but that Patience was the real writer in the family. She'd be famous someday. I looked at my watch and said I really ought to be going and how soon did he think Viking would be sending me a check.

"I'll get them to expedite the check," Gerry said. "Knox says you're broke."

"That's a fact. And—" I almost said *and going to jail,* but I was afraid they'd change their minds. I shrugged.

"Well, that's going to change," Gerry said. "I have a good feeling about this book."

Gerry walked me back to the reception area and we said good-bye.

By dusk the next day, Patience and I were in a cabin on a lake in Maine.

Patience has lots of relatives, and they all come to Maine in the summer. Aunt Priscilla stayed two cabins down the shore, Aunt Pat lived two cabins up the shore. Uncle Roger lived across the lake. Patience's brother Chris lived up the road year-round; her sister Vickie, also a permanent resident, lived three miles away. They all knew me because Patience and I had been here while I was in the Army, before and after Vietnam. Now they knew I'd been convicted, was going to jail, and also that I'd sold a book. Nobody, including me, knew how to act, proud or ashamed.

I had my electric typewriter and a pack of paper. That's all it takes to be a writer. I worked at the kitchen table in the cabin. And as long as I worked, I felt okay. I began part three, which I called "Short Timer's Blues." This was a tough one to remember. Near the end of our tours, the pilots were just plain overworked. I and my buddy, Jerry Towler (who I was calling Gary Resler in the book because I still hadn't heard from him), had each flown close to a thousand missions by the time we'd transferred to the Forty-eighth Aviation Company, called the Blue Stars. As we got closer to our departure date, and as the missions got hotter and hotter, and when the Army forgot about their promise to rotate short-timers back to ass-and-trash duty in Saigon and other places, I began to have real problems: hallucinations. I saw my electric razor burst into flames—as real as life—in the mosquito netting over my cot one night near Dak To. I had weird periods when I'd lose my balance while I walked. I had temporary blackouts when I'd see my face suddenly an inch from the page of a book I was reading and not know how I got there. I was losing it.

And now I was losing it in Maine.

I'd quit writing after lunch and go for walks in the woods with Patience. It was no good. I'd walk a few hundred feet and get breathless.

I felt like a deflated balloon. All my strength left me when I tried to relax. I stayed in the cabin and read. I was reading *The World According to Garp*, which I liked very much. In the evenings, Vickie and her husband, Peter, usually came down to the cabin and we sat around and talked. I played chess with Peter.

When everybody went home, when Patience and I went to bed, I'd sit bolt upright against the headboard, unable to sleep. My pulse raced. I had chest pains. My hearing would mysteriously fade in and out, like someone switching the balance on a stereo. I tried the meditation tricks the VA had taught me. I could relax every muscle in my body to absolute biofeedback perfection and still feel undefined panic take over.

For two months I wrote every morning, read every afternoon, and panicked when it was quiet and I was alone with myself. Even Alan Watts's heartening words about life, the universe, and everything were of no comfort.

In October Patience started cleaning houses in Gainesville to make ends meet.

By Christmas 1981, I'd finished the manuscript and sent it to Viking. Gerry Howard called. He'd found out I was going to jail by reading the last page of the manuscript. He told me he was behind me all the way and so was Viking. He told me that the editing process would take a while—he expected the book would get to the stores sometime early in 1983, over a year after I'd finished it.

I got a letter from Jerry Towler. He sounded just like he had in Vietnam. I don't know why that was so surprising except that sixteen years had passed since I'd last seen him. He said he and his wife, Martie, were taking their two sons to Disney World and why didn't they stop by? I wondered how to break the news to my long-lost brother-in-arms that I was soon to be a convict.

A week later, Jerry called. They were in High Springs. Patience and I drove into town to show them the way to our cabin. When I saw him sitting in his car, I noticed he'd changed. He used to be a young, skinny guy; now he was older, thicker. He remarked that I'd changed, too. In just a few minutes, the changes became invisible and the guy I'd flown with was back, grinning the same impish grin. He introduced me to Martie and his two sons, Greg and Ryan, and we got back into our cars and drove out to the cabin.

I gave them a tour of our woods. I'd cut a mile and a half of trails through it and considered the whole woods a home. Certain clearings were like rooms to me. I showed them the local plants and bugs and especially the spiders. Huge orb weavers, called banana spiders by the locals, and Nephila clavipes in spider books, were special to me. I'd been studying them for years. Their silk is the strongest natural fiber in the world and is used to make string and fishnets in Central and South America. Martie was decidedly unimpressed, even when I showed her you could stick your finger right up to the face of one of these three-inch spiders. "See, it won't bite. Not unless you grab it," I said. Martie shuddered and wondered if we could go back to the cabin now.

We had lunch and talked for the few hours they could spare. I kept trying to think of some smooth way to break the news that I was soon going to jail, but I couldn't. I decided to let Jerry read about it. I promised that I'd have Viking send him an advance copy. "Yeah. Then it's too late for me to make it right," Jerry said.

"I know. Too bad we didn't find each other sooner."

"I bet you didn't even mention how many times I saved your life," Jerry said.

"You saved my life?" I said. I turned to Martie. "Martie, you wouldn't have this guy as a husband or those two handsome boys if it wasn't for me being there to keep him from killing himself trying to fly that helicopter."

"Now I know who to blame," Martie said with a grin.

When they drove away, I felt guilty. Jerry and Martie were the epitome of the middle-class, hardworking, honest American family and I was a convicted drug smuggler.

Editing was completed by June 1982, and Viking published a bound galley they sent out to reviewers. I made a few changes in the galley, including the fact that Jerry had gotten shot down during the Ia Drang Valley campaign, spent the night on the ground with the grunts, was nearly overrun in an all-out Viet Cong attack. I'd forgotten that until Jerry talked about it on his visit.

I started working on my robot book again.

My lawyer called to say the district court of appeals had decided not to overrule Judge Blatt's decision. The vote was three to two. The next step was to take it to the U.S. Supreme Court. "You won't get a hearing there," Bowling said.

"So what's the point?" I said.

"The outside chance they'll hear it," Bowling said. "And you're free until they decide."

John and I argued over whether we should continue the appeal. I was in favor of checking into jail now and getting it over with. John said that if a shred of hope remained, he wanted to wait to see what happened. Patience wanted me with her, too. I wasn't courageous enough to go to jail, so I waited.

CHAPTER 23

August 1983. *Chickenhawk* was officially published.
A first copy came from Gerry by Federal Express. I opened
the package. I'd seen the cover, I'd seen the jacket copy, but seeing
my manuscript as a fresh-paper, wet-ink actual hardbound book gave
me a shot of adrenaline. I put it on a bookshelf with some other books
and waited for Patience to come back from shopping. When she got
home, I pretended to be busy at the table, and said, "Hand me that
dictionary, will you? You know, the one over there." I pointed to the
bookcase. She walked over, looking for the dictionary, and saw *Chickenhawk*. She squealed with delight, grabbed the book, and came over
and punched me in the stomach. It was a happy moment.

I had the book in my hands, but it wasn't yet in the stores. Viking
had sent out review copies. Whether anyone would hear about it was
now up to the reviewers.

Robert Wilson published the first review of *Chickenhawk* in *USA
Today*. Wilson was impressed when I said, about the men in the burn
ward I visited, "I saw 18-year-old boys with their faces burned away,
bright pink skin stretched over strange, stunted noses. Had someone
photographed the men there, twisted and deformed with featureless
faces, by the hundreds, the war might have ended sooner. But probably

not." The cynicism of the last line struck Wilson and he went on to say, "If I sound just a little overwrought, I defy you to read this straight-forward, in many ways underwrought, narrative and feel any dif-ferently."

These first reviews took my breath away. John Del Vecchio (author of *The Thirteenth Valley*) said in the *Philadelphia Inquirer*, "*Chickenhawk* had me trembling in my seat—fidgeting—wanting it to stop—wanting to get those guys up, off the LZs. Powerful scenes in this personal narrative . . . made me cry. By the time I was a third into this book, it had me."

Larry Heinemann (author of *Close Quarters*) titled his Chicago *Sun-Times* review HACKING IT IN A HUEY: A SUPERB MEMOIR OF VIETNAM.

I had always imagined reviewers laughing at my feeble attempts to be a writer. This was amazing. And not one of these reviews mentioned my legal problems and that I was on my way to prison.

The man I figured would be my toughest reviewer, Towler (still known as Resler in the book), sent me a letter. Towler would know if I'd gotten it right. He'd also now know all about my secret life as a crook. The following is an extract of that letter:

I must say I was stunned in what I read in the last two chapters. I laughed and I cried throughout your book and I truly had a hollow, sickly feeling when I finished it.

I too had dreams that would wake me up at night in a cold sweat. I guess I would jump so much that occasionally Martie would have the bruises to show it. Fortunately, I was able to adjust, but then, I had my flying to come back to. You know, I have never been out of aviation since my first solo in flight school. I can't imagine what I would have done if I was suddenly grounded.

What you have accomplished with *Chickenhawk* should make you jus-tifiably proud. I know it can never make up for all the suffering you have endured both during and after Vietnam, but hopefully this book has been your therapy. You no longer need to house all those nighmares within. You've let it out for yourself to look at objectively and hopefully others will do the same for themselves when they read it.

I know I don't have to tell you that someone else suffered, in her own way, right at your side through those many traumatic years and in many ways went through her own private war. I knew by our many conversations in Viet Nam just how much strength your love for Patience and your son provided you when our world seemed like a nightmare. I felt I knew Patience like a brother in Nam and in many ways I envied you. I would watch you read the same letters sometimes five or six times a day. You always carried one from her in your breast pocket.

I pray to God your appeal in court will have a favorable outcome. You've served your time and then some. I hope this country can accept that. I know you never had strong feelings toward the Almighty but I feel he let you survive for a reason, two of them being your loved ones, the next so that your story could be told. You have made yourself and all of us proud, so take strength in those who love you and your friends who respect you. You'll always be a Hawk in my eyes.

Your Buddy,
Resler

The next day, Dan Bowling called to tell me the Supreme Court had refused to hear our appeal.

"Now what?" I said.

"The Bureau of Prisons will be in touch. Count on it. Could be a month. Could be a few days."

Knox called me on the morning of August fourth. "I'm sure you don't get the *New York Times* down there in the swamps."

"I've heard some people saw one in Gainesville, couple years ago."

"Great. You have just been reviewed by Christopher Lehmann-Haupt in the *Times*. And it's a great review. Got a minute?"

"Sure."

Knox read me the review.

Lehmann-Haupt started by calling *Chickenhawk* a "remarkable journal based on a year spent flying assault helicopters . . . in Vietnam." He said, "So compelling are Mason's technical details that only by subliminal degrees do we become aware of his mounting battle fatigue." He ended the review this way:

I wish I could close by quoting in full one of the scenes in which Mr. Mason demonstrates his use of detail . . . But each of these scenes is too long to be quoted in full. Besides, it is the even longer combat scenes that catch the real flavor of *Chickenhawk*. It is to combat that Bob Mason is always drawn, no matter how frightened he feels . . . And in that paradox lies the terror of his hypnotic narrative. It is combat that becomes his natural environment. Combat becomes the only habitat in which he feels alive. Combat possesses his dreams long after he has left the war. And in realizing this, he discovers that he has gone quite mad.

I was stunned. Lehmann-Haupt seemed to get it, and I was happy that I'd gotten through.

To illustrate the power of the *Times,* at noon the same day the review came out a producer from the *Today* show called. She wanted to know if I could be on the show. I said I'd have to check with Judge Blatt, I'd let her know. By two o'clock, *People* magazine and *Time* magazine had called to arrange interviews. By late in the day, a clerk from Sol Blatt's office called me to say that the judge had no objection to me traveling to New York since it was part of my work, but, the clerk stressed, when I was assigned a date to go to prison I had to report immediately, no matter what television show I was scheduled to be on.

Suddenly everybody knew I'd written a book. Almost none of them knew I was also going to jail. None of the reviews mentioned my pending incarceration. The *Today* show people found out when I told the producer that my trip was subject to clearance by a judge.

Towler insisted on flying down from Michigan to help out while all this was going on. He wanted to see what I was going to wear on television. I showed him a blazer I had bought years before in New York. Storage in our cabin had spawned several colonies of mildew. "You can't wear that on the *Today* show!" Jerry insisted.

"Why not? Most of the stains are on the pocket and on the back. I'll be sitting down."

"C'mon, take me into town. You need something to wear. I'm not going to let you embarrass helicopter pilots."

We went to Penny's and Jerry helped me pick out a new blazer, some shirts, pants, and a tie. Knowing I had very little money, he insisted on buying this stuff for me.

That night Jerry brought out a box of slides he'd taken in Vietnam. We saw ourselves, two skinny kids again, filling sandbags for our bunker at Dak To; touring a village where a kid tried to sell me a dead baby; in the cockpit of our Huey; making coffee next to our helicopter in a rice paddy. Time travel. He showed a slide of me standing on smooth red clay, staring into the camera. I didn't remember being there. Jerry said it was taken after the battle at Plei Me, didn't I remember? No. I recognized that it was Plei Me; but I couldn't remember the picture being taken. I couldn't remember being there. Behind me were a score of Vietnamese bodies, men who'd been hit with 20mm cannon fire from strafing American fighters. They were eviscerated, beheaded, twisted, and horrible. I didn't remember it at all. If it wasn't for the slide, I'd still say I hadn't been there. I wondered what else I'd forgotten.

We stayed up until early morning talking. I realized that Jerry and I had become brothers through our shared experience in that war.

The next day, when I did a book signing at Goering's in Gainesville, a *Time* photographer showed up, too. Jerry and Patience stood behind the photographer goofing it up to make me smile. I was feeling the exhilaration that comes from such attention. I'd never had so much recognition in my life.

Jerry left the next day, satisfied that I was prepared for my New York trip. He told Patience that if she needed anything, call.

The court called. I had to report to Eglin Federal Prison at Eglin Air Force Base, Florida, on Friday, August 19. I'd have just enough time to go to New York.

I flew to New York on Monday the fifteenth. I cabbed to the hotel where NBC puts up its talk-show guests. I had phone messages—a reporter from a paper in Texas, another from my childhood home area newspaper, the Palm Beach *Post-Times*, and several others. I did phone interviews for a couple of hours. Then I walked down the street to a restaurant to meet Gerry Howard and some other Viking Penguin people. I met my publicist, my copy editor, and the assistant publisher over a meal. I don't recall what I ate. I don't recall what I said.

After dinner, Gerry took me to a nice bar and wanted to know if I needed more money. I said an extra couple thousand'd be nice. He said, "How about another seventy-five hundred?"

At six-thirty Tuesday morning a young woman, a publicist, picked me up at the hotel and took me to the NBC studios.

I sat in a barber chair while a guy put makeup on my face.

I sat in the Green Room holding a cup of coffee, watching the monitor. The producer told me Bryant Gumbel had read most of my book. Over film clips of helicopters flying in Vietnam, a voice said,

"Coming up, Robert Mason, author of the new best-selling book, *Chickenhawk.*"

"Where'd they get the best-selling bit?" I said.

The publicist shrugged. "Can't hurt."

I was so excited that I was beginning to lose track of reality. I followed a guy into the studio in an apprehensive trance. I sat in a chair behind a desk. The guy next to me leaned over and said he was Bryant Gumbel. "I know this is strange to you, Robert, but just try to act naturally."

I nodded. Three huge television cameras stared at me. I saw a commercial playing on one monitor, Gumbel and me on another, and a close-up of my face on another. My eyes looked puffy, but my new blazer and tie looked okay. I saw a script roll through the prompters on the cameras, Gumbel's lines. I realized then that millions of people, no exaggeration, were going to be watching. I had no lines.

Somebody said, "Five seconds, Bryant." The camera light blinked red. Gumbel asked a question. I answered. We did this for five minutes. I don't know what I said. I do remember the last question, though.

"Robert," said Gumbel, "I understand something special is happening to you in a few days."

I nodded. "Yes, Bryant. Friday I'm going to prison."

CHAPTER 24

The prison had sent us a letter telling us what we were allowed to bring. I decided to take everything they allowed, whether I had it or not. I bought a bamboo flute and a tennis racket simply because I was allowed to have them.

People magazine, interested in the writer-going-to-prison slant, sent writer David Chandler and photographer Lynn Pelham to interview me the day before I was due to report to Eglin. Pelham had me pack up a bag and walk out the door so they could show Patience and Jack waving good-bye: Dad marches off to jail. They promised they'd see me at Eglin to complete the story: Dad arrives at jail.

Patience and I drove over and picked up John and Alice and then drove a short distance to say good-bye to my parents. Dad had retired a few months before, had bought a little seven-acre farm near us, and puttered around growing vegetables and raising chickens, pigs, and cows.

My father was stoic, my mother was in tears. I told them I'd be back soon.

We drove two hundred miles to Fort Walton Beach and found a seaside motel. This was my treat. Gerry Howard had come through with more money against future royalties. They'd sold out the first printing of *Chickenhawk* (five thousand copies); we'd already made back my advance.

I wanted to spend my last night savoring freedom, eating a nice meal, making love. I couldn't taste what I ate. I couldn't seem to concentrate on anything. The fact that I was going to voluntarily walk into a prison the next day produced emotions too powerful to ignore. I felt like I had just before the assaults in Vietnam. I felt myself falling into a dark abyss.

The next day at noon, we drove to the main entrance of Eglin, the largest Air Force base in the world. The guard at the gate asked us what we wanted. I told him we were checking into prison.

The guard looked at me and smiled. "You the helicopter pilot? The guy who wrote the book?"

"Yep," I said.

"Pleased to meet you, sir," the guard said. He stood back and saluted. I returned the salute and drove on.

In one small corner of this huge military installation is a small group of buildings called the Eglin Federal Prison Camp. The camp was indistinguishable from the other buildings on the base. There were no fences, no walls, no guard towers. Just a cluster of buildings with a sign out front. We walked into the administration building. A guy dressed in blue asked us what we wanted.

"We're checking in," I said.

"Everybody's at lunch," the man said. "Take a seat."

We sat.

After lunch, a man came down the hallway. "Robert Mason and John Tillerman?"

"Yessir."

"Welcome to Eglin Prison Camp, men." The man, Captain Raulings, looked at Patience and Alice and said, "You should say good-bye to your ladies now. They can come visit you tomorrow. Visitors can come Saturday and Sunday."

I hugged Patience while tears spilled down her cheeks.

I stood in the hall with my bag and my tennis racket and my bamboo flute, feeling like a recently orphaned immigrant.

"Okay, men," Captain Raulings said. "Let's check in."

While we filled out forms in a small room, Captain Raulings came in and said that the warden wanted to see me. "The warden never sees new prisoners," he said. "You must be a real fuckup."

Although everybody called the head of Eglin Prison Camp a warden, he was officially a superintendent. Superintendent Robert Honsted had a large office. He invited me to sit.

"Mr. Mason," he said, "because of all the publicity about you coming here, you are what we call a high-profile prisoner. That means we have to treat you differently than the rest of the prisoners. You won't be allowed to work on the Air Force base like most of the prisoners do. You'll be confined to the camp. We don't want reporters interfering with day-to-day prison business, as might happen if you're out on the base, in public."

I said I understood, though I thought the designation *high profile* was a little extreme.

"What was the name of that book you wrote?"

"Chickenhawk."

"Is it any good?"

"I guess so."

"Maybe I'll buy a copy." Honsted stood up. I got up. "Okay, Mr. Mason. Good luck."

When I returned to the inprocessing routine, a guard checked my bag. When he found four large vials of Valium he just grinned and said, "Nice try."

"They're from the VA. I need them," I said.

"Naw. You won't need this junk here. We'll get you nice and healthy with good clean excercise."

I also had a dozen bottles of Maalox the VA had given me for my constant heartburn. I'd gone in and told the shrink who I'd been seeing for a couple of years that I was going to jail and asked if she could give me a bunch of my Valium and Maalox. She'd said sure, and I had eight hundred pills with me. The guard said they'd send them home.

An hour later we stepped out the other side of the administration building as processed, numbered, blue-uniformed federal prisoners. John and I wore blue work clothes with pants that didn't come within six inches of the ground, wearing work boots, carrying our stuff in grocery bags. A guard named Thompson, rotund and cherub-faced, led us down a sidewalk toward a low green building he said was Dorm Three. I heard the loud roar of a jet and turned to watch an F-16 fighter making a nearly vertical takeoff. The camp was about a mile from the main runway.

"Whatever you do, boys, be sure you are at your bunks during the count. Don't fuck up."

"When's the count?" John said.

"They announce them on the loudspeakers. Everybody's expected to be in their space. If you're not, you're in big trouble. Now, here in Dorm Three—everybody starts out in Dorm Three—you just got a bed. You're expected to be standing at the foot of your bed during each count except the counts after lights out. At night, you're allowed to be in your bed."

Dorm Three was a low, old, and uneven frame building. "Everybody starts out here?" I said.

"Yeah. You live here for a few months and then they'll assign you a cube in one of the other dorms."

"A cube?" I said.

"Yeah. You'll see. Four by seven feet, shoulder-high partitions, a bed and a chair." Thompson shrugged. "Cube."

Dorm Three was like an oven, the air hot and humid. The ceilings were low. The walls were green. The floors were waxed linoleum tile buffed to a brilliant shine. The long building was divided into four sections: A, B, C, and D. Thompson led us to section A and showed John his bed, the lower bunk of a bunk bed. Then he led me to section D and showed me mine. "Enjoy," Thompson said as he left.

I stared at the bunk. This was time travel back to my days as a private in basic training. I knew what to do. There were about fifty men in the section. Mostly they ignored me as I started to make my bed. That's what a nervous ex-Army person does when he sees an unmade bunk bed: you just naturally shake out the sheets and install hospital tucks and stretch the blankets so tight coins will bounce off.

As I finished, a voice blared from two speakers in the section. "Count time. Count time. All inmates report to your areas. Count time." There were speakers in every section of each of the five dorms and about twenty more mounted on poles and buildings all over the twenty-eight-acre compound. The speakers would become an integral part of my life.

I stood by my bunk and watched my section fill up with inmates.

People were coming in from the porch outside. A man in his sixties nodded to me and stood at the foot of the bunk next to me. I said hello. He nodded and said hello. He said people called him Doc.

A couple of guys loitered by the door, on lookout for the hacks.

I asked a guy on the other side of me, a sturdy, thick man, why they called them hacks.

"I'm not sure why," said the man. "Somebody told me it comes from what they call cabs. And whenever you go anywhere in a real prison—not this fucking place—you go with a guard. You take a hack. Sound right?"

"Sounds fine."

"What's your name?"

"Bob Mason."

"Mine's Don Barnett. You happen to be the writer?"

"I think so. I mean, I'm a writer."

Barnett smiled and called across the isle. "Hey, Lauder, this is the guy."

"What guy?" said a suntanned man about my age. He looked over at me.

"The guy who wrote that book you're reading," Don said.

Lauder smiled. "No shit?"

I nodded.

"Great book," Lauder said. "I didn't know shit about Vietnam. You made me think I was there."

"Thanks," I said, unsure of myself. I was not used to meeting people who'd read my book. They had the advantage of knowing a whole lot more about me than I knew about them. I revealed a lot about myself in *Chickenhawk,* and I figured somebody was going to use my candor against me. I mean, I actually admitted that I'd masturbated in Vietnam. I kept expecting to hear somebody call me a jerkoff.

"They're coming!" the lookout said. He stepped back to his bunk.

We assumed count position. The man on the top bunk sat with his legs draped over the foot of his bed. The man on the lower bunk stood in the aisle.

Two hacks walked in the door and barked, "Count." One stayed near the door and the other walked up the aisle nodding at each inmate, counting. When he'd walked up and down each side, he gave the number to the other guard. The guard checked his count sheet and nodded. The two hacks walked out the door to the porch and were gone.

The inmates crowded around the door, chattering like kids, making jokes. I asked Barnett what what going on.

"We're first for chow this week. It rotates among the dorms." He looked at the eager mob by the door. "They're going to race to the chow line. Not much happens here. This is a big deal."

The speaker blared: "The count is clear. The count is clear. Dorm Three may proceed to dinner."

The doors burst open and I watched the men scramble out on the porch and onto the sidewalks. I'd read part of my *Admissions and Orientation Guide* already. You could not run anywhere in camp except the jogging trail. You had to stay on the sidewalks. The men walked in the hip-swiveling gait of professional speedwalkers, arms swinging, racing to the mess hall. I vowed I would never rush to dinner. I'd prefer starving to letting these people see me that eager for their food.

John came into my section. "Wanna go check out the place before we eat?"

We walked along the sidewalks of the prison. The five dormitories were grouped irregularly in an immaculately groomed landscape. Dorm Three was the worst-looking building in the camp. The other four dorms were single-story concrete buildings that looked like college dorms. Everything was neat and tidy. The hedges were flat as tables. Sidewalks were edged. There were no weeds. The grass was cropped as smooth as a carpet. We came to a service road that led in from the base and formed the eastern boundary of the camp. The service road looped around the buildings in the camp and exited at the west side. We walked south along it. Inmate joggers and speedwalkers passed us. Just past the last dormitory, Dorm Five, was a wooded area, and just beyond it was a finger of water from Choctawhatchee Bay that came into the camp. We veered off the service road, following a woodsy path down to the white sandy beach. The water was dark and uninviting. We walked along the beach until we saw a guy named Jeff who'd checked in when we did. He was standing on the beach, staring at the water.

"Nice beach," I said.

"Yeah, better'n no beach. But I'm from the Virgins."

John and I nodded. We, the three newbies, looked over at the long line of inmates in front of the mess hall which was right in front of Dorm Five.

"Just like the Army," I said. "Find a line and stand in it." Two guys walking the path together rushed past us.

"I hear there's some asshole big-deal writer showing up today," Jeff said.

I smiled. "He's here," I said.

"Really? Where?"

"There," John said, pointing to me.

"Really?" Jeff said, grinning. "Sorry."

"Hey," I said. "You got the asshole part right. I didn't get where I am today by being smart." Jeff laughed. I noticed a Huey flying just over the trees behind him. I felt a pang of embarrassment, imagining the pilot seeing me.

We decided to go eat and continue our tour later.

The mess hall was designed to feed five hundred inmates, the maximum this camp was supposed to hold. The population when John and I arrived was about six hundred and fifty. The result at the mess hall was longer waits and earlier opening of the serving line. Some inmates ate dinner before the four o'clock count.

The long line of inmates that formed outside against two walls of the building, under a metal awning, divided into two lines inside. The place looked like any civilian cafeteria. You got a tray from a stack, silverware (actual metal, as opposed to the plastic variety used in higher-level prisons), and plates. The first serving table held salads on a bed of crushed ice—tossed, gelatin, fruit, five-bean, and so on. Yes, I am talking about a prison. You scooted your tray along the rails and handed your plate to the servers. Our first meal was thin-sliced roast beef, mashed potatoes, spinach, and squash. As you continued along the serving line, you got your choice of Coke, coffee, iced tea, or milk with unlimited refills. We carried trays to an empty table and sat down.

"How'd you get here?" I asked Jeff.

"Stupidity."

"Like?"

"Oh, I got wooed, you know?"

"Screwed?" John said.

"Same thing," Jeff said, laughing. "These guys said all I had to do was to go buy a brand-new yacht in my name, make one delivery with it, and the yacht was mine to keep. I couldn't pass up a deal like that. Naturally, I got busted. Guess who's the registered owner of the boat? Guess who takes the major rap? Five years."

"Plus they took your boat," John said.

Jeff nodded. "Plus they took my boat."

"And you didn't even get kissed," I said, laughing. Jeff looked at me. I shrugged. "Sorry."

We ate in a hurry. The food was okay, typical institutional fare. The problem with the mess hall was that it was pandemonium. The noise of two hundred men talking, laughing, clattering plates, clinking silverware, moving chairs, echoed and reverberated off the tile floors and concrete walls. You had to shout to be heard. John was sweating profusely, complaining how hot it was. It wasn't hot. Every building in the camp, except Dorm Three, was air-conditioned.

Outside, we walked the rest of the jogging trail, a sandy path that ran along the boundary of the camp, beyond the dorms, and around a level grassy field big enough for a couple of football fields and a baseball diamond. We walked along the trail beside the western boundary of the camp, a white rope hung on short posts. Beyond the rope was a shallow ditch. Beyond the ditch was woods. To escape, just step over the rope.

The trail went past the weight shack, which was the busiest place in camp. Inside the open-walled building, thirty men lifted weights, punched punching bags, pedaled stationary bikes, and used all kinds of other exercise equipment. Around the weight shack were a couple of bocci lanes (at which four men on each lane rolled five-pound balls back and forth, seeing which team could get the most balls closest to the end of the lane); four tennis courts, which were always busy; and the softball field complete with bleachers—two sets of bleachers, one for inmates and one for the public. The prisoners were in the local softball league and played the Air Force units on the base. There was a baseball game going on as we walked by. We went past a low building that issued playing equipment, toward the administration building, back on the service road, completing one circuit of the jogging path.

The three of us stood at the entrance of the camp, staring at the white line painted across the road. Nobody said anything. That white line was the barrier. The physical thing that kept us here was a white line, painted over many times until it was as thick as two playing cards.

It seemed absurd that this system worked, but it did. The kind of prisoners sent here were just the kind who'd stay behind a white line if you told them to. You could not be sent to Eglin, or any of the other twenty or so camps in the United States like Eglin, if you were guilty of a violent crime, if weapons were used in the commission of your crime, or if your crime was a sex crime. Minimum-security camps were originally built to incarcerate white-collar criminals. Robert Haldeman of the Watergate era was sent here. The governor of Maryland was here the year before. Several wealthy businessmen were here now. Times change. Now the population was swelled by drug smugglers like us. Roughly seventy percent of the prisoners here were in for drug-related crimes, the rest were in for tax evasion or stock manipulation or union violations, or even any of several federal misdemeanors that can send you to prison. The white line worked because, if you stepped over it, you were guilty of escape and would be sent to a level two (or higher) prison, where they have actual, physical boundaries.

Floodlights atop tall poles flicked on, hazy cones surrounded by dusk. We continued down the service road and walked through the recreation room (pool and table tennis), the library (a living-room-sized place with few books), and the craft shop, which had a complete collection of woodworking equipment. We saw a big line of people going into a building next to the craft shop. We walked up to the door and saw that it was the camp commissary.

When we checked in, John and I had deposited a hundred dollars into our inmate commissary account. We were eager to spend some of it on essentials like soap and cigarettes. We got in line. After about a half hour, we got to the steps of the wooden porch at the front of the commissary building. A sign on the wall listed what you could buy and next to the sign was a box of order slips. You had to fill out the order slip before you got inside. The commissary was like a convenience store except you had to wait in line and clerks got the stuff for you. I studied the list. You could buy soap, soap dishes, combs, cigarettes, cigars, baby oil, soda, candy, shower shoes, towels, tennis balls, handballs, sweatshirts, T-shirts, fresh fruit, portable radios, watches, ice cream, and lots more. The list had a note attached that said special orders for tennis shoes, running shoes, baseball gloves and shoes, table tennis rackets, shorts, and tennis rackets were taken only at the commissary office between eleven and twelve, weekdays.

I decided to buy a watch. They'd taken my old Seiko when I checked in because they said it was too valuable. I'd bought it on my R&R in Hong Kong for five dollars, eighteen years before.

"Yeah," John said. "Me, too. A watch, some Jif peanut butter, some Ritz crackers. Need a bunch of stuff."

We filled out our lists and went inside. By the door was a counter closed off with a Plexiglas panel. You slipped your list through a slot. One of two inmates who worked there would grab it and start loading up a plastic bin with whatever you had on your list. They were both fast. They put your bin in a queue that they shoved along the counter until it stopped next to the cashier. The cashier was Miss Reed, a nice-looking blond woman who ran the commissary. They called her Lady-hack. She looked like most any other clerk you've seen in a convenience store except that she was attractive even wearing the blue Bureau of Prisons uniform. Miss Reed pulled inmate account cards from a portable file drawer and put them in her register. She totaled up the order as the other inmate clerk shoved the stuff through a hole. Bananas and socks and soap tumbled down a chute for the inmate customer to bag. The purchase amount was deducted from the account card. Miss Reed looked for John's account card and shook her head. One of the inmates, called Grumbles because of his gravelly voice, said, "You don't have an account yet."

"What d'you mean?" John said. "I gave them a hundred bucks. Cash."

Grumbles shrugged knowingly. "I'm sure. But the assholes haven't made you an account card yet. You'll have one by Monday. Try then." Grumbles turned around with John's bin and restocked the stuff in it in about ten seconds. I told him I was in the same boat, and we walked outside.

On the way, we passed the camp chapel. Inside, we saw men singing. A choir of prisoners. The chapel was a refuge for many, and I think it was good that they provided one. In keeping with the cynical spirit of prison, people who did not go to chapel called those that did "kneel and squealers."

We were back at our bunks for the ten o'clock count.

I sat on my bunk after the count and just watched. I was feeling sad.

At forty-one, I was feeling the same homesickness I'd felt as a teenage college student away from home the first time. I was a stranger in a strange place. Doc, the man next to me, was reading the Bible. Doc had told me earlier that he was a physician (family practice). Doc believed that the federal income tax was unconstitutional. Protesting this illegal tax, Doc didn't pay his for several years. He got two years, proving that having a medical degree doesn't necessarily mean a person is smart.

Barnett, the guy in the bunk above me, was telling an inmate how to appeal his case. Barnett was an attorney from Atlanta. Jailhouse lawyers, I am told, are common. At Eglin, though, most of them were actually attorneys. Across the aisle, Lauder was reading my book. I nodded at a wild-looking man next to Lauder who was staring at me. He had hollow eyes, long stringy black hair, and looked about fifty pounds underweight. He nodded back and came over to my bunk. He sat on Doc's bed, ignoring Doc. Doc glanced up, made a small sneer, and looked back to his Bible.

"You wrote that book?" the rangy-looking inmate asked.

"Yeah. I did."

"That's great," he said. He smiled. "My name's Fred. Fred Devito."

"Bob Mason. Pleased to meet you, Fred."

"I'm trying to teach myself how to write. You know, learn something useful while I'm here besides how to spear trash."

"That's great," I said. "That's your job? Spearing trash?"

Devito nodded. "That's what they've got me doing now, during this two-week A&O (admissions and orientation) bullshit. I walk around with a bucket and a stick with a nail on the end. I pick up cigarette butts and stuff all day. Not a bad job, really. You'd be smart if you could get it tomorrow."

"Tomorrow?"

"Yeah. First three weeks you're here, before they assign you your regular job? You're an A&O. They have you washing floors, cleaning latrines, digging ditches, shit like that—seven days a week."

"You're kidding."

"Yeah, sure, I'm kidding. Wait until tomorrow. Unless you got a visitor, you'll be fucking working."

"I do," I said. "My wife's coming."

"Lucky," Fred said. "They'll call you out of your work detail when she shows up."

"Man," I said. "I had this image, you know? Me with a typewriter in some lonely cell, typing away. Like in the movies."

"Yeah," Fred said. "You have to go to places like the one I just got out of to do that. These camps are all work camps. Everybody works. In a real prison, it's a big deal to get a job. Mostly you hang out in your cell jerking off and smoking pot. Actually," Fred said, "I didn't mind it too much."

"Why'd they send you here?"

"They send some of us to places like this when we get close to getting out. Kind of a transition zone, I guess. I'll be outa here in six months. How long you in for?"

"I was sentenced to five years," I said, not believing it was me speaking. "Pot smuggling."

"How much pot you have?" Fred asked.

"Three thousand pounds."

"You'll do two," Fred said.

"You think so?"

"Yeah. You'll see. You go before the parole board in a month or so. They have guidelines set up according to how much stuff you brought in. Three thousand pounds will get you two years."

Two years. I looked around the room. The huge fan near our end of the room was buzzing loudly, swirling hot, humid air around the crowded room. Groups of men chattered around bunks and more talked in groups out on the porch. The noise was incredible. There was absolutely no privacy. Two years of this? "How long you been in jail so far, Fred?"

"When I leave, it'll be five years."

"Damn."

"Yep," Fred said, looking distracted. "Bob. About this writing. I was wondering. You think you could look at something I wrote?"

"Sure, where is it?"

"It's still kinda rough, you know?" Fred said. "Maybe I'll have it ready tomorrow."

The showers closed at eleven. I stripped down, wrapped a towel around myself, and walked down the hall. The bathroom was like the ones you see in school locker rooms and in basic training in the Army, public showers and a long row of stalls with commodes. You showered with up to six other men. They had put doors on the toilet stalls, the only concession they'd made for privacy. I showered. I'd forgotten to bring shower shoes. I could feel colonies of foot fungus migrating through the pores in my skin and under my toenails. I dried off and walked back to my bunk and dressed.

I lay in bed after the lights went out at ten-thirty and listened to the fans buzzing. I closed my eyes and begged for cosmic intervention. I needed a miracle. Someone could decide I'd had enough and call and tell the warden to let me out. Or, equally likely, a spaceship might land and take me away. I slept.

Fred was right about us having to work on the weekends. The next morning at eight, the speaker blared that all A&O inmates were to meet at the television room in Dorm Two for checkoff. Jeff and John found me on the porch of Dorm Three. We walked to Dorm Two together.

We gawked at the luxury we saw inside the dormitory. Air-conditioning. Shiny and clean aisles, carpeted floors in the sleeping sections. There were glassed-in recreation rooms where inmates played chess and checkers and cards. Each inmate had his own stall, a cube. The bathrooms were completely tiled, brilliantly clean, with private shower stalls. It was like a hotel compared to Dorm Three.

The TV room was packed with new inmates. At one end of the room, the TV, a big-screen projection model, was off, but I found myself staring at the gray screen. After a five-minute wait, a hack showed up carrying a clipboard. "Tarzan," somebody said. Somebody else laughed. The hack ignored them. I'd already heard the story. Tarzan got his name a year before by hiding in a tree in the woods next to Dorm Five trying to catch inmates smoking pot. He'd fallen out of the tree and broken his arm.

Tarzan was a compact man, wore his tailored uniform well, and seemed to enjoy his work. I'd seen him pat-searching an inmate the night before on the porch of my dorm with cool, professional, hawklike interest. Random body searches were part of the drill at Eglin. They were looking for drugs or money. Of course you couldn't have drugs. I was surprised that you couldn't have more than a dollar in change on you, either.

Tarzan looked at his clipboard and called out a few names, including

John's and mine. "You men have visitors." The inmates booed and hissed. Tarzan looked at us dispassionately, continued. "After visiting hours, report to inmate Harris and clean up the visiting room." The inmates cheered and laughed. As we left, we heard Tarzan calling off names for the work details.

The visiting room was actually two large rooms that made an L-shaped building next to the administration building. The open sides of the L were walled off, making the visiting area a separate compound from the rest of the camp.

Wives and families lined up and waited outside until the place opened at eight. Then they brought in picnic baskets and books and kids and toys and gathered together chairs and tables inside the rooms and out in the yard, establishing small enclaves where they could visit with their men. Most people stayed until closing at three. In the yard outside, inmates dressed in their blue prison uniforms sat around circular concrete picnic tables talking to their gaily dressed wives. Children played tag.

Guards watched to see that the rules against physical contact were enforced. You were allowed to kiss upon meeting and upon departure. Holding hands, as long as they were in view, was permissible. When a hack told me that having a hole in your pocket was against the rules, I had to ask. "We got guys who'll let their wives play with them through their pockets," said the hack. His disgust reminded me of a school-teacher who told us to ignore whatever it was the monkeys were doing during a trip to the zoo.

Some inmates and their wives strolled together around a short walk-way that meandered through the yard. Against the farthest wall from the visiting rooms was a sandy play area filled with kids who played on seesaws and spring-mounted rocking horses. With all the blue uniforms mixed with bright civilian clothing, it looked like a weekend picnic for a bunch of gas-station attendants.

Patience and Alice had set up a table inside where it was cool. Patience brought some coffee and doughnuts and yogurt. We hugged and kissed under the watchful eyes of the hacks and sat down.

"I love you," Patience said.

I winced.

"What? You don't think I should love you now?"

"No."

"Just because you're a convict?"

"That's a pretty good reason, don't you think?"

"Maybe if you'd killed somebody, or robbed a bank at gunpoint. Maybe then I'd have trouble."

"We have at least two more years of this, Patience. It's going to get old fast."

Patience looked at me carefully. "I love you," she said.

Before I finished my coffee, I heard my name called. I went to the hacks at their desk near the entrance.

"I'm Mason," I said.

"They want you at control," said a hack known as Rocky. Rocky was a three-tour Marine Vietnam vet who, I later learned from him, thought guard duty at Eglin was about the pussiest job he could imagine. He was surly to inmates, with the amiable fierceness of a drill sergeant.

"What's the deal?"

"Deal?" Rocky said. "The deal is you get your ass up to control. That's the deal." Rocky made me miss the Army.

I went outside and walked to control. I went up to the window on the side of the glass booth and told them I was here. The hack nodded, motioned to come around the other side to the door. I walked around and went inside.

"What are you doing in here, inmate?" the hack said.

"You just told me to come in here."

"Wiseass, eh? What's your name?"

"Mason."

"What's your number?"

"Eight-one-three-four-nine-dash-oh-seven-one-ay."

The hack nodded and said, "Wait right there."

I stood against the wall in the hallway. Hacks passed me like I was wallpaper. In a minute I saw the photographer from *People* magazine walking toward me with Superintendent Honsted.

"Hey, Lynn, how you been?" I said. I remembered his name because while he'd been photographing me at home, we had talked about photography: the kind of film he used, the cameras he liked best, and so on.

"Fine, Bob. They treating you okay?"

I looked at Honsted. "Here? It's like staying at a resort, Lynn. Great place."

Lynn smiled and asked Honsted if there were any restrictions for the photography session.

"No. Not as long as I'm with you. I suggest we go outside. You can start out there."

I posed next to the big sign out front. I had to cross the white line to get to it, but I had Honsted's permission. Next we walked to Dorm Three. The other A&O guys were mopping floors and scrubbing the latrine. Jeff looked up from his mopping, shook his head, and smiled. The inmates watched me, their faces filled with curiosity. An inmate, the warden, and a photographer are walking around here? Who's that guy?

Lynn photographed me standing by my bunk and then we went out on the porch. He had me sit on one of the benches and mug for the camera while he ran off a roll. I stood up and leaned against the porch railing for another roll. While he took pictures, I watched the other inmates staring. In that few minutes, half the camp finally knew exactly who the asshole, big-deal writer was.

By three o'clock, I was ready to snap from aggravation. I hated the visiting room. I hated being a prisoner, but that wasn't why I was so pissed. I deserved humiliation, but having Patience subjected to it made it much worse. I was selfish. I wanted isolation to sulk, to forget where I was. Visitors from the *outside*, even Patience, reminded me that I was *inside*.

We hugged by the door. I gave Patience the one legal kiss I was allowed and we said good-bye. She promised she'd be back the next day. I smiled, trying to suppress my disappointment. "You want to see me, don't you?"

"Yes. You know I do."

I watched her walk with Alice out to the parking lot.

When the visitors were gone and the inmates were gone, the A&O inmates remained. The hacks left when inmate Harris arrived. Harris, a greasy guy with broken teeth, hurried around the place, earnestly pulling buckets and mops and brooms out of closets. "We got to clean this place up before the four o'clock count," Harris said seriously. "If we don't, we got to come back and do it tonight."

John and I were assigned to police the visiting yard. I had wondered who was going to pick up the few thousand cigarette butts I'd noticed collecting on the ground; now I knew. We hauled plastic garbage bags around and filled them with drink cans, Styrofoam cups, half-eaten sandwiches, cigars, and even a few disposable diapers. In half an hour, we had cleaned up the trash. Harris then had us hook up water hoses and wash down everything. I was beginning to understand just why this prison always looked so spotless. It's the kind of thing you just take for granted.

The fifteen A&O inmates made the place as shiny as new: floors mopped and buffed, tables and chairs wiped and set back in place, bathrooms scrubbed, coffee urn washed, all trash in trash cans, and the whole yard washed down—all with five minutes to spare. Harris thanked us distractedly as he carefully inspected our work before letting us go to our dorm. Harris, a former bureaucrat from Jacksonville, had totally focused his mind on the condition of his visiting room. He had escaped.

Count.

Watch the race to the mess hall.

John and I and Jeff walked around the camp, trying to find people we might know who lived in the regular dorms. John and I were especially looking for somebody who'd lend us some cigarettes until the commissary opened Monday. We were both going to quit smoking, we said, but the time wasn't yet right.

Because of the *People* photography session, a lot of guys stopped me and said they'd heard about my book, or heard me on the radio, or read about me. By this time, nearly every major newspaper in America had reviewed *Chickenhawk* or reprinted the *New York Times* piece. When we met an older guy who'd read my book, I noticed he had a couple of cartons of cigarettes in his locker; I asked him if he'd lend me one. He was pleased to. Proud to.

Amazing, isn't it? Even as a convict, I was living proof that you could take five dollars' worth of paper and turn it into a book. *Chicken-*

hawk wasn't yet an official best-seller, and I wasn't making tons of money. At the moment, though, my fame was worth a carton of cigarettes.

The Sunday visit was worse than Saturday's and I wondered how I was going to tell Patience I wanted to see her less than the every-other-week visiting schedule she said she'd maintain.

CHAPTER 25

Monday I woke to see everybody bustling around getting dressed and rushing off to breakfast. During the weekend, breakfast was served at ten. During the regular weekday routine, the kitchen opened at five-thirty. At six-thirty, the loudspeaker blared, "Work call. Work call," and the inmates who worked on the Air Force base gathered at their checkpoints at the entrance to the camp. They were met out front by their Air Force bosses, usually young technical sergeants, and driven off to work. Some inmates—the phone repair people and others—actually had their own Air Force trucks parked in the parking lot which they jumped into and drove to work. I was witnessing a workday at Eglin.

At seven, all the A&O inmates were called to the visiting room.

Superintendent Honsted welcomed us to Eglin. He was a good-looking guy, and considered very fair. He said he was approachable if we saw him walking around the camp, but the best way to get our needs known was to go through the chain of command. The camp was divided into two units, north and south. Each unit had a unit manager. Each unit was further divided into six teams. Each team was comprised of a case manager, a counselor, and a secretary. These teams had offices where we applied for furloughs, job changes, and relief from whatever grief we wanted to complain about. The forms used for these various requests were called "cop-outs." He finished with: "You may be surprised to know that the Bureau of Prisons does not consider your stay here, in any way, as rehabilitation." Honsted waited to let that sink in. "It is the common belief, mostly from movies, that the state is trying to somehow rehabilitate its criminals. The Bureau of Prisons considers that you are here to be punished. Plain and simple. If you want to further your education, learn a trade or something; these things are possible, but whether you do them or not is your responsibility. Not ours."

The warden left and the assistant warden, younger and not nearly as friendly as the warden, lectured us on the various rules of the camp. He said that Eglin was created in 1962 under a maintenance contract with the Air Force. That's what we'd be, most of us, contract laborers working for between eleven and thirty-four cents an hour. The Air Force paid the prison camp minimum wages ($3.25 an hour) for our time, which helped make the camp self-sufficient. It only cost taxpayers half what it would cost to put us behind bars. We'd read that in our pamphlets. What we wanted to know about was the furloughs.

"You are eligible for your first furlough, a one-day pass in the local area, when you've been here at least six months and you're within two years of release, assuming you have no points against you and if your counselors recommend it," said the assistant warden. "Within eighteen months of release, you're eligible for an overnight furlough in the local area. Every six months after that, you are eligible for a five-day furlough to your home community. These furloughs are not automatic; they are granted to help an inmate keep his family together and to help his transition back into society as he gets near the end of his sentence. They must be applied for, your family has to request your visits, and each request has to be reviewed before it is granted."

"Does anybody ever not get a furlough?" asked an inmate.

"Almost everybody gets their furloughs. We weed out real troublemakers and send them to higher-level prisons," said the assistant warden. "Like Superintendent Honsted said, you're here to be punished, but we realize that it's to everybody's benefit that you have some opportunity to readjust to normal society."

After that, a man called Coach told us about the athletic program; the director of education told us how we were going to be tested, screened for job suitability and educational level. All prisoners would work every day, all day, except those not having a high-school diploma or those who didn't demonstrate a high-school level of competence. They would have to attend the camp's school in the mornings and work in the afternoons. He said also that it was possible to take courses at the local community college. We heard from the food service director, the finance manager, and the chaplain. Lady-hack, Miss Reed, told us how the commissary worked.

By ten, we'd heard from most of the people who ran the camp. The director of education, Mr. Gossen, said that the following morning we'd begin the testing. Now we were excused to go have lunch. After lunch, we would report to Dorm Two and get our work assignments.

During lunch I talked to some inmates who'd been in camp for a year. They said that while we were in A&O, the counselors and hacks would be deciding what our permanent jobs would be from the forms we filled out. They never let doctors work at the clinic, or dentists assist the dentist, or lawyers work in the business offices. Usually, however, they assigned plumbers and carpenters, phone installers, mechanics, machinists, and air-conditioning men to their respective trades. I had a useful trade for a prison career: I could type. I figured I might be able to get a job as a clerk or as a teacher's assistant at the school. Either one would give me access to a typewriter.

That afternoon, Tarzan assigned me to landscape detail, known as "landscrape" in camp. I hung around the landscape shed in the shade of an oak tree. The shed was next to the service road that looped around the south end of the camp, and about twenty inmates were sitting in the sweltering heat waiting for Officer Simpson, the hack in charge of landscape. His regular team of a dozen inmates were there, including Barnett, along with about ten temporaries like me from the A&O gang.

"How come they got you on landscape?" I asked Barnett.

"I'm a troublemaker, Mason. This is where they put us."

"I'd go nuts," I said.

"It's not so bad," Barnett said. "It'll get you in shape. It's like working in your yard except you do it every day, seven to three."

Officer Simpson showed up driving his blue pickup truck. He stood on the tarmac, pushed his baseball cap back revealing a sweaty brow, and began calling off names from his clipboard. Everyone was present. Simpson ambled toward the door to the shed and walked inside.

The shed was packed with riding mowers, mulchers, push mowers, gasoline-powered blowers, rakes, shovels, edgers, and big push brooms. "Okay, Taylor," Simpson said to an inmate. "You and Barnett will be in charge of the edging team today. We're going to the village." The village was a group of houses near the camp in which many of the hacks lived. The inmates mowed the yards and trimmed the hedges there, too. Barnett and Taylor nodded and began loading Simpson's truck. Simpson then called off names and assigned inmates to a trench-digging team, a gravel-spreading team, and a sod-planting team. The regulars marched off toward the dorms carrying buckets and rakes and brooms. I saw Devito, the man from my section, and two other guys headed off carrying buckets and trash spears. A tall Cuban named Fredrico was in charge of all the hedges on camp and had an assistant who helped him. They used taut strings and long thin boards as guides to keep the hedges perfectly flat and square. Other inmates cranked up their riding mowers and chugged off to mow the camp. I heard my name called. "Mason, you take a hand mower up between Dorm One and the visiting room and mow that section," Simpson said. He was pointing to a lawn mower. I nodded.

The mower was a power mower, but it had to be pushed. I pushed it to the other end of the camp and cranked it up. The sun beat down so hard that my shirt was soaked before I'd pushed the mower one lap around the section. By the time I got the first piece finished, I was feeling faint. I wasn't used to working in the sun. Hell, I wasn't used to physical labor at all.

It took about an hour to mow the area Simpson had assigned me. I pushed the mower back to the shed, weak, seeing stars, drenched with sweat. Back at the shed, Simpson was gone, out with Barnett's team at the village. An inmate whose job it was to sit at Simpson's desk and answer the phone and to check equipment in and out told me to wash the mower off and put it back with the others. I washed the mower with a hose and parked it.

Simpson's clerk said, "Simpson wants you to trim around the posts and crap at the recreation building, Mason. You'll need a bucket and some shears."

Most of the buildings at Eglin had little white posts and white rope fences around them. When they mowed around the posts with the riding mowers, tufts of grass stayed. There were about fifty posts around the building. I started out front and worked around back, pulling the grass out by the roots next to the posts and trimming the small swatches the mowers missed with the shears. I put the grass trimmings into the bucket. By two in the afternoon, I was behind the recreation building, across the service road from the building called the clothing room. I was sitting by a post pulling grass when Grumbles, the commissary guy, who was sitting in the shade of the laundry room overhang, yelled, "Hey Mason, how does it feel? One day you're a famous writer, the next day you're a fucking landscrape artist!" A few guys sitting with Grumbles laughed. I looked up and smiled.

"Life's like that," I said.

Simpson drove by in the landscape truck with Barnett and Taylor and three other inmates in the back. He stopped beside me. "Better get your tools together, Mason. We're about ready to pack it up."

I nodded and Simpson drove down the service road.

I was walking along the posts next to the sidewalk carrying my plastic bucket and my shears when the warden came around the corner from behind the recreation building. He walked up to me. "How you like it so far, Mason?"

"Swell," I said. "I think I'd be better as a clerk, though. I'm a very good typist."

Honsted smiled and shook his head. "No writers around type-writers," he said.

I nodded. We'll see.

The warden looked up toward the clothing room. I looked. The inmates that'd been loitering out front had disappeared. The warden smiled and said, "You know, Mason, I've noticed something interesting when I read your personal history sheet. You and I are the same age."

He was dressed in a crisp white shirt, a tie, pressed slacks, and loafers. He was smiling. I was dressed in high-water blue pants, a blue shirt, both drenched with sweat, and wore a pair of stiff boots, the tattered insides of which I was afraid to explore with my hand for fear of something biting me. I was smiling, too. I nodded. "Pretty ironic, all right," I said.

After the four o'clock count, I went to the clothing room to see about getting some different boots. There was a complaint window just off the service road. I got in line behind two inmates. A white-haired old man was inside the window. The guy in front of the line called him Deacon and was saying that his pants were worn out. Deacon said, "They look fine to me. What do you think this is? A fucking resort?" He looked past the inmate and said, "Next."

"Hey," the inmate said. "What about my pants? I work in an office, and they want me to have nice-looking clothes."

"If you don't like your pants, fill out a cop-out and get your counselor to authorize an exchange because you need new pants for your job."

"You crazy? My counselor? That'll take forever. Why can't you just hand me another pair, Deacon? You got hundreds of pants in there," the inmate said, pointing behind Deacon to the floor-to-ceiling shelves packed with clothing.

"You heard me," Deacon said. "Next."

"You prick. You act like you own this shit," the inmate said, walking past me, his face burning with anger.

The next inmate held up a pair of underwear with a dozen holes peppering the seat. "You have some kind of flatulance problem?" Deacon said.

"No, Deacon, these are worn out," the inmate said, smiling, intimidated.

Deacon nodded, tossed the underwear into a bin inside, and yelled, "John. Give me a pair of Jockeys, medium. Stamp 'em three ninety-seven."

Inside, I saw John, a tall blond guy, grab a pair of new underwear off a shelf, break open the package, and put them in a stamping machine. John limped when he walked. Most of the people in the clothing room were either old or handicapped. He set the number on the machine and hit a switch. The inmate's laundry number was impressed in black characters on the waistband of the Jockeys. John gave them to Deacon.

"Here you go," Deacon said, tossing the underwear to the inmate. He looked at me and said, "Next."

"Hi," I said. "Deacon?"

"Yeah?"

I stood back a little and held up my foot. "These fucking boots were worn out a couple of years ago. Really hurt my feet."

"Yeah?" Deacon said, looking at me carefully. "You the new guy? The writer?"

"Yeah," I said, smiling. I figured I was looking at a favor coming up, considering I was a celebrity and all.

"This is prison, Mason."

"Really?" I said. "This is prison? I know it's prison. So what? I see people wearing new boots around here."

"You haven't been here long enough for new boots. Next."

"Are you kidding?" I said.

An inmate behind me said, "C'mon, man, I'm late for chow. Deacon doesn't kid."

I got out of line and stood by the door to the clothing room, seething. Deacon'd been here so long he figured he owned the clothes. I watched the traffic in and out of the clothing room, trying to understand how it worked. Somewhere in there, they had boots. New boots.

Inmates waited in line and walked in a door and up to a counter and called out their clothing number. Other inmates inside, one of them the old guy from my dorm, Doc, would go to one of the hundreds of bins behind them and get the inmate's laundry. Then the inmate walked out the other door. I saw another door at the far end of the building. I walked to it and peeked in through the screen. I heard the chatter of a sewing machine. I went inside and saw a guy working on a sewing machine in a closet-sized room. The bottom half of a Dutch door with a shelf on top was closed across the doorway. I leaned on the shelf and said, "Hi."

The guy looked up from his work. "Hi. Need some alterations?" he said with a strong accent. Sounded English to me.

"No. That's what you do?"

"That's right, mate."

"You British?"

"Me, mate? No way. I'm Australian."

I grinned. Seemed funny to me. "What—"

"Got caught at sea, mate. Your Coast Guard nabbed us in international waters and towed us back."

"Tough break," I said.

The man shrugged. "Better jail here than in Australia, mate."

"Why's that?"

"They take a sterner view of this drug-smuggling business than your blokes do. I got five years here. I'll serve maybe two. In Australia I'd have gotten ten and served ten."

"Man," I said. "That's tough." I looked at the sewing machine.

"You knew how to operate that before you got here? Ah—" I said, prompting him for his name with raised eyebrows.

"Tom. Tom Carpenter," he said. "I was a sailmaker on the outside. You?"

"I was a writer."

"Oh. You're the bloke they been saying was showing up. Robert Mason, right?"

"Bob."

"Bob, then. I'm reading your book right now, Bob. Nice job, that. You know a lot of our boys were there, too."

"I know. I met some Australian pilots over there. I remember they used to carry change purses made from kangaroo scrotums."

Tom nodded. "Yep. That's them, all right. What do you need, Bob? Something altered?"

"No. I was trying to find out who's in charge of boots."

"Boots?" Tom jutted out his chin. "Right behind you, Bob. That old fart in there, Timmy. He's the bloke you want."

I turned. Across the hall from Tom's alteration room was another doorway. I walked to it and saw an old man inside holding a shoe up against a buffing machine, his back to me. I stepped inside. When the man turned around to set the shoe on his work counter, he saw me. "Yeah?"

"You Timmy?"

"Yeah."

"I hear you're in charge of boots and shoes here."

"Yeah."

I pointed to my boots. "These things are beyond fixing," I said.

Timmy looked down at my boots and grinned. "That's the shit they issue to the new guys. You're supposed to go through the exchange window to get new ones. You try getting Deacon to exchange 'em for you?"

"Yeah. He told me this is prison."

"That old fart's acting more like a hack every day. He's been here almost five years, and I don't think he'll leave when he's free. If he does, he'll probably open his own fucking jail. Prick." Timmy looked at my boots again. "Elevens, right?"

"Right."

Timmy stepped into a small storeroom and came back with a brand-new pair of work boots, size eleven. "Here you go. The least a body should have around here is some boots that're fit to wear."

I sat on a wooden stool and changed boots. "You work on shoes on the outside?" I said as I laced up the new boots.

"I used to own a shoe shop," Timmy said.

"How'd you get here, owning a shoe shop?"

"Shoes had nothing to do with it. I got stupid and agreed to fly a fucking DC-6 load of pot from Colombia."

"DC-6?" I looked at Timmy skeptically. He looked at least sixty-five. He was gray-headed and stoop-shouldered, the least likely looking pilot I'd ever seen.

"Yeah, used to fly 'em for the airlines. I retired ten years ago, opened up my shoe store with my brother. We were doing fine. Not getting rich, you know? But a good living. Greed got me. Some kids asked me did I want to make a hundred thousand on one flight. Said they owned a DC-6, heard I used to fly 'em."

I tightened up the laces and tied them off. I stood up and walked around experimentally. "How they feel?" Timmy asked.

"Great. So how'd you get caught?"

"It was an old ship, most of the instruments were broken," Timmy said. "Got caught in the soup and couldn't find the damn cow pasture where they wanted the stuff. When I got low on fuel, I just flew the fucker to the nearest airport and landed. Damn near made it, too." Timmy grinned at the memory. "But they were watching the airport, Customs guys. Came aboard."

I nodded. "I know what that feels like," I said, standing on tiptoe to stretch the new boots. They fit perfectly, a little stiff from the newness. "Well, thanks, Timmy. These are great. Any time you want a favor, let me know."

"I don't care nothing about favors. There's nothing in this camp I want except to get out of it."

I was lying on my bunk after I'd showered, watching life in Dorm Three. A Cuban across from me coughed so hard I thought I'd see chunks of lungs coming up any second. When he finished hacking, he looked up, blinked, wiped his mouth, shook his head like a fighter who'd taken a hard punch, and lit up another cigarette. It was disgusting. I pulled my pack of Winstons out and tapped out a cigarette and lit it. I was going to quit, but I hadn't gotten to it yet.

Barnett's feet dangled off the edge of the bunk above me, and then he jumped down to the floor. He leaned over and said, "You read much?"

"Some," I said.

"Here," he said, holding a mail-order book catalog toward me.

I took the catalog. "Thanks."

"Sure," Barnett said, walking away.

I opened the catalog and heard, "Mason? You Mason?" An inmate on crutches swung across the waxed tile floor, his crutch tips squeaking and chirping. His left leg was in a cast from his ankle to above his knee.

"Yeah," I said. "What about it?"

"I'm a Huey pilot, too, that's what about it!" The inmate laughed and sat down on Doc's bed.

"No shit?"

"No shit, brother. Jack Cantrell," he said, holding out his hand. "There's at least three of us here."

I shook his hand. "Three of us? Three Huey pilots?"

"That's a fact. Above the best!" Jack Cantrell yelled the Army Aviator's motto.

"All right!" I said. "Pleased to meet you, Jack. Who were you with?"

"Flew guns with the Americal." He immediately rolled up his pants leg and showed me gnarled scars on his good leg. "Got raked in my cockpit, Bob." He rubbed the puckered skin around his knee and shin. He crossed his arms, raised his sweatshirt, and showed me a pencil-thick half-inch-deep indentation in his chest. "A fucking tracer came through my chicken plate just far enough to stick into my chest. Sat there and burned into me." He let his shirt drop and rolled his pants leg down. "You?"

"You make me feel bad, Jack. I just wrote a book about my tour, and the worst I got was the clap."

"Hey," he said, laughing. "Lucky for you. I don't mind. I'm glad you wrote it. People need to know what it was like over there."

I made a face that dismissed the compliment and shook my head. "What's the cast for?"

Jack laughed. "Would you believe it? Baseball? Broke it sliding into third base last week. And I'm due to leave yesterday!"

"Yesterday. You serious?"

"Like a fucking heart attack. They won't let me go until it's healed. You believe it? I ask them what the fuck difference it makes if I go home with a cast. They say they're responsible for my health here, and I'm not well. Can't leave prison if you're sick. Bastards. They're lifers here, every one of them. I told one of my hack buddies that when I'm out of here, I'll be thinking of him every day. I said, 'I'm gonna spend a minute each day, take a whole minute off, just to think about this place. And I'm gonna laugh my ass off, old buddy, 'cause you'll still be here.' "

We talked for an hour. Jack talked about flying Hueys with infectious enthusiasm. I realized I missed them, too, missed the tough missions, the tricky flying we had to do to survive. He told me about the day he was wounded. He was flying low-level down Route 19, a road I knew, and got caught in an ambush. Two machine guns raked his cockpit, shattered his shins and knees. His copilot was killed.

Jack knew all about flying Hueys in combat. He also knew the ins and outs of Eglin. I told him I wanted to work at the school. He said that was smart. Teacher's assistant was a piece of cake. He told me the name of a guy to go see, the same procedure we used in the Army. Everything worth doing in the Army was done outside the usual channels, through the clerks and technicians, the people who actually did the work. If you needed new boots, you made friends with the supply sergeant with a bottle of whiskey. If you wanted a leave request approved, you walked it through the chain of command's clerks in a day. If you waited for official Army channels to process a request, you'd have gray hair first. I figured Jack was a good contact.

I settled into life at Dorm Three. I didn't see John Tillerman much. He was in a different section, and we never got assigned to the same work details. I talked to the inmate Jack Cantrell had suggested. He explained that I was a hot property in camp, and wouldn't have any trouble getting the job I wanted in the school. That was a relief; landscrape was getting hard. We'd finished the morning talks and testing, so we worked all day. I mowed, weeded, dug—it's not that I didn't like this kind of work, I just didn't like doing it all the time. I talked to the education director, Mr. Gossen, in front of the education building while I was pulling up weeds. My inmate connection had told him I wanted to be a teacher's assistant. He said he had arranged everything.

After mail call, Barnett showed me a copy of *People* magazine, the September twelfth issue, with a picture of Chevy Chase on the cover.

"Yeah?" I said.

Barnett flipped it open. "Looky here. You're in trouble," he said, grinning.

It was a picture of me looking pissed off, standing on the porch of Dorm Three. The section was entitled TROUBLE and the headline said: AUTHOR ROBERT MASON, JAILED FOR DRUG RUNNING, WATCHES HIS LIT-ERARY TRIUMPH, *Chickenhawk*, FLY THE COOP. The headline didn't make much sense, but Chandler's two-page article was pretty accurate. It was a strange feeling to see me and Patience and Jack in *People* magazine.

I called Gerry Howard in New York the next day. He told me to call every Friday to find out how the book was doing. Phones were scattered all over the camp. The permanent dorms had one pay phone at each end, some inside and some outside. Dorm Three had phone booths on the porches on each side of the dorm. To make a call, you roamed the camp or sat in line. I called Gerry, collect, during lunch.

"To date . . ." Gerry paused; I could hear some paper shuffling. "Let's see. Oh, yeah. We've sold twenty thousand books." Gerry paused again. I felt a jolt of surprise. I heard Gerry laugh and then say, "Kind of beats the hell out of our prediction of five thousand, eh?"

I laughed. "Twenty thousand?"

"Yep. And we're selling an average of a thousand a day. A day."

I walked back to work, dazed. While I helped unload gravel from a pickup truck that we were spreading over a drainage field we'd dug, I multiplied twenty thousand times $2.50, the royalty I got for each book. It came to fifty thousand dollars no matter how often I figured it, but that couldn't be right. I'd never dreamed I'd get that much money for the book. Fifty thousand and growing? Gerry said we were selling a thousand a day? That meant while I was here, in jail, shoveling this gravel, I was making twenty-five hundred dollars a day? I couldn't help it, I grinned.

I started chattering with Kurt Vierthaller, another of the A&O guys. I was bubbling over with joy and took to laughing and horsing around with Kurt, knocking the gravel off his shovel and stuff. Simpson came up behind me and said, "This isn't a fucking lark, Mason. This is prison." I turned around and saw Simpson glaring at me. I nodded. Simpson was telling the truth. I threw a shovelful of gravel into the drainage field, but I was laughing inside.

I heard an inmate in the hall yell to someone that our permanent work assignments were posted on the bulletin board. I breezed down the hall toward the mob crowded in front of the bulletin board next to the bathroom door. The other A&O guys were pressed around the board, reading their assignments. I heard bitching and moaning. I smiled smugly. If you had your act together, like I did, you didn't have to depend on luck. Smart people make their own luck, suckers. I stood behind the crowd and lit a cigarette. As the inmates thinned out, I moved closer to the board. I read "Mason, Robert, 81349-071A" in the name column and followed the little dots across from it to the job column. I read "Landscape."

I traced the dots across the page with my finger. It was landscape, no mistake.

I went to the education building and found Mr. Gossen sitting in his office. He waved me in. "What happened?" I asked.

"The superintendent. He approves all the job assignments, Bob. The staff does the picking. His signature is just a formality. But this time he was looking for yours. He saw you assigned here and denied it."

"Is there any recourse? Can I do anything?"

Mr. Gossen shook his head. "Not really. You can go through your counselor. If you can prove your job is bad for your health or something, they can get your job changed. You have a health problem?"

"Not unless you count going fucking nuts when I see a rake."

Mr. Gossen smiled. "I'm sorry, Bob. We were looking forward to having you around here. Bob Haldeman used to work here."

"The Watergate Haldeman?"

"Yeah. He wrote a book. I thought it'd be nice to have had you here, too."

CHAPTER 26

Dorm Four is mine. I am supposed to keep every blade of grass and every leaf and every lump of dirt around Dorm Four cut, arranged, and smoothed to perfection. I have tools: a bucket, a stiff push broom, a springy leaf rake, a sharp edging tool with a new hickory handle, a nice new snippy pair of shears, and—that's it.

I start in the morning by emptying all the butt buckets at each of the four entrances. There are cigarette and cigar butts in the sand in each butt bucket and all around each butt bucket. There are wads of stuff people who chew tobacco spit into the butt buckets, gelatinous and brown. People who use tobacco are pigs.

I curl up a piece of cardboard to scoop the sticky messes out of the sand. I make a swirl design in the sand of each butt bucket when I am finished, like you see in posh hotels. Next, I sweep two hundred yards of sidewalks and patios around Dorm Four with my broom and gather together hundreds more cigarette butts. I put all this into my bucket.

The grass is freshly mowed, so all I have to do is manicure the shrubbery beds on all four sides of the building. The beds are dirt extending eight feet from the walls. In this dirt are various kinds of plants. Some are grouped together as hedges, which I trim flat and square with my shears. Some are individual plants which I trim to shape with the care of a sculptor and from whose interiors I pluck unsightly dead leaves. The lawn attempts to intrude into these dirt beds and has to be trimmed to a definite, knife-edged boundary. I shove the edger blade through snakes of Bermuda grass shoots which are infiltrating *my* pristine dirt beds. When I have finished edging the grass, it is ten, time to get ready for lunch.

At eleven-thirty, I am back at my post. It is now very hot. I thought it was hot earlier, but I was wrong. It is hot now. Panhandle Florida in August and September is hot and humid enough to bake bread.

All the twigs and leaves and grass clippings I've trimmed are now lying, in horrible disarray, in the plant beds. I rake every inch of the dirt, leaving careful parallel marks in the sand running smartly, perpendicularly, from the walls to the grass.

Then—I'm finished? I check my new Casio watch I bought at the commissary. It's only two o'clock. Simpson works us until three. I see Simpson driving toward me on the service road. I put my rake on my shoulder and go fetch my bucket while Simpson drives by. He nods to let me know I'm doing okay. Of course I'm doing okay. I'm good at this stuff.

I'm sensitive to the proper order of grass and leaves and twigs and dirt; Dorm Four will look like a Zen garden someday.

I notice that my predecessor, an aesthetic dullard, has let the grass grow up wildly around each and every one of the hundreds of white-painted stones that line the border of the service road and *my* grass. I begin working to correct the problem.

At two-thirty, I see others of the Eglin landscrape corps ambling back to the landscrape shed, known to our proud few as "the shop." I stand up and review my progress. I have gotten a dozen rocks looking up to snuff. I fetch my rake and broom and shears and edger and my five-gallon plastic bucket and walk to the shop.

I wash off my tools and put them back on the racks. A couple of new A&O guys look bewildered and lost and I point out where the stuff they're carrying is supposed to go. Outside, I sit on a low rock wall under the big oak, next to Barnett, and light up a Winston.

"Whatcha think?" says Barnett.

"I think I will be nuts very soon."

Barnett laughs. "You don't like this? Hey, Bob, this is back to the land, close to nature. Fresh air, excercise—"

"I hate nature," I said. "It makes me sneeze. You know what else I hate?"

Barnett is laughing and doesn't answer.

"I hate grass because it never stops trying to fuck up my shrubbery beds. I hate it when that happens."

"You're really getting into this," Barnett says.

"Yes. I am. But it's not all bad. I think I've made a scientific discovery about that slimy brown stuff you see in the butt buckets—you know what I'm talking about?"

Barnett can't talk. This kind of humor gets to him.

"That stuff, as slimy and revolting as it looks—it looks exactly like hawked-up, disease-infested, tobacco-chummed sputum, I know—is actually a previously unknown species of slime mold I have discovered. It is alive."

It is the habit of those 150 of us who work in the camp and get sweaty to shower in the few minutes before those 500 of us who work off camp return. It is our good fortune, because the camp is not crowded then and the showers are not packed with dangerous elbows that fly around as men suds up. I can shower and change and still be ready for mail call at three forty-five, fresh and happy as a fucking clam. After mail call, I stand in front of my bunk waiting for the hacks to come count us again in case someone has thrown a ladder over the white line and escaped today, taking solace in the fact that I only have to work on Dorm Four for another couple of years.

John and I are together in the gang of fifty inmates who are standing outside the visiting room Saturday morning waiting to be called inside. We have heard our names on the speaker, but we already knew Patience and Alice were coming. This is our third visit. We've been here a month. We've gotten rid of our high-water pants and managed to get at least two pairs of new socks each. We are each wearing our new socks and our running shoes, which we are allowed to wear when we are not working. New socks are a premium in camp because the clothing room rarely issues them and buying them at the commissary is expensive on sixteen dollars a month. We've both noticed that some inmates have entire wardrobes of new clothes as well as new socks and new boots. There is a hierarchy of prisoners here, some kind of power elite exists, but the workings of this fellowship are invisible to us so far. I point to a Cuban inmate standing fifteen feet ahead of us whose tailored, ironed shirt fits like a glove. "Look at that guy's uniform, John."

"Looks like the guys in basic who had their uniforms tailored," John says.

"Who the hell wants to tailor a goddamn prison uniform?" I say.

"He does, Bob."

I look at John. He's springing up and down on his toes, then twisting his torso, stretching, then feeling his biceps. "You look like you're getting in shape, John."

"You can tell?" John said.

"Yeah, but it's kind of annoying, you know, watching you fondle yourself in public."

"You're a real happy guy, Bob," John says. I've hurt his feelings. John has decided, as have many others, that if he's going to be here, he will get in shape. He's starving himself, eating celery and ice cubes between modest meals (we have an ice machine in each dorm), jogging five miles every day, and working out at the weight shack. He's losing weight and firming up, no doubt about it, but being around him during this process is like being around a born-again Christian who's just quit smoking so he won't offend the other guys at the AA meetings while he talks to them about quitting coffee.

I wasn't going to do that. I knew that every one of these guys would revert back to being normal beer-drinking, potbellied Americans the minute they got back on the street. I didn't want to waste my energy starting robust new habits I'd only break later. I walked every day for thirty or forty minutes, but I had been doing that at home.

The hack in charge of the visiting room this weekend, Rocky, calls our names. We go inside.

Patience and Alice were standing in the crowd of wives who were greeting their men. I went to her and we hugged. We kissed our official greeting kiss. I followed her to the table she and Alice had prepared for us. This being their third visit, they now knew the ropes—the ins and outs of visiting your man at Eglin. They had brought in a big bowl of fresh fruit, half a dozen croissants, yogurt, instant Bustelo coffee, and more, and that was just for breakfast. Patience showed me the new freezer chest she'd bought, inside of which were the makings of a gourmet lunch.

The sight of all this plenty was both heartening and depressing. I like this kind of food—it was just that it offered the contrast that I was able to avoid when I was in camp tending Dorm Four. Here in the visiting room, the fact that I was a prisoner in a prison—whose wife worked cleaning houses to support herself and our son (she had not yet gotten enough of the money I'd made on the book to quit) and drove two hundred miles and camped out in a tent at a nearby campground—was obvious. It made the punishment all the more painful.

After coffee and a croissant, Patience and I went outside and walked laps on the concrete path around the yard. I told her of my adventures as keeper of the grounds around Dorm Four, which she took to be funny.

Patience told me how nice everyone was back in High Springs. We'd wondered how the people of High Springs, a small (population five thousand) rural southern town, would react to the news that I was a convicted drug smuggler—and had been walking, unknown as such, among them for two years. It turned out they were very supportive. One man told me, just before I'd left for prison, that I shouldn't worry. "Hell, Bob, there's a lot of people in this town made their living making moonshine. People understand about pot. You don't have to worry about nothing." Another man, Bob Ryan, who operated the country store up the road from us, sent this message with Patience: "Tell Bob I'm feeling real safe now; knowing he's up there in prison and not able to sneak into my house some night while I'm asleep and stuff one of them marijuana cigarettes in my mouth." Patience told me she'd met a couple—Mike Costello, a Vietnam veteran, and his wife, Patti Street, who had been one of Jack's teachers. Mike had written a novel about Vietnam called *A Long Time from Home*, which he was in the process of getting published. She told me Mike was cutting firewood for her so she'd be ready for winter. Patience had passed a petition around town, which hundreds of people signed, and sent it to Judge Sol Blatt, asking him to give me an alternative sentence.

In conjuction with the petitions, we had hired (with the extra advance from Viking against my royalties) a group known as the National Center for Institutions and Alternatives (NCIA), which was preparing an appeal of my sentence to the judge. In support of their work, people—readers and friends from all over the country—were sending hundreds of letters to the NCIA, which would be submitting them to Judge Blatt. The goal of NCIA was to have me released to work in my community as an alternative to incarceration—there are Dorm Fours in every community. Tom Wolfe, the chief of police of High Springs, even wrote a letter saying he'd watch over me personally, make sure I did my work.

I had not much hope in the success of this appeal, and the fact that so many people supported me was both exhilarating and heartbreaking. I'd never had so many friends in my life. I was guilty as hell and paying the price. I did not believe I deserved to be helped.

We walked slow laps around the short path, Patience clinging to me like I was going to be snatched away any second. I was feeling miserable. I had come to some kind of adjustment, a balance with myself about being in prison that this walk was upsetting. "Patience. Do you realize that if you keep coming up here every other week, we'll have to go through this at least fifty times?"

"How do you know? You haven't even seen the parole board yet. And the NCIA petition, you don't know how that will work, either."

"True, I don't know anything for sure, but I have a strong feeling about it. Everybody here figures he shouldn't be here. And they're probably right. If God considered each person's whole life and compared it with the fuckup that got him here, most of these guys wouldn't be here. But that's not how it works. I'm going to get the standard two years, what they give people who smuggle three thousand pounds of pot. They don't care if I'm a nice guy and this is my first crime."

Patience nodded. "We'll see. In the meantime, I'll come see you every other week."

"Patience, having you come here is killing me. I hate the visiting room. It's like a fucking bus station—no, it's worse; it's like waiting in a dentist's office for two days with one *Elks* magazine. It took me three days to get over the last visit."

We stopped on the walkway and she stared at me. "Well, how often do you want me to come?"

"The truth?"

"Yes."

"I don't want you to come. I'll see you when I get a furlough. I want to work at Dorm Four and never know what's going on outside until they tell me I can walk out of here. That's what I want."

Patience looked like she was going to cry. She shut her eyes and said, "I have to come, Bob. I have to. I have to see you to believe you exist."

We started walking again. Damn, this was so complicated: other people's feelings. It was easy for me, I didn't have any. I was numb. Why couldn't Patience just go numb, too? "Okay," I said. "How about once a month?"

"Every two weeks, Bob. That's what I need. That's all you can do for me now."

John and Alice were strolling toward us, John chewing on one of an endless chain of puffed-rice crackers he ate between celery stalks during the visits. Abreast of us, John said, "How you doing, Bob?"

"Fine," I said. "Fucking fine, John."

Sunday afternoon, after twelve hours of visiting spread over two days, I was lying on my cot trying to disappear. I wanted to go to sleep and wake up in two years.

In addition to extreme boredom and humiliation in conjunction with visiting, another of the problems of sitting with your wife for such long periods is that the subject of sex invariably rises. If you watched carefully, and God knows I had the time, you could see couples playing skillfully disguised, tender sex games: A wife turns to look out the window and brushes her hand across her husband's lap. The husband does the same. A skirt overlaps a man's pocket and you can see the movement of her hand when the hack is not looking—that old hole-in-the-pocket routine. These people were sex-starved and were doing things in public they'd never dream of doing normally.

There is the stump of a large oak tree in the visiting yard sawed off level with the ground that, before it had been toppled, had shielded some daring couples who, with friends on lookout, would enter into coital bliss while the hacks wandered around unaware of the fact. Eventually some actual criminal—a Christian zealot, it was said—blew the whistle on a couple of fornicators and the prison administration sent the guy to a real prison over in Tallahassee and took vengeance on the oak tree.

Well, Patience and I played these games, too, with the result that the young male malady known as "lover's nuts" or "blue balls," depending on where you're from, struck me. It was not sexy. It was painful. The only cure I knew of was to go hide in one of the stalls in the bathroom with a bottle of Johnson's Baby Oil (a popular product in camp) and work it out. If I didn't do that, I'd have an embarrassing reaction to the water spray when I showered which was impossible either to hide or to attend because, as I mentioned, our showers were public. My great fear was that some hairy, two-hundred-and-fifty-pound, weight-shack faggot (no gays were allowed in Eglin, but who knows?) would smile and take as an invitation—trolling with live bait, if you will—my predicament. All in all, visiting was not profitable for me.

Two months later. I was sitting in one of the two park benches behind Dorm Four smoking a cigarette. Dorm Four was now perfect. I had even taken to combing tiny tree detritus from the lawns with my rake as fast as it landed, falling from the overhead and totally uncontrollable tree branches. I was having a hard time coming up with much else to do. Dorm Four could have been put in a glassed-in diorama at a museum, it was so perfect. Across from me, sitting on the other park bench behind Dorm Four, was George Allen, the caretaker of Dorm Five, which was identical to Dorm Four, right next door. George and I, both being custodians of entire dormitory grounds, had a lot in common and had taken to meeting like this daily, just before lunch, to have a smoke break and talk about new things to do to our dorms.

"I saw you washing your sidewalks today," I said to George.

George smiled sheepishly. "You like it? The way it looks?"

"Yeah," I said jealously. "It looks nice while the concrete is wet—"

"I know," George said, looking exasperated. "If only there was some way to keep that wet look—"

"And, of course," I added sharply, "these pigs get their feet wet and track up the halls and stuff. Bet that pisses off the inside cleaning crew."

"Yeah," George said, shrugging. "It may not work out." He reached into his shirt pocket, brought out a pack of smokes, and leaned forward to offer one. I crushed out mine—it was short—in my five-gallon

plastic bucket so as not to ruin the swirls I'd made in the sand of my
butt bucket, and took a new one from George. We lighted up.

We sat and puffed contentedly for a while. George was a real skinny
guy, jumpy and serious. He puffed sharply and looked over his shoulder
often. "You don't have to worry about Simpson," I said. "He told me
our dorms were the pride of the camp."

"He did?"

No, but what the fuck. "Yes. Yesterday."

George nodded happily, gazing over at Dorm Five. I could see he
was eager to get up and attend to a fallen leaf or something. I wanted
just to wait the fifteen minutes or so until lunch, so I said, "So, George,
you never talk about how you got here. Everybody knows how I got
here."

George smiled, looking embarrassed. "I know, but it's so stupid.
You'd laugh."

"I promise," I said, shaking my head.

George puffed quickly, deciding, and said, "Sporting goods."

"Say again?"

George spoke so softly I could barely make it out. "Got arrested for
buying stolen sporting goods."

Naturally, I laughed.

George looked away and stared at a couple of guys—cooks, by their
whites—walking down by the water. "Sorry. Sorry, George. It wasn't
funny. It must be the way you say it."

George nodded. "Oh, I know what people think," he said. "Compared to you guys—dope smugglers and crooked attorneys and rip-
off stockbrokers and busted politicians and stuff—it must sound real
wimpy. But I got five years for buying a truckload of exercise equipment
from a guy. I had no idea the stuff was stolen. It was cheap, sure, but
that's business. Isn't it? Looking for a good deal?"

"Yeah, sure is. I was in business once myself, George."

"Really?"

"Yep. Manufactured mirrors in New York."

"Huh." George grunted. "Sounds interesting."

"Oh, it was. Fascinating," I said. "So, George. You buy the stuff
from this guy. How do the cops know about it?"

"Oh. That's easy. The guy is working for the cops."

"What?"

"Yeah," George said, leaning forward, all embarrassment gone, getting into the story. "See, this guy hijacks this big semi truck full of stuff somewhere in New York. Then he takes it over to New Jersey to sell it. He gets caught—I don't know how. Then the cops tell him if he drives down the East Coast and sells the same truckload of shit to sporting goods places, they won't prosecute him."

"The guy who stole the stuff?"

"Yes. So he goes down the road stopping everywhere, offering the stuff at a third of what it's worth. Anyone who goes for it gets busted the minute they say okay."

"You didn't actually buy the stuff?"

"Nope. I *agreed* to buy it. Then the cops come swarming out of cars parked nearby. Guy has a bug on him, you know?" George looked real sad suddenly. "I got five years, and then my business starts to fail because I'm in jail and my wife doesn't know how to handle it and then she gets pissed off because I was away so long and she finally left me about a year ago."

Now I was really not happy I asked. But I had to know: "George. What happened to this guy? The original thief?"

"Him? Oh, nothing. They kept their promise. They let him go for cooperating with the police."

We sat smoking cigarettes for a while, not saying anything. I was beginning to think that the government spent most of its time setting up crimes and corraling the suckers who'd go for it. George's was just one of many stories about a technique for crime control that is illegal in all industrial nations except our own. In England, for example, George could not have been arrested because the criminal act he was involved in had been set up by the police. You have to actually commit a crime on your own to get arrested in England.

But George could have been lying. People sought me out to tell me their stories because, they said, I was a writer and people ought to know what happened to them. When listening to these stories, I'd wonder, Why's this guy telling me this? Does this story have anything to do with the truth? But I listened. You can learn a lot about people from the stories they tell and how they tell them. It's all interesting.

"How long you been in charge of Dorm Five, George?" I asked.

"Coming up on a year," George said.

"I think that if I have to work on this dorm that long, I will go nuts."

"Yeah? I don't mind. It's easy work and I like making the place look good. I do that all the time at home. Jane is always saying—" George stopped talking and flicked his cigarette out on my yard and stared at it. The smoke swirled lazily in the still air. I'd have told him to pick it up, but this was a bad moment for George.

"I don't know exactly why I hate it," I continued. "But I hate it. I don't care how this place looks. I want to get to a typewriter."

"You can type?" George said, interested.

"Yeah. I've always been able to type. Learned in high school."

"Well, Deacon just asked me if I knew anyone who could type. His boss is looking for a replacement for him."

"Deacon's leaving?"

"Yeah. In about a month."

"Who do I see?"

"Deacon or that guy, what's his name? The guy who helps him run the clothing room?" George stared at me, then his eyes rolled up looking in the top of his head, searching for the memory. I didn't know who he meant. I thought a hack ran the clothing room. "Foster. Don Foster. He's the guy. He and some of the others eat early chow. You probably can see him right now."

"What's he look like?"

"Heavy guy, black hair, short; acts like he owns the place."

I jumped up. "I'm gonna try it, George. Thanks." I left my tools out next to a tree and walked up the sidewalk behind Dorm Five and went into the mess hall. About thirty men were still eating from the ten o'clock lunch period. The regular line didn't start until eleven. I saw three men sitting at a table with a guy that matched George's description. I walked over.

"You Foster?" I said.

"Yeah," Foster said, looking piqued because I'd disturbed him at lunch.

"I hear they're looking for somebody who can type over at your place."

"Yeah. Typing's part of the job. You also have to know how to run a small business."

"I'm your man," I said. "Where do I sign up?"

Foster shrugged. "Okay. Come over to the clothing room after lunch. I'll get you in to see Mr. Baker and you can talk to him."

"What time?"

"Say about two?"

"I'll be there."

CHAPTER 27

Baker was a tall guy, probably six feet four. He spent most of his time smiling. He sat in his executive's chair behind a gray government desk, fidgeting with a wooden puzzle that could be made into the letter L, if you knew how. I stood in his office while his inmate lieutenants questioned me. The inmate cadre of the clothing room was Deacon, the head boss; Foster, next in line; and a guy they called Rusty, a crackly voiced old guy who seemed to be kind of a Gabby Hayes sidekick for Baker.

I told them about my business experience in New York.

Deacon finally said, "I think we could give him a try, Mr. Baker. I'm not leaving for a month; we got time to find somebody else if he doesn't work out."

Baker nodded, smiling. He had just put the puzzle together. "Deacon, we'll do whatever you think is best." Baker turned to me. "We want you to start as soon as you can, Mr. Mason."

"Okay. But I'm not sure how you go about it, you know?"

"Oh. Well, you have to apply for a job transfer. Through your counselors," Baker said.

I guess my face dropped. I'd heard of guys trying to get job transfers for their entire stay at Eglin. Deacon said, "Don't worry. We can get that done fast enough. You just get the blank paperwork from your counselor and bring it back here."

I hung out in the hallway by the counselor's office in Dorm Five, the dorm I would be going to when I got out of Three. My counselor, Mr. Josephson, whom the inmates called Waterhead, finally came down the hall after lunch. I was in a rush because I had to be back at my post before Simpson noticed I was gone. I'd waited until he drove by on the service road. Usually I didn't see him again for an hour, but there were no guarantees. Simpson didn't miss much, and there were so many ball-busting jobs, like digging ditches, planting trees, or shoveling gravel, that he had going on all the time, that he had plenty of fun things to keep you busy if he thought you were fucking off. I almost called Mr. Josephson by his nickname, Waterhead, because the hacks' nicknames were what we knew them by, but I managed to say, "Mr. Josephson, can I get a form from you?" as soon as he was close to his door.

"What kind of form?"

"A job-transfer request."

Waterhead nodded for a second. "Sure, come on in." Waterhead was actually a very nice guy. He looked a little loopy, and he wasn't going to give you an answer to a math problem real fast, but he was fair with the inmates, actually tried to help them. He unlocked his door with a key he kept on a recoil reel chain attached to his belt. Inside, he pulled out a big file drawer and flipped through the folders. He pulled out a form. "Here we go," he said, handing it to me. "You realize the chances of you getting a transfer are pretty slim?"

"Yeah, I've heard."

Waterhead nodded. "You have to have some good reason, Mason, not just some whim."

"I understand. I just thought I'd try."

"Sure. Why not?" Waterhead said. He stared at me for a minute until I realized my business was over. I said good-bye and left.

I checked my watch. I'd been gone five minutes. I walked across the camp to the clothing room as fast as I could walk. This time, I didn't see Baker. Deacon took me to his desk in the back room, just behind the complaint window, and sat down. Sitting at a table was the blond gimpy guy, John; a short dark guy named Joe; a one-legged kid named Griffis; a guy in his sixties, Tony Abruzzo, said to be in the Mafia; and Don Foster. Joe and John and Griffis were sorting underwear into piles of small, medium, and large, while Foster talked to Abruzzo. Foster, who owned a car dealership in New Orleans, was an executive in the clothing room and didn't have to actually work. Abruzzo was telling stories about his early days as a young hood in New York. I tried to listen in while Deacon turned on his typewriter, since I'd never been around a Mafioso before, if that is what he was.

Deacon had a typewriter, an IBM Selectric. Deacon took the form and twirled it into the carriage, began typing. I had never seen anybody type that fast in my life. *Brrrrrip!* and he rolled the form out, held it up, and read it through the bottom of his bifocals. "Yeah. Looks good," he said. He told me to wait a minute, got up, and went into Baker's office. I watched him take the form to Baker through the window next to his desk. He put the form in front of Baker, who was busy talking to Rusty. Deacon put his finger on the form where he wanted it signed. Baker glanced down, nodded distractedly and signed it. Deacon came back and handed it to me. "Okay. You've requested a transfer, and the head of the place where you want to work just approved it. Take it back to your counselor and get him to sign it. Do not give it to him. The usual chain-of-command bullshit could take weeks, months. Just have him sign it; then take it to the south unit manager, Mr. Thompson."

"I give it to Thompson?"

Deacon stared at me for a second. "Yeah. Give it to Thompson. He'll have gotten a phone call by then."

I nodded and walked back to Dorm Five. I found George and checked to see if he'd seen Simpson yet. No, maybe he wouldn't be coming around for another hour.

I went inside and knocked on Waterhead's door. It was really fortunate I was getting this done during the normal working hours. Usually, after hours, the chairs in the hallway outside the office were filled with inmates waiting to see him.

"Come in."

"I brought that job transfer request back for you to sign, Mr. Josephson."

"Huh? I haven't even sent it to wherever you wanted to transfer to yet," Waterhead said.

"No need," I said. "It's already been approved."

"What?"

I put the paper on his desk. He read it. "Inmate requests work transfer to the clothing room." Waterhead looked up. "That's it? You didn't put down why and Mr. Baker signs it?"

"Yessir. They need a clerk real bad."

Waterhead nodded and picked up his phone. I looked out his window and saw Simpson's blue truck cruise by. Simpson was talking to Barnett, who was riding in the cab with him. "Larry?" Waterhead said. "I have a transfer here, from an inmate Mason. You approved his request?" He listened for a second and nodded. "Huh? Oh, nothing. I just thought this was too fast to be true, you know?" He listened for another second. "Okay. Sure, I'll sign it. If you need a guy, you need a guy."

After work I dropped the form off at the unit manager's office. He didn't say anything, just nodded and said that was all; I'd hear from them later.

After dinner, Foster came by my bunk and told me to report to work the next morning at nine.

"It's approved?" I said.

"Sure. Baker needs you because Deacon's leaving soon. Deacon's going to need the time to train you. You'll have to know how to run the clothing room. The assistant warden already signed it. You'll see it posted on the bulletin board tonight."

"He wants me to run the clothing room? Somebody told me you ran the clothing room," I said.

"Naw. Deacon does. I do the receiving for the commissary."

"Receiving?"

"Yeah, when the stuff shows up from the vendors. I check it in. I calculate the markup. I do inventories now and then. Like that."

I was actually getting out of landscrape? I wondered what the warden would say when he found out. Maybe he'd never notice.

Baker's office was an air-conditioned box in the middle of the clothing room fitted with five big windows. From his desk, Baker could watch the inmates who ran the clothing room line on his left and the inmates who ran the back room, where the complaint window was, on his right. He could not see Tom in the alteration shop, Timmy in the shoe shop, or the several inmates who did special washes and ironing.

Inmate clothing was washed at the Air Force laundry. The clothing room sent big rolling bins filled with dirty clothes in a blue van. The van brought back the clean laundry from the previous day when it returned. The ten or so men in the clothing room line sorted the truckload of clean clothes by laundry number and put it into the inmate boxes.

Inside the office, Larry Baker sat behind his desk and mostly talked with his inmate bosses, who sat in a couple of leather chairs which used to be in the inmate quiet rooms (which were now noisy recreation rooms).

Baker assigned me a desk next to the door at the front of the office. Actually, I shared this desk with Foster, but he seldom used it. Deacon's desk, and presumably mine when he left, was in the issue and repair room, in sight of Baker.

Deacon showed me his system of books in which he logged in every required task and checked it off when done. He managed everything, a kind of master sergeant for the company commander, Baker. All Baker wanted to know about anything was where he was supposed to sign. If he got questions back from the front office, he was briefed by Deacon. Usually Baker would ask Deacon to compose and type the responses to queries from administration. Among my first tasks was to write a report to administration about why we needed to order some new boots.

Deacon loaded me up with typing jobs and kept a careful watch on my output. When he figured I could type well enough, he began to teach me how to conduct inventories of the stockrooms. Inventory reports were due every quarter, but we did one when I'd been at the clothing room for a couple of weeks so I could start off with a fresh slate. Everything in the warehouses was stacked neatly, labeled. The inventories were professionally done. Deacon took his job very seriously.

The only time it was wildly busy at the clothing room was in the afternoon when the inmates returned from work. Lines of inmates, sometimes a hundred or more, formed up in the afternoons to get their laundry. The rest of the day was fairly slow. Inmates sorted clothes and bullshitted, keeping an eye out for intruders from administration who expected to see inmates working at a feverish pace no matter the work load—just like anywhere else.

While Deacon trained me, we became friendlier. Deacon was a curmudgeon, a proud and ornery man in his late sixties. When we walked back to his dorm one afternoon, he told me he'd been in jail once before, during World War II, for resisting the draft. He had gone to jail at that time for his beliefs, but this incarceration was a setup. Deacon was a biochemist. He'd shown me two texts he'd published. As head of the anthropology department at a large university, he'd been making his own psychotropic drugs with which to test his lab animals. He claimed he could guarantee consistent quality in the drugs by making his own—stuff like LSD. Being around the utterly serious and caustic Deacon, it wasn't difficult to believe that he had made a lot of enemies at the university. He was very abrasive, impatient, not at all given to platitudes and encouragement. A graduate student he'd refused to accommodate—something about low grades and a delayed graduation if Deacon wouldn't help—turned him in for making the drugs. In court, Deacon didn't deny making the drugs, claimed it was his professional right to make them if he wanted to, called the female prosecuting attorney at his trial a Nazi whore, and generally behaved like Deacon. He was famous in camp for refusing to go before the parole board to get his sentence reduced. He felt it would be groveling before inferior men. That cost him a couple of extra years. Deacon stood up for himself when most people at camp would call what he was doing pissing into the wind. I had to respect him.

Two weeks into the job, I was typing a letter for Baker when I heard "Warden's coming" from the guys out on the porch. I looked up and saw the warden and his assistant walking down the service road toward us, the same warden who had said, "No writers around typewriters." I jumped up from my desk and told Baker I had to leave for a minute. He nodded, but he was himself getting organized for the impromptu inspection. His bosses had run out to their respective crews, and in seconds the clothing room was bustling with activity. Twenty inmates moved stacks of clothes from where they were to where they weren't and then back again. It was all very impressive. I ran through the issue room and into the stockroom, where I hid behind a tall stack of Army blankets.

It took about five minutes for the warden to get to the stockroom. I heard him talking to Baker in the hallway, his voice muffled. His voice got louder as he came into the stockroom. He looked around quickly, said the place looked good, and left. When I heard the all clear, I went back to my desk.

"Where'd you go, Bob?" Baker said.

"Had to go to the john. Stomach," I said.

"Too bad," Baker said.

I fell into step. My days had become routine, which I could follow while thinking of other things. Up at seven. Breakfast at seven-thirty. Read from eight to nine. Go to work at nine. Lunch at ten-thirty. Back to work at one. Dinner at four-thirty. Walk and shower, one hour. Free time until sleep.

In November, Viking sent Knox a check for more than a hundred thousand dollars, and *Chickenhawk* was still selling well. When Knox told me this, it felt like he was talking about somebody else's book.

Patience would get the money and could finally quit her house-cleaning work. I was grateful she could stop. Maybe she'd finish that novel she'd been working on. Anyway, that was her world.

I was here. I lived on my twenty-five dollars a month. I had a full-time job. I had dropped out of the real world.

I'd brought my robot book manuscript to Eglin with the intention of finishing it. I wouldn't be allowed to publish it while I was in prison, but I visualized myself walking out the front gate with the completed manuscript under my arm—making the best of a bad situation.

Writing, however, was problematic. There was never time at the clothing room. As Deacon trained me ("No, Bob, not form twenty-eight. Form twenty-one. You really have a college education?"), I realized just how much he did there. I was expected to do the same, and I was willing, especially considering the alternative, landscape, but I still had to get a place to write. Dorm Three was a nightmare. It was the only dormitory without air-conditioning. Two giant fans buzzed constantly, men argued, laughed, talked until lights out at ten. The place was noisy beyond belief. The reading rooms—the last quiet places on camp—were now all game rooms. The library was a converted closet with no room to spare. The legal library had three typewriters, but they were restricted for use to prepare legal briefs. Inmates waited in line to type up their appeals. The one thing I could do in the noise was read. Since my robot book was going to be an adventure novel, I checked adventure novels out of the inmate library. I read *Aztec, Eye of the Needle, Little Big Man, Marathon Man, The Key to Rebecca,* and many others. I read John Gardner's *Art of the Novel,* and learned the word *denouement,* which means the solution, the end, of a novel, and now had a professional writing term to use in conversations with inmates, along with suggestions to not split infinitives or leave participles dangling. My inability to write in prison applied to my letters home as well. The ones I did manage were short and essentially incoherent.

Problems at the clothing room occupied my mind. Inventory coming up in a week, need to order new shirts, socks getting low, Deacon leaving soon, and so on.

I'd been in the clothing room for three weeks when, just before Christmas, the warden discovered me. I was typing a report for the commissary because, although Foster did their receiving for them, he could not type up the reports. Foster's big job, I observed, was operating an ancient, programmable adding machine with which he calculated the retail prices for the stuff the commissary received. It took him maybe a half hour a day to figure the twenty percent markup for the stuff on the receiving tickets, and then he handed the stack to me for typing and left to do whatever he did. I didn't care. I liked typing, and Foster had helped me get my job. I typed. Baker was out of the office. I heard the door open, figured it was Baker coming in, kept on typing. Felt someone staring at me. Looked up. The warden. I stopped typing. The warden smiled the slightest smile and shook his head. He nodded at me sternly, turned, and walked out of the office. I watched him walk up the sidewalk toward the administration building. Baker returned. I told him the warden had been here. He was surprised; there had been no inspection. I told him that I thought he might be getting a call from the warden about me because the warden had told me he'd never let me work around a typewriter.

"Really?" Baker said, shocked. He saw his new clerk evaporating before his eyes.

"Sorry I didn't tell you before," I said.

The phone rang.

"Wally?" Baker said into the phone. Wally was Baker's buddy, a counselor in Dorm One. Baker laughed his southern, good-old-boy laugh, which meant Wally had a new fuck joke.

I returned to my typing.

By dinner no one had called.

The next day, no one called. I met the warden in camp, said hello. He didn't mention the incident. Maybe he thought I showed admirable ingenuity and spunk by sneaking past him. Maybe he knew they needed a competent clerk in clothing.

Deacon was gone the next day. I smiled when I realized he hadn't said good-bye. That was his style.

The tall blond guy in the issue room, John, assumed that as the head of the issue room, he'd be getting the desk in that room. Deacon had used the desk, so I figured it would be mine. I walked into the issue room and saw John going through the drawers. I sat in a chair and watched him. John had been working here for almost two years. John looked up a few times, but mostly he was sorting through the stuff Deacon had left behind. We were contesting the ownership of this desk without saying a word.

"I know Deacon said you could have this desk," John said after a while, "but I've got seniority. I need a place to run this room. This is going to be my desk."

I looked through the window into Baker's office. The only other desk was the one in there. To be cooped up with a hack all day was really asking too much. I figured I had enough clout, even being new, to force John to give up the desk. I watched him. I noticed that Joe and Tony Abruzzo, the two guys who work with John, were watching me to see what I'd do. Technically, John worked for me. He managed the clothing issue and repair room efficiently. He was probably the only guy in camp who knew how to do it and cared enough to do it right. It was to my benefit that I didn't have to monitor him and also to my benefit that I didn't have to learn his job to be able to monitor him. All I really wanted was not to have to sit in Baker's office all day.

"How about if I just borrow your typewriter now and then? When you're not using it?"

John smiled. He'd been tensed up, ready for a confrontation. I could see him relaxing. "Sure. I'm usually up and working anyway. Help yourself."

As I walked to Baker's door, I could hear Tony Abruzzo, the Mafioso, laughing. "Good job, John. You defended your fucking territory like a man." I guess it looked like I'd lost.

"There he is. There he is," Baker said, smiling a huge smile, as I walked into his office. Rusty, his almost constant companion, grinned. "So, Bob," Baker said. "What does it all mean? Really?"

I sat down at my desk and flipped on the typewriter. Baker asked the same question every morning, and every morning I'd give the same answer: "I just don't know, Mr. Baker."

Baker laughed like this was the funniest thing he'd ever heard, every day. What he was laughing about was all the oddball reasons people were sent to this prison. He collected incarceration histories like people collect stamps. His friend, Wally the counselor, kept him up-to-date on all the strange ones.

Baker said a guy had just arrived in camp for scaring a bear. "Imagine that, would you?" Baker laughed hard enough to make his face red. "This fellow scares a fucking bear. I mean a bear, you know: four legs, black and hairy, long snout? A fucking bear! He scares this bear, you know? Boo!" Baker put his thumbs in his ears and wiggled his fingers. "And now he's in Eglin for six damn months." Baker laughed more and finally added his ultimate comment: "Bob. What does it all mean? Really?"

"I just don't know, Mr. Baker."

On Christmas Eve, many of the staff of Eglin—guards, secretaries, counselors—distributed gift packages donated by the government and by local citizens. We lined up, walked outside to get our packages, and walked back inside. We got a vinyl notebook with a pad of paper, two Bic ballpoint pens, a box of envelopes, two bars of Zest soap, two handkerchiefs wrapped in plastic, a six-pack of Juicy Fruit gum, and a calendar you could use to mark off the days.

CHAPTER 28

By New Year's 1984, I had quit smoking. I was walking forty-five minutes a day.

I think I must have been healthy, but I didn't feel healthy. I woke up every morning with a new, insidiously minor, malady. Usually I felt some new pain in my head which I assumed was a new tumor. The pains got worse over the course of several weeks until I woke up one morning with a migraine. The pain was so intense I couldn't open my eyes. Light hurt, even the dim light inside the dorm. I staggered to the infirmary, where they gave me aspirins and told me to go back to bed. My head felt like it was expanding. I lay in bed with a cold washcloth on my forehead and hung on. Then I got nauseous, went into the bathroom, and threw up. I went back to the infirmary, and while I was trying to explain to the aide there how bad I felt, I threw up again. They told me that there was nothing they could do, I just had to hang on. The next time I felt one coming on, they said, come over and they'd give me something to prevent the attack. By dusk the headache was gone. I walked outside and felt like I'd just been reborn. I took a deep breath, smiled at the squirrels, marveled at the rosy glow of the sunset. Not having the pain was like feeling exquisite pleasure. Ordinary life, I realized, is constant, exquisite pleasure which I take for granted. I resolved never to forget again. Life, just being alive without pain, how wonderful. The next morning, I'd forgotten my revelation and went back to work.

We were sitting around the issue-room table telling stories one after-noon when a man appeared in front of John's desk. He stood at ease—I mean, the "at ease" you're taught in the military, feet apart, hands clasped behind your back. When John looked up, the man straightened to attention.

"Yes?" John said.

"Johnson. I'm here to pick up my clothes, sir."

"You don't have to call that asshole sir," Tony said, laughing.

Johnson glanced at Tony, turned back to John. He said nothing.

I said, "When did you go?"

Johnson's eyes met mine. "1967 through 1969, sir."

John got up to get the bundle of clothes already picked out for the new prisoner.

"You don't have to call him sir, either, Johnson," Tony said, making a face at me, signifying the guy was a little off.

The man ignored Tony, something Tony was not at all used to.

"When were you there?" Johnson said to me.

"1965. First Cav."

"You flew helicopters," Johnson announced.

"Yes. What did you do?"

"I killed Vietnamese, sir."

"What unit?"

"I was a Seal, sir."

"Too bad," I said. "I heard that was a tough job."

"I liked to kill Vietnamese, sir."

John plunked down the bundle of clothes. The man picked it up, about-faced, and walked out the door.

"That guy isn't back yet," Tony Abruzzo said.

Later, Mr. Baker told me about Johnson. It seems the staff all knew about him.

"The guy was a Seal," Baker said.

I nodded.

"Well, he lived in Key West, heard about a pot bust, heard that the boat, still loaded, was at the Navy base there. This guy gets dressed in black—black face paint and stuff—sneaks into the base at night. He attacks, subdues, gags, and ties up the two sentries guarding the boat loaded with the evidence and then he steals the fucking boat! All by himself!" Baker started laughing. "I mean, this is one tough fucker."

"How'd they get him?"

"Well, it was by accident," Baker said. "The relief guards showed up early, and in a few minutes they were chasing this Seal guy down with patrol boats, searchlights, loudspeakers telling him to stop, all that. He wouldn't. They had to shoot the boat to splinters, blow up the engine, to get him." Baker shook his head in admiration. "Not many people like him in the real world."

As February drew near, I began to look forward to my first furlough, one day in the local area. John and I had both applied, our wives had requested the furlough, all things that had to be done were done. We waited.

John got his approval and came to my new cube in Dorm Five to tell me. I checked the bulletin board. Nothing. I went to the counselor's office and waited in the hallway. After an hour wait, I asked Waterhead what had happened. "They wouldn't approve it. You're considered a high-profile prisoner, Bob. They're afraid the press might make a big deal about the furlough program if they let you go," Waterhead said, not able to look me in the eye.

I met John in the mess hall and told him. He looked very upset. He was caught in the middle of one of the few good things that could happen to you at Eglin, a furlough, and a bad thing: his codefendant and friend was denied the same furlough. We ate in silence.

I walked longer than usual that evening and went to bed early. The next day, at lunchtime, I went into Waterhead's office and told him, "This is about the most chickenshit operation I've ever seen. You idiots furloughed the captain of the fucking boat I was on as a crew member, a man who's got a third longer sentence than mine, and refused to furlough me because I wrote a book. You are all assholes." Waterhead said nothing. I slammed his door as I left.

I still didn't feel any better, though.

Patience and I visited in the visiting room while John and Alice stayed at the beach.

The next possible furlough was in August.

I felt nails going into my skull, over my left eye, and went to the infirmary. They gave me Cafergot, a drug that constricts blood vessels.

The pain vanished. The side effect of the drug is nausea, which, in comparison, is a delight.

I saw Johnson, the Seal, buffing the floor while I was at the infirmary. I asked him how he was doing. He said fine, they had him on Thorazine. "That makes me feel calm, sir." I nodded. When I left, I saw Johnson still buffing the hall, face placid. He'd already polished the whole length of the hallway to a gleaming mirror finish; he had now started over.

I went to work.

Officially I was the inmate in charge of the clothing room, but Foster seemed to be getting the perks. For one thing, he got Post Raisin Bran at breakfast when no one else could. I tried being right behind Foster in the breakfast line, but there was never any Raisin Bran when I got to the bin. I asked Foster about it.

"I make a deal here, a deal there," he said.

I didn't know what he was talking about. I spent nearly every minute at work working. I didn't have time to make deals. And what kind of deals could I make anyway?

"Rags are good," Foster said.

"Rags?"

"Yeah," Foster said, nodding toward an inmate kitchen worker. "See that rag hanging out of his pocket?"

I looked. Sure, all the guys who worked in the mess hall had rags to wipe the tables and stuff. "Yeah. What about them?"

"Where do you suppose those rags come from?"

Foster, a wealthy businessman on the outside, was a rag broker in Eglin?

"I wouldn't be telling you about this, Mason, except I'm leaving in a month. I might as well let you in on some of my contacts."

After we ate, Foster took me back behind the serving counter, into the mess hall kitchen, and introduced me to the hack who ran the place, Evans. Evans nodded when Foster told him I was taking his place. "He can get the rags?" Evans asked.

"Yeah, I'm setting him up today."

"Good. We need some. Like yesterday."

We walked out the back door of the kitchen, onto the service road, and up to the clothing room. "Mason, I know you're a capable guy, but you don't seem to get it, you know?"

"Get what?"

"That's what I mean. You're all the time typing and doing your job. You're blind to the action going on all around you."

"Action?"

"You'll see."

Foster took me on a tour of my own clothing room. We went back to the three washing machines. Two guys were there washing clothes. "Now, who do you suppose these clothes are for?" Foster asked.

"I don't know. Never cared."

"Well, people pay for the service, Mason. Some guys don't want their clothes washed in with all the other who-knows-what's-in-them stuff. They want their stuff hand washed and ironed separately. We provide the service, and we all get presents from the commissary."

I'd heard how the payment plan worked. No inmate was allowed to have more than ninety dollars sent to him in a month. Some of the richer inmates would enlist the services of poorer inmates as "shoppers." The deal was that the shoppers would receive ninety a month, every month, half of which was theirs to keep. To earn their forty-five bucks, the shoppers had to go shopping for their benefactors. Some of the richer inmates, I was told, had as many as ten shoppers because they spent heavily in the nightly poker games. Foster and his employees were getting paid in cigarettes, ice cream, and tennis shoes. There were other services. When I moved into Dorm Five, I noticed that one inmate never made his bed or swept out his cube in the morning; he just dressed and walked out. Two guys who cleaned the dorm would come in every morning and straighten his cube up to inspection level in five minutes—made the bed, even vacuumed the carpet.

Foster called one of the laundry guys over. "Stevie. Bob here's gonna take over for me when I'm gone."

Stevie nodded.

"Evans says we need more rags," Foster said.

"When?"

"I'd like to have a couple of bundles this afternoon."

"You got it," Stevie said.

As we walked back to the office, Foster told me the rags came from the sheets the inmates turned in every day. They washed them with lots of Clorox and ripped them to dish towel size. In time, the rags were washed again and again, eventually wearing out. They just converted more sheets.

"Doesn't anybody ever miss the sheets?" I asked.

"Sure. Like on the largest Air Force base in the world, they notice they're short a few hundred sheets a year out of a million."

I nodded. "Right."

That afternoon, Foster came to my desk to get me. He'd been cool to me since I'd arrived, but now that he'd decided to pass his operation on to me, he took to it with enthusiasm. We went back to see Stevie and got the two bundles of rags, all folded and tied and packed in mattress liners. As we walked down the service road, Foster wanted to know what I wanted the kitchen to do for me.

"Raisin Bran."

Foster laughed. "You noticed, eh? No Raisin Bran in the serving line?"

"Right. That's what I want."

We gave the rags to an inmate who was waiting for them.

The next morning, I went to breakfast as usual, except that when I got in the serving line I noticed one of the inmate kitchen workers behind the coffee urn nod slightly. I got a tray and scooted it along the rails. People ahead of me were asking for Raisin Bran. One guy said, "Out? How can you be out? The stuff comes in an assortment. See the box?" the inmate says, pointing behind the counter. "Says Post Assortment Pack. But you're always out of Raisin Bran, no matter how early I get here."

"I don't know why," said one of the servers. "Talk to Post's legal department."

When I moved in front of the cereal bin, a hand shot out beside it with a box of Raisin Bran in it. I took the box and put it on my tray. When I got to a table, I created a sensation. I told them I'd gotten the last box.

The prison population had grown—swelling to over 750 men. They were arresting so many people for drug violations that the place was getting stuffed. A dozen guys from Steinhatchee, Florida, a small fishing community, showed up one day. As a consequence of the flood of new prisoners, the prison staff converted all the recreation rooms (the former quiet rooms) into bunk rooms. The inmates sleeping in them called them aquariums because they lived behind glass. That still wasn't enough space, so they had also installed double bunks in the cubes that were against the back walls of the sleeping sections so that two guys shared the twenty-eight square feet, the same desk, and the same chair. I'd been sent to such a cube when I first got to Dorm Five. My cube mate was seldom there, and being back against the wall, I had privacy and, compared to Dorm Three, quiet. I spent most evenings reading.

I felt someone watching me. I looked over my book and saw Johnson, the Seal, standing at the entrance to my cube. He wore a T-shirt. His arms were wiry, strong. His stomach flat. His dark eyes piercing.

I sat up. "Hi, Johnson."

"Hello, sir. May I enter?"

I wanted to tell Johnson to stop calling me sir, but you could tell that was how he wanted it, how he saw the world, I think. He sat across from me on my folding chair. I sat up against the headboard of the lower bunk.

"I'll be leaving soon," Johnson said.

"Really? You just got here. I heard you got five years. Judge give you a break?"

"My employers are getting me out."

"Your employers?"

"Yes," Johnson said with finality. I was not to ask for details. Either he was a total looney, or he was telling the truth.

Johnson said nothing for a long moment. Then: "I have bad dreams, sir."

I nodded. "I understand. So do I."

"I know. That's why I'm here. Civilians can't understand. I've always had them, but they're getting worse. I have them while I'm awake. I see people. People I've killed."

This guy was messed up. I was the only one he could talk to? "Do you have a wife, Johnson? A girlfriend? Someone close?"

"No, sir. No family. I had a wife. I woke up strangling her, sir. I am afraid to fall asleep with a woman, so I don't make friends with them."

I swallowed. I thought I had it bad? "What did you do there, Johnson? What'd they make you do?"

"I am an assassin, sir. I worked alone, mostly. My specialty was taking out individual targets. They'd want a particular man, in a Viet Cong–controlled village, usually a village elder or leader, killed. Just the one man, usually. The idea was not just to kill the man, but to scare the rest of the villagers."

"You could sneak into a Viet Cong village, kill a guy, and get back out?"

"Yes. I never bathed. I smelled like the jungle. I'd get into the man's village, past their trip wires and punjis. I'd get into his house. I can see him sleeping on his mats. His wife is only a few feet away. I hold him down, sink my knife under his sternum, into his heart, hold him until he stops jerking, and leave. The dogs don't bark. I am the jungle. When they find him the next day, it scares them because it shows that no one is safe at night. I once stayed to watch, it was so close to dawn. The whole village wailed and cried. I was in a tree, watching them like you do ants. Women, kids, screaming in terror. I didn't feel a thing."

I nodded. Johnson was staring at me. "You're traumatized, Johnson. It's part of the trauma, not feeling."

"Yessir, so I've been told. But I think I'm just evil, sir. I *liked* to kill. I preferred killing alone, though. Sometimes, in teams, the leader would have us surround the village. Then they'd set it on fire. We'd just snipe the people as they ran away from the fire. Wasn't much to it."

"Except for the people being killed."

"Except for the people being killed," Johnson said, nodding. "I know something's wrong. I should feel something. I remember they, the officers, started thinking I was taking my work too seriously, I was collecting ears. They made me stand down. Three days. Ordered me to rest, R&R in the camp, have some beers. I hated it. I don't drink. I sat around camp the first day, not knowing what to do with myself. I cleaned my rifle, sharpened my knives. I went into the jungle that night. I came back the next morning with ears. Took them to the CO and tossed them on his desk. I said, 'Three less for you to kill, sir.' The CO, all of them, figured I was crazy, but I was also good at my job. They never made me stand down again."

"You did this for three years straight? No leaves?"

"I never left. Only when I was transferred. My new employers wanted me to work elsewhere."

"Where?"

Johnson shook his head. "Lots of places. You don't want to know, sir."

I nodded. I think I already knew too much. "You say these . . . these employers . . . they're going to get you out of here?"

"Yessir. In two days. A job has come up."

I swallowed. "How do you feel about that?"

"I hope he kills me, sir, but I'm afraid he can't," Johnson said. His eyes pierced mine. If ever a face looked truthful, Johnson's did.

Two days later, Johnson, having served three months of a five-year sentence, was gone. I sincerely hope he got his wish.

CHAPTER 29

In June they assigned me my first permanent cube. It turned out to be one next to the main aisle, closest to the back door to the mess hall, and ten feet from the phone booth.

I accused Waterhead of picking it especially to torment me. I'd complained that the noise was giving me headaches. I just *thought* it was noisy before. Now it was cacophony. I applied for a transfer which was never granted. I traded some new socks for a set of earplugs from a tree-trimmer inmate. That didn't work. I could hear myself swallow, the ringing in my ears, and the soft rumble of the noise I was trying to avoid. There is nothing louder than sound avoided.

Jeff, John Tillerman, and I were walking our laps one afternoon. Jeff said he'd been on a work detail at the Air Force warehouse where he worked with six other inmates. They had spent the day unloading all the brand-new cans of paint stored inside, throwing them into Dempster Dumpsters.

"They threw new paint away?" I said.

"Yep. Then they had us saw up strapped pallets of plywood with chain saws into chunks we could fit into the Dumpsters."

"Naw," I said. "Really?"

"Really," said Jeff. "It's a fucking crime."

309

John said, "Hell, some guys told me they buried a two-million-dollar jet engine. And remember when the Army was here a couple of months ago for some joint training operation? Well, they left all the C-rations and stuff they brought—excess. They have inmates digging huge trenches to bury whole fucking truckloads of food."

I knew that the staffs at every military and government installation we supported all over the world were at this very moment doing very much the same thing. If they had any supplies left over at inspection time, their budgets would be cut. If their budgets were cut, it would imply that they were not doing their jobs. This could slow advancement among the military personnel and government civilian employees. The only thing to do, in this kind of system, was to get rid of the excesses, thereby proving that one's agency was operating as described in the books. A commander or manager only had to point at his empty supply shelves; his requisite collection of office memos; his efficiency reports for every member of the staff; the monthly safety meeting reports, each with the signatures of all the staff, proving they had all been there; fire-drill maps that showed people how to walk out the doors; OSHA posters on every wall, and their one hundred percent participation in the payroll Savings Bond plan, to prove to the Inspector-General that everything was up to snuff. I knew this, and I tried to explain it to Jeff, but he didn't seem to understand. John, being a veteran, knew what I was talking about.

Jeff was obsessed with the subject of government waste. He started to say something, but his voice was drowned out by a jet fighter taking off. It's a stunning sight and we stopped to stare as the plane rose vertically on a column of smoke and disappeared into the deep blue upper atmosphere. Wow! What a kick that must be, I thought.

"How much does one of those things cost, Bob?" Jeff asked.

"F-16? I'm not sure. Somewhere around twenty million, I'd guess."

Jeff nodded and we continued our walk. By the time we got by the weight shack, Jeff said, "Okay. If you figure that the average middle-class American family pays, say, five thousand dollars a year in taxes, then it takes four *thousand* families to buy that one plane we just saw, right?"

I nodded. John nodded. "Seems right," I said.

"They say a person works three months to pay his federal taxes. Can you see it?" Jeff points out beyond the fence by the tennis court. "Four thousand families, twelve thousand people, each having given every penny of three months of their wages, all standing out there, beaming, as they watch the result of their labor blasting up into the sky?"

"Makes you feel proud, don't it?" I said.

"Makes me sick," Jeff said.

John laughed. "Think of this," he said. "It costs about twenty thousand a year to keep each of us here. That's about four taxpaying families for each of us, right?"

Jeff and I laughed, too. Jeff pointed out at the field and said, "Yep, there they are, over there next to the twelve thousand people who bought that plane. Twelve families, sitting on the grass over there, having a picnic, nodding with satisfaction every time they see us walk another lap. 'Yep,' Fred Taxpayer says, 'getting our damn money's worth, Edna. I worked three months to keep one of them foul fellows behind that white line for three months, and damned if I don't feel just fine about it, too. Damn drug dealers. Pass me a beer, Edna.' "

" 'Why couldn't we buy part of that plane, dear?' " John said, mimicking a woman's voice. " 'We might, Edna. Next year. This year, we take care of these fellows,' " he said gruffly.

We were laughing like kids by now. I could almost see them, the taxpayers, grimly watching us paying our penance, believing they were winning some war on drugs our leaders said we were fighting. The thought was funny, but also depressing. I was a taxpayer, too.

Another F-16 blasted into the sky. I saw this flight differently because of Jeff. I wondered how many people had had to give good money for that one flight. There are thousands of such flights every day, all over the world. God! And what about all the *people* who work for the government? There are hundreds—no, thousands—of government departments. The money wasted! It boggles the mind.

When Foster left, he threw a giant ice-cream party, one of the biggest the camp had seen. Most of the inmates who left Eglin cashed in their commissary accounts in ice cream, had a party and invited their friends. Foster must have served ten gallons of ice cream. He also had a big bowl of fresh fruit salad and a huge chocolate cake from the kitchen. He collected much status as a prisoner doing this, but who was going to remember? He was leaving.

I now had custody of Foster's programmable adding machine and the job of figuring the markup on the receivables. It only took me an extra five minutes a day doing it, and it got me into the commissary.

I hand delivered the commissary receiving forms to the commissary office in the afternoons. Miss Reed read them and signed them. I usually lingered there because it was interesting to be somewhere besides the clothing room, and Miss Reed was friendly. I could sit at a visitor's chair in front of her desk and we'd gossip. I kept her up on what was happening at the clothing room; she told me the latest stuff going on in the administration building. Grumbles often joined in our conversations. Grumbles had his own desk across from Miss Reed, a radio, and his own IBM Selectronic typewriter, which he didn't know how to use. I watched him type. Two fingers? No wonder I did all the typing for the commissary.

Two other guys, Frank Short and Joe Leone, worked as stock clerks in the commissary storeroom, which was piled floor to ceiling with boxes. They seldom came into Miss Reed's office. If they had work to do, they were very busy. When they didn't, Miss Reed let them off because they had to work every night in the commissary line. Grumbles and these two guys were the highest paid inmates in the camp. I made fourteen cents an hour at the clothing room, which adds up to nearly twenty-five dollars a month. Grumbles earned fifty a month, Frank and Leone split fifty, the other half of the hundred-a-month budget the prison provided for inmate pay at the commissary.

I liked being in the commissary. They needed me. I helped them do inventories. They needed to get organized. I was, after all, a school-trained former U.S. Army supply officer. Much of the stock was packed sloppily, leading to incorrect counts and inefficient restocking; there were several brands among rarely used items like chewing tobacco—a wasteful repetition; unnecessary duplication of ice-cream brands, which only took up more space; they needed better inventory forms. I might get a chance to straighten this place up—Grumbles was leaving. He'd told Reed they offered him two months at a halfway house, but he told them to stuff it. He was leaving in four months.

Despite our initial confrontation in the clothing room, John and I became friends over a period of a couple of months. He and I had to work closely together to manage the place for Baker. John and I did all the inventories in the clothing warehouses and decided what to order and how much to order for Baker. John and his crew did the grunt work. I handled the paperwork. We never mentioned the desk incident again, and I spent most of my free time sitting at his desk bullshitting with him and his team while they worked, like Foster used to do.

Tony Abruzzo had been a member of a New York street gang in the thirties, saw combat in World War II, eventually ended up working for the Mafia after the war. Crime, he explained, was his salvation. He grew up poor, his father a carpenter. He'd hijacked his first truck, in Manhattan traffic, when he was fourteen. When he was sixteen, his father gave him fifty cents pocket money. He had forty dollars in his pocket at the time and a car parked around the corner. His dad didn't own a car.

"We didn't know what the fuck we were doing," Tony said. "We just figured a whorehouse was a place we'd see some money." Tony folded shirts while he talked. "You know, a guy comes into these places to get laid, he's *got* to have some money on him. So we, three of us, march up the stairs to this cathouse on Eighth and go inside. We timed it so we'd be the first. We tell the girls, 'Hey, we're taking over for a while.' The madam says, 'What?' Joey, my partner, says, 'You know, we're the bosses now. Get to work.'

"The madam says, 'Nobody's here,' and Joey says, he's grinning like a kid, he says, 'I'm here, sister. Start on me.' " Tony broke into laughter. "That fucking Joey was always a gas," Tony said, tears welling in his eyes.

"So what's the point? That's the crime? You raped some whores?" John said.

"No, you dumb fucking cripple," Tony said. Joey and John and I laughed. Abruzzo was abrasive and rude and everyone liked it. He called Baker a hillbilly redneck to his face and even Baker laughed. "Besides," Tony said, "Joey pays the whore. Of course, he takes the money back, but that's robbery, not rape. Anyway, what we did was to wait until the customers showed up. I'd pull my gun when they got inside, tell them to empty their pockets. They'd go, 'Hey, you can't do that,' and I just smile and wave the gun. The gun does all the talking. They empty their pockets. Then I send them back to the girls,

saying, 'Hey, maybe you're getting fucked, but at least you'll get laid.'
I'm feeling like Robin Hood, here." Tony stopped while we laughed.

John, my clothing room partner, and I were having early dinner at
three. I'd had Baker put us on the list because John and I liked coming
back to the clothing room and having coffee during the four o'clock
count. It allowed us to think we were special not to be counted in the
dorms. I filled out an "out-count" form every morning, which Baker
signed, with our names and four others who worked in the back,
including Jed Wilson, a new guy who was helping Timmy in the shoe
room. During the count, John and I brewed instant Bustelo espresso
and sat back in our swivel chairs in the issue room and bullshitted
while we monitored the count's progress on the loudspeakers. We
talked about our crimes, our families. John had a brand-new son and
showed me his picture often. After count, we managed the complaint
window for an hour, told people they couldn't have anything, and
then we'd be off. It was pleasant.

John was in for smuggling marijuana, too. On his last trip he got
caught in a storm, got beached at night, miles from his drop-off point.
After a frantic night of getting a truck, unloading the pot, he set a fire
to scuttle the boat. But the boat didn't burn and sink like he'd planned
and the police were able to trace him. Pot residue in the boat convicted
him. John was appealing his case. The government only had a few
ounces of pot as evidence, a misdemeanor, but the feds had calculated
that the boat was carrying two tons, based on the size of the boat.
John was outraged because he'd only had half that. Anyway, he had
made successful trips, and I'll never forget his description of how he
felt after his first trip.

"I almost didn't make it, Bob." John was smiling, shaking his head.
You could tell by the happy twist of his mouth and the shine of his
eyes that he really loved smuggling. "Shit, I really didn't know what
I was doing. I was lost half the time. But I got the stuff here. Delivered
it to my partner. A week later he comes by my place, plops down a
grocery bag on my coffee table. I look inside. Money. Bales of it.

"A few days later, I'm driving down U.S. 1 on my way to Fort
Lauderdale. I'm driving a brand-new Mustang convertible that I bought
with cash. The top is down. Jimmy Buffet is playing my favorite song

on the tape player. I'm smoking some very nice weed, not the stuff I brought in. The sun is shining. I have over a hundred thousand dollars in a canvas tool bag in the trunk of the car. I am free." He sighed. "Life can be *good.*"

Jed Wilson was sitting at our table in the mess hall telling John and me that he thought drugs were the ruination of America.

John said, "Jed, they put you in here for smuggling cocaine. Where do you get off?"

"Sure, I smuggled it, but I never once used it," Jed said. "It was strictly business with me."

John and I rolled our eyes.

"The truth," Jed said, smacking his fist against his sternum. "God strike me fucking dead."

John nodded. "You ever smoke any pot?"

"None of that, neither. Send you straight to hell."

"Do you drink or anything?" John said.

Jed shook his head and said, "None of that. You want to know a *legal* way to get stoned that *won't* send you to hell?" Jed leaned close to us.

"What's that?" John said.

Jed smiled. I saw something black in his mouth, like his lower gum was dead or something. "Simple and legal," Jed said. "You take a piece of fishing leader—you know, that clear kind? And you stick it into a cigarette. That's it. Smoke that. That'll fuck you up."

John and I looked at each other.

I said, "Jed, that shit can kill you."

"Better'n going to hell," Jed said. "I been doin' it for years." He smiled and I saw the crescent of black stuff peeking over his lower lip again.

"Jed," I said, "you got something in your mouth? Besides food?"

Jed nodded and finished chewing a mouthful of chicken. He swallowed and said, "Yeah. My chew."

"Tobacco? You mean you keep that shit in your mouth while you eat?" John said.

"Sure. Where else am I going to put it?"

"That's disgusting, Jed," I said.

Jed smiled, encouraged. "I sleep with it, too."

"You're kidding."

"Nope. Works great. I wake up feeling nervous? I just take a couple chaws and stash my chew back inside my lip. Sleep like a baby."

"God," I said. "What does your wife think of that? Like when you try to kiss her."

"Her?" Jed said, looking sheepish. "Hell, Clarice won't let me chew when I'm home."

CHAPTER 30

Two good things happened on my first anniversary in Eglin. In August 1984, I got my first furlough, and *Chickenhawk* became a *New York Times* paperback best-seller.

Patience came to the prison Saturday morning. I'd changed into my set of civilian clothes kept in the administration building and was waiting for her outside. I saw some staff coming to work and started worrying, wondering if they'd think I was trying to escape. I was dressed like a civilian and armed with a letter that said I could walk around like a civilian until eleven o'clock Sunday night. But they could change their minds, couldn't they?

Patience drove up in our Escort. I mentioned that the dashboard was dusty. A mess like that would get you demerits in prison, I said. Patience nodded with a worried look on her face. She'd spent hours cleaning it up.

We drove to a seaside motel in Fort Walton Beach, known as the "Redneck Riviera" because it was popular with tourists from southern Alabama. We spent the day making love and walking on the purest, whitest beach I've ever seen. I'd asked Patience to bring my camera. I had an inexplicable urge to take pictures—I really missed making photographs. I guess I wanted to absorb myself in something I could control. I had thirty-nine hours of freedom and Patience was watching me photograph sand dunes. That night, we saw *Ghostbusters* and ate at a posh restaurant that served worse food than I ate in prison.

At ten o'clock Sunday night, Patience drove me back home.

I walked through the administration building, changed my clothes, and, less than fifteen minutes after she dropped me off, I was once again a prisoner. I felt relaxed. I'd felt uncomfortable at the motel. You could do anything you wanted—the choices were endless and intimidating. Meals were confusing—you had to tell them what you wanted from a huge list of possibilities. You had to decide how to dress. There was no count to positively establish that you belonged anywhere. It was also deathly quiet.

Prisoners were supposed to visit in visiting rooms.

It was no surprise that my book was going to be a best-seller in paperback. Gerry Howard told me *Chickenhawk* would be a best-seller before it was printed because Penguin had already gotten huge orders from the two big bookstore chains, B. Dalton and Waldenbooks. Penguin printed "National Bestseller" on the cover of the first paperback edition, and so it was.

At the end of the first week of publication, my cube neighbor, ex-stockbroker Walton, who subscribed to the *New York Times* (and the *Wall Street Journal*), showed me the best-seller list in the *Book Review.* Number five, on the nonfiction side of the list, read: "*Chickenhawk,* by Robert Mason. (Penguin, $3.95) The experiences of a helicopter pilot in Vietnam." Walton said that was great, and maybe I ought to be reading some of the books he had about managing money and investing. He said, "Know what the hell you're doing, and never trust your stockbroker. He's trying to make money. For him." Walton's advice came from personal experience. He was convicted of fraud because, he said, some salesmen at his firm, an international investment company, made outrageous promises to their clients and a lot of people lost lots of money. The government claimed Walton knew what his salesmen were doing, but Walton just shrugged at that. "Salesmen will say anything, Bob. Just remember that."

Walton was a frank kind of guy. He once admitted to me that he was really nervous about being in a prison filled with drug dealers. But, after he got to talk to them, he discovered they were just regular people, most of them.

I used to ask the inmates if they thought this was working, this

incarceration, for people like us, people who had committed nonvi-
olent crimes. Walton just shrugged. "When I get out of here, Bob, I'll
still be a rich man. My tennis game will be better; I'll have lost twenty
pounds; I own a house in Connecticut and one in Florida. You really
want to hurt me? *Take my money.*" He smiled.

Walton's smile said, *If you can find it.* There were quite a few financial
crooks in Eglin, and I asked them how money was really hidden. I
didn't have any to hide, but I figured the information might come in
handy someday for a book. I had come to believe in Bill Smith's motto:
Don't do it; write about it.

I read the description in the best-seller list over and over, not really
believing it was me they were talking about. It felt like it was some
kind of trick. I kept expecting someone to yell, "Surprise." I sat on
my bunk trying to comprehend what this meant, aware that I was due
to go back to work in a half hour. I took Walton's copy of the *Book
Review* around to show a few of my friends, but I wasn't free to celebrate. Having a book on the best-seller list had nothing to do with
reality. I was a prisoner who ran the clothing room. I went back to
work and wrote a letter for Baker about the status of our last clothing
inventory.

Viking Penguin sent Patience on a big book tour in my place. She
sent me her itinerary, and I called her at hotels all over the country.
When I phoned her in Detroit, a man answered the phone, breathing
hard. I said, "Who's this?"

The voice, panting, says, "That you, Bob?"

I recognized Jerry Towler. I laughed. "What the hell you doing,
Towler?"

"I told Patience to ask me if she ever needed anything, Bob. She
took me up on it. Pant. Pant." I could hear Patience laughing in the
background.

I laughed and said, "Can I talk to my wife, asshole?"

Towler spoke away from the phone: "You okay?" Patience was
giggling. "She's okay. I was kinda worried. I always leave 'em gasping,
you know?"

Later, when she got to San Francisco, I called her at Bill Smith's
place. Talking to Bill and Emmy from inside prison was weird. They

sent me a postcard of Alcatraz which said, "Having a wonderful time. Wish you were here."

I walked down the jogging trail. A volleyball game was going on at the sandy court near the water. The sun was getting low; the heat on my face felt good. As I passed the mangrove marsh where the water from the bay disappeared into the woods, I saw a feral mother cat and her two kittens backlighted on a tree branch, looking like lions in the Serengeti. I'd called to them often, but they'd always ignored me. I made a squeaking noise through my pursed lips and they looked at me curiously. One of the kittens yawned. I increased my pace.

I heard a thunderous roar coming from the airfield. A F-16 fighter was making a maximum-performance takeoff. The pilot had the plane in a perfectly vertical climb, afterburners on. He was climbing at nearly fifty thousand feet per minute, a fact that was completely astounding to me. Hueys can climb at two thousand feet per minute, on a good day. The sound shook my chest. In seconds the plane was invisible at the top of a long contrail. What a thrill that pilot must feel. A minute after takeoff, the plane was gone. I saw the four thousand taxpayer families who owned the plane and, over there, the three families who'd paid for this one flight. They were all applauding.

I recognized an inmate walking toward me. His name was Jones, but everybody called him Biafra. He'd come to Eglin weighing three hundred pounds and decided that his project would be to lose weight while he was here. Eglin was known, after all, as a fat farm for crooks. Biafra was now down to two hundred. His skin hung in folds and flapped around his legs as he walked. Each day I saw him, it looked like he was deflating. You wanted to cinch him up, take up the slack somehow. Biafra puffed past me, nodding slightly, his mind calculating the number of calories expended at each step. I saw Biafra every day and watched his progress. The consensus among the inmates was that his skin would never tighten up, and that he should stop. He was, after all, a big man. A healthy weight for him might've been 220, but he announced he would not stop until he reached his ideal weight, 150 pounds.

I walked past the weight shack and watched the guys inside grunting and puffing, pumping weights with grim determination. Up and down. Sweat pouring, muscles rippling. I circled past the tennis courts as I looped around to reverse my track for my second lap. It was easier to reverse course than to walk through the camp, or at least it was habitual for us to do so. I stopped at the bocci courts, picked up three of the heavy balls used in the game, and tried to juggle them. I'd taught myself how to juggle in New York when I dreamed up a product, a set of bean-bag balls to learn how to juggle. I claimed the bean bags would make learning to juggle easier because if you dropped them you wouldn't have to chase them. To prove this, I used them to teach myself to juggle. They worked, but like so many things I've thought of, I never pursued it. My real work in life then was to make mirrors.

Mirror maker. That seemed so long ago it had probably happened to somebody else. It was like a fantasy that I'd once been an executive in a business. Each bocci ball weighed five pounds, and I figured juggling them was good exercise for my arms. I juggled for a couple of minutes, dropped the balls on the hard-packed clay lane, and continued my walk. Halfway down the west boundary of the camp, I stopped and did as many chin-ups as I could on the chinning bar set up along the trail. The most I could do when I started was two. Now I did ten. Continuing down the trail, I felt my biceps. Soon I would be a gorilla.

I came to the white line across the service road. I walked beside it carefully, like it was a precipice. I noticed some people driving by, maybe some of *my* taxpayers. That was outside. I turned and walked back along the service road for my second lap.

The Steinhatchee boys, twelve fishermen who'd shown up a few months before for running pot in their boats, were sitting on benches under some trees next to Dorm Two weaving fishnets. They watched their work intently through squinted eyes in their weathered, leathery fishermen's faces. Their line-burned, scarred, and gnarled hands knotted string into a web so complex it made you dizzy. The Steinhatchee boys were standoffish. I only overheard them a few times. They talked about how they were ever going to replace their boats the government had taken. They shipped the fishnets home for their wives to sell.

I walked along the wooden fence, down the jogging trail. You could roll under this fence; it wasn't for security, it was a privacy fence. There was a trailer park next door. Some guys did roll under the fence at night, to visit some enterprising girls at the trailer park who entertained sex-starved, and courageous, inmates.

When my watch showed that I had been walking for the forty-five minutes I allowed myself for exercise, I stopped. I walked into the small woods beside Dorm Five and did stretching exercises and cooled down.

I walked toward the side entrance of the dorm and saw Doodle Harris, the millionaire land developer who'd arrived at Eglin the day after John and I. They'd gotten Doodle for not paying taxes. He finally did. The local paper announced it on the front page. He'd paid the half million dollars the government wanted, thinking he'd made a deal, but the IRS threw him into jail anyway. His wife and his partners showed up every week in his Rolls-Royce, and they spent the whole visit going over Doodle's plans. He claimed he'd be out in a few weeks, didn't really unpack for a month. Now, a year later, his confidence had disappeared. Doodle looked very despondent sitting on the park bench beside Dorm Five. He nodded, but he was lost in worry. I'd heard him talking on the phone to his "people" and I knew he was trying to lock up a deal on a piece of beach property. The deal wasn't going well, according to what I heard, and Harris wasn't able to get out and kick some ass to make it work. I went inside to my cube.

Walton, my stockbroker neighbor, and Doug Norton, the inmate tennis pro, were in the aisle with a tennis racket. Norton was showing Walton the importance of a follow-through with the racket. Norton had a client list of about ten inmates he was teaching to play tennis. Like Walton had said, he wanted to improve his game. I watched them, interested, while I undressed. I'd tried playing a few times with Tony Abruzzo. He kept telling me, "No, Bob, the idea is to hit the fucking ball *over* the net." I smiled. Tony, at sixty-five, could slaughter me in tennis. I watched Norton show Walton how to hold a racket for a backhand. I stripped down, wrapped myself in a towel, and went to the showers.

I always used the same shower stall, and I noticed that so did most people. Inmates would actually wait if "their" stall was busy. I think it must have been a small way to personalize our lives here. I liked my stall because it had a showerhead that delivered a thick stream of water which felt like a massage. There was no worry about running out of hot water at the camp, and I spent at least fifteen minutes letting the water stream beat on my shoulders and neck. While I basked in the steam, I noticed plastered on the tile wall a new soggy fuck-book foldout page. There was a different one every day. Today it was Nancy.

Nancy was wet and wrinkled on the tiles, but she was still smiling as she exposed herself to viewers who needed to see one again. I wondered if she knew where her picture would end up when she posed for the shot. Probably. She seemed to be thinking: Here it is, jerkoffs. I tried not to pay attention to Nancy. The pose was brazen, vulgar. Cheap titillation. I faced the shower and lathered my hair with Johnson's Baby shampoo and things went normally until the shower stream hit low. I could feel myself stiffen. I looked down. I was standing out like a coat peg. It was really impressive to me that I could consciously be offended by pictures like Nancy while my body was clearly in love. I wanted to be home where I could give Patience some loving hints like: "Feel like fooling around?" But I wasn't. I wouldn't be home for a year. I felt myself getting stiffer. Apparently Nancy was plenty good enough for my dick. I rinsed off the shampoo and stood back and watched the stream of water hitting me. In two minutes, I went off like a gun. Well, that was sex for another three or four days. The average was three or four days, at the end of which time I must have had testosterone saturating every cell in my body. I had sexy dreams like I did in high school and sexual urges so strong I could think of nothing else until I did something about it. I would be a failure as a monk; or did monks take a lot of showers, too?

I soaked in the steam awhile longer and then turned the water off. I thought, Thanks, Nancy. I hope it was as good for you as it was for me, and stepped out to towel off.

I went back to my cube and put on a clean set of clothes. All my clothes were new—as you would expect of the guy who runs the clothing room. I put on a new pair of pants and a sweatshirt I'd bought at the commissary and stood for a minute, watching the section buzzing with inmates, deciding how I'd spend my evening. The section had a homey quality about it. I knew most of the twenty-five men there, and they all knew me. It was home.

I unlocked my locker and got out my big radio and the earphones. I hung the radio on a hook on the partition above the head of my cot. I had made the hook with coat-hanger wire so the radio was up high enough to get the PBS station in Pensacola.

The loudspeaker called an inmate to the control room. That meant a urine test. It was random. They called up two or three men every night. Some of the inmates who had been here a few years said the piss tests really cut down on the pot smoking. Not like the good old days, they said, when the guys had parties in the woods next to Dorm Five where Tarzan fell out of the tree.

I listened to the radio no matter what I was doing. Sometimes I answered mail. I was getting about fifty letters a week from readers, most of whom, I was surprised to know, weren't Vietnam veterans. I read them all, and tried to answer them, too, but I was falling behind. I got a thousand letters from readers while I was at Eglin.

Sometimes ideas for new inventions popped into my mind, and I made drawings. I sent an attorney friend of mine, Tony LoPucki, in Gainesville, my idea for a quartz wristwatch that didn't need batteries. LoPucki, who used to be a patent attorney, liked my ideas, but he thought the world was doing okay using batteries in their watches. Fine. The only reason LoPucki talked to me at all was that when I first met him, I showed him my scheme for three-dimensional television. I got the idea looking at the display of a quartz wristwatch, oddly enough. I'd experimented with 3-D movies in New York. I exposed single frames of a still life in an 8mm movie camera, moving the camera left or right for each frame. I projected this film and tried looking at it through a spinning disk with one hole near the edge. The idea was that if the disk spun at the right speed, then my left eye would see a left image in one frame of my film, and then, if everything was timed right, my right eye would see the next frame, a right image. Persistence of vision, I figured, would create a 3-D picture. I mounted the disk on a hand drill, and by varying the speed, I got it to work. But I couldn't figure an easy way to synchronize the disk with the flickering left and right images. The blinking seconds on the liquid crystal display of a watch gave me an idea: Wear glasses with liquid-crystal lenses. Then send a signal from the TV to the glasses, and the lenses could be switched alternately from opaque to clear in synch with the thirty images per second on the TV screen. I had no idea how to build something like this, so I sat on the idea for a year before I met LoPucki. LoPucki was going to Washington anyway, so he said he'd do a search free, because he knew I was poor. He came back very impressed. The idea was patented, yes, but only three months before. I didn't know where these ideas came from, but they weren't coming tonight.

I decided to read. I selected a book out of the dozen or so I had on the shelf over the built-in desk. I picked out *The First Circle*, by Aleksandr Solzhenitsyn.

I'd finished *At Play in the Fields of the Lord,* by Peter Matthiessen, a book Bill Smith sent me. Smith had been sending me books to improve my essentially illiterate background. So had Larry Heinemann. Heinemann sent me *Life on the Mississippi* because he said I wrote like Samuel Clemens. Heinemann was gracious as hell. *At Play* was stunning, and I wondered how Matthiessen ever got to be so smart. His writing is like poetry, every page of it. The book was written in 1965, while I was living in a pup tent in Vietnam. I missed it, though I probably wouldn't have read it had Bill not sent it. At Eglin, in addition to the technical books I read—layman physics stuff about fundamental particles, black holes, artificial intelligence, computers, and so on—I read a lot of novels, hoping that some of what makes writing a novel possible would rub off on me.

I put on my headphones and tuned in the classical music station. That made the rumble and rush of the crowded dorm fade to the background. I read.

The irony of *The First Circle,* for me, was that it took place in a *sharashka,* a minimum-security prison in Russia. I got lost in the life of Nerzhin and the other well-educated inmates of the *sharashka* because Solzhenitsyn made me feel I was there with them. Naturally, you can't learn how to create stories like Solzhenitsyn or Matthiessen do by copying their writing techniques, but you can see grace in action and learn a few nuts and bolts about how they handle the mechanics of the presentation. All it took was time to do careful reading. I had plenty of time. I was now around day three hundred and ninety. I had another two hundred and ten to go. Lots of time.

Just before ten, the guys who'd been watching television came wandering back from the TV room to be in their cubes for the count. I put my book away and turned out my desk lamp.

After count, a lot of the inmates returned to the TV room. We had cable, and they wanted to see *The Hitchhiker,* a popular program on HBO.

Now the thing I dreaded the most happened. Someone whose voice had become a nightly torment got on the phone in the phone booth that was conveniently located ten feet from my bed. I covered my head with my pillow, but I could hear every word.

The guy on the phone had a problem. He'd said his wife could date while he was inside. I heard him explaining this to his buddy one day in the chow line. He said, "She gets lonely, and I trust my friends."

His friend looked at him incredulously and the guy quickly added, "Well, hell, it doesn't wear out, you know," and laughed to show his friend he was kidding.

Tonight, as usual, he talked loudly, as though he were home instead of in a prison bedroom where twenty-five men were trying to sleep. I heard: "Yeah, Sam's okay. Sam's a good guy. Where'd you go?"

"The Tin Lizzy? What'd you do?"

Pause. I could only imagine what his wife was saying. I was hoping she'd talk long enough for me to get to sleep.

"Yeah? You never wanted to dance with me."

Pause. I pressed my hands against my ears.

"Me? I dance. I love to dance."

I was groaning under my pillow. I couldn't stand it. I'd been plotting to take the phone apart and throw the little microphone in the mouthpiece into the swamps where the cats lived. A phone repair inmate told me they had a problem with that: guys were throwing them away for the same reason I wanted to—peace. The idiot talked. And talked.

"Sure. When I get home, I'll take you dancing."

Pause. I was so happy for him. Dancing? My, my.

"So what'd you do after Tin Lizzy?"

He took her home?

"Took you home? I know he took you home. What did you do when you got home? That's what I want to know."

He kissed her?

"What?" the idiot says real loud. I heard "Shutthefuck up!" from somewhere in the section.

The idiot ignored the request. He said, "Yeah. Then what?"

More than a good night kiss?

"Yeah. *Then* what?" His voice was changing, higher in pitch. He listened for a long time, almost long enough for me to drop off.

"What?" the idiot yelled suddenly. I jerked back from the brink of sleep and heard, "You sucked his dick? You sucked *Sam's* dick?"

A pause while idiot's wife, Mrs. Idiot, explained.

"Sure, I said you could date my friends. When you had to. I know I said that. But I didn't say you could suck their dicks! That's personal!"

I heard a loud crash. Someone had thrown a work boot at the phone booth.

The idiot lowered his voice so only those of us lucky enough to be right next to the fucking phone could hear. "Did he come? In your mouth?" he said softly.

"Enough!" I groaned. I got out of bed and went to the phone booth. "Hey," I said. "You mind? I'm trying to sleep."

The idiot said, "Wait a minute, hon," put his hand over the mouthpiece, and said to me, "This phone is for anybody to use."

"Yeah, I know. But most people phone when most people are awake, you know? This is bullshit. Get off the phone."

"You want to try to make me?" said the idiot loudly. He was stupid, but he was very large.

A voice behind me said, "I'll fucking make you." I turned around. It was my neighbor across the aisle. He was a former professional football player who'd got caught selling cocaine to his fellow players. He was a linebacker. Very big.

The idiot was intimidated. He nodded and said quietly into the phone, "Look, honey. I'll call you back from another phone, okay?" He paused. "No, I don't. I understand. You know I love you. I'll—"

The linebacker, who looked as tall as the phone booth, stepped up close to the idiot. The guy looked up, nodded quickly, said "I'll call you back in a minute," and hung up the phone. We both watched him leave. The linebacker said, "Is that guy as stupid as he sounds?"

"Yes. Every bit as stupid as he sounds. Possibly he's a vegetable."

Luckily, I fell asleep before the next call.

CHAPTER 31

Ine of the guys who worked the clothing room line was called Professor because he read all the time and talked about philosophy. He was a black guy and a cripple. His ankles were fused, for some reason I forget, and he hobbled when he walked. I lent him *The Holographic Paradigm*, a book about the mind as an illusion that I could barely follow. He loved it and we became friends.

When it was lunchtime three of us from the clothing room, Professor and John and I, usually walked to the mess hall together. Since we were with Professor, John and I had to walk slowly so he could keep up. One day Tony Abruzzo came up behind us and said, "What the hell's the holdup here?" I turned around and saw Tony grinning and shaking his head at Professor's pitiful gait. Suddenly Tony reached out and shoved Professor off the sidewalk. "Get out of the way!" he yelled. Professor stumbled off the sidewalk, tottering, barely able to keep his balance. Tony turned to him as he passed us and said, "Professor. You know what your trouble is?"

Professor, amazingly, was laughing. He said, "What?"

"Not only are you a nigger, you're a fucking cripple."

I was horrified, but Professor started giggling like a kid. I still couldn't figure out how Tony did it.

For some reason, I often ended up in line at the mess hall standing next to an attorney from New York City. Mike usually told me how he had the government on the run with all his fancy legal maneuvers. Mike had robbed his clients of money they invested with him and took the position that they should've known better. Today Mike was talking about a hot new business scheme he had for when he busted out of here.

"You hear about how they can implant a fertilized egg from one woman to another?"

"I've read that, yes," I said. "Like they do with cattle, right?" The line moved ahead and I took a step. Mike followed.

"Right. But with people? Wow! There's a fortune in this," Mike said.

"Yeah, I guess a lot of women will have that done. Infertile couples, and all that."

"Naw. That's not what I mean. There's some money that way, too, but you have to be a doctor to cash in on that. What I want to do is even more brilliant. Attorney work."

I asked how an attorney could cash in on fetal transplants.

Mike grinned. "Simple. You buy fertilized eggs from beautiful blond couples, you know? Good stock; they make just the kind of kids that're in demand. Then you take these eggs to someplace like Haiti and hire native women to carry the fetus to term. Get it?"

"Black women give birth to blond babies?"

"Right! Do you have any idea what blond babies are worth on the adoption market?"

I shook my head.

"Hundred, two hundred thousand. That's what. You use these niggers like ovens. They hatch the kids; I arrange the adoptions. Millions."

I stared at Mike. He was smiling like he'd discovered how to turn lead into gold. I think he was a sociopath.

"What do you think?"

"Millions," I said, nodding.

"Right!" Mike said, laughing.

When we got into the mess hall, I made sure we were in separate serving lines.

I didn't see Mike in the chow line for a few days. I heard from John Tillerman, who worked as a clerk in administration, that they'd sent him out for "diesel therapy." Mike had succeeded in getting a judge in New York to review his case and the judge called him before his court. That happened now and then, and the Bureau of Prisons had busses traveling all over the country transferring prisoners from prison to prison and sometimes delivering them to court dates.

If you were not a troublemaker like Mike, they usually gave you a legal furlough and let you fly to wherever you had to go. Mike had pissed off too many people; the prison elected to send him by bus to New York. Normally that might take a few days. But when diesel therapy was prescribed, the route was not direct. They switched you from one bus to another, making your trip an arduous zigzag tour of the whole country with extended visits at county jails while you waited for the next connection. John said they'd put Mike on the bus two days ago to make his court date in six weeks. Mike would be spending his days on a prison bus, in handcuffs, his nights in one squalid county jail hole after another. I figured it was justice.

At work one day, we heard that Tony Abruzzo had a heart attack while playing tennis. They shipped him to Lexington, to the Bureau of Prison's main hospital. We heard he was doing okay, but he'd miss the big talent show, the Eglin Frolics.

The inmates had built a stage across the salad bar and set some patio clamplights up all around it. It was standing room only when I got there. I sat on the low serving-line wall with John Tillerman. Everybody was hooting and waving, having a great time. I saw Red the counterfeiter sitting with Joe the materials engineer. Red told everybody he was here for making his own money. He owned a print shop and got curious about how they printed money one day. He went to a bank and, as a businessman, asked them how he could detect counterfeit bills. They told him how and gave him a pamphlet about it. Red took this information and started making money that'd pass. His money wasn't a work of art, he said. The bills all had the same serial number. He claimed it didn't matter. The secret, Red said, was to condition the money so it looked circulated. He'd come up with just the right mixture of dirt and oil and stones that he dumped into a washing machine with his freshly minted hundred-dollar bills. A couple of hours later, he said, the bills looked like they'd been in circulation for years. He sold this handmade money to people for twenty to forty cents on the dollar and made real money. He told me he knew he'd be caught eventually, but he'd been saving up for it.

I seldom got to see everybody in one place like this. Joe the engineer listened to Red for a while and then turned to argue with Chuck, another engineer. Chuck and Joe had fundamental disagreements about stuff I didn't understand. Each one thought the other was a quack. Joe was in materials; Chuck was a mechanical engineer. Chuck was also designing an airplane. I had seen the model he made in the woodshop, and it looked like it would work as a full-sized plane. He was having his kid run computer programs at home to design the airfoils for the wings. He was not joking. He said he was going to build it when he got out, and I had no doubt he would.

The show was late to start. The inmates were loud, yapping happily. I looked around for more people I knew. I knew a lot of inmates and I knew all their stories. They came to me with them. That guy, sitting two guys down from Red. Danny? Danny something. He shouldn't be here. He should get an award for what he did.

Danny was a pilot, in his late twenties. He had been approached by two guys who asked him if he wanted to make a hundred thousand dollars for one flight. Danny was nervous, but he listened. They said, "Look, we're not bullshitters with some junky plane. We have a DC-6 that's like new. We need a good pilot and we hear you're great. Take it for a ride, check it out, see what kind of equipment we have." Danny did. He told me the plane was in first-class shape. When he landed, the two guys gave him ten thousand in cash as a down payment.

Danny went home, told his wife what he was thinking of doing. They stayed up all night talking about it and the next morning he found the two guys and gave them their money back. No deal, Danny told them, something I should've done.

A year later Danny was arrested. The two guys were DEA agents. Danny's crime was that he failed to inform the authorities about the offer these men made. That's conspiracy. He got five years.

The guys were chanting, "Start the show! Start the show!" The hacks were smiling, getting into the spirit of the thing. I saw Simpson, my old boss from my landscape days. He was not smiling—looked a little anxious, in fact. He and I had become friendly since he was no longer my boss. He looked at another hack seriously, but the hack just smiled. The place was looking like a riot to Simpson, I guess.

Simpson had come to Eglin from Marion Prison. Marion is the only prison in the system with a level six section. The most vicious, the vilest, the most heinous criminals our society produces all live in perpetual lock-down in cages at the level six section at Marion. Simpson once told me he still had a hard time seeing inmates wandering around loose. He'd jump if you came up behind him.

Simpson was on a detail one day at level six with two other guards. They were to escort a completely insane murderer to his daily shower. The inmates at level six get an hour a day out of their cells for a walk in the halls and a shower, all under heavy guard. The guards are not armed because weapons could be taken away and used against them. This murderer, Simpson said, used to call the guards filthy names the whole time, but they ignored him. Part of the job. This day, however, the guy had a surprise. He was standing in his cell holding a towel wrapped around his waist, ready for his shower. They let him out. They did not search him. As the guy walked by one of the guards, Simpson's friend, he dropped the towel, exposing a three-foot piece of broomstick. He'd sharpened one end of the stick, and in one blurred move, Simpson said, he jammed the stick up into his friend's belly with both hands. Simpson said he shoved it up deeper and deeper, forcing it up into his friend's chest while all the guards beat him wildly with their clubs. He said the guy didn't notice, just kept screaming and shoving that stick deeper. When Simpson's friend collapsed in the hall, a bloody mess, the guy stood up straight and laughed like crazy. "Guards zero! Inmate two!" the guy screamed. He'd killed a guard once before. There wasn't a federal death penalty for murder then, and the guy was already in for a couple of lives. They couldn't do a thing about it. Simpson said he had to go tell his friend's wife. I understood why Simpson was looking anxious. I wouldn't want his job for anything. The hacks at Eglin had it easy, but they would eventually rotate to real prisons.

The inmate band—we had all sorts of musicians here—played an introduction. The chaplain's assistant was the master of ceremonies. The first act was an inmate who played the guitar beautifully. We heard a singer, watched a tap dancer, and then a comedian who did impersonations of the hacks.

The last act. The chaplain's assistant announced, "And now, ladies (a few female staff were present) and gentlemen—" he paused while an inmate drummer who had missed the cue started a drumroll, "the luscious, the vivacious, the beautiful—Coquette!" A single spotlight flashed on the stage. The band launched into a saucy bump-and-grind tune and into the spotlight leapt Ernest the black homosexual. I know I said they didn't allow gay guys at Eglin, but I think they tolerated Ernest because he was just so damn open about it that nobody felt threatened. Ernest was always on. He was more effeminate than most women, and I'd seen him moan at guys he thought were attractive. The rednecks thought he was kind of bizarre, but they didn't kill him—a testimony to Ernest's charm.

Ernest did the best striptease act I've ever seen. He was wearing a mop for a wig and a costume of filmy cheesecloth. He whirled around with the music, swishing, tossing the veils into the crowd until he was down to a gold lamé brief. It was so convincing, I forgot Ernest was a man. The crowd went wild.

Ernest won the talent show by a big margin.

I spent the summer of 1959 in Havana, living with a Cuban family. I saw Fidel Castro there and met Camilo Cienfuegos, a senior general under Castro whom Castro later had killed. I met General Cienfuegos by running past his armed guards when I saw his helicopter landing at the house he'd commandeered across the street from where I stayed. When I got close to the helicopter, I saw Cienfuegos first look surprised and then laugh. I was bounding, barefooted, across his huge yard with his armed guards in hot pursuit. He held up his hand and the guards dropped back. He walked up to me carrying a .45-caliber pistol he fitted with a stock and a long banana clip and asked me, in perfect English (he'd gone to school at the University of Miami), who I was.

I told him I was living with the Uriartes across the street, and I loved helicopters. He laughed and let me walk around and look at his chopper. Then he had one of his guards come over and take our picture together with my camera. After he left, the guards, who were called *barbados*, became my friends because I had shown such courage. For a boy, they said, I had the *cojónes* of a man, which is a terrific compliment for an adolescent boy.

I knew Cubans, you see, and I liked Cubans, so it was a painful disappointment to me that they were the most unpopular ethnic group in Eglin.

These Cubans were mostly drug smugglers or money launderers, two of the more lucrative industries that have sprung up around the drug business our drug laws have created, and most of them had grown up in Miami. Some of them brought bizarre religious practices like Santeria that involved sacrificing, especially trained white doves, and some of the poorer Cubans made sure there was a glass of water under their beds at night to ward off evil spirits. I'd seen none of this in Cuba. These habits added a threatening element to Cuban culture from the Anglos' point of view. The real problem, though, as the Anglos in camp saw it, was simply that the Cubans were rude. Anglos are seldom rude, even if they are about to kill you. Cubans at Eglin were thought of as loud and pushy. In our crowded living conditions, the Cubans would often pack ten of their friends into one cube and have a noisy party over espresso and cookies. That produced much friction. Anyone making a complaint to them met with surly glares and loud advice on what sorts of things they might shove up their assholes.

There were few fights in Eglin because the penalty for fighting was that all participants in a fight were shipped off to higher-level prisons regardless of who started it. The one exception I knew about was one famous fight in Dorm Three just before I moved to Dorm Five. I didn't see it but the story got around. A hillbilly from Tennessee, Sammy McGuire, had asked the three Cubans next to his bunk who were having a meeting after lights out if they minded terribly shutting the fuck up. The Cubans got mad and threatened to put the hillbilly's lights out if he didn't mind his own fucking business. This usually worked because, as I said, everybody goes to a real prison who's in a fight, and Eglin is a camp full of wimps. But Sammy McGuire didn't seem to be impressed. Since it was dark, no one could see the action, but the result was three injured Cubans, one of whom had to be treated at the infirmary.

To the Cubans' credit, they refused to admit that there had been a fight, claiming they'd all fallen down in the shower. The prison officials, having no witnesses or confessions (after an all-night grilling), were forced to accept the story, but the inmates knew what happened. McGuire became a hero among the Anglos. Even the Cubans respected him.

I had very little to do with the Cubans because they were so hard to get along with. The only one I talked to was a dentist in my section named Antonio. One Sunday afternoon, while I lay in bed reading, a group of Cubans were just outside the dorm, about ten feet from my cube (all major noise in camp was ten feet from my cube; only the airplanes were farther away), talking loudly and playing their radio. The windows were open because the weather was perfect. I tried to ignore the music, even put my headphones on, but it was really loud. I endured for a half hour and finally got mad. I went outside and asked one of the guys, Eduardo, who lived down at the end of my aisle, if they might consider turning the radio down.

Eduardo stared at me sullenly and said, *"No hablo Inglés.* I don't speak English."

Well, of course he did. I'd talked to him a couple of times.

"C'mon, Eduardo. It's way too loud. I can't think. Besides, you aren't even allowed to use a radio without earphones."

"No hablo Inglés," Eduardo said. His two friends snickered and looked at me like I was from the Other Side.

I said, "Eduardo, *por favor,"* and held my hands over my ears.

Eduardo just glared at me as if I had just suggested that his sister fucked donkeys.

I felt my heart pounding in my ears and I was beginning to get into a rage. Didn't anybody understand the importance of quiet in this fucking place? I mean, we had *rules* here! I went inside and found my friend Antonio. I told him about Eduardo, and he volunteered to act as my envoy. I watched through the window as Antonio explained to them my side of the issue. Eduardo told Antonio to mind his own business. Antonio came back inside and shrugged. If a Cuban couldn't make them shut up, then the only people who could were the hacks. However, going to a hack about this kind of problem was worse than the problem; it just wasn't ethical to rat on an inmate, even if the inmate was a total asshole. I took a walk.

As the population of Cubans grew, so did incidents between them and the Anglos. Cop-outs flooded the counselors' offices. Even George, the sporting goods felon—the meek and apathetic soul I used to tend grounds with—lost it one night and got into a fight with two Cubans in Dorm Four. A hack saw it, and George and the Cubans were shipped to the federal prison at Tallahassee. That fight and the continuing complaints caused the hacks to cruise the dorms more frequently. They were breaking up the Cubans' parties, which made the Cubans resent the Anglos even more. A real schism was developing and peace in our little crook farm was jeopardized.

I had cooled down about the radio incident, but when I passed Eduardo in the aisle and tried to be friendly, he just glared at me and said nothing. My transgression, asking for peace and quiet, was not forgivable.

Three weeks after the radio incident, Antonio came to me one night and said he'd heard that the prison was going to ship Cubans, lots of them, out of Eglin. He wanted to know if I'd heard anything about it. I hadn't. However, the rumors persisted and grew to the extent that the Cubans sent a spokesman to the new warden. Superintendent Honsted had been sent to open a new prison a few months before. The Cubans requested that the warden meet with them outside the administration building to talk about the rumor. On a Friday evening, the warden did. He told the Cubans he'd heard the rumor, too, but that it was only a rumor and they had nothing to worry about. They believed him.

When I woke up Saturday morning, Eduardo was gone. So was Antonio. So was every Cuban in our dorm. At the mess hall, I learned that nearly every Cuban in camp had been rounded up at three in the morning by hacks carrying shotguns (which is amazing, since hacks never carry weapons in a prison unless there's a riot or something). They were already on buses going, it was claimed, to Atlanta. Being sent to Atlanta Federal Prison, I was told by people who'd been there, is the same as being sent to hell—it's huge, overcrowded with crazy *and* pissed-off Marielitos who chant and scream twenty-four hours a day, demanding their freedom, creating a literal bedlam. As much as I didn't like Eduardo, I wouldn't wish Atlanta on anyone, especially a pot smuggler who was considered harmless enough to be sent to Eglin.

At the visiting room, there were a lot of Cuban women crying and screaming at the guards, pleading to know where their husbands were. It was sad to see.

The few remaining Cubans were noticeably quiet. They no longer gathered in the cubes and even responded positively to the normal requests for quiet that came up every evening. The consensus among the Anglos was that the warden did the right thing shipping those forty or so Cubans. This action didn't establish a ban on Cubans coming to Eglin; they continued arriving a few at a time and the population slowly began to rebuild. But it took a long time to reach critical density again.

I began having migraine attacks twice a week after my book became a best-seller. Maybe watching it move up and down the list for fourteen weeks made me tense. The clinic had brought in an injectable version of Cafergot for me. It only worked some of the time, and I was getting depressed. When I wasn't having migraines, I was having strange pains in my head. I went to the clinic and complained. Shouldn't they check out my head to see how many tumors there were?

They agreed to send me to a civilian doctor in Niceville.

A week later, I got into a blue Air Force van driven by an inmate named Jennings, a veteran of World War II, who'd gotten caught trying to smuggle some pot in his airplane. I had not left the camp except for one visit to the base hospital for my initial physical and my overnight furlough with Patience. It was weird to me that Jennings just waved to the base guards as he drove through the gate. In minutes we were cruising among civilian traffic on our way to town. Think of it, two federal prisoners driving alone among real people. The fact was astounding to me.

"I do it every day, Bob. Everybody knows who we are," Jennings said. "We're everywhere. A lot of inmates are drivers; we got guys who go the officer's club every day to take care of the club; we got guys who work at the golf course, the yacht club, you name it. Everywhere."

"I just can't shake the feeling that a cop's going to pull us over and take us back to prison," I said.

Jennings laughed.

Twenty minutes later, Jennings pulled into a parking lot in front of a medical center. "Here you are. I'll come back in an hour," Jennings said.

I got out and watched Jennings drive down the street. I saw an elderly couple get out of a car and walk into the building. The woman smiled at me and I smiled back, feeling very out of place. I read the name on the note they'd given me at the camp and looked up the

office. I walked inside. I figured as soon as people saw my blue mechanics' uniform they'd start shrieking and stand up on the chairs or
something, but nothing happened. I went to the window and told
them my name and who I was supposed to see.

"Robert Mason," said the nurse. "From the prison?"

"That's right," I said quietly, trying not to alarm anybody.

The nurse smiled and told me to have a seat. The doctor would see
me in a minute.

Dr. Johnson, a neurologist, asked me a bunch of questions and then
told me he knew all about migraines and how much they really hurt
because he was a doctor and also because he had migraine attacks,
too. "I became a specialist in migraines because I get them, and I hate
them. I've been looking for a cure for years."

That meant he hadn't found it yet. Dr. Johnson got out a picture
of a human head sliced in half and for the next half hour described to
me the nature of the ailment. His descriptions of the symptoms matched
mine perfectly. He told me that the warning symptoms almost always
happen the same way, and the trick was to take the Cafergot as soon
as I felt the first twinge. That didn't always work, he said. When it
didn't, lying still in the dark with a cold compress on your head was
the only practical answer. They could, he said, give me narcotics, but
my being at a prison camp probably excluded that possibility. When
he wrapped up the examination, he said, "You the same guy who
wrote *Chickenhawk*?"

"Yessir. That's me."

"That's one helluva book. My son-in-law was a door gunner over
there. Didn't really understand what he went through until I read your
book—he won't talk about it, you know? Thanks for writing it. They
treating you okay at the camp?"

"Yessir. If you have to be in prison, Eglin's the place to be."

Johnson laughed. "Good. Listen, Mr. Mason, I predict that when
you get out of there, these migraine attacks will stop. They usually
come when you're under a lot of stress."

I checked out at the nurses' window and they just said good-bye.
Didn't have to pay anything, taxpayer's treat. When I turned around,
I saw Jennings sitting in the waiting room reading a magazine. He
looked up. "Man. What was wrong with you? You've been in there
over an hour."

"Doc said I have to have a brain transplant," I said.

On the way back to camp, we spotted a blue Air Force pickup truck parked at a convenience store. Two inmates were sitting in the cab drinking Cokes. "You want to stop and get something?"

"We can do that?"

"Well, not really," said Jennings. "But they don't hassle you if you don't abuse it."

"You can stop if you want," I said. "But I don't want anything. I have everything I need at camp."

In a half hour I was home, feeling relieved to be there.

A month after his heart attack, Tony Abruzzo came back. He was a little thinner, but he had a tan, and he was filled with stories about life at Lexington. "The place is co-ed," Tony said. "Can you imagine that? I didn't know they had such a thing in the prison system. It was disgusting."

"What d'you mean?" John said. "I'd like having some girls around to talk to."

"John, these women are not interested in talking. All they want to do is fuck."

"So what's wrong with that?" John said.

"These girls? You don't know where they've been, John. I wouldn't fuck them with your dick."

John laughed and said, "How do they get the chance? They all aren't in the same dorms, right?"

"Right. They have separate dorms, but everything else is shared. You're allowed to walk around and hold hands. You can hug and stuff. You can go to the movies together—" Tony stopped to laugh and said, "I'm in the movie, right? *The Godfather*—God, was that one great movie—and this girl comes crawling along the row—you know, between your knees and the seats?—asking guys if they want a blowjob. She comes to me and I say, 'Get out of here!' "

"Right, Tony."

"Right, John, you schmuck. I can hear you now. 'Oh,' " Tony mimics John in falsetto, " 'she wants to give me a blowjob. She loves me.' Jesus! Me, I don't need whatever she's passing around. She's crawling around on her hands and knees giving blowjobs to perfect strangers for cigarettes," Tony said.

"She gave a blowjob for a cigarette?"

"No, John, this is a high-class girl, someone you'd respect. She charges a whole pack of cigarettes."

John said, "Man, she's got a real smoking addiction."

The back room crew laughed.

"And that's not all," Tony said, grinning. He was enjoying the story. "These people are fucking all over the place. It's like I'm in a zoo during a rut. These women have nothing else to do. They've figured it out. They sew their zippers in along the inseams of their pants, you know; not vertical like normal, but along—" Tony put his finger six inches down on the inseam of one leg of his pants and followed the seam across his crotch and back down the other inseam, "that way, sideways."

"Why?" John asked.

"'Cause they don't wear panties and they can unzip that zipper and then when they're hugging their boyfriend, he can just slip it in. When a guard's around, they're not moving, just leaning up against a wall, hugging. But the guy's plugged in. The guards think they're just making out. When the guard leaves, the guy starts humping, real slow. Pretty soon, they're fucking their brains out. I saw this with my own eyes! I couldn't believe it! Fuck, fuck, fuck. That's all they do at Lexington. Animals."

Who knows if it was true? It was exactly what we wanted to hear.

We heard they were coming a week before they got there. People were talking in the chow line. Four guys were coming to Eglin. A sheriff from a county jail and three of his deputies. Rumor said these guys were convicted of depriving a couple of black guys of their civil rights by beating them to death at the jail they ran.

Wait! Everybody was saying. You can't let murderers into Eglin! This is a nice camp! A hack told me the bureau was sending them here because they knew they'd be killed in a real prison.

The day they arrived, the Eglin wimps were prepared. The guys in the clothing room made sure that their pants were short enough to look like knickers, their shirts were too small to button, and their shoes were the oldest, foulest pairs they could find. The new prisoners walked into prison looking like they'd fallen into a vat of some chemical that shrank all their clothes and rotted their boots. They also looked very nervous. By dinner they couldn't go anywhere without somebody pointing them out. One black guy ran up to the ex-sheriff in a dorm hallway. "You like to kill niggers? Well, kill me, motherfucker!" he yelled, jabbing his chest with his thumb. "C'mon. Kill me!" He glared at the ex-sheriff, and the ex-sheriff shrank up against the wall, petrified. The black guy shook his head in disgust and said, "Damn!" The ex-sheriff slinked away.

The ex-sheriff had nothing to worry about. Nobody at Eglin would actually hurt him and his deputies. We pecked at them, true, but it was like being pecked by ducks. For a few weeks the former cops couldn't get new clothes or shoes until the staff came over and made us issue decent stuff. Okay, the clothing room gang said, they have good clothes. Try wearing them! Ha! They sprinkled fiberglass insulation into their underwear and "lost" the rest of their laundry. Every time their laundry came back from the base, the clothing room team just sent it right back. After a month of petty harassment, everybody lost interest. Eglin inmates were a real disappointment if you were looking for really nasty crooks. Eventually the cops were left alone. Nobody would talk to them, but they weren't harassed, either. They were lucky.

Actually, I think there was another murderer at Eglin, but I can't be sure. He was there for income tax evasion. Jules worked internationally, knew a lot about hiding money. He seemed a very friendly man, knowledgeable about intriguing criminal matters and willing to talk. I enjoyed our conversations. I mentioned something about how hard it was to get the seed money for the kinds of banking crimes with which Jules was involved.

"It's not hard, Bob." Jules said. We were walking beside the beach, on the jogging trail.

"C'mon," I said. "You say you need a few million dollars. How can a person get that kind of money together?"

Jules nodded, looked at me seriously. "If you are willing to do what has to be done, then it is easy."

"Yes?" I said. The way he said it made me wonder if I wanted to hear the rest.

"Yes. I've been busted before, Bob. Ten years ago, when I got out of prison, I was flat broke. A year later I had five million dollars in a bank in Austria."

I laughed nervously. "What'd you do? Rob a bank?"

"Exactly," Jules said.

"C'mon," I said. "That never works."

"It is child's play. Do you want to know how?" Jules and I were at the lonely stretch of the trail, beside the swamp. The feral cats watched us. Jules's tone of voice made my skin crawl.

"Why would you tell me? I might write it down someday."

"Fine. Do it. You don't know if I'm lying."

"Are you lying?"

"No."

I shrugged. There is no way out of a cycle like this. It's an example of a self-referential conundrum I'd been reading about, like: "This sentence is false."

"You walk into the bank, after you have found out who is the president, and—"

"You're telling me how?"

"Yes. It's part of the real world, Bob. In the real world power rules. Powerful people take what they want."

I saw John Tillerman in the weight shack. He was bench pressing a very large set of weights. He didn't see me. "You promise me you're lying, and I'll listen."

"Everything I am telling you is a lie," Jules said.

"Tell me."

"You know who the banker is, you know where he lives. You have grown a full but distinguished beard, dyed your hair. As you walk in the front door of the bank, your two partners are inside his house, with his family. When the secretary asks your business, you give her an envelope to give to the president, an envelope with a picture of his wife and kids. A minute later the secretary says he will see you.

"When you are sitting together, in his office, discussing how much money you want, you suggest he call home. He does. One of your partners answers."

We passed the bocci courts. We were once again skirting the swampy side of the camp. Long shadows of sunset enclosed us.

"The banker is not a power person. When your partner answers, the banker is pissing in his pants. He makes a couple of calls. A clerk delivers the money, gives it to the 'important client' in the office. You pack it carefully in your briefcase."

"What keeps him from calling the police when you leave?"

"He leaves with you. He is going to lunch with the important client."

"Where do you go?"

Jules smiled slightly. "Fishing."

I nodded, quickly. Why did I know what that meant? "The family?"

"Nothing. You are not a brute. They know nothing. They have been with two men wearing ski masks for a couple of hours."

I nodded. We walked in silence.

"It is shocking to you? This real world?"

"I've seen people killed. Women and children have died because of me. That's real. I've just never met anyone who'd kill in cold blood, except in war—that's not . . . well, it has a purpose. I'd be shocked, if I thought you were telling the truth," I said, staring at Jules.

Jules laughed, but his smile wasn't happy. "Yes. Luckily, nothing like that *really* happens."

I turned away from Jules and shrugged.

"Isn't that nice?" Jules said.

One morning, out of the blue, Baker told me that Grumbles the commissary clerk was leaving in a week and Miss Reed wanted me to come work for her. "I'd really like you to stay, Bob. You know how to do everything around here. But Miss Reed has a lot of clout with administration. I think she can get you even if I don't agree." Baker leaned back in his big executive chair and rested his chin on his fists. "I've talked to her about it, and the deal is that it's up to you. You say you want to go, and I'll agree. You want to go?"

Baker was pulling my strings. It wasn't that he was dependent on me, personally; he just dreaded the hassle of finding somebody to take my place. "Well, Mr. Baker. I like working here—"

"Good—"

"—but I wouldn't mind a change, you know?"

Baker looked very sad. "Who's going to take your place?" he said.

I thought for a minute. "Well, we got that new guy, Winkler, the college professor?" Winkler, a tenured professor, was sent to Eglin, he said, over a three-hundred-dollar discrepancy in his tax return. He claimed he made a mistake, deducted the same business trip twice, but the government chose to prosecute. He got a year, would serve eight months. Because he wasn't able to honor his teaching contract, he lost his job and his tenure. He was collecting stories about how people get into places like Eglin.

"Winkler? The shrink?"

"He's a psychologist. Anyway, he can type great—good as me. He's just being wasted now."

"What's he do here, anyway?" Baker asked.

"Nothing, really. I set him up with his own desk, you know, that little table in the supply room? He's working on a book or something."

"How long would it take? To train him?"

"A week, maybe. He's real smart; he's got a Ph.D., you know. Besides, Mr. Baker. I'd be just across the street. I'd be around to help him out if he had questions."

"You'd do that?"

"Sure. I don't mind."

Baker nodded to himself for a while. "Well, if you think Winkler can do it, and you're around—"

"Right across the street."

"Okay. I'll tell Miss Reed you'll be there next week. You can start training Winkler right away." Baker shook his head and sat forward on his chair. He smiled. "I'm going to miss you, Bob. You're the best clerk I've ever had."

I said thanks.

Baker grinned and said, "Bob. What does it all mean? Really?"

"I don't know Mr. Baker. I just don't know."

The following week, instead of showing up at the clothing room, I knocked on the door to the commissary. I heard a key working the lock. The commissary was the only place in the camp that kept the doors locked. The door opened and Miss Reed was smiling at me. "Come in," she said. I walked inside and watched her lock the door. We were alone in her office. "Where's Leone and Frank?" I asked.

"They don't show up until after lunch," she said. "They have to work the line at night, you know."

"Right," I said.

"Grumbles left you quite a mess," she said, pointing at the desk. "I wish you'd go through his stuff and figure out what you need."

Grumbles's desk was piled with stacks of file folders, order forms, notebooks. I couldn't get a clue what he did by looking at his records. But I knew most of the job already because I'd been typing up receiving reports for a year. As it turned out, that's about all the commissary clerk did, and since I was doing it for Grumbles, he'd spent most of his time working in the stockroom with Leone and Frank. The only thing he'd been doing that I didn't know about was typing up the orders for the stuff the commissary bought. I went through a loose-leaf notebook of the orders to see how it was done. There was a chart on the wall listing the suppliers, their phone numbers, and the days of the week that they brought their stuff. Ice cream came on Wednesday. Fresh fruit came on Monday, Wednesday, and Friday. The local tennis shop came every Friday to deliver tennis shoes and rackets and to pick up rackets the inmates brought in for restringing. The other stuff, like radios and combs and playing cards, came from about twenty different suppliers, some local and some out of state. The job, essentially, was to keep track of the inventory and to submit the appropriate orders, timed so that the commissary's storeroom didn't get too crowded and we never ran out of anything. Piece of cake.

I had a lot to do to get the commissary up to snuff. I was appalled at the haphazard way Grumbles had done the inventories, so I designed and printed an inventory form that had all our products arranged in the same order that they were stored on the shelves in the storeroom. I also changed which products we carried. I canceled Sealtest and had Häagen-Dazs delivered instead—a popular move in camp. When somebody told me about a new instant Japanese soup called Oodles of Noodles I asked for a case to try out. They sold out in a day. I stocked it, bringing it in by the pallet. We sold a lot of stuff. The commissary, I soon learned, did fifty thousand dollars of business each month.

I was becoming popular in camp because of the changes I was making. The compliments felt good, and I spent a lot of my time researching our catalogs finding better products to offer. I looked forward to going to work every day. The commissary was my life.

CHAPTER 3 2

I heard my name called on the speaker in my dorm. Patience wasn't
due to visit until next week. I guessed it was Towler: he once said
he'd try to visit. I walked through the visiting room door and saw Jerry
there, beaming. I was instantly aware that I had stepped into The
World. What I was doing in the commissary seemed suddenly incon-
sequential and pathetic. Jerry was dressed in a spiffy flight jacket. He
was a corporate jet pilot. I was a convict. It was hard to believe we
once flew a Huey together in some of the most vicious combat flying
ever done in helicopters.

"Like your clothes," Jerry said.

"Oh. Thanks. Blue is my favorite color. I'd pick this even if I had
a choice."

Jerry nodded, smiling, and we walked outside and sat at a picnic
table.

We talked. He wanted to know how they were treating me. I said
they were just people doing their jobs. I had nothing to complain about.

"How's the appeal doing?" Jerry said. He meant the barrage of
letters sent to Judge Blatt petitioning him to either release me to do
an alternative sentence or to reduce my sentence.

"Well, Blatt was impressed, I guess. He reduced my sentence from
five years to forty months; cut off a third."

"Does that mean you'll get out sooner?"

"Nope. The parole board set my sentence at two years."

"They don't care if your judge reduced it?"

"No. They have their guidelines. Based on the amount of pot we had, their guidelines say two years."

He shook his head. "Damn."

"Hey," I said. "I don't mind. The fact that so many people tried to help is enough for me. Most of these guys have no friends anymore. A lot of them have lost their wives. I'm lucky."

"It's really a crock," Jerry said. "I read about a guy in California who murdered two people, getting five years. I think they should've factored in what you did for your country, you know?"

I nodded. I disagreed, but I didn't say so. I didn't do anything for my country. I flew for the troops. We were all victims of that bullshit war started by idiots; the least I could do was help the victims. Between us, Jerry and I saved hundreds of lives. "They did, Jerry. They put me here instead of a real prison."

Jerry nodded. "I guess that's something."

"It's a lot. I think being in a penitentiary would've broken me. This is bad enough."

"Hey," Jerry said, "I almost forgot. Congratulations on being a best-selling author. Imagine, my friend the big deal!"

"Thanks, but I'm no big deal."

"You're telling me? I know that, but it's got to make you feel proud, right? I fly all over the country, and I check all the bookstores. *Chickenhawk* is everywhere. When my friends found out I'm the Resler in the book, they had me sign their copies."

"What you sign as? Resler or Towler?"

"Resler."

I smiled. "I wish I'd known where you were; I could've used your real name."

"Yeah, and I could've corrected all the mistakes you made about me!"

I laughed. "Like what?"

"That story you told about me spending the night in a whorehouse made me real popular with Martie," Jerry said, grinning. He and Martie were married after the war. "You got it wrong."

"Wrong? I remember you telling us all about it. You and twenty nubiles trapped all night—"

"Yeah, I told that story because the truth was too embarrassing."

"You're serious? You weren't in the whorehouse?"

"Naw. You know how I used to get drunk on one beer? Well, I had about six that night in Pleiku. When I saw I was five minutes from curfew, I panicked and tried to find my way out of town. I was so messed up, I ended up in some dark neighborhood on the outskirts of town. I knocked on a door and asked the mamasan if I could stay there. I can't believe I did that. I probably slept in a Viet Cong's house. Anyway, I spent the night there, and when I got back to our camp, I made up that whorehouse story so nobody'd know how stupid I was."

I laughed a long while. "That's a much better story. Teach you to lie."

"Well, who would've thought that the guy you're telling a story to twenty years ago is going to put it in a book?"

We talked all day, going over the past, projecting our futures. Jerry is one of the few guys with whom I can freely share my fears and dreams. Jerry understands about waking up in sweaty panics. He understands that it is normal to check for snipers, even in a park. He understands what it feels like to face death in combat. He seemed totally unimpressed that I was a convict. We tried to figure out where the guys in our old company were. Maybe we'd have a reunion one day. For a while I forgot where I was.

At three the hacks announced visiting was over. I walked Jerry to the door. While wives and children filed past us out to the real world, Jerry said, "You'll be out of here before you know it. I want you to come visit us. Stay as long as you like. Martie says to leave your spiders at home, though."

He smiled that goofy smile of his. He kind of looks like Stan Laurel when he tries to look happy. I nodded and we hugged. As I walked to the back of the visiting room, I suppressed tears. This prison life was turning me into a whimpering fool. I missed Patience and Jack. I missed Jerry. I even missed my damn spiders.

I stood in the line of inmates waiting to leave. We had to be checked off the roster and then pat-searched in the hallway before we left. I looked back at the door to the world, and Jerry was gone. When I got into the small hallway with two other inmates, a hack said I was going to be strip-searched. They strip-searched inmates at random, and this was my turn. I went into a closet-sized room with a hack and took off all my clothes.

The hack said "You have a nice visit?" while he checked the seams of my pants for whatever you can hide in the seams of pants.

"Yeah. My buddy from Vietnam."

The hack nodded while he pulled out my pockets to check for the forbidden holes. "You have a Vietnamese friend?"

"No. He and I flew a helicopter together in the Army." The hack was now checking my running shoes, to see if I'd stashed anything under the insoles.

"That's great that you and your buddy are still in contact," the hack said.

"Yeah," I said. "We didn't see each other for sixteen years."

"Wow, sixteen years," the hack said, after checking my clothes. "Okay. Hold up your penis, please."

I reached down and held up my penis. This is standard procedure. A crook can supposedly hide stuff there. He nodded, "Fine. Now turn around and bend over."

I nodded and did.

"Spread your buttocks, please," the hack said. While he was inspecting, he said, "How'd you locate him?"

I was standing bent over holding my butt apart thinking, Is this fucking real? "Ah, I sent a letter to the Pentagon. They forwarded it."

"Oh. Good idea. Okay, you can put your clothes back on."

"Thanks."

I think I must have looked ruffled. The hack shrugged. "Just doing my job," he said.

Since I'd gotten the commissary job, I'd started going to the commissary every night while Miss Reed and Frank and Leone ran the commissary line. I'd go in through the exit door. Miss Reed would see me and nod and unlock the door beside her. I'd go inside, say hi to Leone and Frank, and then walk through the storeroom to my office in the back. This was the only private place for me in camp. Nobody could come in here except Miss Reed or Leone or Frank. And since the line to the commissary never dwindled, they were always busy. I seldom saw them.

After a year of trying, I was finally sitting at my own desk in front of my own typewriter. It was quiet and private. No more excuses. I had my robot manuscript and I was trying to continue where I left off.

I read what I wrote and I couldn't remember how I did it. It seemed to me it was written by somebody else. I put a sheet of paper in the machine and stared at it.

Stare.

I turn on the radio and tune in the public station.

I stare at the blank page in the typewriter.

I reread the last two pages of the manuscript.

I stare at the blank page.

I put the manuscript away and write a letter to Patience, experimenting with the different type styles you can use on a Selectric by just changing the type ball.

When Miss Reed was ready to close up the place, Leone stood by the door after Miss Reed unlocked it to let them out. "What are you waiting for?" Miss Reed said to Leone.

"You're supposed to pat-search us, Miss Reed." Miss Reed was supposed to pat-search us every time we left the commissary. Instead she searched us randomly, which kept everybody honest.

Miss Reed nodded, smiled. Leone pulled this gag now and then. "Well, I'm not. I've been watching you all night. Get going."

"Miss Reed, it's a regulation. Who knows what all I have stashed on me? If you don't pat-search me, I'll pull my pants down. I'm no lawbreaker." He laughed, adding, "Anymore."

"Go ahead, Leone. I need a laugh," Miss Reed said.

We all laughed and Leone and Frank left.

Miss Reed was extremely quick on the uptake with inmates and hacks. Rocky the hack once complained to her that he hated visiting-room duty because, he said, the inmate wives would stare at his bulge.

I asked her what she said to that.

"I told him maybe he needed a new wallet."

I waited while she locked up the storeroom and the front door and then walked with her up the sidewalk beside the building.

"You're looking pretty glum tonight," she said.

"Am I?"

"Tried writing again, right?"

"Right."

"Don't worry. When you get out, it'll come back to you." We stopped at the sidewalk intersection where our paths separated. She would walk left, to the parking lot. I would walk right, to Dorm Five. "You haven't got too long to go, have you?"

"Getting short," I said. "They accepted my application for a halfway house. If I get a four-month halfway house, I'll be out of here in May."

"That's only eight more months," Miss Reed said.

"I know. I really can't complain. What's eight months?"

I work, eat, read, walk, have independent and extremely safe sex, and receive visitors. That's what I do.

They say you learn who your real friends are at times like this. Many of the prisoners have gone to great effort to hide the fact that they are here. Their families often claim they're working "overseas" or are "on assignment." I have no such refuge, but it's better. I know everybody knows I'm here, and it's a big relief. My friends do not desert me. John O'Connor, the drawing professor who almost witnessed my exploding drawing, and his wife, Mallory (my former art history teacher), come to visit several times; Joe Leps and Nikki Ricciuti visit me with their daughter Zubi; Merv Wetherley, a childhood chum who taught me to fly in high school, a bush pilot in Alaska, saw my story in *Time* magazine at an Eskimo trading post and comes to visit; my parents come several times. I have a picture of my mother and me together in the visiting room; it looks like the one in which we posed together on the occasion of my being a new freshman at college, except we're both older and I'm in prison blues. Jack and his girlfriend, Wallie, come with Patience now and then. Wallie is like a daughter to Patience. Jack started going to the University of Florida when I came to prison, but dropped out. He claims he isn't bothered by my being in jail, but I don't see how it could not have affected him. He is very bright, but he is distracted, isn't sure what he wants to do. He loves music and practices guitar regularly. He loves playing Ultimate Frisbee (a team sport played something like hockey except with a Frisbee). He loves Wallie, too. He does not love going to school to learn things he doubts he needs to know.

Some of the press visit, though I am not now much of a story. The local paper, the Fort Walton Beach *Daily News,* sent a reporter, Bruce Rolfsen, to interview me. The warden accompanied us while we walked around the camp. Rolfsen asked me how long I'd been at Eglin. I told him thirteen months and that "I'm now more than half reha- bilitated." I smiled at the warden. "In another year, I will be a hundred percent safe for society."

The warden looked sour. He did not like jokes like that. When Rolfsen asked me what I thought about people using marijuana, I said—quoting a line from Jeff MacNelly's cartoon strip, *Shoe*, "Smoking marijuana will cause your body to be thrown into jail."

The warden didn't like that, either, but this is a free country. The remark was printed as I said it.

Miss Reed worked every day in the commissary office and every night running the commissary line. She petitioned the administration for help and, after several months, they hired someone.

One day Miss Reed showed up with the new guy in tow. His name was Holbrook. Holbrook was quiet and nervously observant of us, the inmates. He'd gone to hack school and knew all the rules. He told us he'd worked at the FBI.

"An FBI agent?" Leone asked.

"You might say that," Holbrook said mysteriously. Inmates are not allowed to grill hacks, so we left it at that. His nickname became Elliott Ness.

Elliott Ness was an intrusion into our comfortable relationship with Miss Reed. When he first ran the line without Miss Reed, he pat-searched Leone and Frank when they left. They were outraged: What? You don't trust us? Elliott Ness explained that it was the rule.

Holbrook's nickname became especially ironic when we finally got him to tell us what his job had been at the FBI. He had been a file clerk. On Miss Reed's days on, we made jokes about Elliott Ness the wastebasket monitor, Elliott Ness the file duster. Miss Reed told us she didn't want to hear that and to leave the poor man alone. Whatever Miss Reed said, we did. No more Elliott Ness jokes in front of Miss Reed.

At the next commissary inventory, we came up short two thousand dollars' worth of goods. The shortages were blamed on Elliott Ness, he being the only new variable in the operation. This was a source of great mirth to Leone and Frank. After an investigative inventory, and after the dust cleared, Miss Reed told us she knew we must be stealing stuff when Mr. Holbrook was running things. "It's not just illegal," she said, "it's downright nasty. That man can't help it if he was a file clerk. He's just trying to make a living and you guys want to hurt him for that? He could lose his job if we come up short again. You leave him alone, or you'll answer to me."

The next inventory was right on.

On December 27, Waterhead called me out of work. He told me my father had had a stroke. "I just talked to his doctor. He says he probably won't make it," he said.

I nodded, looking down at the floor, feeling the helplessness piling up. Nannie, my dad's mother, had died three months before and I wasn't allowed to go to her funeral.

"You aren't due for a furlough for two months. We can let you take one now, a five-day furlough, but it'll replace the one you've got coming. You want to do that?"

"Of course I do. My father's dying."

"I figured you would. I already talked to your wife. She'll be here tomorrow morning. You'll be cleared to go as soon as she arrives."

Patience picked me up the next morning at eight. She said that the doctors said it was bad, but if my father made it through the next three days, he might live. She also said that she'd stayed in a motel last night and she still had the room. Why should we waste it? "In your condition, I'll bet you'd finish in a couple of seconds. Wanna?"

After a ten-minute delay at the motel, we were on the road for the six-hour drive to Gainesville.

My dad lay in bed, pale. He couldn't talk, but he knew we were there. Patience told him we'd stopped for a minute to get laid and he smiled. I sat beside the bed and held his hand. He didn't seem to notice. His whole right side was paralyzed. I told him they were going to let me stay around for five days and he smiled again.

There wasn't much to do except wait. My emotions were in an uproar. I felt good that I was walking around like a real person again, but I felt terrible seeing my dad like that.

I went out in the hall and listened to my mother and my aunt talking over and over about the attack. "He was feeding his chickens," my mother said. "I wondered where he was; he was later than usual. Then I looked outside and saw him lying on the ground."

Later my mother asked, "Are you going to spend the night here?"

"I'll stay around until I get tired," I said. "I don't see what staying here will do for him."

"He'll know you're here, Bob," my mother said.

"He's asleep most of the time, Mom. He needs the rest."

"You never do what I want you to do," my mother said.

"Mom," I said, "I've been in jail for sixteen months. I won't get another furlough. I'll be here most of the time, but I want to spend some time with Patience and Jack. You know, try to patch my life back together?"

"Your dad is lying in there dying and all you can think about is yourself," my mother said.

"Mom. You're his wife. Where will you be?"

My mother glared at me. "Nobody cares how I feel," she said. "You just don't know how this has affected me. Everybody's worried about him. What about me? Now I have chest pains. I have to go home and take care of all those damn animals he collected."

"Don't worry about the animals, Betty," my aunt said. "I know what to do. I was helping Jack—"

"I need to rest," my mother said. "Chest pains. I have to go home."

My aunt shrugged at me. I nodded.

I called my friend, Joe Leps, now a nursing student, and asked him what he would charge to stay with my father for a few nights. He said he'd do it for a nursing book he needed. "That's all?" I said.

"Yep. Just the book. I'll watch him for you."

With Joe on watch at nights, I slept with Patience in our own bed in the upstairs of our cabin. During the days, I attended to a few details to get ready for my eventual homecoming. I went to the driver's license bureau at the highway patrol station to renew my license. They had a computer at the highway patrol station, and it knew I'd gotten a speeding ticket in South Carolina seven years earlier doing eighty-eight miles an hour, but it didn't know I was in jail. When the clerk asked me if my address was the same, I said yes, expecting her to say something like, "What? Says here you're a convict!" But she didn't.

At the end of three days, my dad was improving. He still couldn't talk or move his right side, but the doctors said he'd probably make it and started him on a regimen of physical and speech therapy. I felt relieved.

When my five days were up, Patience drove me back to Eglin.

I seldom saw John Tillerman. He worked in camp at the administration building, ate at different times, and lived in a different dorm. He stopped by my cube occasionally and visited. His obsession with getting in shape had worked. He now weighed 165 pounds, and it was 165 pounds of muscle. He could bench press 280 pounds at the weight shack. When we talked, it was usually while we walked laps on the jogging trail. John usually talked about Dave, going over and over the foul-up that got us busted. John complained that Dave and the gang had done nothing to help us. There was an understanding, John said, that Dave would help our wives while we were locked up. Patience didn't need the help because of my extraordinary luck with my book, but Alice did. John claimed he was going to find Dave when he got out and make his life miserable. It was all he talked about, and I think that having that focus was actually good for him. Life in camp was mentally stultifying. Revenge gave him a healthy goal.

In May, when I had about a week left before my release to a halfway house in Ocala, I was reading in my cube when two Cubans started a loud argument in the hall right next to me. In the intervening eight months since the big Cuban roundup, their population had returned to its previous level. It was noisy again. I'd had one blessing in the meantime: the prison had removed all the phones from the dorms and installed a calling center in a small shed attached to the administration building. It was not as convenient, but it was quieter.

I tried to ignore the chatter. Then I heard some guys in the section yell "Shutthefuckup!" but the Cubans ignored them. I was looking at my book, but I wasn't reading. Anger welled within me. I had endured, for almost two years, what I considered bedlam, and now these two guys were pushing me over the edge. I concentrated on the book. They yammered away, louder. Finally I threw down my book, stomped out of my cube, and approached the two Cubans.

I recognized one of them. He'd been here as long as me. "Hey. How about a break? There's got to be a couple of miles of hallways in this camp. Why here? Better yet, why not outside?"

They stared at me like I'd accused them of being too friendly with their mothers, faced each other, and started talking again. I don't know what they were talking about. They spoke Spanish.

"Hey," I said. "Didn't you understand me?"

The guy I recognized said, "We understand you. We can talk any-where we want. This is a public hallway."

Something snapped inside me—the insanity fuse, I suppose. I walked up to them and pushed my face into theirs like I'd learned to do in the Army. "You want to talk?" I yelled. "Then let's fucking talk!"

They backed up a little. I'd surprised them. I'd surprised myself. "Hey. What's wrong with you, man? You crazy?"

"Crazy? Me? No, you assholes, I want to talk, too. I can talk any fucking place I want to. Why not here? This is a *public* hallway!"

"You're asking for big trouble, man," said one of the Cubans.

"Trouble?" My voice was getting louder as I spoke. "For talking in a fucking public hallway?" I yelled. "C'mon, let's talk. I like to talk."

"I'm gonna take you to Tallahassee with me if you don't leave us alone!" yelled one.

"Fine!" I yelled. "I'd love to go to Tallahassee! Talk, goddamn it! Let's talk!"

If I had a fight, we'd all go to a real prison, maybe Tallahassee, and I'd stay there for my full term, possibly longer. I knew that, but it didn't seem to mean anything to me. What I wanted was to be left alone. I wanted some peace in the bedlam, and these guys were in the way.

The guy I knew stepped away from my intruding face and yelled, "Okay, motherfucker. You asked for it. You and me. You and me are going on a trip, motherfucker!"

"Fine," I yelled, closing on him. "Let's go!" This was all the more absurd when you consider that I'd never had a fight with anyone since the third grade, unless you consider pummeling your buddies in basic training fighting. "C'mon," I yelled.

I thought my ferocity was finally getting through to them because I saw their eyes widen as I snarled like a lunatic. They moved farther away, edging toward the door. Hey, I was tougher than I thought. "Whatsa matter, assholes? Don't want to talk anymore?" I yelled.

The Cuban stuttered with rage, glaring at me, and also glancing over my shoulder. "Lucky for you, motherfucker," the Cuban said. "I'm going on furlough tomorrow. But when I come back—you and me. You and me, motherfucker. We're going to Tallahassee," he screamed. And then, miraculously, they turned and left, pausing only once to shake their fists. I heard cheering in the section. I turned around and saw twenty smiling heads bobbing over the cube walls. I turned farther around and saw that Sammy McGuire was standing behind me. Sammy McGuire the famous Cuban killer from Dorm Three. He'd come up to help me. It was him they'd been staring at. It was Sammy they were afraid of. "Hey, Sammy," I said, "thanks a lot. I didn't know you were there."

"That's okay, Bob. Those boys just don't have the simplest fucking manners, you know? I don't know how they get that way." He smiled and said "You did all right, Bob" and walked back to his cube.

CHAPTER 33

Early Friday morning, May 17, 1985. I'd been awake since two A.M. In the dim light of the exit sign, I double-checked my cube. Everything was gone except a few books. My sheets and blankets were all packed into one pillowcase, my prison clothes and work boots were stuffed in another. I wore the last set of blues I'd wear in prison. I'd change into my street clothes on the way out.

I'd just shipped all my personal stuff home, including my untouched robot manuscript. When I took the boxes to the administration building for inspection prior to shipment, the hack there said good-bye and asked what I was going to do when I got out. "I'm going to get a faster boat," I said, and laughed with him.

I took the books and put them on Walton's desk. He'd be here for a few more months. I sat down on my bunk. Four-thirty: that's what time they were coming for me. My watch said four. I walked over to the water fountain and drank. I went to the glass doors and leaned against the frame. The mess hall was lit up, the inmate kitchen crew was making breakfast. I went back to my cube and lay down on my stripped mattress.

I waited.

Maybe they forgot. I stood up and checked the section. No hack in sight. I lay down. Maybe they did forget. They forgot lots of things.

I waited. I remembered my ice-cream party. I had it the previous

Sunday. It was a sign of my status in the prisoner hierarchy that I could have an ice-cream party on a Sunday. The commissary was closed during the weekends, so you had to have a party during the week or you couldn't get the ice cream. I used my connections in the kitchen and stored about forty pints of Häagen-Dazs in the kitchen freezer. Further proof of my power was that the ice cream was still there when I went to pick it up. It was a good party, I thought.

I got the ice cream on Friday. Elliott Ness was working the register when I went behind the line and started loading up a shopping bag with pints of Häagen-Dazs from the ice-cream freezer. He said, "Getting ready to leave, Bob?"

"Yeah, Mr. Holbrook. I'm going to zero my account."

He nodded and pulled my account sheet. "You have twenty-four dollars left, enough for ten pints and some change."

"Keep the change."

"Can't. We'll send you a check."

I nodded and continued packing the ice cream into the bag. Leone, who was working the line with Frank, came over and asked if I needed any help. I said no, put the twentieth pint in the bag, set it aside, and popped open another bag. "How much you taking, Bob?" Leone asked.

"I have enough money for ten," I said. Leone blinked and stared at the bag I had just filled. He glanced over his shoulder at Elliott Ness and grinned. I filled up the second bag and picked them both up, freezing against my body. I walked toward Elliott Ness, toward the door. "You got your ten?" he asked.

"Yessir," I said. At least ten. I didn't know why I was doing this. I was risking a lot, stealing in a prison camp in full view of a guard— after never having stolen anything for nearly two years—a few days before my release. It just happened. Maybe I'm incorrigible. Elliott Ness, who knew me as the squarest and most trustworthy of the commissary crew, didn't even look up. He put my account sheet in the machine and charged my account. I walked outside, grinning. As my last official act in Eglin, I had committed larceny in front of the FBI.

That afternoon at the mess hall, Leone came over and sat at my table. Leone never sat with me; I wasn't in his clique of friends, they being mostly Mafia and other serious crooks. My being a writer and small-time pot smuggler was okay, but it certainly wasn't something you'd want to brag about. My impression was that Leone thought I

was the straightest wimp he'd run into. He once accused me of running
the commissary like I owned stock in it. Leone sat down, grinning. He
leaned over his tray and said, "Bob. That was really something. *Now,*
now I respect you."

It had been a long twenty months. It was actually ending? Knox
had written me earlier, comparing my incarceration with his collection
of tropical fish. He said, "I got some guppies just for movement, and
now they've given birth, so the population rises—and none of these
guys get out on weekend passes. Ever. The only way they leave is fins
first." I was leaving, and I was still alive.

I was grinning to myself when Tarzan walked by with his flashlight.
I stood up and watched him checking each cube on my aisle. He walked
back to me. "Ready?" Tarzan said.

"Yeah. I'm ready."

He shined his light around inside my cube. "All cleaned up?"

"All cleaned up."

"Okay, grab your sheets and stuff."

I picked up the two pillowcases and followed Tarzan out the door.

Dawn was a faint glow in the east. I followed Tarzan over to the
clothing room and dumped the pillowcases into the piles of clothes in
the bins. Then we walked together up the long sidewalk to the administration building. Tree frogs croaked, crickets chirped. Our footsteps
crackled sand on the sidewalk. Tomorrow, and for all tomorrows, an
inmate would be sweeping it clean. I looked around as I walked, trying
to memorize the scene: the shadow of a huge oak barely perceptible
against the early glow of dawn; dim lights in dorms filled with seven
hundred and fifty sleeping men; Tarzan strolling ahead of me, still
unapproachable after almost two years; men moving as shadows
against dim lights inside the guard shack. I didn't want to forget any
of this.

Tarzan didn't talk. Of all the hacks I'd known, Tarzan had the least
to do with the inmates. "I'm sure going to miss this place," I said.

"Sure," Tarzan said.

CHAPTER 34

After an eight-hour ride from prison, I met Patience at the bus station in Ocala. You can ride home in your car on furloughs, fly if you want, but you have to take the bus when you leave. Technically, you're still in custody when you're transferred from the prison to the halfway house. It's a rule.

We drove to the address and found a white brick house with a sign out front that said SALVATION ARMY. When I saw this, I began to have regrets that I'd fought so hard to get a four-month halfway house. The counselors said I already had a job. The idea of the halfway house was to help a convict get a job and get back into society. I had argued that I couldn't live forever on one book, I really had to get back to work, try to write another book. They gave me the halfway house. Now, looking at the Salvation Army building, I began to have doubts.

A woman inside showed me the bunk room where I'd be staying five nights a week for the next four months. The room was down the hall from where the normal clients of the Salvation Army, the homeless and destitute, stayed. There was room for ten men in the bunk room which the Salvation Army provided on contract with the state and federal prison systems. The bunks were equipped with lumpy, plastic mattresses.

The woman said I'd have to go check in with the head of the place, Captain Eugene Gerber, at his office in another part of town. Patience and I drove to Gerber's office.

Gerber knew all about me. He sat behind his desk under a picture of Jesus Christ and lectured me and Patience for two hours about the kind of "ship" he ran. He was a Navy veteran, a sailor. Now he was captain of the local Salvation Army. Gerber ran a tight ship.

Gerber read from a whole list of regulations: I'd have to be at the Salvation Army every night by ten except Friday and Saturday night. On weekends, the felons got passes if we hadn't fucked up by breaking any of the rules. I was to keep my bunk straight; I'd also be responsible for keeping the bathroom clean; I was subject to random urine checks, which, if I failed, would send me back to prison. I could, however, drink if I didn't get drunk. Gerber had more regulations than Eglin, and read them all. Finally he said I had to get a job.

I said, "Captain Gerber, I have a job. I'm a writer."

"I've heard. Do you get a paycheck every week?"

"No. Writers usually get paid twice a year. Royalty payments."

"I have to see a paycheck every week," Captain Gerber said.

I was about to say I'd made a hundred and eighty thousand dollars in less than two years, but I knew that would only piss him off. So I said, "I'll get a paycheck every week."

"Fine. Where will you work?"

I'd heard I might run into this problem, so I'd already called Knox about it. "I'll be working for my agent, at home."

Gerber nodded. "That's okay with me. Have him send me a letter saying you're employed by him. I want to see a Xerox copy of each paycheck, each week. Also, keep in mind that you have to check in here before six every day."

"I thought you said I'd have to be here at ten."

"That's right. But we have to see you punch in at the time clock after work. You're free from then until ten."

"I live in High Springs, Captain Gerber. That's sixty miles from here. Couldn't I just call you and tell you I'm finished working for the day?"

"No. I have to see that card punched every day. Before six."

This guy was going to show me what power was all about. I already knew one guy in Gerber's halfway house, a former inmate from my section at Eglin, who worked in Gainesville, thirty miles away, and he didn't have to check in after work. There was no way around this guy—it was a rule. He was simply being selective about enforcing it. I could feel my face getting red. I said, "Fine. Is that all?"

Gerber smiled. "Yes. You follow the rules to the letter, Mr. Mason, and we'll get along just fine."

On the way to a restaurant in Ocala, I went into a rage and told Patience I wanted to go back to prison, where people were reasonable. Patience said I didn't love her, and I shut up.

I fell into a new daily routine: I got up at five-thirty in the felon's bunkhouse, made a cup of coffee in the kitchen, got into our Escort, and drove sixty miles to High Springs. I stopped off at my parents' at six-thirty and had coffee. My dad was improving. He couldn't walk or use his right arm, but he was talking well enough to understand. My mother wanted to sell the farm and move to Gainesville, closer to the doctors.

By seven-thirty, I was home. I'd make Patience a cup of coffee, drink another cup myself, read the paper, and be at work by nine. I worked on my robot book in the attic of our cabin. Patience had bought a computer while I was in prison, so now I had a new way to write. I trashed the manuscript I'd carried with me for two years because, as Knox said, it wasn't "up to the standards you set in *Chickenhawk*, Bob." As a matter of fact, Knox not only hated what I'd written, he hated the idea. Knox doesn't like science fiction, and he especially hates robot stories. That was okay. My goal was to write a robot story that Knox would like because I didn't want the book to be considered strictly science fiction. I wanted the average reader to experience my robot as though it were real, now. Knox would be my litmus test.

I wrote from nine to twelve every day and then spent time working on the cabin. I'd left it unfinished and Patience was reluctant to have anything done until I got back.

At four-thirty in the afternoon, I left for Ocala, where, at five-thirty or so, I put my time card into the time clock and put the card back in the rack. Now I was free until ten, but I was in Ocala.

Ocala is a small place but it had a nice library. I spent most of my time in the library. If there was a movie playing I hadn't seen, I went to see it. I saw every movie released from May to September 1985. I also tried to shop for new clothes. All my stuff was old before I went to prison. It was even worse now.

Shopping was really difficult. The big department stores were incredibly intimidating. I saw how much stuff people really needed when I ran the commissary. Nobody needs all this stuff, I thought. The stores were overstocked. They had way too many brands of duplicate products. It was a tragic waste.

I spent hours looking at shirts, checking prices, trying them on. The result of most of my shopping trips was that I agonized for hours and ended up buying nothing. I couldn't decide; I'd freeze trying to decide to buy a shirt for twenty-five dollars or one for twenty. I worried myself sick that I'd run out of money. I'd been living on thirty-three dollars a month. Just one decent shirt cost more than that. I had lots of money in the bank, but I had no confidence I'd ever sell another book, and how long would I get royalties from *Chickenhawk*? It took me four months to buy four shirts and four pairs of pants. I spent two weeks stalking a mall before I got the courage to buy a pair of running shoes.

By ten I was checked in at the Salvation Army. The television in the front room was permanently tuned to the Christian Broadcasting Company. Jim and Tammy Bakker were the drill on Captain Gerber's ship. Each night the people in the front room were different. The rule was that indigents could stay one night. They got dinner after a prayer meeting. They got breakfast before they had to leave the next day, no prayers required. These people, men mostly, sat staring at Jim and Tammy telling them how God would help them just like He'd helped Jim and Tammy. Homeless men stared at the effervescent, clown-faced Tammy Bakker with vacant eyes.

One morning, while I made my coffee, I watched a young mother with a baby and a two-year-old eating breakfast. I asked her where she was going. She said she'd go as far as she could walk. One of the benefits of capitalism is that it offers constant reminders of the consequences of failure, especially if you hang around places like the Salvation Army. I felt terrible. I wanted to do something for her, but deciding what to do about her and the others that drifted into this place every day was even tougher than picking out a shirt. I wasn't able to help. I nodded, poured my coffee, and left. That, I figured, was where I was going to be if I didn't get another book published.

The routine changed on Friday. Patience came with me to Ocala in the afternoon. I turned in my Xeroxed paycheck from Knox, punched in, and punched out for the weekend. Then we drove to Gainesville and went to the Wine and Cheese Gallery. There, in a small courtyard behind the restaurant, I saw old friends and met new people—none of them felons—musicians, attorneys, professors, computer programmers, and so on. The Friday meetings became a regular thing and I began drinking beer. The Wine and Cheese had a hundred different brands from all over the world, and I probably tried them all over a period of four months. I hadn't had a drink or a joint or even a cigarette for nearly two years. I'd been detoxed. I wanted to get retoxed.

Saturdays I worked on the cabin. On Sundays I lay around and read until about eight-thirty. Then I'd attempt to choose some clothes to wear at the bunkhouse. I found the task frustrating and irksome. Why do I have to pick what I wear every day? Why doesn't everybody just wear the same thing?

One Sunday night, after spending an hour agonizing over just what I should wear at the Salvation Army, I said, "Patience. What High Springs needs is a clothing room."

"What?"

"You know. A place that does all your laundry and gives everybody uniforms. You wouldn't have to worry if you were in style. The clothes would be cheaper. People would be a lot happier if they had a clothing room."

Patience looked at me sadly and shook her head.

During July, John Tillerman showed up for his four-month halfway house. He, too, had to get a job, and he chose to be a free-lance carpenter. I hired him to help me finish the cabin. He put in wallboard upstairs, a cypress ceiling downstairs. I installed two air conditioners so our papers and books wouldn't mildew.

On August 12, 1985, I was released from the halfway house to the custody of the parole office in Gainesville. I met my parole officer, Jack Gamble, at his office in the courthouse. He had been my presentencing investigator, and was a fair man. He told me I couldn't use drugs. I asked if that included alcohol and tobacco. He said those were fine. I said they kill a thousand times more people than all illegal drugs combined. Gamble nodded and said, "That may be true, but they're legal." He continued, saying I had to expect unannounced visits from him; I'd be free to travel anywhere I wanted, with permission. Everywhere except Central and South America. They were afraid I'd smuggle in another load, I guess. All I had to do on parole was submit a monthly statement saying I still lived at the same place and how much I earned that month. Again, the fact that I was paid only twice a year brought complaints from Mr. Gamble's bosses. "Bob, it looks bad when you say you earned nothing for months at a time," he said after I'd turned in three reports indicating zero income. When I got my royalty statement from Knox, I made a copy and sent it to Mr. Gamble. I'd made over a hundred thousand and I included a note saying: "In case anybody asks you why I don't report a monthly income, show them this." I wanted them to know that I was equally capable of being snotty.

I wrote about 150 pages of the second version of my robot book. I'd changed the whole story. I invented an undercover Russian agent to come to Florida (where the robot was built) to nab the machine. I thought it was pretty good; so did Patience. Knox sent a note back saying, "I just don't get this, Bob."

I was invited to give a reading in Chicago in June. Larry Heinemann had arranged it and invited us to stay with them. I was going to meet Larry for the first time and worried that we might not get along. I mean, he'd been wonderful and generous to me, writing to me in jail, sending me books, but what if he turned out to be an asshole in person?

Gamble gave me travel papers and we flew to Chicago, took a cab to Larry's house. He came out wearing a baseball cap and said, "Welcome to Chicago, Bob. I'm glad you're out of jail. We got rules here, too. Never pick a fight in a strange bar. Never cheer for the Yankees. And never, ever park your car in the same place twice." We got along great. His wife, Edie, and Patience clicked, too.

Chicago was having a better-late-than-never welcome-home parade for Vietnam veterans. Neither Larry nor I wanted to go. The Chicago Sun-Times sent Tom Fitzpatrick over to get our feelings about the parade. When Fitzpatrick asked us if we were going, Larry said, "Nope. It's just another fucking formation to me."

I said, "Nope. Pilots don't march."

Patience was disgusted with us and made us go. "You don't have to march," she said. "Just watch. But go."

We did, and I'm glad. It was heartwarming to see the hundreds of thousands of people who turned out to applaud and whistle and generally behave as though Vietnam vets weren't losers after all. General Westmoreland gave a speech which Larry and I boycotted. Westmoreland, to me, was a fool whose strategy of attrition—killing people without taking territory—was responsible for that war lasting ten years and costing fifty-eight thousand American lives plus millions of Vietnamese, Cambodians, Laotians, and even Thais. Now he was an old man and I just wanted to leave him alone. Heinemann said I was too kind, and held Westmoreland in such contempt that he probably would've choked him if they'd met.

Larry had just published his second book, *Paco's Story*, which later won the National Book Award. He knew what he was doing. I talked to him about the trouble I was having with my robot book. He said that my strongest skill seemed to be in first-person narrative, like *Chickenhawk*. Maybe I should think about that.

I spent a month writing a hundred pages of a new robot book, version three. This time, the robot told the story. Clever, eh? First-person narrative. I sent this to Knox and then we drove to Maine to spend a month at my mother-in-law's cabin on the lake. While I was there, Knox sent me back the manuscript saying, "I just don't get this, Bob."

I called him up and we talked. "You aren't getting the reader involved, Bob. I kept falling asleep with this thing. You have to make people care about a machine, and I don't think you can do it." He paused. "Well, what are you going to do next? Get a job?"

"I don't know. I guess I won't write any more robot stories."

"Good," Knox said.

We stayed another two weeks in Maine. I concentrated on refining my sailing skills with a little Sunfish. In the evenings I sat on the porch and watched the lake, listening to waves rustling the sand, hearing loons wail. I was feeling like a freak, a one-book flash in the pan. I wasn't really a writer, I'd just been lucky. I couldn't think of anything else I wanted to do, and my money would run out in a year or so.

One evening a few days before we left, while I daydreamed by the lake, I saw my robot, a black plastic mannequin-looking machine, stalking silently through a jungle. Wet leaves plastered its eye covers, spider webs and jungle debris covered its body, but the robot (I had no name for it) ignored the stuff clinging to him and moved stealthily and purposely among the shadows of the jungle, stalking. The image was very exciting. My high-tech robot was contrasted against the organic lushness of the jungle, emphasizing its alien nature. I'd been telling my robot story set in laboratories where the robot just blended in with the rest of the high-tech gadgetry. The image stayed with me.

When we got back to High Springs, I decided to work on the cabin. I didn't write a word. I spent a month installing a brick patio around the cabin. I built an upstairs deck which opened out of the eight-foot-square office Patience and I shared and made it seem larger. John and I put on a catwalk out front, a ledge to stand on to wash the bedroom windows, and built a small shed to house the washer and dryer.

The image kept returning, always the same: the robot was stalking something in a jungle and disappeared into the darkness. What was it tracking? Where was it? Who made it? Why?

When I finished my cabin improvements, a plot jumped into my head. The robot was in a rain forest in Costa Rica. The robot was being tested by the Army. (I had read about the Defense Advanced Research Projects Agency sponsoring research for such a weapon.) It was stalking a man as part of the test. That's all I knew. I started writing.

In every version of the robot story prior to this one, I'd spent a lot of time developing a detailed outline, following it carefully, because that's how I thought you were supposed to do it. I had only a vague idea what the plot might be for this book, and I wanted to try an experiment: I was just going to start writing and see what happened.

I worked for four months on the first 150 pages. During that time, Knox called and wanted to know what I was doing. He said, "Please don't tell me you're working on another robot book."

"I'm working on another robot book."

"Jesus, Bob. You don't give up, do you?"

"Nope."

"Well, send it up when you have something to show me," Knox said, his voice reeking with pity.

I had no name for the robot until the first human character, the soldier it'd been stalking in a test, talked to it when it flunked the test by becoming more interested in a dragonfly than in killing the soldier. The soldier approached the robot and said, "Nice bug you got there, Solo." Ah. Solo was the robot's name. I had wondered what it might be.

I rewrote the manuscript (I was using a Macintosh, and the rewrites were fast) two times until I thought it could take Knox's criticism. I knew it worked this time. I sent it to Knox.

A week later Knox called. His voice was filled with enthusiasm. "I don't believe it, Bob. I actually gave a shit what happens to this thing, and I hate robots. You've actually done it."

I decided to finish the book rather than try to sell it based on the first part, as I had done with *Chickenhawk*. Much of the story took place in a small Nicaraguan village where the robot hid from its makers. I'd never been to Nicaragua, and I wanted to know at least what it looked like. I wanted to talk to Nicaraguans to see how they talked, lived, what they ate, how they cooked, what color the sand was at Lake Nicaragua, where the story was set; I wanted to see the two mile-high volcanoes, Las Maderas and Concepción in the lake, and a hundred other things.

I called Mr. Gamble and asked him what my chances were of getting permission to go there—a business trip, I said. He said I could try, but he knew the parole board would refuse. I didn't want to spar with bureaucrats who make life tedious, so I spent a few months doing extensive research in the Latin American Library at the University of Florida. I read nineteenth-century explorers' journals (in which I discovered a whole section on Nicaraguan superstitions), I read travel books, I read several histories of Nicaragua. (In my research, I discovered that the reason Nicaragua had always had so much trouble with the United States was that they happened to own the very best spot in all of Central America to build a sea-level canal. Their history is filled with broken treaties over the building of this canal on what the U.S. government still considers to be a strategic site. Nicaraguans didn't like the idea of an American-owned canal crossing their country, and were not easily pushed around. We even sent in Marines to enforce our will. In five years of fighting, the Marines were defeated by Agusto Sandino.) I had plenty of book information, but I wanted eyewitness details. I put an ad in the paper requesting interviews with Nicaraguans. I talked to several families who told me things I couldn't find in books. The kinds of beds peasants sleep on. Favorite country meals. I learned that Nicaraguans loved a coffee and cocoa drink, *piniolio,* that was so common in that country that other Central Americans called Nicaraguans Piniolios. Armed with these details, I invented a peasant village, a cooperative, and populated it with whole families. Eusebio, a teenage boy, became a major character. I modeled his mother, Modesta, on a woman, Sebastiana, we'd known in Spain. I invented life in the village, basing it on the seven months we'd spent in the village of Almonaster La Real. Everything was coming together. Solo would have a place to hide, people to talk to—people who'd use a two-billion-dollar machine to gather firewood and work on their trucks. I had a plot.

Two years after I got out of prison, I sent the completed book to Knox. I decided to call it *Weapon*. Knox sent it to Viking because Viking had the right of first refusal as part of my contract for *Chickenhawk*. Gerry Howard refused to buy it, which astounded me. Hey, I thought. Remember me? I'm a goddamn best-selling author, here. What the hell's going on? Gerry said Viking wasn't publishing science fiction, which was a nice way of saying he hated the book.

Knox sent it to other publishers and it was rejected. Most of the editors expressed surprise because *Weapon* had nothing to do with Vietnam. Mason is supposed to be a Vietnam writer, isn't he?

I sent a copy of the manuscript to Bill Smith in California. A week later, he sent me back a two-page letter pointing out a few weak points, but saying, "If this is science-fiction, then I love science-fiction." He said that I might try writing a new opening chapter that would introduce the location of the story and some of the main characters more gradually than I'd done.

I agreed with Bill's suggestion about a new opening chapter. I called Knox and told him to withdraw the book. I was rewriting it.

A month later, I sent him the new version. Gerry Howard said he wanted to read it, and did, and rejected it a second time. This writing business is not a piece of cake.

Months went by. I was getting the same kinds of rejections: I like it, but it has nothing to do with Vietnam. With *Chickenhawk*, they'd said no one wanted to read about Vietnam; now everybody did. It looked like I had to write about Vietnam or nothing.

Even if I was not having much success *being* a writer, I *acted* like one. I enjoyed being around writers. Mike Costello, the writer who'd cut firewood for Patience while I was gone, and his wife, Patti, were now two of our best friends, and we saw them almost every Saturday night. I met Padgett Powell (who wrote *Edisto*) at a reading I gave at the

University of Florida. I met Jack C. Haldeman II, a science fiction writer, and through him, his brother Joe Haldeman, the author of a science fiction classic, *The Forever War*. These three guys lived in the Gainesville area and became my friends.

Padgett liked my robot story well enough to recommend that I teach his writing class at the university while he took a year's sabbatical. The writing faculty at the university vetoed that idea, saying I was too commercial. I knew what they meant. I'd gotten a degree in fine arts, majoring in photography. During my art school days, we were taught that anyone making money selling their work, not in galleries, was highly suspect of not being a fine artist at all, but an *illustrator*, a common tradesman like Norman Rockwell. Writing popular books, for many members of the literati, borders on prostitution.

The accumulation of rejections, being considered too commercial by the academics, and the fact that I was running out of money were making me depressed. I left Solo to wander around New York to find a publisher while I began research for a book I wanted to write about Arabia.

A group of Vietnam veterans at the Union Correctional Institution, a very serious state prison near Raiford, Florida, invited me to give a talk to their group. Reluctantly, I agreed. I brought Patience with me. The idea of going into this prison was daunting. Raiford is not Eglin. It is surrounded by high walls, guard towers, and barbed wire. Our escort said the *average* sentence there was life. I enjoyed talking to the prisoners, but was very happy to leave. I found the place scary as hell.

On the drive home, Patience told me that one of the inmates had said he wished his wife had been as understanding as she—it might've kept him out of prison. It made her cry. She decided that she'd write a book for the wives of Vietnam vets, called, she announced in the car, *Vietnam: A Woman's Guide*.

She wrote a proposal immediately. I was happy to see her doing it. She's a great writer, and *somebody* in the family had to publish a book. She sent her idea to Knox, who sent it on to Gerry Howard, the editor who hates robots, and damn if he didn't buy it. He offered Patience an advance of fifteen thousand dollars, twice what they'd given me, and she was ecstatic. So was I, but why did he give her more than me? Knox sent a note later saying, "Jeez—don't let this Viking Penguin business go to Patience's head! Keep her in the kitchen as much as possible . . ."

Joe Haldeman and his wife, Gay, were visiting us at the cabin one afternoon soon after Patience sold her book. The chatter was happy. Joe had just sold his sixteenth book, *Tool of the Trade;* Patience had just sold her first. I lurked in the corner forcing smiles when they looked my way. It's tough being around successful people when you aren't, especially if you claim to be in the same profession. They'd poured some champagne to toast their successes. I declined because, I said, champagne gave me a headache. As they drank their goddamn champagne, the phone rang.

It was Knox. "I've got some interest from Putnam, Bob. I'll know in an hour. How do you want to get paid?" He meant did I want all the advance at once or did I want to break it up into payments. My heart was beating wildly in my throat. I said I'd like installments.

I had a glass of champagne, and in half an hour Knox called back and said it was a deal. Lisa Wager, a senior editor at G. P. Putnam's Sons, a very discerning and intelligent woman, who obviously had great taste, loved *Weapon.*

Finally, after ten years of trying, Solo lived.

While *Weapon* was still an unedited manuscript, it was optioned by Twentieth Century-Fox to be a movie. Knox sold it to publishers in England, Japan, and Germany. In a few months, I'd gathered in a whole bunch of sheaves, as they say.

The book wasn't a best-seller, but the reviews were great. The *New York Times* (which did not consider it science fiction, but a techno-thriller), said "Put it at the top of your list" and later included it in their list of notable books for 1989. What did Gerry Howard know about robots, anyway? I had broken the one-book barrier.

Patience's book came out as *Recovering from the War: A Woman's Guide to Helping Your Vietnam Vet, Your Family, and Yourself* in 1990. Viking sent her on a book tour. I went with her and got some of the writer's perks I'd missed while I was in jail. We were on the *Today* show together and stayed at posh hotels in twelve cities all over the country. Patience is now working on a new book.

Jack, now twenty-eight, is a musician. His group, NDolphin, was very popular in the Gainesville area until they broke up. He writes all of his songs, a talent which Patience and I assume he inherited from us, but he also writes and plays his own music, something that is totally mysterious to two people who can't carry a tune in a bucket.

I've written *Solo*, a sequel to *Weapon*, and this book you are now reading.

In March 1989, the U.S. Parole Commission released me from their supervision, and in May the Florida Office of Executive Clemency sent me a piece of paper entitled CERTIFICATE OF RESTORATION OF CIVIL RIGHTS.

Officially, I am just like everybody else. Back in the world.

E P I L O G U E

I'd given quite a few talks at universities, been included in a BBC
television program on helicopters; but I'd never given a talk to my
peers, the pilots who flew in Vietnam, the ones I wrote about.

I am a member of the Vietnam Helicopter Pilots Association, the
VHPA, which now has over six thousand members. I went to my first
reunion at their annual meeting in Washington, D.C., in 1987.

Almost no one in the association mentioned my felonious past except one former captain who said he hoped I'd learned my lesson. I
said that I had: get a faster boat. He didn't like that. There were, in
fact, several members who thought that, though my book was good,
I was still a drug smuggler. I was really surprised when Dave Owens,
the president of the VHPA, invited me to be a speaker at the next
reunion, in Texas.

On Friday, July 1, 1988, Patience and I flew to Fort Worth and met
Jerry Towler and his wife, Martie, at the hotel where the reunion was
being held. The next day five hundred of us were going to be bused
to Mineral Wells, where we'd all gone to flight school. They said the
whole town was going to throw us a party.

That night, Jay Elliott, a member of the board of directors, told me
that my speech was scheduled for the big luncheon Sunday. He also
said, "There might be an incident, Bob."

"Incident? Like what?"

"Some of the guys gave us a bunch of flak about having you give a speech. You know, your smuggling thing. They said they'll get up and leave as a group when you're speaking."

"So why the hell did you and Owens invite me?" I asked.

"Because I think you did a hell of a job with *Chickenhawk*. You made a mistake, I'm sure you know that. I just wanted you to know not everybody agrees with us so it wouldn't take you by surprise."

Saturday morning we loaded up in twelve buses and drove the fifty miles to Mineral Wells. The buses drove through the main gate of the former flight school. The two helicopters were gone; only their pedestals remained. Fort Wolters, former home of the U.S. Army Primary Helicopter School, was now an industrial park.

The buses parked in the drill field where we used to practice marching for endless hours. The barracks, long two-story brick buildings, were empty, abandoned on a weedy field. We got out and wandered around the buildings, remembering. You could almost hear the shouts that used to echo in the yards, "Give me twenty, candidate." "You call that a clean belt buckle, candidate?"

Jerry and I went into a barracks, walked down a hallway, trying to find our old rooms. The building was dusty, spooky, quiet. It had once bustled with eager young men determined to become pilots. We used to spit-shine our floors and wax the sinks. We used to sit up nights in the latrines, studying for the next written test. We braced to attention and slammed against the walls when an upperclassman or, God forbid, an actual TAC officer met us in the hallways. The place never rested. Now our footsteps echoed in the emptiness.

Outside, tumbleweed drifted between the barracks.

As promised, the town gave us a party. They'd reopened the old mess hall. They served barbecue and beer, all the beer we could drink.

After lunch, we sat through a couple of hours of speeches given by former flight school instructors and the mayor, and saw a movie describing the opportunities of starting a business in the industrial park.

When a speaker asked someone to stand up at the back of the audience, the man in front of me turned around. It was Woody Woodruff. I called him Decker in *Chickenhawk*. He and Captain Phillips (Morris in the book) were shot down when Phillips, Woody's best friend, was shot through the heart during an assault landing in Happy Valley. I'd gotten caught in the same ambush, gotten shot down, but didn't get a scratch.

"Mason!" Woody said, beaming.

"Woody!"

Jerry, sitting beside me, said the same thing. We hadn't seen each other since Vietnam. After the meeting, we traded addresses with Woody and got back on the buses for a tour of Mineral Wells before heading back to Fort Worth.

The buses looped around this small Texas town and our guide, a local volunteer, pointed out the new library and showed us that the old hotel was closed. In the country outside of town he pointed at some buffalo grazing in a field, said ranching buffalo was a burgeoning industry in this part of Texas. The truth was, when the flight school closed, Mineral Wells shriveled up and became the small central Texas town it had been before the Army arrived in the fifties.

The train of buses stopped at the Holiday Inn on the way out of town. Here, two rotor blades were set up as an arch at the entrance to the pool. In the days after Jerry and I graduated, the new pilots were thrown into this pool when they first soloed, not in the cattle ponds like we'd been. More beer was available, as much as you could drink. Soon people were throwing one another into the pool. After a couple hours of play, the pilots, many dripping wet, boarded the buses for the trip back to the city.

When one of the other buses passed us on the highway, everybody in our bus booed and demanded the driver catch them. Who knows why? The driver ignored us. Finally one of the pilots walked up to the front of the bus and held out fifty dollars saying, "You beat these other assholes back to town and you get this."

The driver sped up and the race was on.

One bus passed us on a downhill run, and we saw two forty-year-old men with their naked butts pressed up against the windows. Everybody was laughing. Patience and Martie were giggling. One guy yelled "Pressed ham!" Martie yelled "I'm in love!" It was crazy, it was juvenile, it was fun.

The pilots raced and mooned each other all the way to Fort Worth, prompting calls to the police from offended motorists. The police called the hotel and were informed by the manager, "That's impossible. These men are all over forty!"

When we got back to the hotel, the drivers were all given their prizes, for being good sports and for giving it their best.

I woke up early Sunday morning wondering what I was going to say in the speech. I'd given talks at universities, but those were usually about Vietnam and helicopters in combat. What could I tell these guys about that? Also, I knew there was going to be some kind of demonstration.

I decided to write a short story about our trip to Mineral Wells. I spent a couple of hours at it and it seemed like it would probably work, though I suspect you would have had to have been there to appreciate it. I still didn't know how I was going to handle the protesters.

Jerry and Martie Towler and Patience and I sat at a table near the dais. Dave Owens, who was sitting with us, leaned over and said, "You know what you're going to say?"

"Yeah, pretty much."

"Bob, I want you to do me a favor and not get mad."

"What's that, Dave?"

"Show me your notes when you come up to the dais, just a glance."

"What for?"

"Because that was one of the conditions for you speaking here. They said I had to see your notes before you speak."

"That's bullshit, Dave."

"I know. I won't read them. Hold them up when you walk by me. That's looking at them, isn't it?"

I laughed. "Sure, okay."

Dave went to the podium, made a few brief announcements, and then introduced me.

As we passed each other on the steps, I held my notes out to Dave, who looked at them and then out at the audience. He nodded and said, "Thanks, Bob. Give'm hell."

I turned on my pocket tape recorder, put my notes, my story, on the podium. There were over a thousand people in the room. The applause was thunderous. I waited.

I said:

"I thank you for inviting me to be your speaker today. I feel kind of odd about that. I'm a member of the organization; I'm not from outside.

"I'm here because I wrote a book about what I, and many of us, did in Vietnam, and subsequently gained some celebrity because of it.

"I feel odd about that, too, because almost anybody here could have written *Chickenhawk*. Many of you certainly experienced more harrowing adventures than I did. But I'm the one who wrote the book." I paused. "I'm the one that's getting the recognition," I said quietly. I looked across the audience.

"I'm the one who gets the letters."

"I get letters from grunts thanking me for having been a helicopter pilot in Vietnam.

"They thank *me* for the pilot who pulled them out of a hot LZ and saved their lives.

"They thank *me* for the pilot who got the Huey in, at night, without lights, under fire, bringing in ammunition and supplies that saved their unit.

"They thank *me* for the things we *all* did in Vietnam.

"Being, I suppose, the more well-known of the Vietnam pilots here, the one who gets the mail, the one who gets the attention we all deserve, I hereby pass that thanks on to you." I stood back, held up my arms, and said, "You deserve it. Give yourself a hand."

There was much applause. I scanned the room. I saw smiles. I saw tears. Nobody got up to walk out.

I then read them the story I'd written, "The Race," which, as I had hoped, met with success. Racing buses filled with mooning forty-year-olds is just naturally funny, especially to the participants. I brought the house down.

I talked about some early experiences I'd had as an adolescent pilot trying to teach myself to fly and got a lot of laughs.

Then I faced the issue of my controversy.

"A situation that irks some of my fellows here, and is an issue of curiosity for others, is, what did happen at the end of the book?

"For those of you who haven't read *Chickenhawk*, I say, at the end of the epilogue, that I had been arrested for smuggling marijuana and I was appealing the conviction. That sounds pretty serious. It was. In fact, I lost the appeal. I went to jail."

It was quiet in the auditorium. Someone coughed.

I launched into a quick-paced summation of selling the book and going to jail. I told them what it was like being sent to Eglin. I told them about the white lines that marked the boundaries, that it was a prison for wimps, that if you had to go to prison, Eglin was the place to go. I made Eglin seem like a lark. I made them laugh.

I paused.

"But it was still prison. I couldn't leave.

"When my book became a best-seller, it didn't seem real. Because, while I was experiencing the highest moment of life, I was also experiencing the lowest moment of my life. I was not proud of what I'd done or for going to prison. I was humiliated and embarrassed. Yet, at the same time, I was experiencing this wonderful success. It was a tough mixture of emotions for me.

"But it's over now, or nearly so. For those of you who think I haven't paid enough for what I did, I'm still on parole. As a matter of fact, I'm here courtesy of the U.S. Parole Commission. It's been seven years since I committed my crime. I'll be off parole this December. I'm looking forward to that."

I made Jerry Towler stand up, introduced him as my flying partner and the Resler in the book.

When I finished, the applause was astounding.

I wasn't able to walk anywhere for the rest of the reunion without someone coming up and telling me I was okay. I needed that.

In August 1989, David Hunt and Kevin Bowen of the William Joiner Center at the University of Massachusetts (which is trying to get decent medical care to the Vietnamese) invited me to come to Boston to meet a group of Vietnamese writers—former Viet Cong and North Vietnamese regulars, VC and NVA, as they were known to me. Philip Caputo, Tim O'Brien, and other American writers of the Vietnam War were also coming. They wanted to know if I'd give a reading with Tim O'Brien. I agreed.

Patience and I flew to Boston. During the drive from the airport, David Hunt told us that their public meeting with the Vietnamese the day before had ended in disaster. South Vietnamese refugees broke up the meeting, injured some of the guests. Now, he explained, they were holding the rest of the conference at Kevin Bowen's home in the Dorchester section of Boston.

We climbed the stairs up to the attic of the three-story house where the meeting of American and Vietnamese writers had already started. Three Vietnamese sat together on a couch at the front of the room: Le Luu, who wrote a Vietnamese best-seller, *The Humorless Colonel*; Nguyen Khai, a writer and the deputy general secretary of Vietnam's

Writers Union; and Nguyen Quang Sang, who'd written a novel, four short-story collections, and produced several films about the war. About ten people sat facing them in folding chairs, five of them writers: novelists Philip Caputo, Wayne Karlin, Tim O'Brien, and two poets, Larry Rottman and Bruce Weigl. They stopped talking for a second when Patience and I walked in, and then continued after we sat down.

In this first meeting, the discussion was about the war as seen by the different sides. It was an opportunity to ask questions of your former enemies. An American asked, "What did you think of the American troops' fighting ability?"

Le Luu, the most popular novelist in Vietnam, shook his head and smiled. "Generally," he said through an interpreter, "they weren't very good fighters."

I felt myself getting excited; I had wondered how I'd react. I had been against us being in Vietnam, but then, these guys had *killed* some of my friends. I had never seen a living North Vietnamese regular, and very few living Viet Cong. One of them might have been the guy who shot me down. It was an eerie feeling to face former enemies.

Philip Caputo, a former Marine lieutenant, replied, "You're saying we were *bad* fighters?" Caputo looked pissed off.

The interpreter, a young man who wasn't born until after the war, shrugged, translated. Nguyen Khai, the leader and diplomat among the Vietnamese contingent, smiled nervously. There was great pressure in Vietnam to regain normal relations with the United States. I think he sensed the tenseness in the air.

"Not bad in the sense that you were cowardly or unprofessional," Khai answered. "You were simply not as well motivated as were we. We, after all, were defending our country—"

Sang broke in, his voice deep, his smile wide. "When you did not have your fighters and helicopters and B-52s to support you, you were easy to beat."

Caputo answered grimly, "I saw plenty of firefights where we took you one on one, no outside support, and we won."

Sang shrugged. "Certainly there were exceptions. I was speaking in general. You did win some battles; some, like the Tet Offensive of 1968, were devastating for us. But you must admit, we *did* win the war."

I said, "I don't see it that way. You didn't win the war; we stopped fighting it. There's a difference."

"Not if you realize that it was our sustained effort against an over-whelming force that convinced you to stop fighting," Sang replied. "Of course, you could have blown us back . . ." the interpreter paused, getting an idiom right, "back to the Stone Age, I think you say; but your hearts weren't in it." Sang smiled and added, "For which I am eternally grateful."

The whole group laughed. Kevin Bowen took the opportunity of the break in mood to suggest we stop for a while.

We went downstairs for coffee and beer on Bowen's back porch. Hunt told Sang I was a former helicopter pilot, and he came over to me with the interpreter, who introduced himself as Ha Huy Thong. Sang spoke. Thong said, "You flew the Huey?"

"Yes. First Cav Division."

Sang smiled warmly. "Yes. The famous First Cavalry. I used to shoot you down."

"Yes," I said. "You were pretty good at it. But we still got the job done."

Sang nodded. "Yes. Many brave young pilots died, I am afraid."

The interpreter, Thong, said that Nguyen Sang had made a movie about the American helicopter pilots and wanted to do another. He said that Sang had gotten a lot of the details of his first film wrong. He wanted to know if I'd be willing to be interviewed by Sang the following day. I agreed.

Sang wanted to know if he could have his picture taken with me. We stood side by side on the porch, grinning at the camera. I was at least a foot taller than this wiry, wily Viet Cong. While one of the Vietnamese fiddled with his camera, Sang said something. Thong said, "Sang wants to show his friends back home the kind of people he was shooting down."

I turned to Sang and shook my head. This sturdy little man, my former enemy, in the middle of his former enemy's country, on the other side of the planet, was bragging about killing us. You had to respect this guy.

During the break, I met the other American writers. I told Philip Caputo that *A Rumor of War* was partly responsible for me writing my book. He said he liked *Chickenhawk*. I told Tim O'Brien how much his first book, *If I Die in a Combat Zone*, influenced me, made me realize I, too, had something to say. I also told him I really enjoyed *Going*

After Cacciatio. He was used to that, having won the National Book Award for it.

After the break, we went back to the attic and talked about the writing business. The Vietnamese were fascinated by the fact that American writers seemed to make so much money. They wanted to know how much money we made on our books. Caputo and O'Brien weren't at this meeting, so I volunteered that I had made nearly a half million dollars so far on my book. They had the interpreter repeat this several times to make sure they were hearing right. I understood what the problem was when Le Luu, the author of the number-one best-selling novel in Vietnam, said that he had made enough money on his book to buy a new German bicycle. I felt embarrassed.

As we were leaving, Sang reminded me about our interview the next day. He was starving for authentic details from the other side. I shrugged. "I'll be here."

When I got to Kevin Bowen's house the next morning, the Vietnamese were having a kind of soup they called *pho* for breakfast. While they slurped bowls of noodles and fish, I sat and drank coffee with the interpreter, Thong, whom I found fascinating. He was not a former enemy; he was not a threat to me. He was twenty-three, educated entirely in Vietnam. His English was beautiful. I asked him how he liked America. He said he wasn't allowed to leave New York City (this trip was a special exception), where the Vietnamese mission was located, but he liked the city, had American friends there.

Bowen said that he had to go to the university, and left. In a few minutes I realized that there was no one in the house except me and two Vietnamese: Ha Huy Thong, the interpreter from Hanoi, and Nguyen Quang Sang, the tunnel-rat Viet Cong who'd shot down a lot of helicopters.

We sat at Bowen's kitchen table. The table was wood, old, pleasantly worn. Sang sat across from me and switched on his Sony tape recorder, flipped open a notebook. Thong sat between us.

Thong told me that Sang had gotten a lot of criticism of his movie when some Americans had seen it. For one thing, Thong said, Sang showed the American pilots returning home to their base and partying with whiskey drunk from champagne glasses. I laughed.

Sang looked at me seriously. I could see he was studying me, sizing me up. I suppose he was struck by our polarities as much as I. He spoke. Though what he said was incomprehensible to me, his voice was deep, authoritative. This was a warrior who, with others like him, had fought the mightiest country on earth and survived. Thong said, "How many helicopters were in your unit?"

I looked at Sang. He waited for the answer, pencil poised over a notepad. I looked up at the kitchen window and back at Sang. Morning light filtered across the old table. The ridges showing on the rustic, worn wood, the smell of Vietnamese food, the confident look on Sang's face made me feel suddenly queer. It was like I'd been shot down, captured.

Name, rank, and serial number. That's what came to mind. That's crazy, I thought. It's all public information now. I said, "Our battalion had four companies of about twenty ships each."

Sang nodded, made a note.

"You called them 'ships'?"

"Yes. It's a general word for a craft, air or sea."

Sang nodded. "And how many aviation battalions were in the First Cavalry?"

"We had two assault helicopter battalions of Hueys, a battalion of heavy-lift Chinook helicopters, and an independant group, the Ninth Air Cav. Altogether, the Cav had about four hundred helicopters."

Sang nodded, scribbled. "What kind of food did you eat?"

"C-rations, mostly," I said.

"The pilots did not eat better at their home bases?"

"Some did. We didn't. The First Cavalry lived in the field. At our base at An Khe we were served canned food called B-rations."

Sang nodded, spoke. Thong said, "He said he was lucky to get a fish head with his rice."

Sang's confidence, and now his professed Spartanism, irked me. "How many villagers did he kill to get the rice?"

Thong looked at me intently, shrugged, turned to Sang, and spoke. Sang's face darkened. He shook his head and spoke, his voice angry.

Thong shrugged. "He says he never killed his own people. Only you."

"Oh. The *other* Viet Cong killed the villagers," I said.

Thong answered without translating. "Yes. It was unfortunate."

That night, I shared billing with Wayne Karlin and Tim O'Brien at the Boston Public Library. Karlin read from *Lost Armies;* I read a few passages from *Chickenhawk,* all having to do with the Vietnamese. O'Brien read outtakes from his forthcoming book, *The Things They Carried.*

It didn't occur to me until later that night, in bed, that people must consider me to be an important writer, to have invited me to that reading. Imagine that.

The next day, David Hunt asked me if I'd return to Vietnam with the other writers, a reciprocal meeting with the Vietnamese writers. I said I would.

My mother was in the hospital while I wrote most of this book.

On August 29, 1990, Patience and Jack and I, along with my sister, Susan; her husband, Bruce; my nephew, Sean; and my niece, Bevan, took a boat out into the Gulf of Mexico and sprinkled her ashes on the waves. My father refused to come. None of her brothers or sisters attended or even came to see her in the hospital. There was no love in her family, a sad thing to see.

We drank a toast of dry martinis, a drink she asked for as she lay dying, unable to drink anything. I tossed a full glass, with olive, into the water for her.

My mother, despite having a heart condition most of her life, was an energetic woman. She grew up believing the woman's place was in the home, but had worked as a grocery checkout clerk when we first moved to Florida in 1945. Once, when my parents were struggling to make ends meet, she suggested that she go to school and become a nurse, but my father refused to allow it. He believed he should be able to provide for us himself. From 1951 to 1958, my mother did physical work on the chicken farm my dad started west of Delray Beach. We had a hundred thousand chickens on this farm, and we— my mother and father, my sister and I—did most of the work. After my dad sold the farm in 1958, moved us to Delray Beach, and became a real-estate broker, they were sufficiently well off that she could become the ideal of her culture—the wife of a successful businessman. She fulfilled her role by keeping our house as neat as a museum display and giving a cocktail party almost every Friday night.

At the age of sixty-four, a disease called lupus, and the drugs used to treat it, destroyed one of her hip joints. After spending nearly a year in a wheelchair, she decided to have the operation for an artificial hip joint. She was frail; the operation nearly killed her.

She called one day, a few weeks after the operation, said to come over, she had a surprise. When we got there, I saw her standing in the living room wearing a brand-new dress, beaming. After a year in a wheelchair, it was a miracle.

Two days later, she suffered a blood clot in her arm and had to have another operation.

She came home for a week, then went back in for other complications. She never left. I see her standing in the living room, smiling, happy just to stand up. I see her in the hospital, withered, in pain, dying. I see a cardboard box of granular ashes and dust.

My father, who had had another stroke, was now an invalid. With his caretaker gone—my mother had actually cooked for him as a cripple—he made conflicting demands of me and my sister. Depending on the whims of his depression, he wanted a new apartment, he wanted to go to a nursing home, he wanted a companion to live with him, he wanted to move in with us.

I had already started drinking scotch, drank more while my mother suffered, but I noticed with alarm that I was now drinking at least a bottle a week and increasing. I'd thought that drinking was a habit of the past, something I'd grown through.

As the date to leave for Vietnam drew near, I began to have more and more symptoms of distress. I refused to acknowledge them. I had made a commitment and I would stick by it. I called Larry Heinemann, told him I was having problems. He told me to try to hang in there.

The symptoms got worse. I began to have chest pains, dizziness, irregular heartbeats. I couldn't sleep. I really believed that I had overcome all this bullshit, yet here it was, a monster from the past, revisiting. I drank more. If I drank enough, I slept, but I also remembered where that had once led. I was retreating down an unfortunate path. This could not be.

Two weeks before our scheduled departure, I called David Hunt. I told him I wasn't going with them.

"What? Why?"

"I'm having real problems," I said. "Stuff is happening to me that hasn't happened for years. I'm a mess. I don't want to go over there and be a drag to the others."

"You know, Bob, this might be an opportunity to face your fears, overcome them."

"Yeah. Maybe. Or go completely nuts. You don't know how bad I feel right now, David, and I'm not there yet. I don't think I harbor any resentment toward the Vietnamese. I might, but I think the idea of just seeing that country—remembering the waste—I think I'm not ready yet. I will go, when I'm ready. Not now."

"A lot of people are going to be disappointed, Bob. Your book is being translated into Vietnamese. You know who's going. Everyone's a respected writer. This is a historical trip. Even Larry Heinemann is coming; he's your friend, right?"

I nodded. "I'm sorry, David. Please tell everyone that I'm sorry. I've got to go with my gut feelings now. I've ignored them in the past, and I was wrong."

I slept that night through.

The next day I felt better. In a week—though I felt badly about missing the trip—I felt the tension subside, I became calmer, more comfortable. While the writers made their tour, I stayed home and wrote.

Someday I will return to Vietnam, find Nguyen Quang Sang—the man who shot down Hueys—and take him for a ride.

I drink, not as heavily. I don't smoke cigarettes except when I forget at a party or during the holidays. When things are going well in my life, I feel pretty good. Stress brings on the symptoms I've lived with since Vietnam.

I have come to realize that Vietnam did affect me, that I'm not crazy.

The effects are losses, mostly.

I lost my career as a pilot.

I lost the children Patience and I wanted when we were first married, brothers and sisters for Jack. Jack lost a normal childhood and adolescence.

I lost a feeling of fellowship. I am different from people who have not seen combat, especially combat in which people died for a politician's ego.

I lost the belief that I could trust my government.

I very nearly lost Patience. And by staying with me, Patience has become a veteran of another kind of war.

Finally, I have come to realize that the most significant thing I lost in that war was peace.

When Polynesian sailors sail their canoes for weeks at a time on boundless seas without charts or compasses, they believe that they are sitting still, on a vacant earth, and that by moving their paddles correctly, by setting their sails properly, an island, their destination, will arrive on the horizon and come to them.

I move my body carefully and watch the ground pass beneath me and hedges and fences move by me until the steps of my house come to me and touch my feet. I experience the sensation that I am at the center of the universe, focused on what I'm doing, now.

I am looking for peace to arrive.